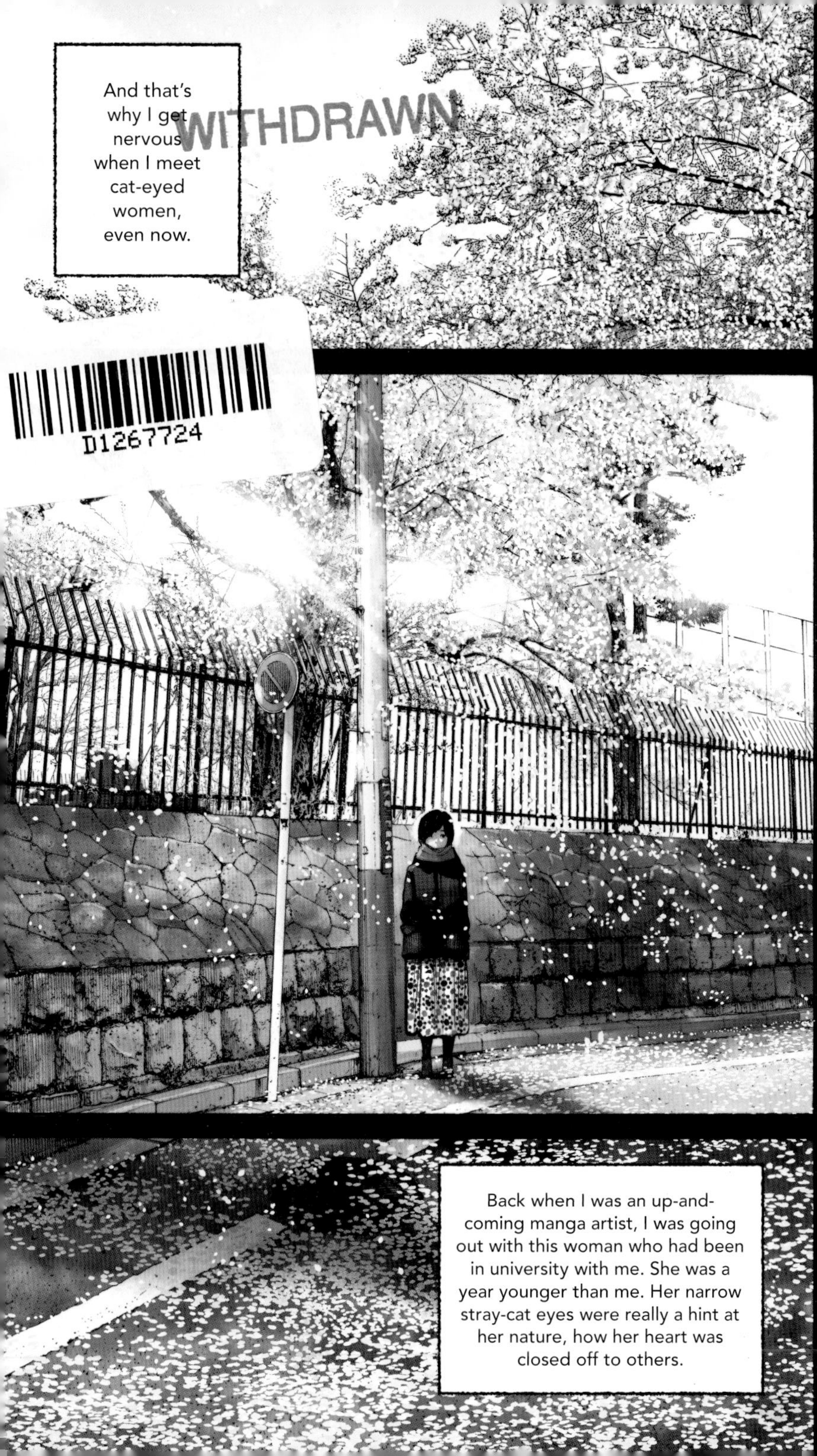
And that's why I get nervous when I meet cat-eyed women, even now.
Back when I was an up-and-coming manga artist, I was going out with this woman who had been in university with me. She was a year younger than me. Her narrow stray-cat eyes were really a hint at her nature, how her heart was closed off to others.

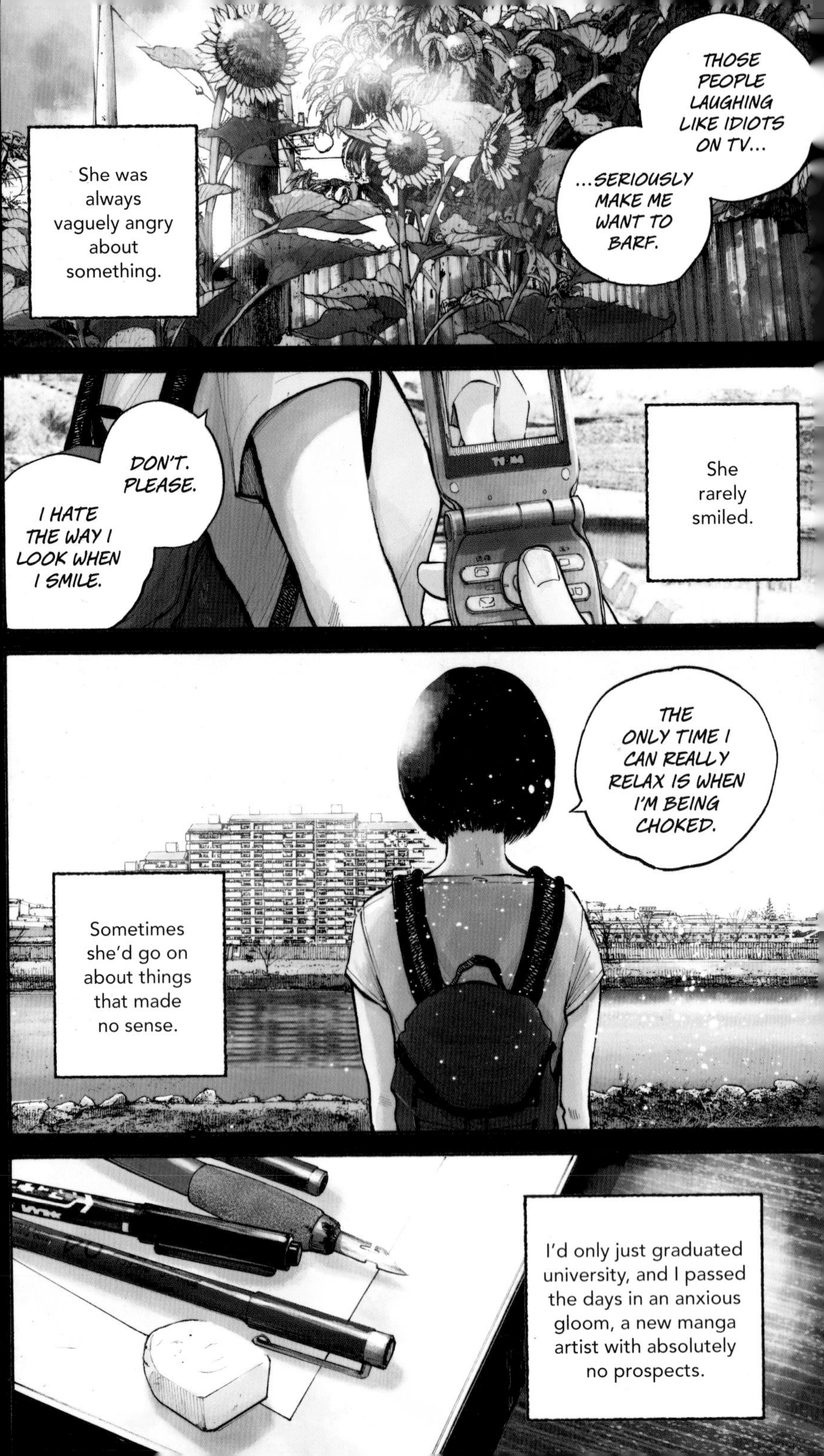
THOSE PEOPLE LAUGHING LIKE IDIOTS ON TV...
...SERIOUSLY MAKE ME WANT TO BARF.
She was always vaguely angry about something.
She rarely smiled.
DON'T. PLEASE.
I HATE THE WAY I LOOK WHEN I SMILE.
THE ONLY TIME I CAN REALLY RELAX IS WHEN I'M BEING CHOKED.
Sometimes she'd go on about things that made no sense.
I'd only just graduated university, and I passed the days in an anxious gloom, a new manga artist with absolutely no prospects.

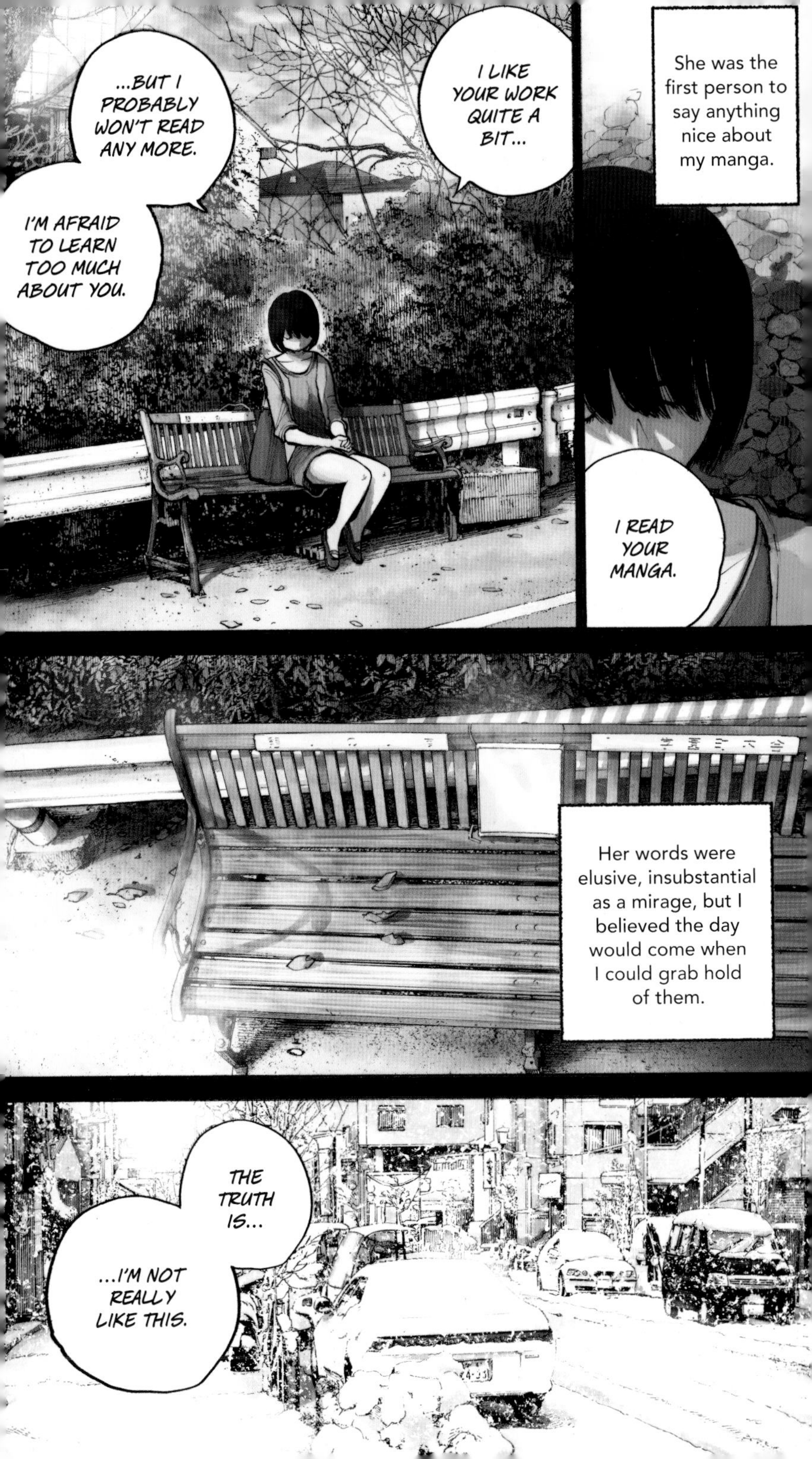

She was the first person to say anything nice about my manga.
I READ YOUR MANGA.
I LIKE YOUR WORK QUITE A BIT...
...BUT I PROBABLY WON'T READ ANY MORE.
I'M AFRAID TO LEARN TOO MUCH ABOUT YOU.
Her words were elusive, insubstantial as a mirage, but I believed the day would come when I could grab hold of them.
THE TRUTH IS...
...I'M NOT REALLY LIKE THIS.

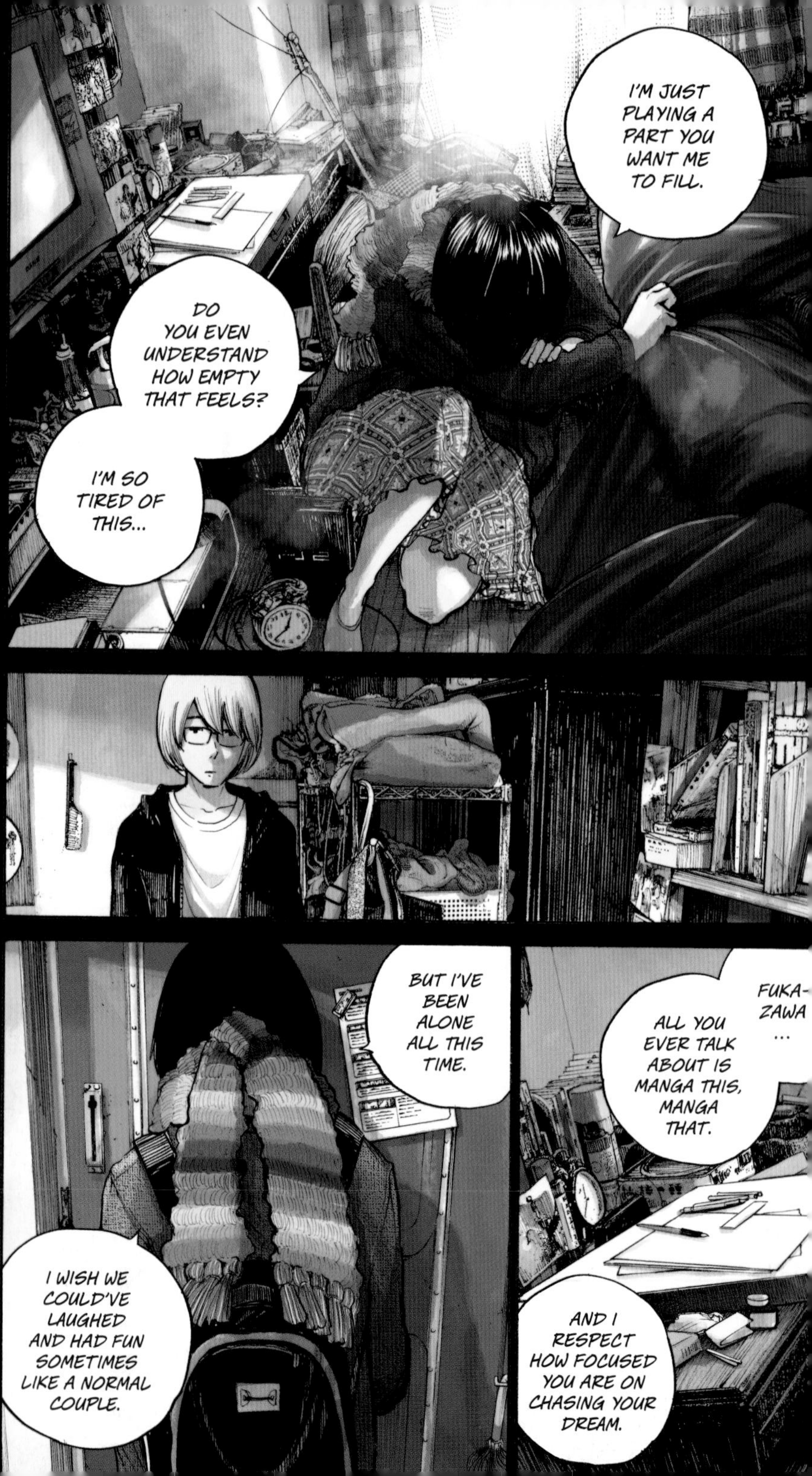
I'M JUST PLAYING A PART YOU WANT ME TO FILL.
DO YOU EVEN UNDERSTAND HOW EMPTY THAT FEELS?
I'M SO TIRED OF THIS...
FUKA-ZAWA...
ALL YOU EVER TALK ABOUT IS MANGA THIS, MANGA THAT.
AND I RESPECT HOW FOCUSED YOU ARE ON CHASING YOUR DREAM.
BUT I'VE BEEN ALONE ALL THIS TIME.
I WISH WE COULD'VE LAUGHED AND HAD FUN SOMETIMES LIKE A NORMAL COUPLE.

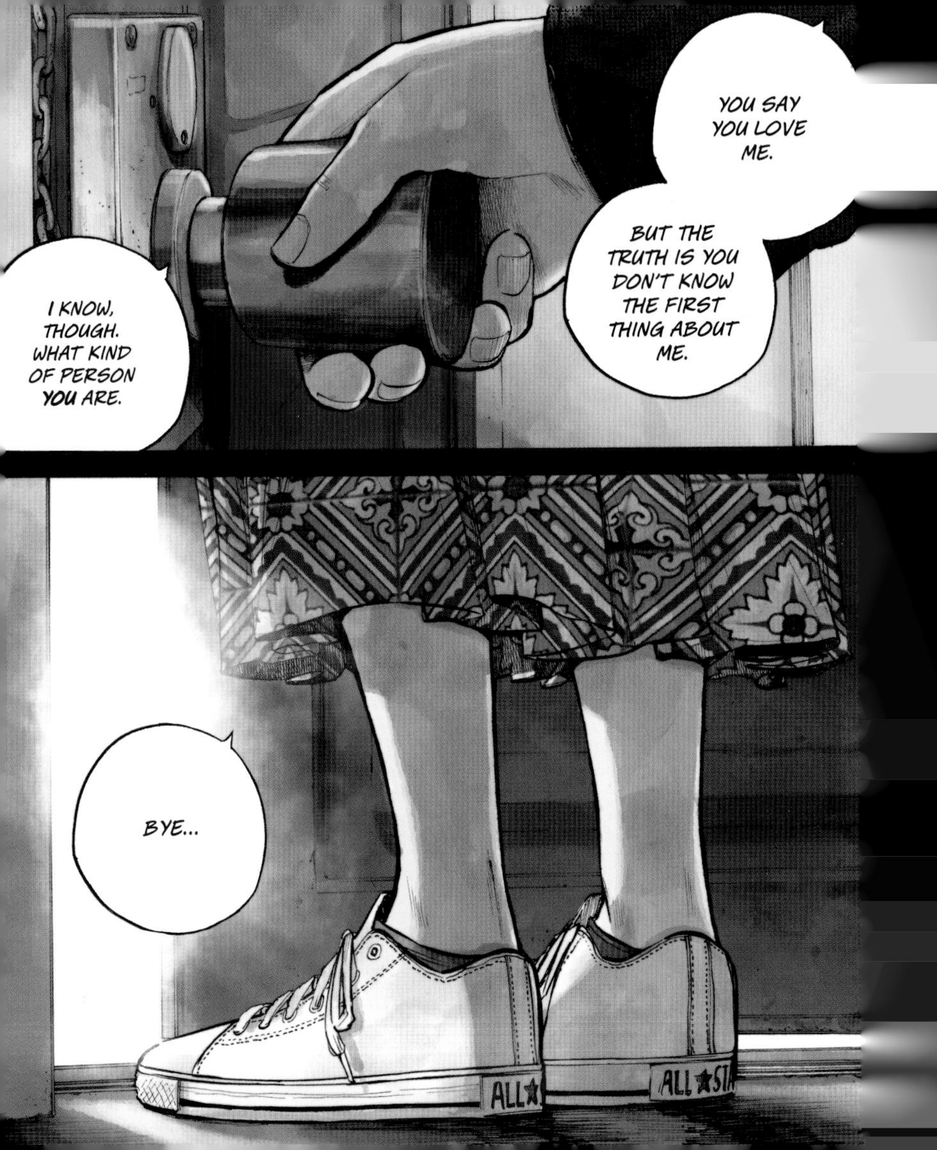
YOU SAY YOU LOVE ME.
BUT THE TRUTH IS YOU DON'T KNOW THE FIRST THING ABOUT ME.
I KNOW, THOUGH. WHAT KIND OF PERSON YOU ARE.
BYE...

DOWNFALL

INIO ASANO

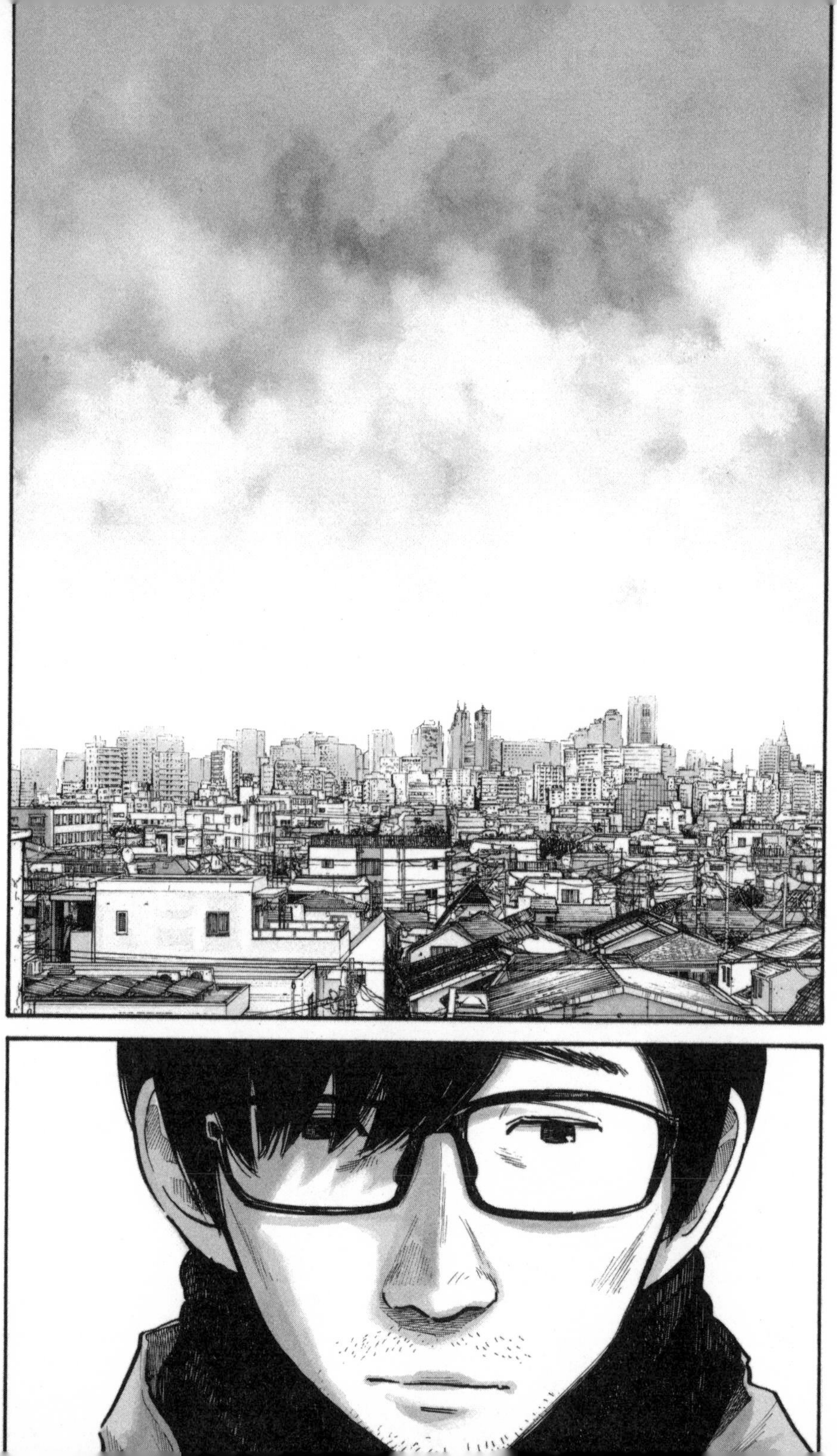

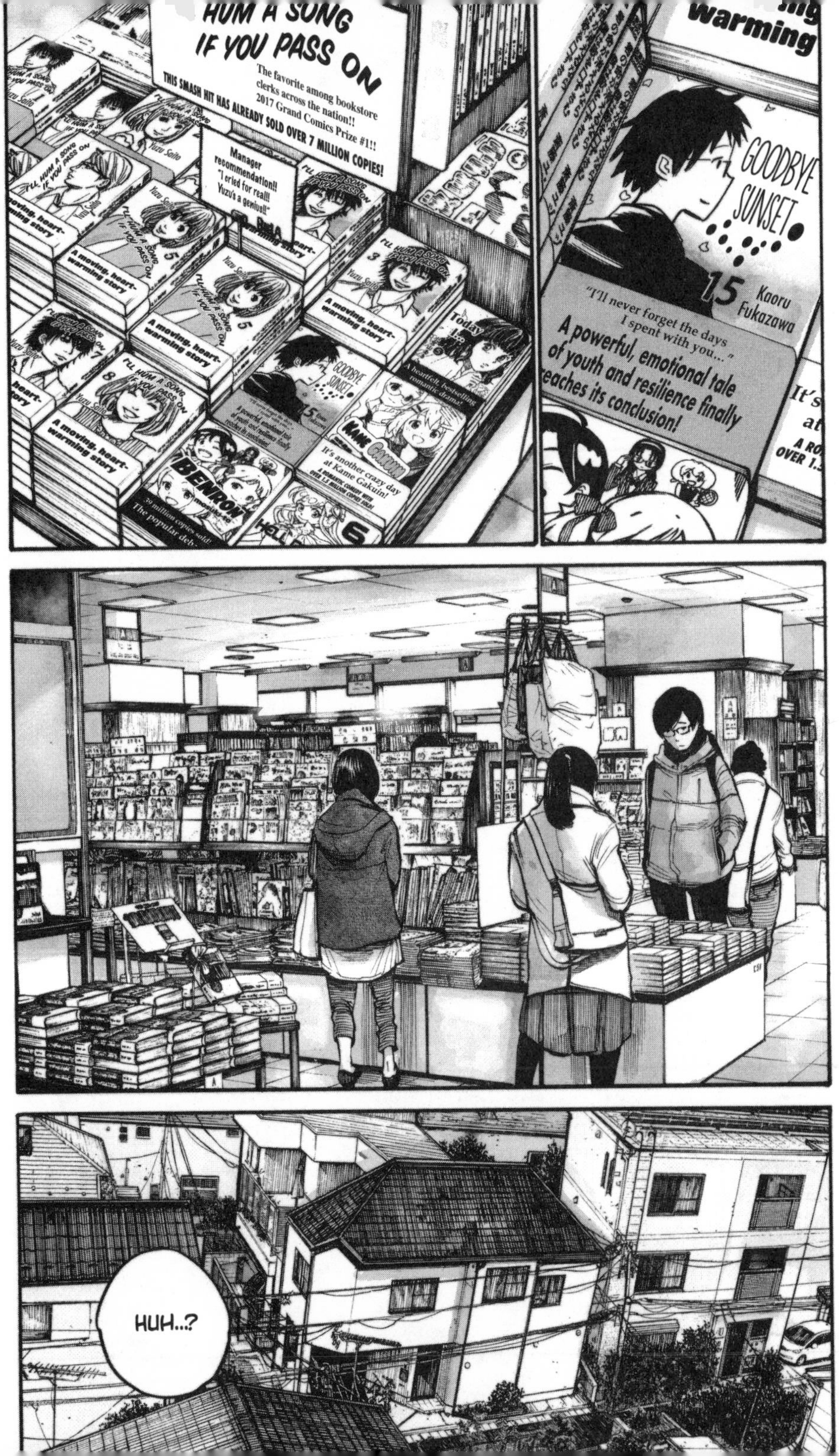
warming
GOODBYE SUNSET
15
Kaoru Fukazawa
"I'll never forget the days I spent with you..."
A powerful, emotional tale of youth and resilience finally reaches its conclusion!
HUM A SONG IF YOU PASS ON
The favorite among bookstore clerks across the nation!! 2017 Grand Comics Prize #1!!
THIS SMASH HIT HAS ALREADY SOLD OVER 7 MILLION COPIES!
Manager recommendation!! "I cried for real!! Yuzu's a genius!!"
I'LL HUM A SONG IF YOU PASS ON
Yuzu Saito
A moving, heart-warming story
Today I...
A heartfelt, bestselling romantic drama!
KAME GAKUIN
It's another crazy day at Kame Gakuin!
A ROMANTIC COMEDY WITH OVER 1.5 MILLION COPIES SOLD!
BENRON
HUH...?

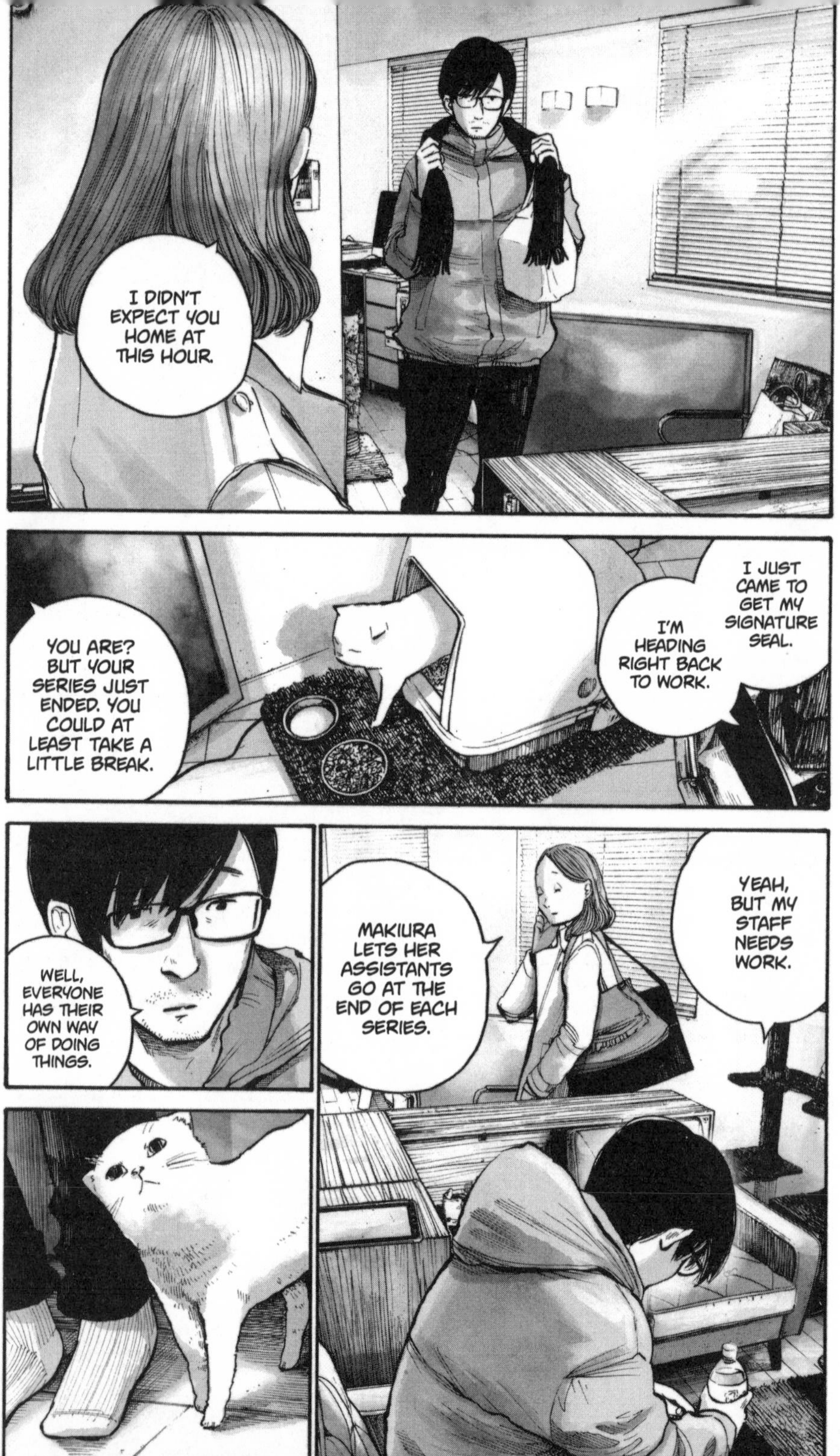
I DIDN'T EXPECT YOU HOME AT THIS HOUR.
I JUST CAME TO GET MY SIGNATURE SEAL.
I'M HEADING RIGHT BACK TO WORK.
YOU ARE? BUT YOUR SERIES JUST ENDED. YOU COULD AT LEAST TAKE A LITTLE BREAK.
YEAH, BUT MY STAFF NEEDS WORK.
MAKIURA LETS HER ASSISTANTS GO AT THE END OF EACH SERIES.
WELL, EVERYONE HAS THEIR OWN WAY OF DOING THINGS.

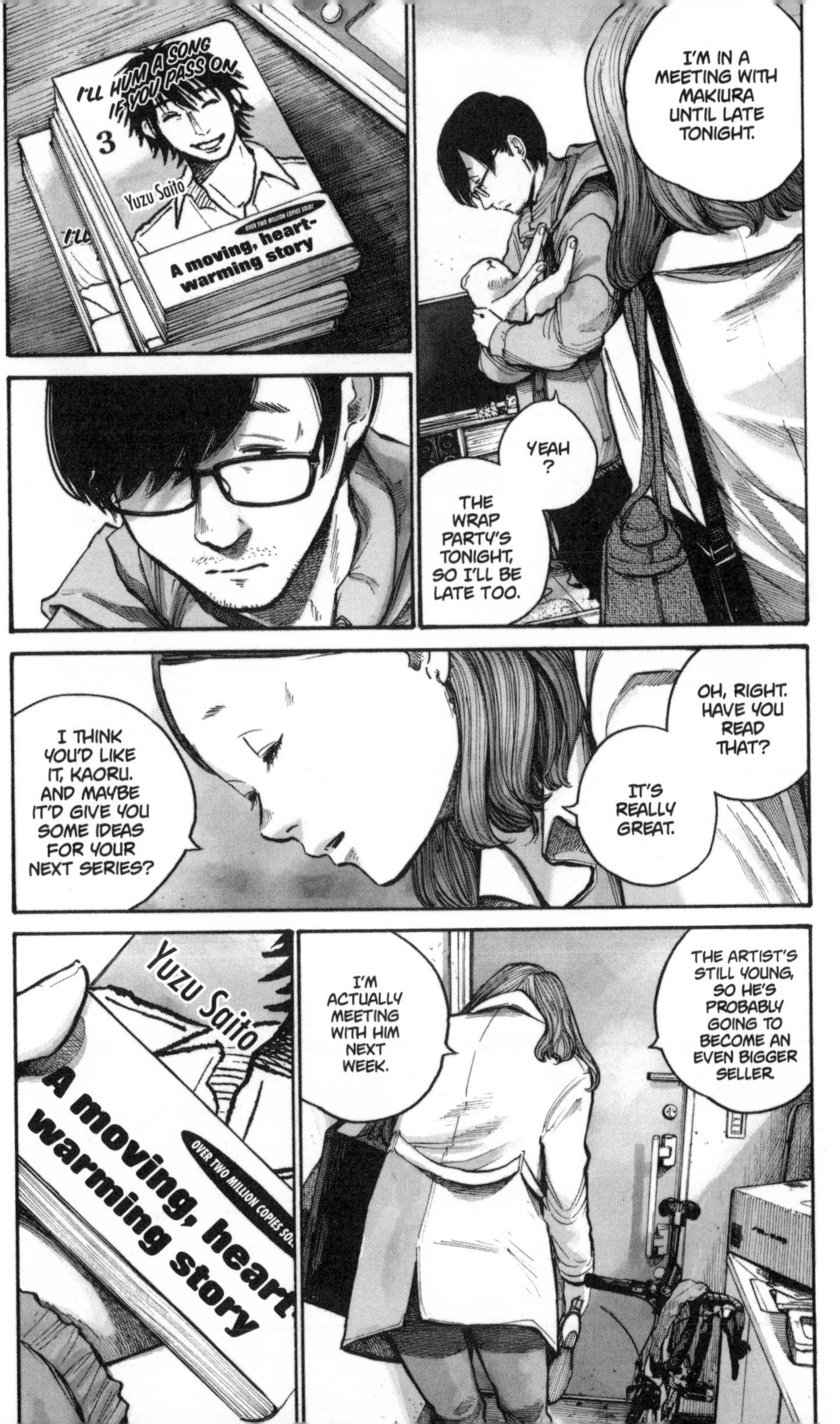
I'M IN A MEETING WITH MAKIURA UNTIL LATE TONIGHT.
YEAH?
THE WRAP PARTY'S TONIGHT, SO I'LL BE LATE TOO.
I'LL HUM A SONG IF YOU PASS ON
3
Yuzu Saito
OVER TWO MILLION COPIES SOLD!
A moving, heart-warming story
OH, RIGHT. HAVE YOU READ THAT?
IT'S REALLY GREAT.
I THINK YOU'D LIKE IT, KAORU. AND MAYBE IT'D GIVE YOU SOME IDEAS FOR YOUR NEXT SERIES?
THE ARTIST'S STILL YOUNG, SO HE'S PROBABLY GOING TO BECOME AN EVEN BIGGER SELLER.
I'M ACTUALLY MEETING WITH HIM NEXT WEEK.
Yuzu Saito
OVER TWO MILLION COPIES SOL
A moving, heart
warming story

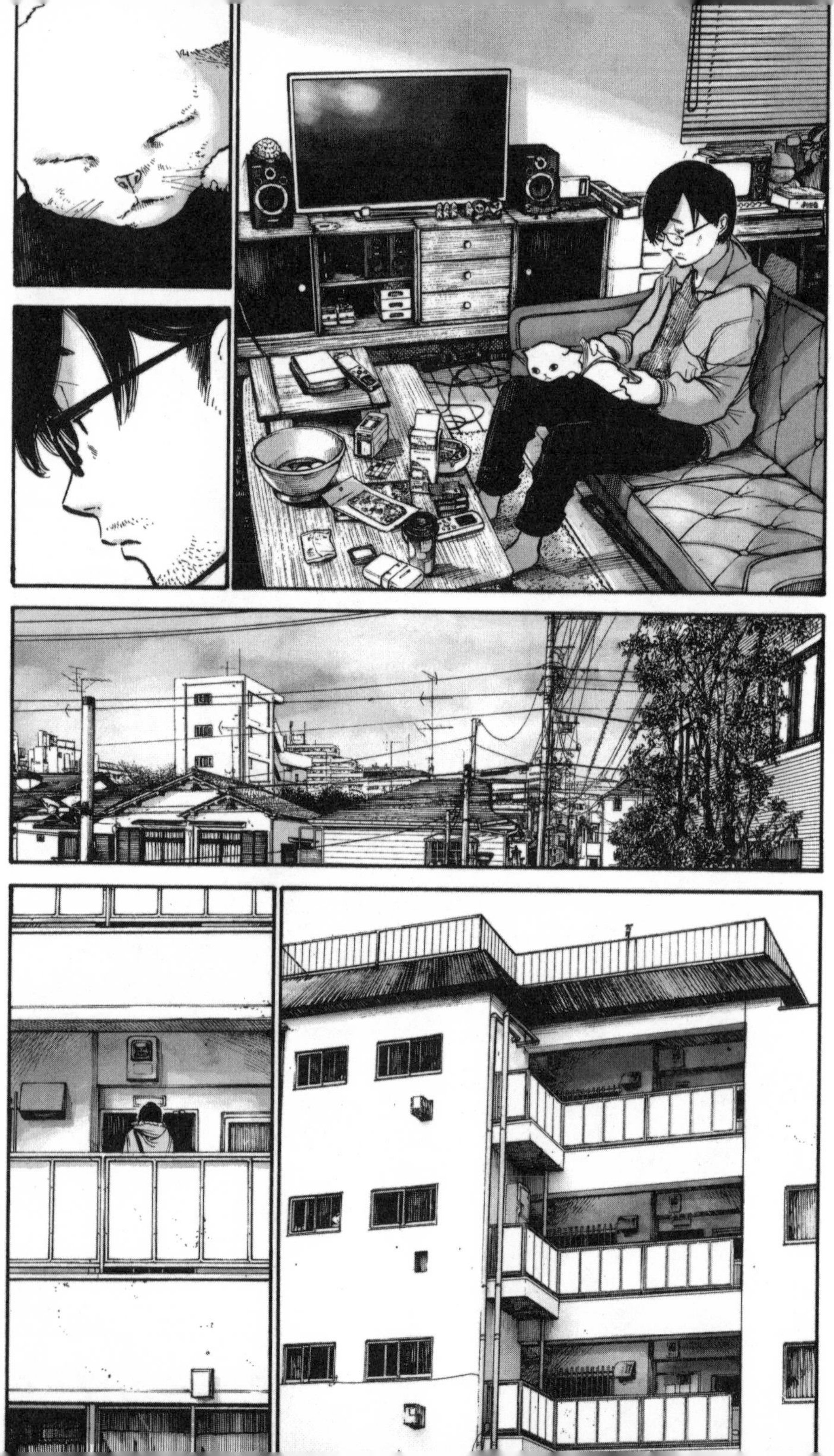

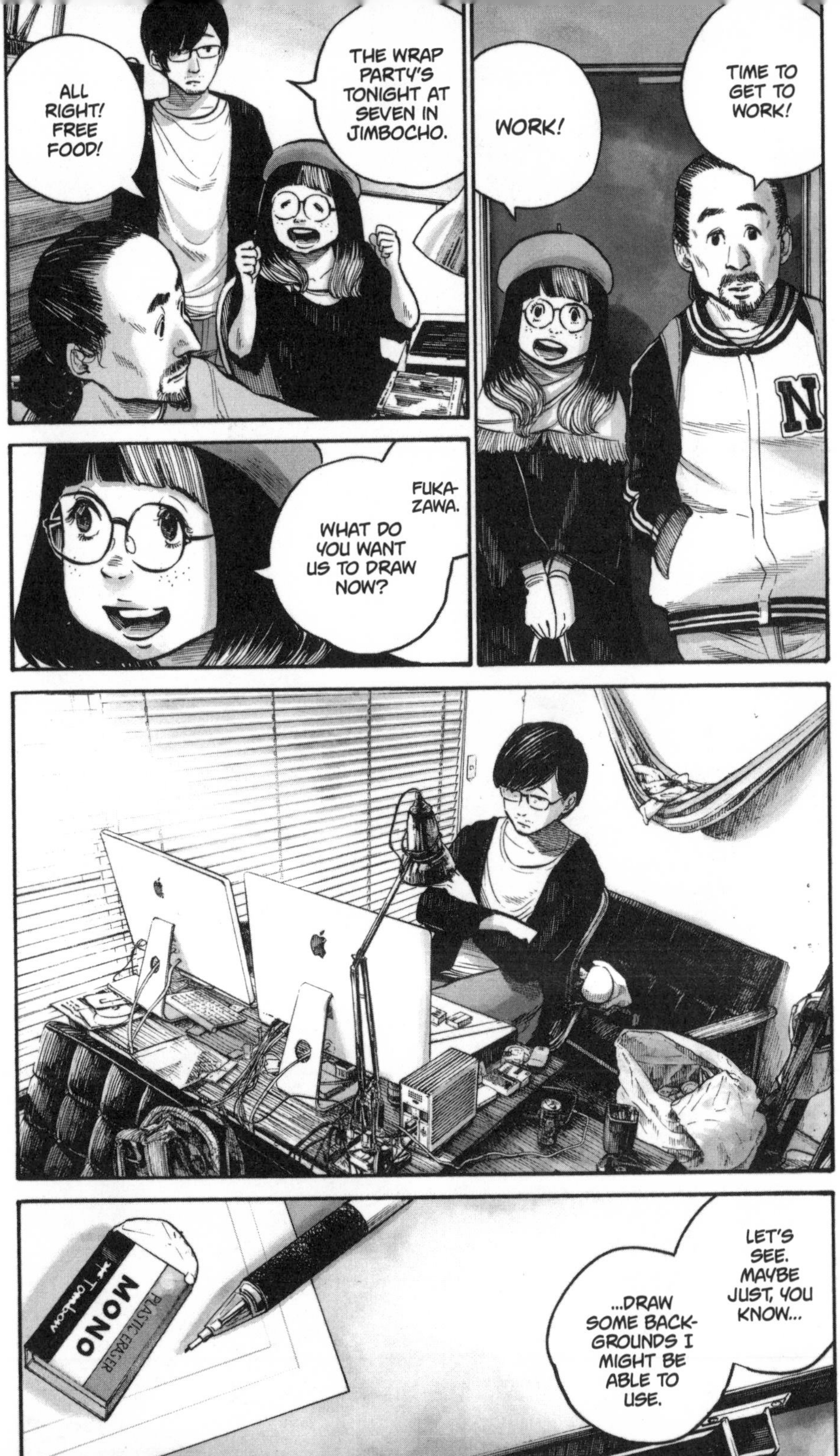
TIME TO GET TO WORK!
WORK!
THE WRAP PARTY'S TONIGHT AT SEVEN IN JIMBOCHO.
ALL RIGHT! FREE FOOD!
FUKA-ZAWA.
WHAT DO YOU WANT US TO DRAW NOW?
LET'S SEE. MAYBE JUST, YOU KNOW...
...DRAW SOME BACK-GROUNDS I MIGHT BE ABLE TO USE.
MONO
PLASTIC ERASER
Tombow

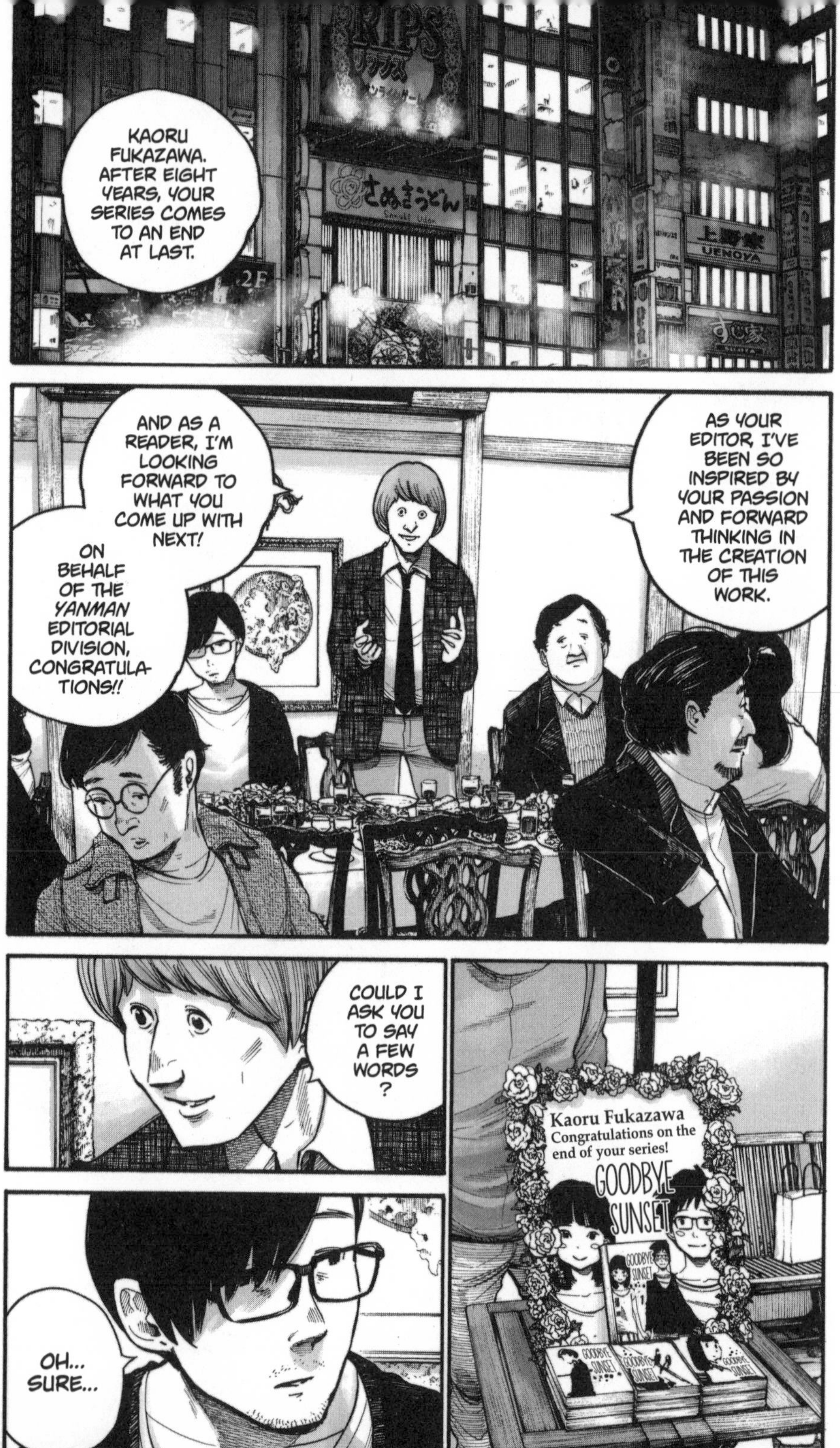
RIPS
UENOYA
2F
KAORU FUKAZAWA. AFTER EIGHT YEARS, YOUR SERIES COMES TO AN END AT LAST.
AS YOUR EDITOR, I'VE BEEN SO INSPIRED BY YOUR PASSION AND FORWARD THINKING IN THE CREATION OF THIS WORK.
AND AS A READER, I'M LOOKING FORWARD TO WHAT YOU COME UP WITH NEXT!
ON BEHALF OF THE *YANMAN* EDITORIAL DIVISION, CONGRATULATIONS!!
Kaoru Fukazawa
Congratulations on the end of your series!
GOODBYE SUNSET
GOODBYE SUNSET
COULD I ASK YOU TO SAY A FEW WORDS?
OH... SURE...

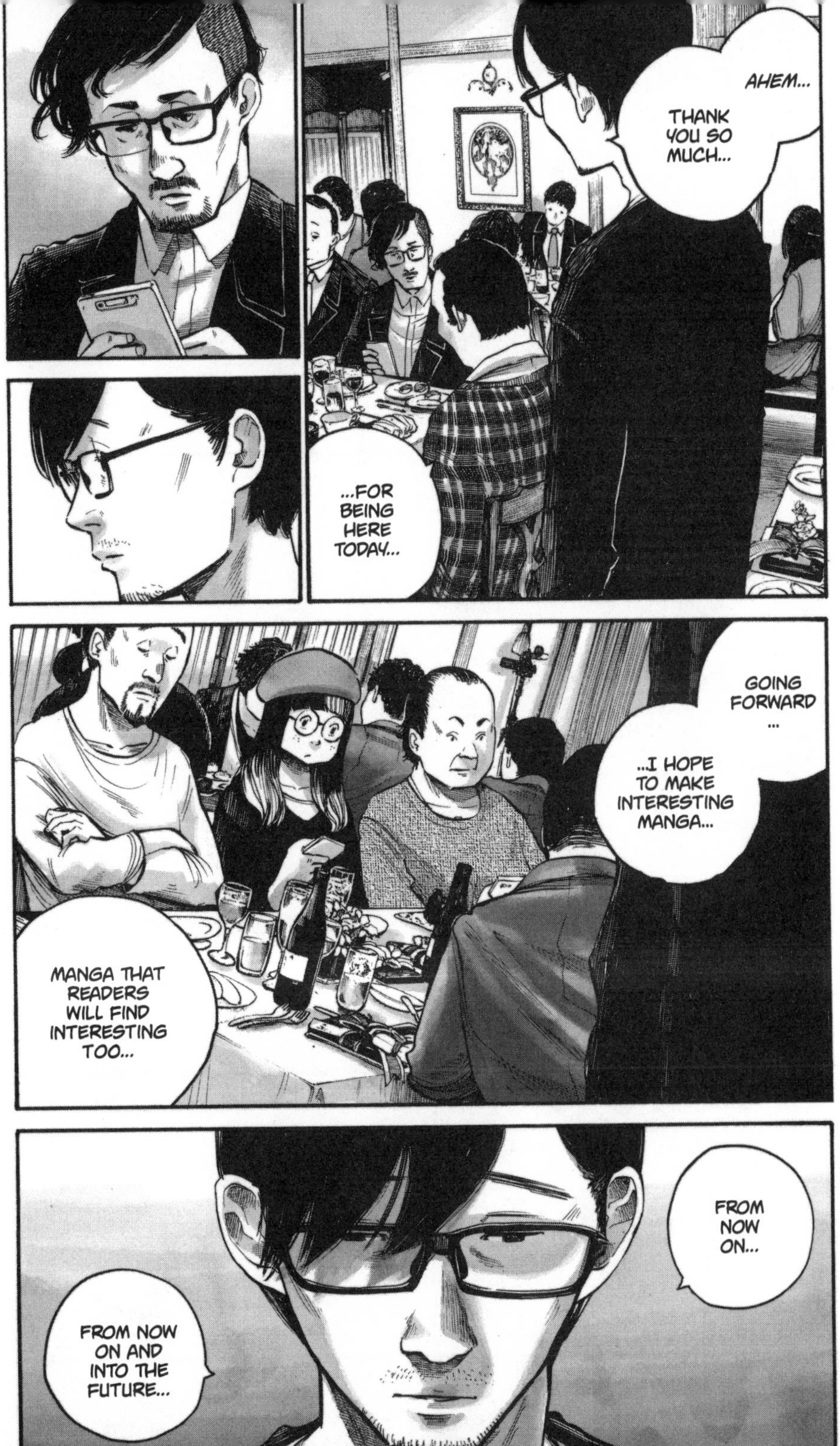
AHEM...
THANK YOU SO MUCH...
...FOR BEING HERE TODAY...
GOING FORWARD ...
...I HOPE TO MAKE INTERESTING MANGA...
MANGA THAT READERS WILL FIND INTERESTING TOO...
FROM NOW ON...
FROM NOW ON AND INTO THE FUTURE...

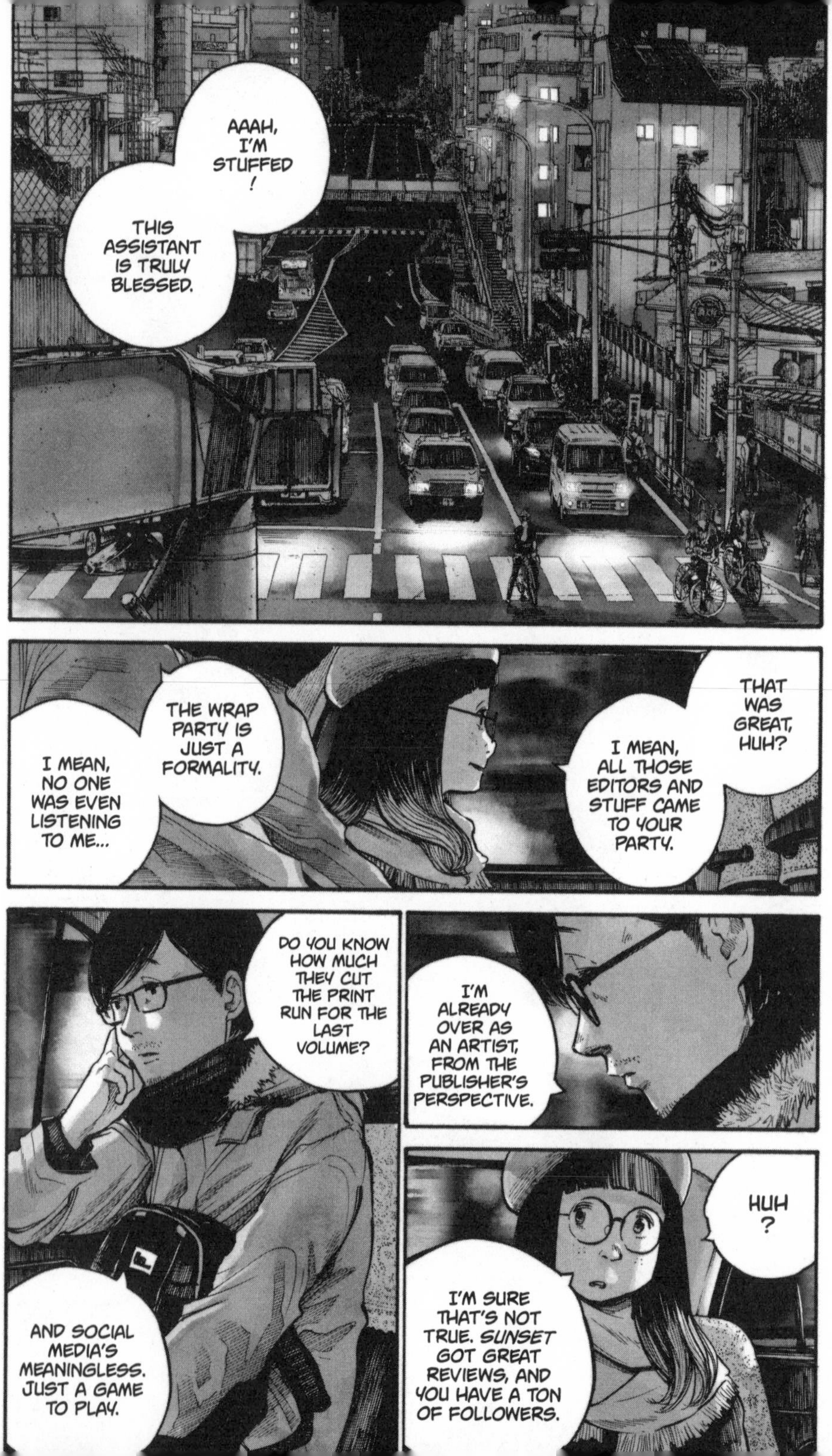
AAAH, I'M STUFFED!
THIS ASSISTANT IS TRULY BLESSED.
THAT WAS GREAT, HUH?
I MEAN, ALL THOSE EDITORS AND STUFF CAME TO YOUR PARTY.
THE WRAP PARTY IS JUST A FORMALITY.
I MEAN, NO ONE WAS EVEN LISTENING TO ME...
I'M ALREADY OVER AS AN ARTIST, FROM THE PUBLISHER'S PERSPECTIVE.
HUH?
I'M SURE THAT'S NOT TRUE. *SUNSET* GOT GREAT REVIEWS, AND YOU HAVE A TON OF FOLLOWERS.
DO YOU KNOW HOW MUCH THEY CUT THE PRINT RUN FOR THE LAST VOLUME?
AND SOCIAL MEDIA'S MEANINGLESS. JUST A GAME TO PLAY.

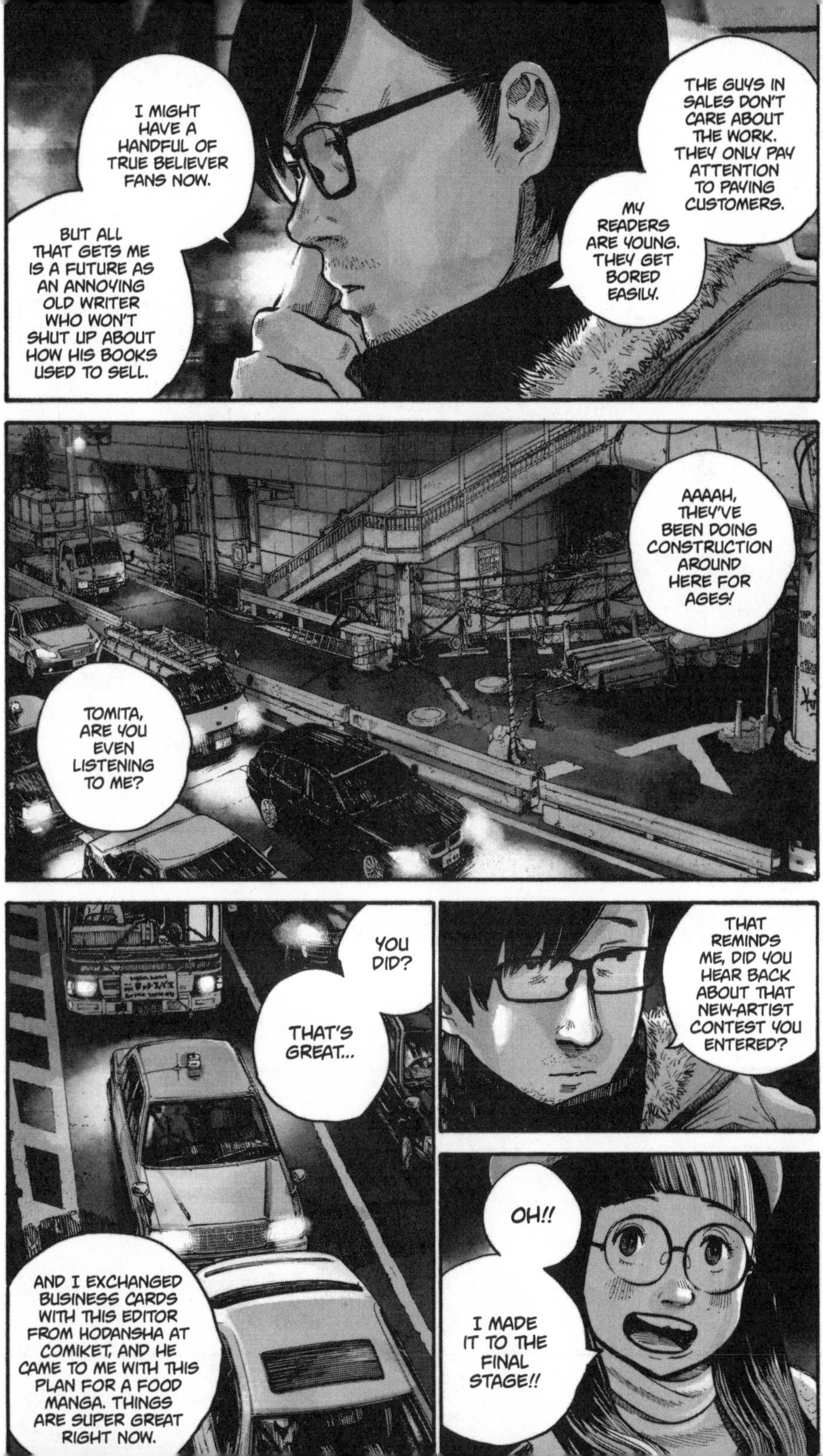
THE GUYS IN SALES DON'T CARE ABOUT THE WORK. THEY ONLY PAY ATTENTION TO PAYING CUSTOMERS.
MY READERS ARE YOUNG. THEY GET BORED EASILY.
I MIGHT HAVE A HANDFUL OF TRUE BELIEVER FANS NOW.
BUT ALL THAT GETS ME IS A FUTURE AS AN ANNOYING OLD WRITER WHO WON'T SHUT UP ABOUT HOW HIS BOOKS USED TO SELL.
AAAAH, THEY'VE BEEN DOING CONSTRUCTION AROUND HERE FOR AGES!
TOMITA, ARE YOU EVEN LISTENING TO ME?
THAT REMINDS ME, DID YOU HEAR BACK ABOUT THAT NEW-ARTIST CONTEST YOU ENTERED?
OH!!
I MADE IT TO THE FINAL STAGE!!
YOU DID?
THAT'S GREAT...
AND I EXCHANGED BUSINESS CARDS WITH THIS EDITOR FROM HODANSHA AT COMIKET, AND HE CAME TO ME WITH THIS PLAN FOR A FOOD MANGA. THINGS ARE SUPER GREAT RIGHT NOW.

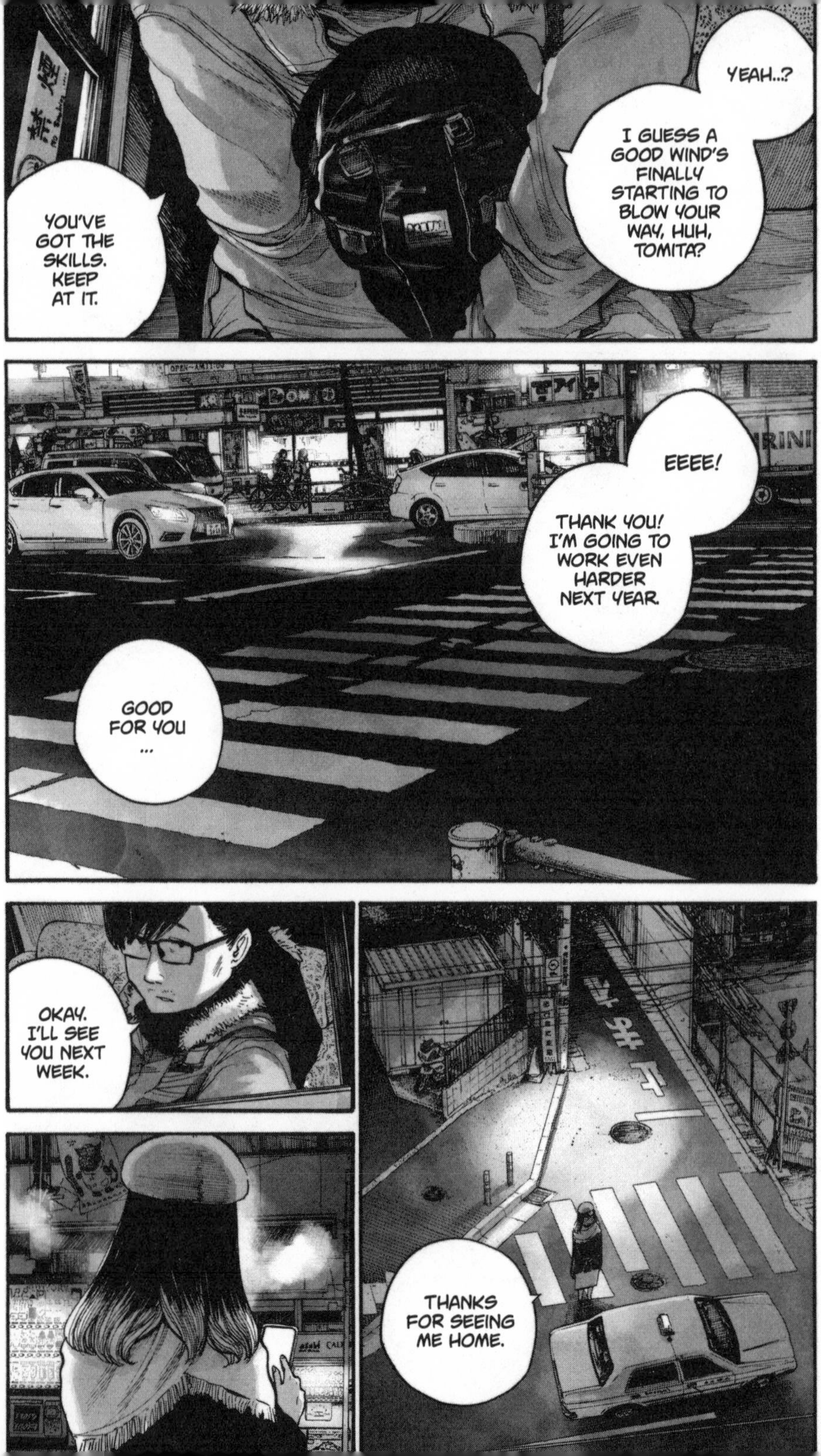
YEAH...?
I GUESS A GOOD WIND'S FINALLY STARTING TO BLOW YOUR WAY, HUH, TOMITA?
YOU'VE GOT THE SKILLS. KEEP AT IT.
EEEE!
THANK YOU! I'M GOING TO WORK EVEN HARDER NEXT YEAR.
GOOD FOR YOU ...
THANKS FOR SEEING ME HOME.
OKAY. I'LL SEE YOU NEXT WEEK.

DID YOU WANT TO TAKE THE ROAD THAT PASSES THE WARD OFFICE, SIR?

SURE...

Nozomi Machida: Just now
Makiura's drunk and invited herself over, so could you kill some time somewhere else?

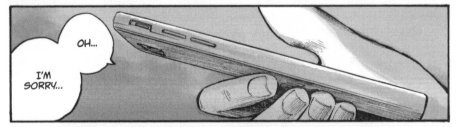

OH...

I'M SORRY...

COULD YOU ACTUALLY HEAD BACK TO SHINJUKU?

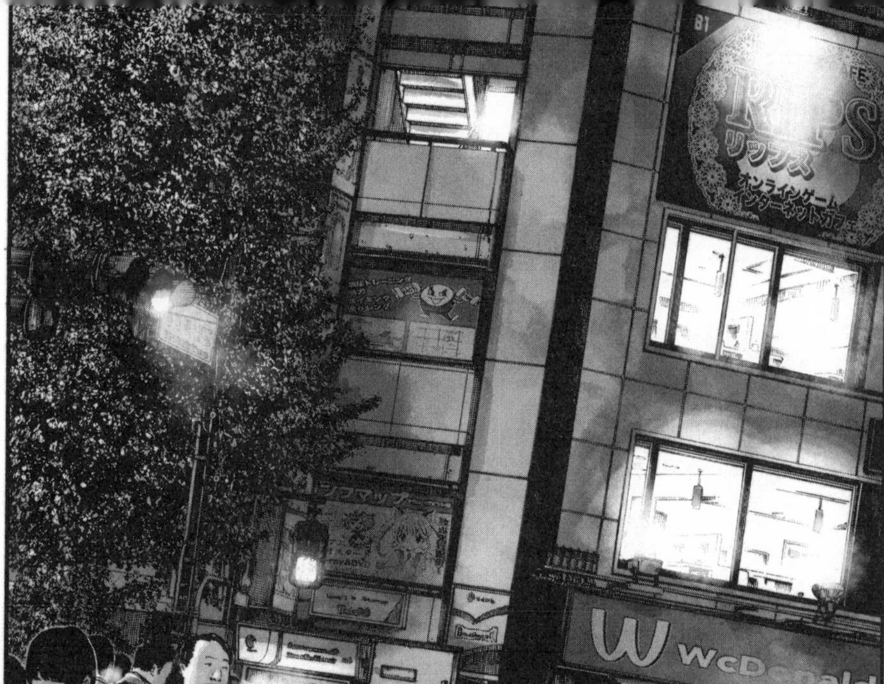
WcDonald

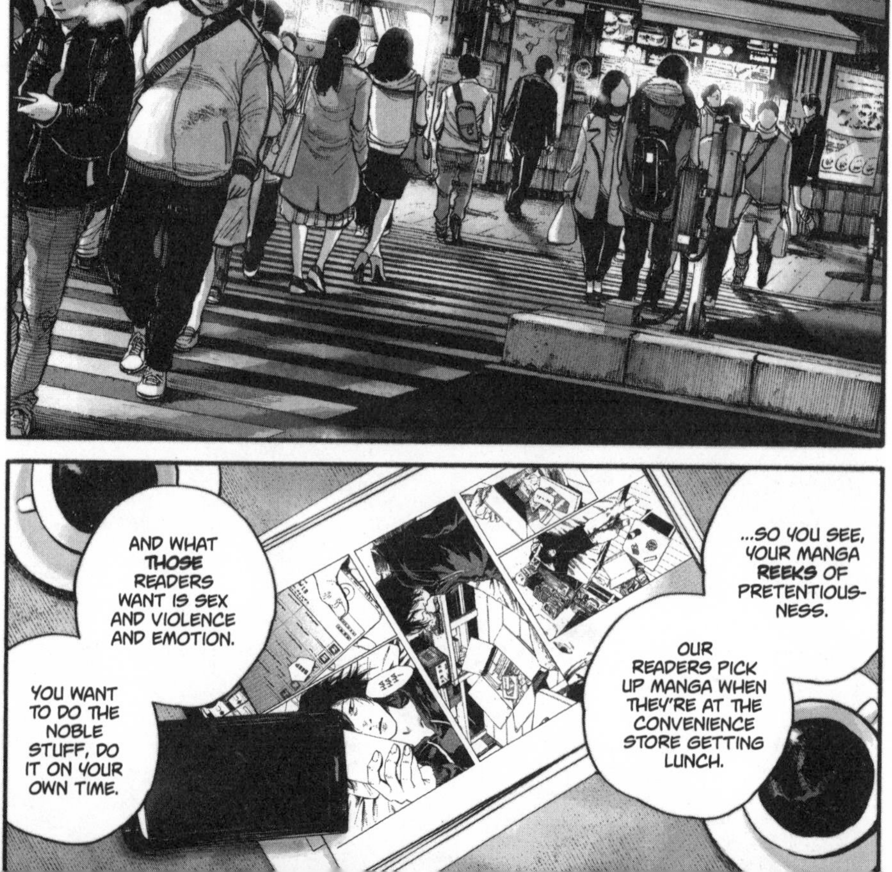
...SO YOU SEE, YOUR MANGA **REEKS** OF PRETENTIOUS-NESS.
OUR READERS PICK UP MANGA WHEN THEY'RE AT THE CONVENIENCE STORE GETTING LUNCH.
AND WHAT **THOSE** READERS WANT IS SEX AND VIOLENCE AND EMOTION.
YOU WANT TO DO THE NOBLE STUFF, DO IT ON YOUR OWN TIME.

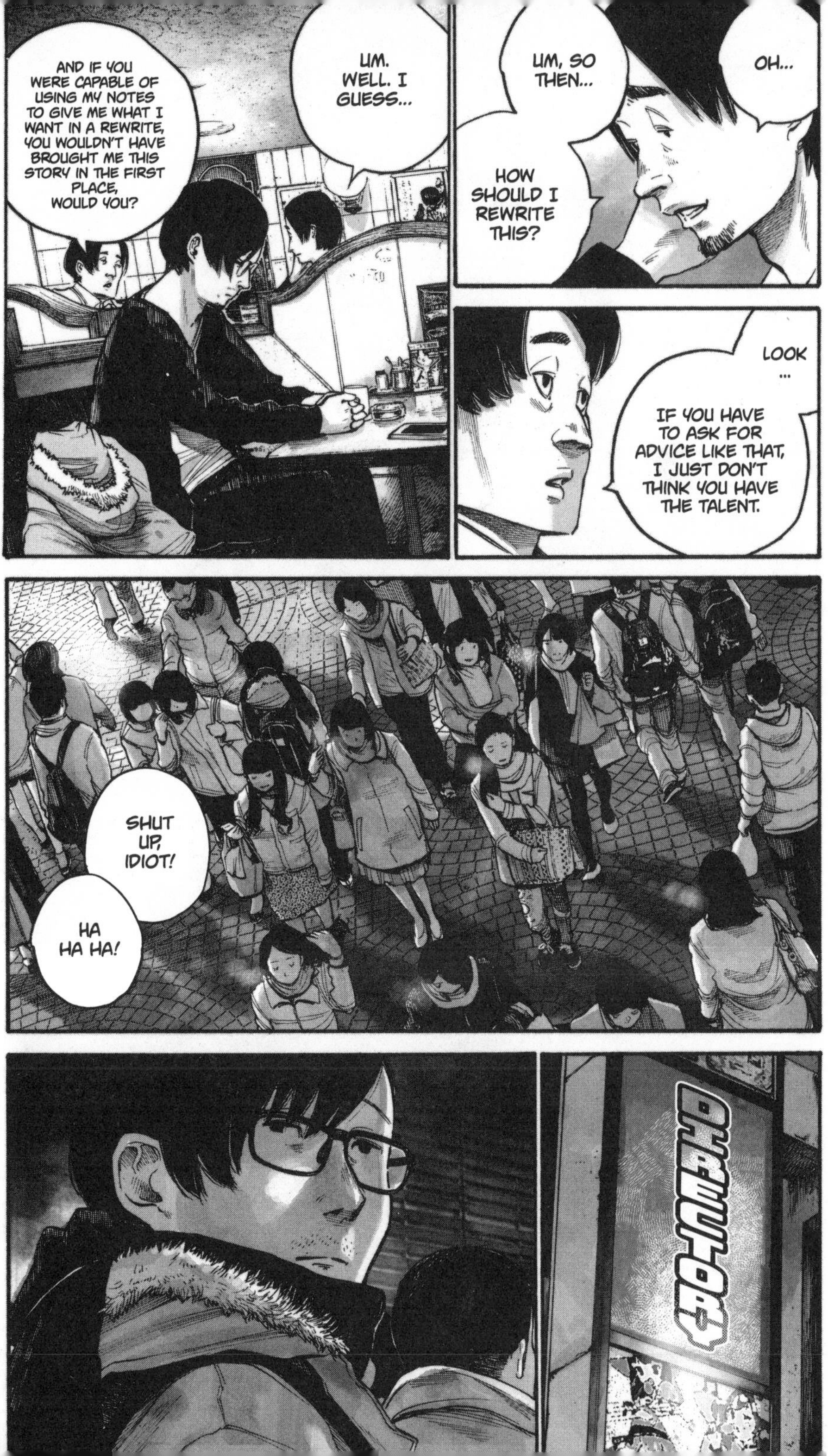
OH...
UM, SO THEN...
HOW SHOULD I REWRITE THIS?
LOOK ...
IF YOU HAVE TO ASK FOR ADVICE LIKE THAT, I JUST DON'T THINK YOU HAVE THE TALENT.
UM. WELL. I GUESS...
AND IF YOU WERE CAPABLE OF USING MY NOTES TO GIVE ME WHAT I WANT IN A REWRITE, YOU WOULDN'T HAVE BROUGHT ME THIS STORY IN THE FIRST PLACE, WOULD YOU?
SHUT UP, IDIOT!
HA HA HA!
DIRECTORY

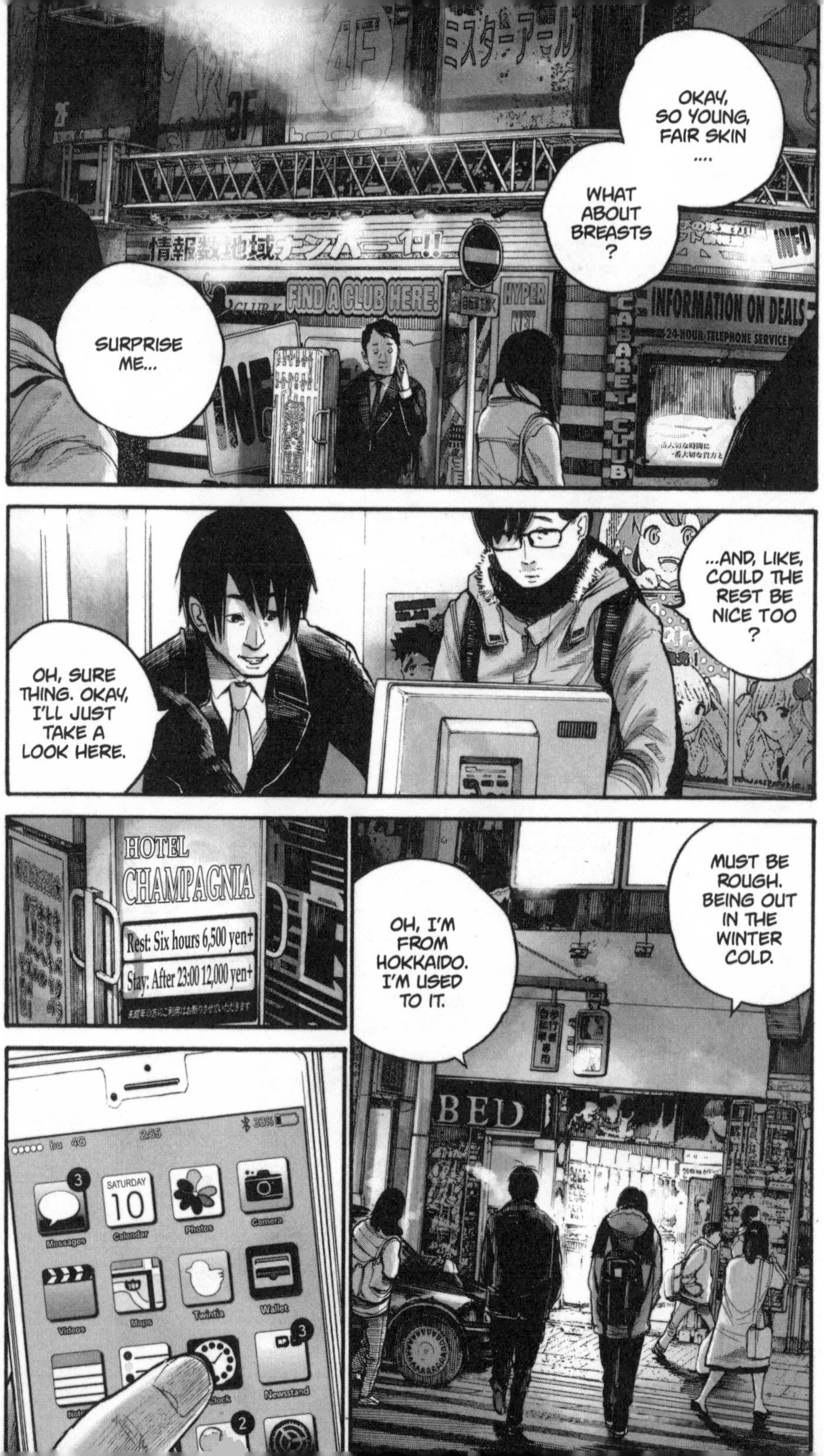
OKAY, SO YOUNG, FAIR SKIN ....
WHAT ABOUT BREASTS ?
SURPRISE ME...
INFO
INFORMATION ON DEALS
24-HOUR TELEPHONE SERVICE
CABARET CLUB
HYPER NET
FIND A CLUB HERE!
情報数地域ナンバー1!!
...AND, LIKE, COULD THE REST BE NICE TOO ?
OH, SURE THING. OKAY, I'LL JUST TAKE A LOOK HERE.
MUST BE ROUGH. BEING OUT IN THE WINTER COLD.
OH, I'M FROM HOKKAIDO. I'M USED TO IT.
BED
HOTEL CHAMPAGNIA
Rest: Six hours 6,500 yen+
Stay: After 23:00 12,000 yen+
SATURDAY
10
Messages
Calendar
Photos
Camera
Videos
Maps
Twintia
Wallet
Newsstand

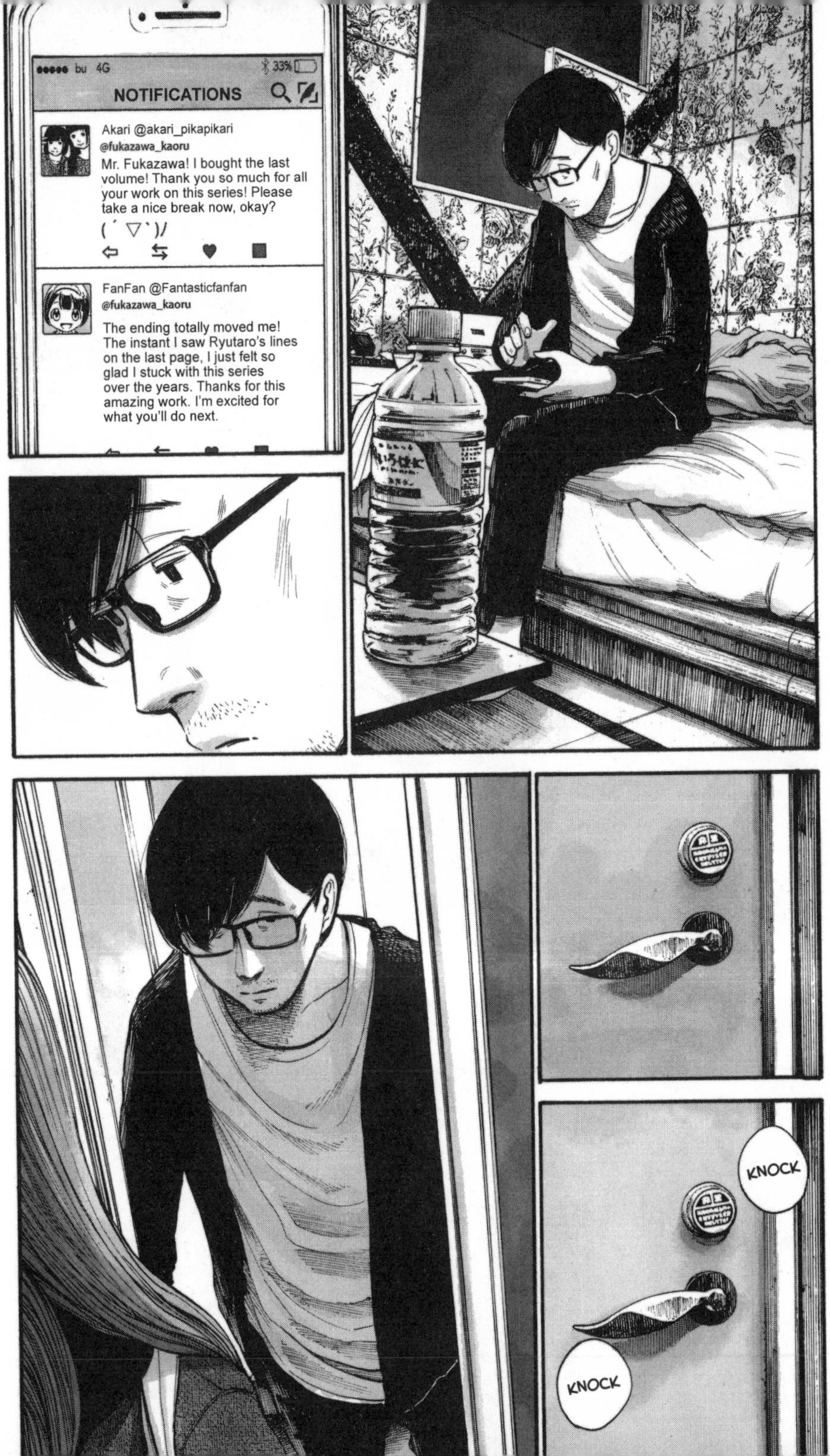
bu 4G
33%
NOTIFICATIONS
Akari @akari_pikapikari
@fukazawa_kaoru
Mr. Fukazawa! I bought the last volume! Thank you so much for all your work on this series! Please take a nice break now, okay?
(´ ▽ `)/
FanFan @Fantasticfanfan
@fukazawa_kaoru
The ending totally moved me! The instant I saw Ryutaro's lines on the last page, I just felt so glad I stuck with this series over the years. Thanks for this amazing work. I'm excited for what you'll do next.
KNOCK
KNOCK

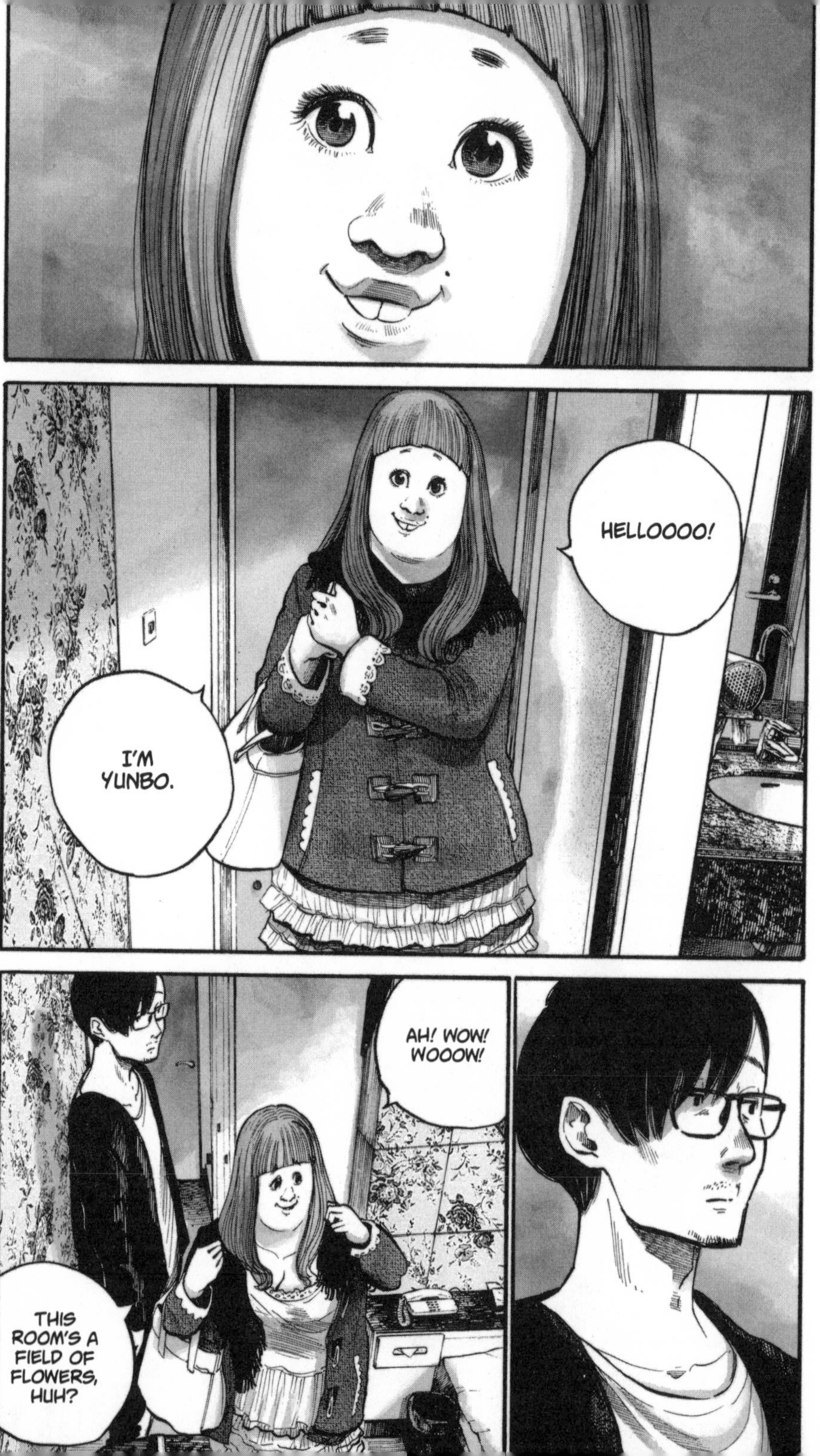
HELLOOOO!
I'M YUNBO.
AH! WOW! WOOOW!
THIS ROOM'S A FIELD OF FLOWERS, HUH?

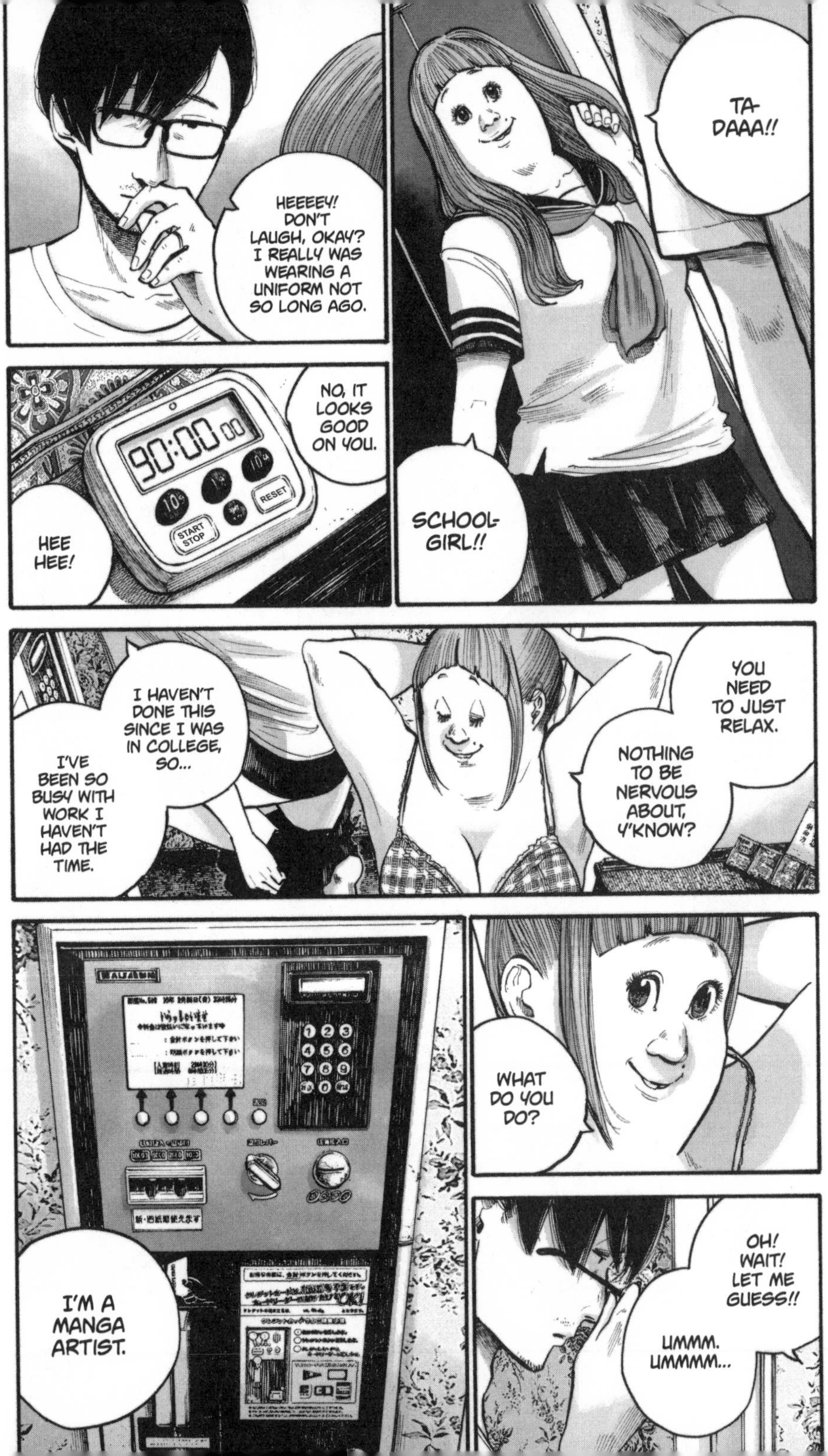
TA DAAA!!
SCHOOL-GIRL!!
HEEEEY! DON'T LAUGH, OKAY? I REALLY WAS WEARING A UNIFORM NOT SO LONG AGO.
NO, IT LOOKS GOOD ON YOU.
HEE HEE!
YOU NEED TO JUST RELAX.
NOTHING TO BE NERVOUS ABOUT, Y'KNOW?
I HAVEN'T DONE THIS SINCE I WAS IN COLLEGE, SO...
I'VE BEEN SO BUSY WITH WORK I HAVEN'T HAD THE TIME.
WHAT DO YOU DO?
OH! WAIT! LET ME GUESS!!
UMMM. UMMMM...
I'M A MANGA ARTIST.

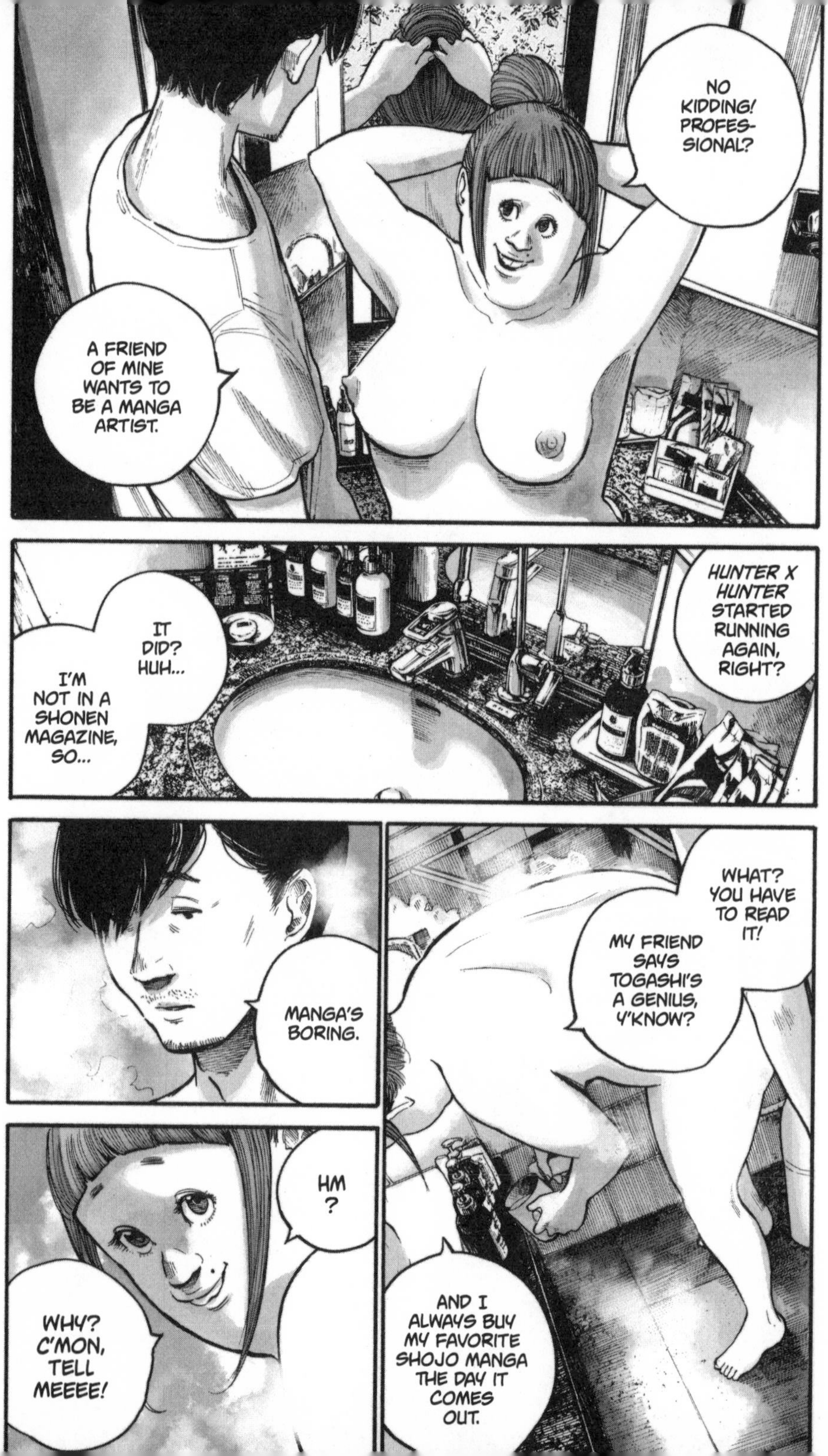
NO KIDDING! PROFES-SIONAL?
A FRIEND OF MINE WANTS TO BE A MANGA ARTIST.
HUNTER X HUNTER STARTED RUNNING AGAIN, RIGHT?
IT DID? HUH...
I'M NOT IN A SHONEN MAGAZINE, SO...
WHAT? YOU HAVE TO READ IT!
MY FRIEND SAYS TOGASHI'S A GENIUS, Y'KNOW?
AND I ALWAYS BUY MY FAVORITE SHOJO MANGA THE DAY IT COMES OUT.
MANGA'S BORING.
HM ?
WHY? C'MON, TELL MEEEE!

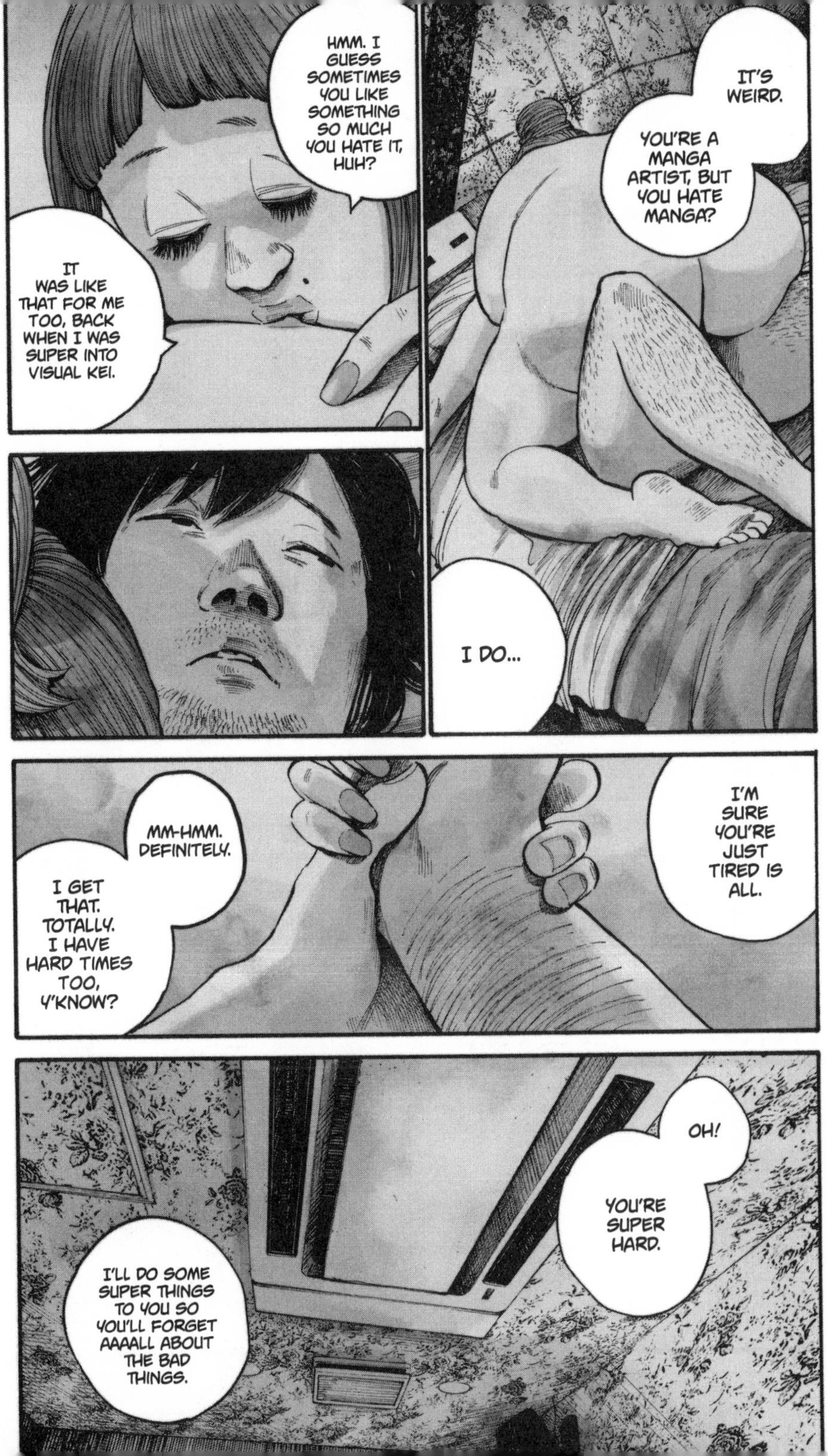
IT'S WEIRD.
YOU'RE A MANGA ARTIST, BUT YOU HATE MANGA?
I DO...
HMM. I GUESS SOMETIMES YOU LIKE SOMETHING SO MUCH YOU HATE IT, HUH?
IT WAS LIKE THAT FOR ME TOO, BACK WHEN I WAS SUPER INTO VISUAL KEI.
I'M SURE YOU'RE JUST TIRED IS ALL.
MM-HMM. DEFINITELY.
I GET THAT. TOTALLY. I HAVE HARD TIMES TOO, Y'KNOW?
OH!
YOU'RE SUPER HARD.
I'LL DO SOME SUPER THINGS TO YOU SO YOU'LL FORGET AAAALL ABOUT THE BAD THINGS.

YOU'RE A NICE GIRL...

YEAH. THANKS ...

WHAT'S WRONG? DON'T CRY.

THERE'S A GOOD BOY. GOOD BOY.

OH, WHOA!

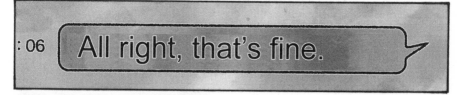

: 06

All right, that's fine.

< 1   Nozomi Machida

Feb. 2 (Wed.)

I have a meeting until late, so I won't be home until morning.   02 : 15

Read 04 : 46   Got it.

Feb. 11 (Fri.)

I'm going to Osaka for research tomorrow. I'll be back at the end of the week, so please make sure to feed the cat.   20 : 38

Read 14 : 22   Okay, I will.

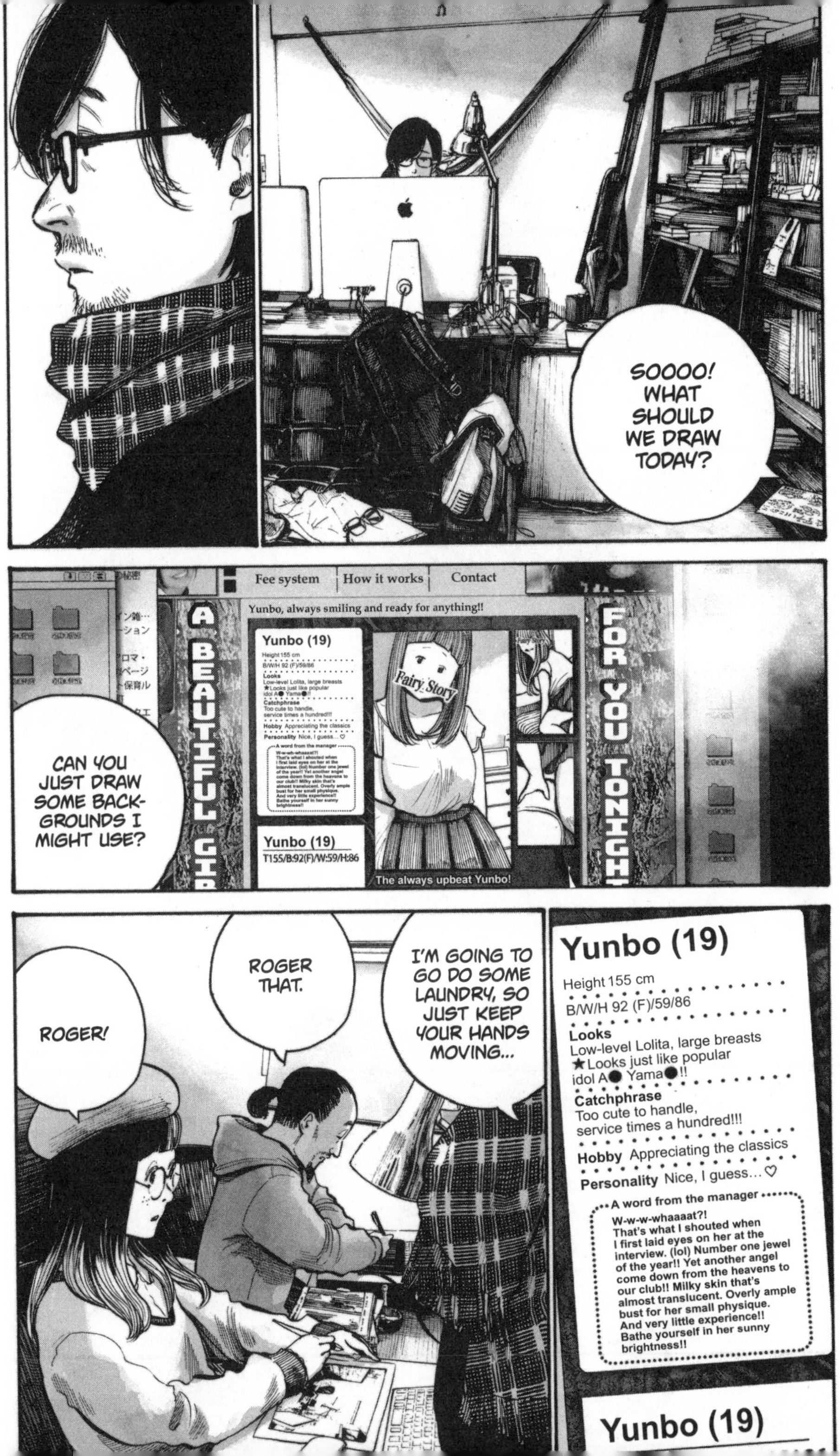
SOOOO! WHAT SHOULD WE DRAW TODAY?
Fee system
How it works
Contact
Yunbo, always smiling and ready for anything!!
FOR YOU TONIGH
A BEAUTIFUL GIR
Fairy Story
The always upbeat Yunbo!
Yunbo (19)
T155/B:92(F)/W:59/H:86
CAN YOU JUST DRAW SOME BACK-GROUNDS I MIGHT USE?
Yunbo (19)
Height 155 cm
B/W/H 92 (F)/59/86
Looks
Low-level Lolita, large breasts
★Looks just like popular idol A● Yama●!!
Catchphrase
Too cute to handle, service times a hundred!!!
Hobby Appreciating the classics
Personality Nice, I guess…♡
A word from the manager
W-w-w-whaaaat?! That's what I shouted when I first laid eyes on her at the interview. (lol) Number one jewel of the year!! Yet another angel come down from the heavens to our club!! Milky skin that's almost translucent. Overly ample bust for her small physique. And very little experience!! Bathe yourself in her sunny brightness!!
Yunbo (19)
I'M GOING TO GO DO SOME LAUNDRY, SO JUST KEEP YOUR HANDS MOVING...
ROGER THAT.
ROGER!

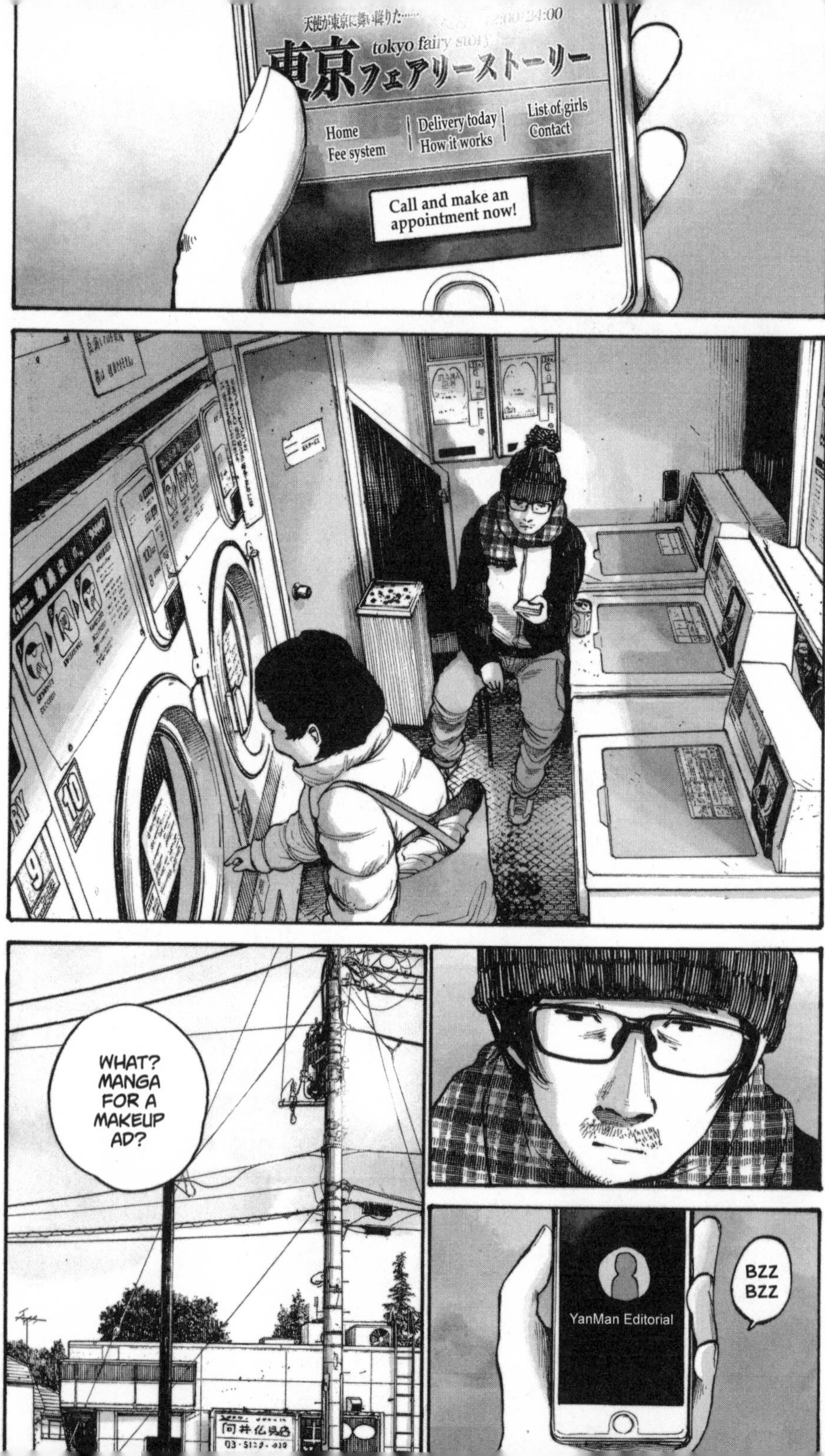
天使が東京に舞い降りた……
東京フェアリーストーリー
tokyo fairy story
Home
Fee system
Delivery today
How it works
List of girls
Contact
Call and make an appointment now!
YanMan Editorial
BZZ BZZ
WHAT? MANGA FOR A MAKEUP AD?

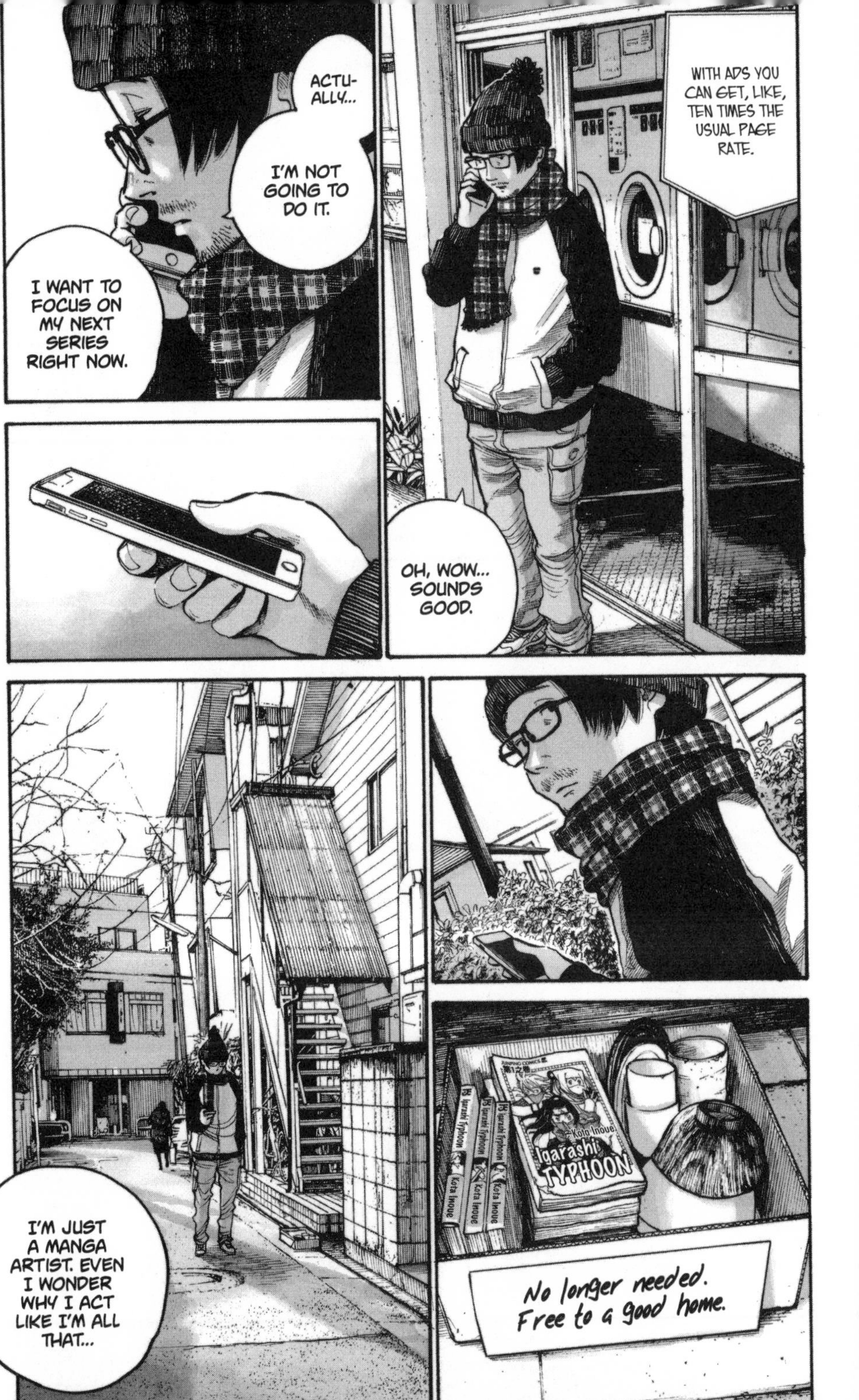
WITH ADS YOU CAN GET, LIKE, TEN TIMES THE USUAL PAGE RATE.
OH, WOW... SOUNDS GOOD.
ACTU-ALLY...
I'M NOT GOING TO DO IT.
I WANT TO FOCUS ON MY NEXT SERIES RIGHT NOW.
Igarashi TYPHOON
Kota Inoue
No longer needed. Free to a good home.
I'M JUST A MANGA ARTIST. EVEN I WONDER WHY I ACT LIKE I'M ALL THAT...

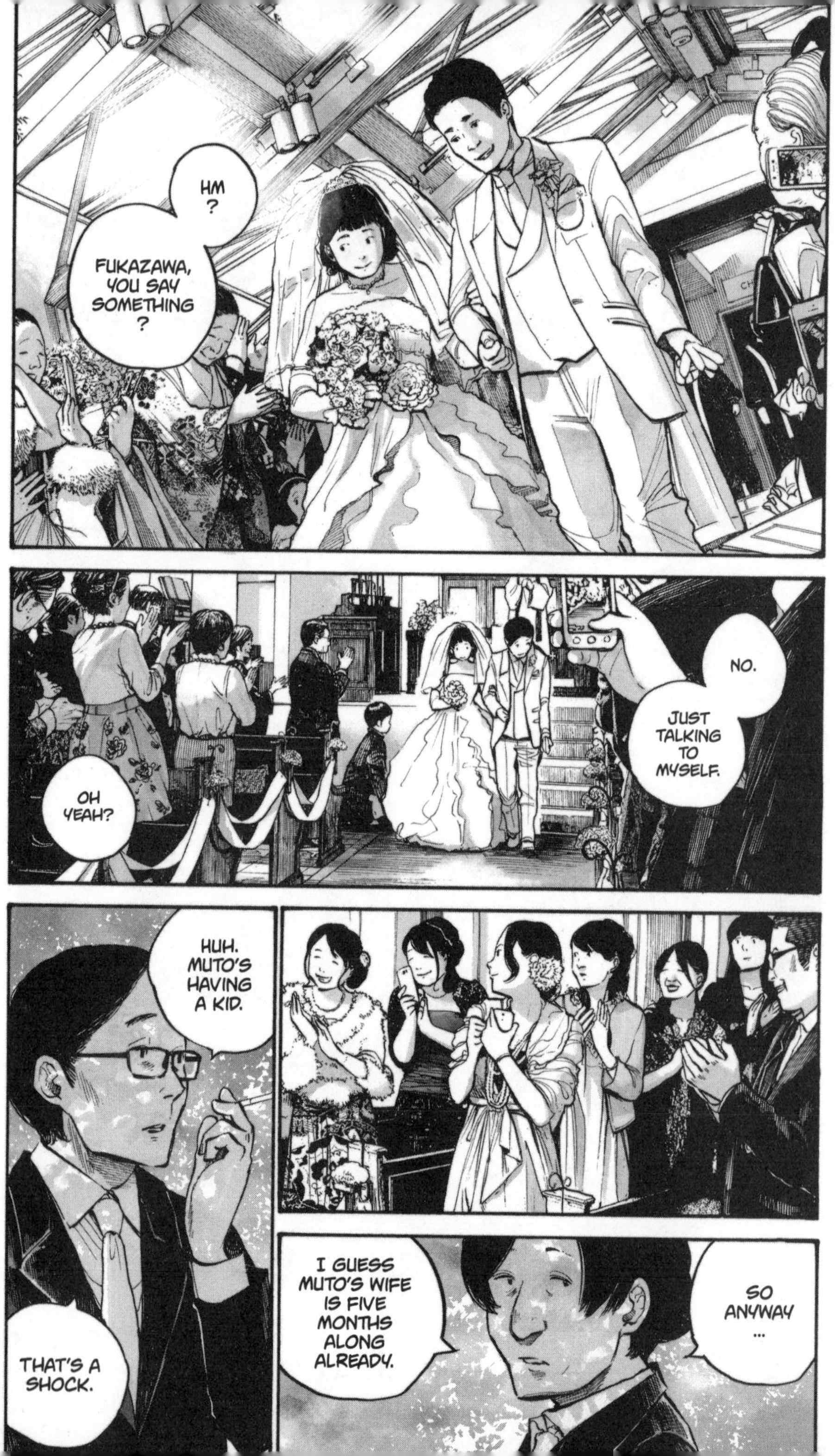
HM?
FUKAZAWA, YOU SAY SOMETHING?
NO.
JUST TALKING TO MYSELF.
OH YEAH?
SO ANYWAY ...
I GUESS MUTO'S WIFE IS FIVE MONTHS ALONG ALREADY.
HUH. MUTO'S HAVING A KID.
THAT'S A SHOCK.

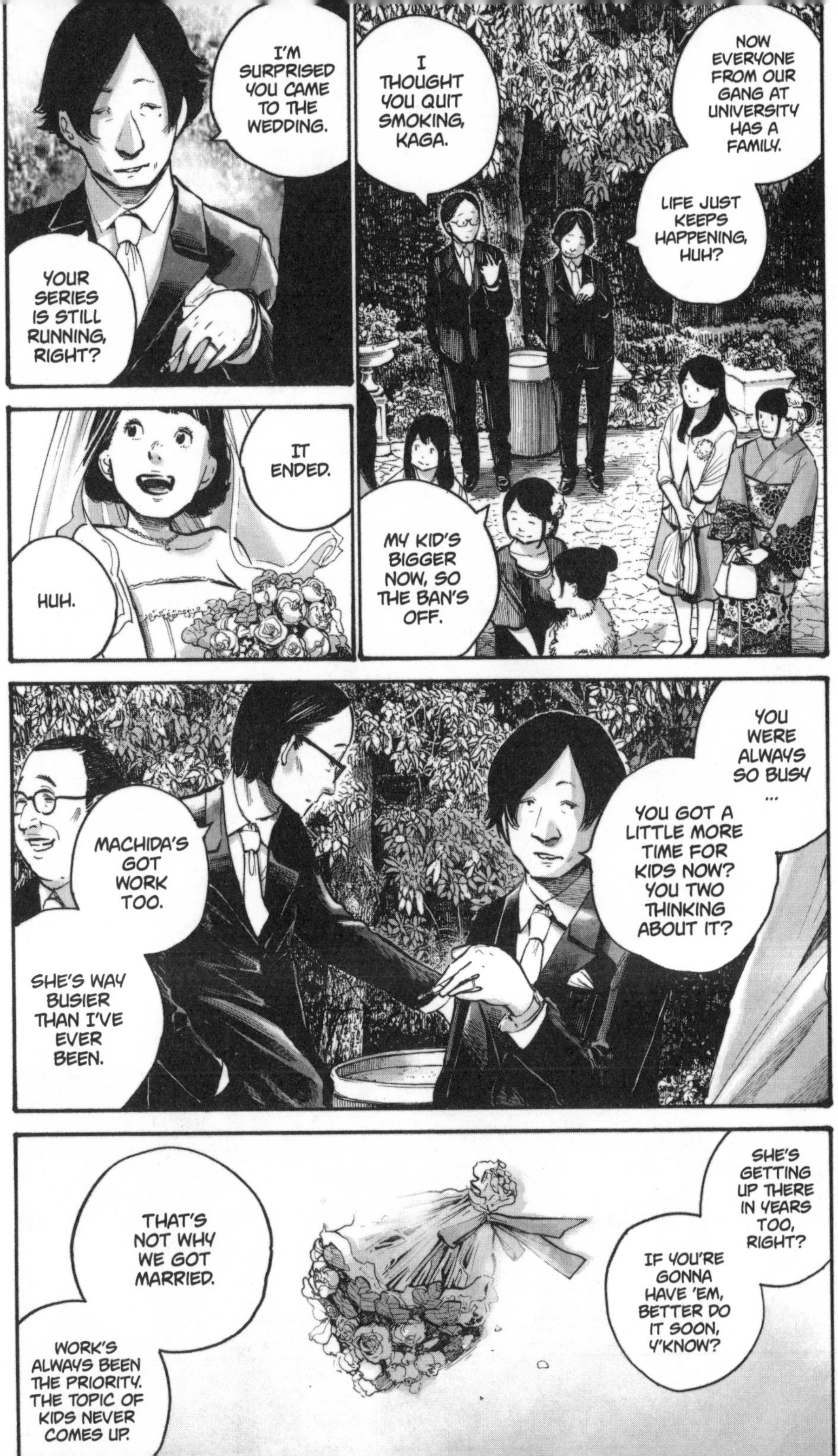
NOW EVERYONE FROM OUR GANG AT UNIVERSITY HAS A FAMILY.
LIFE JUST KEEPS HAPPENING, HUH?
I THOUGHT YOU QUIT SMOKING, KAGA.
MY KID'S BIGGER NOW, SO THE BAN'S OFF.
I'M SURPRISED YOU CAME TO THE WEDDING.
YOUR SERIES IS STILL RUNNING, RIGHT?
IT ENDED.
HUH.
YOU WERE ALWAYS SO BUSY ...
YOU GOT A LITTLE MORE TIME FOR KIDS NOW? YOU TWO THINKING ABOUT IT?
MACHIDA'S GOT WORK TOO.
SHE'S WAY BUSIER THAN I'VE EVER BEEN.
SHE'S GETTING UP THERE IN YEARS TOO, RIGHT?
IF YOU'RE GONNA HAVE 'EM, BETTER DO IT SOON, Y'KNOW?
THAT'S NOT WHY WE GOT MARRIED.
WORK'S ALWAYS BEEN THE PRIORITY. THE TOPIC OF KIDS NEVER COMES UP.

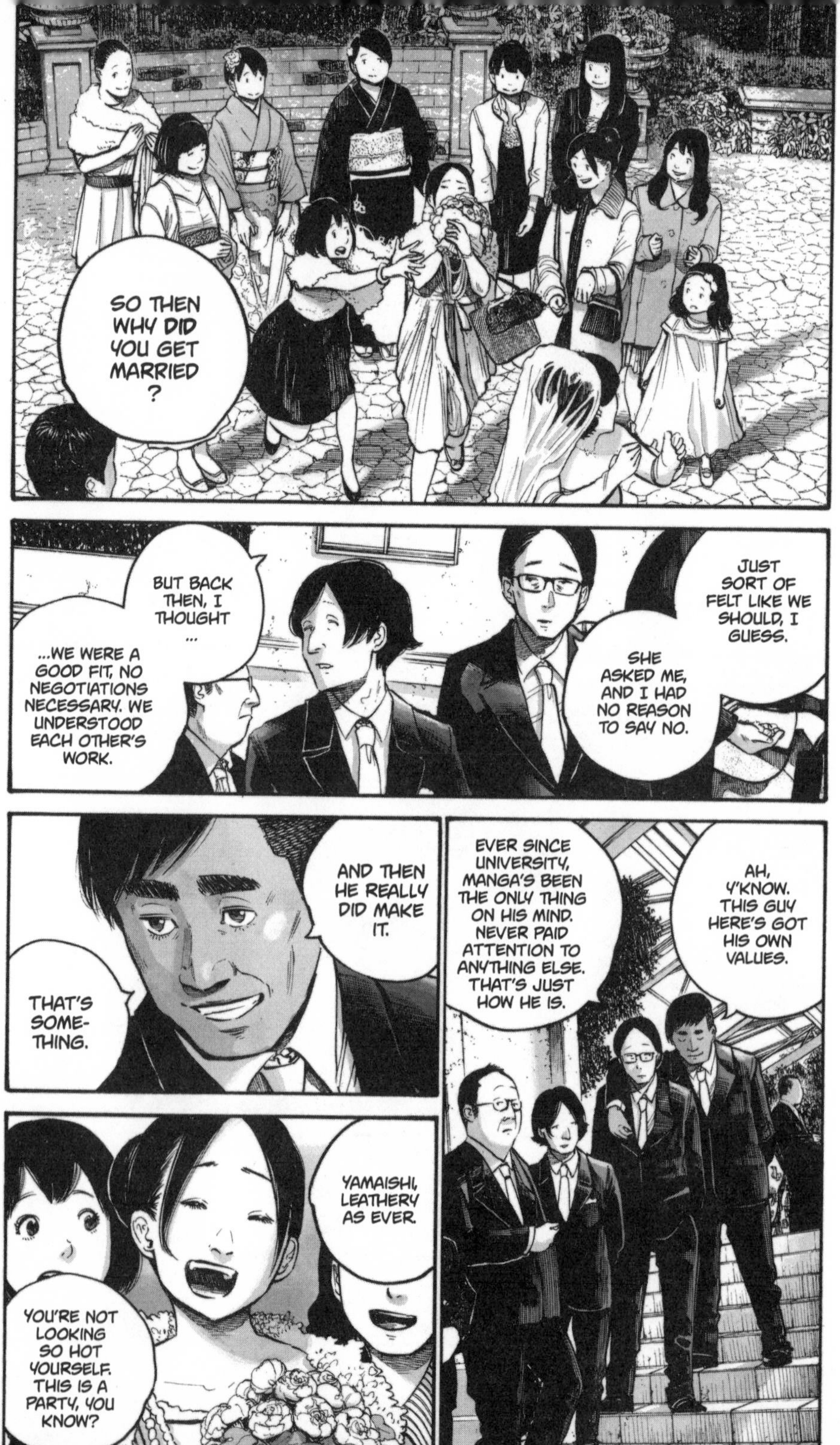
SO THEN WHY DID YOU GET MARRIED?
JUST SORT OF FELT LIKE WE SHOULD, I GUESS.
SHE ASKED ME, AND I HAD NO REASON TO SAY NO.
BUT BACK THEN, I THOUGHT...
...WE WERE A GOOD FIT, NO NEGOTIATIONS NECESSARY. WE UNDERSTOOD EACH OTHER'S WORK.
AH, Y'KNOW. THIS GUY HERE'S GOT HIS OWN VALUES.
EVER SINCE UNIVERSITY, MANGA'S BEEN THE ONLY THING ON HIS MIND. NEVER PAID ATTENTION TO ANYTHING ELSE. THAT'S JUST HOW HE IS.
AND THEN HE REALLY DID MAKE IT.
THAT'S SOME-THING.
YAMAISHI, LEATHERY AS EVER.
YOU'RE NOT LOOKING SO HOT YOURSELF. THIS IS A PARTY, YOU KNOW?

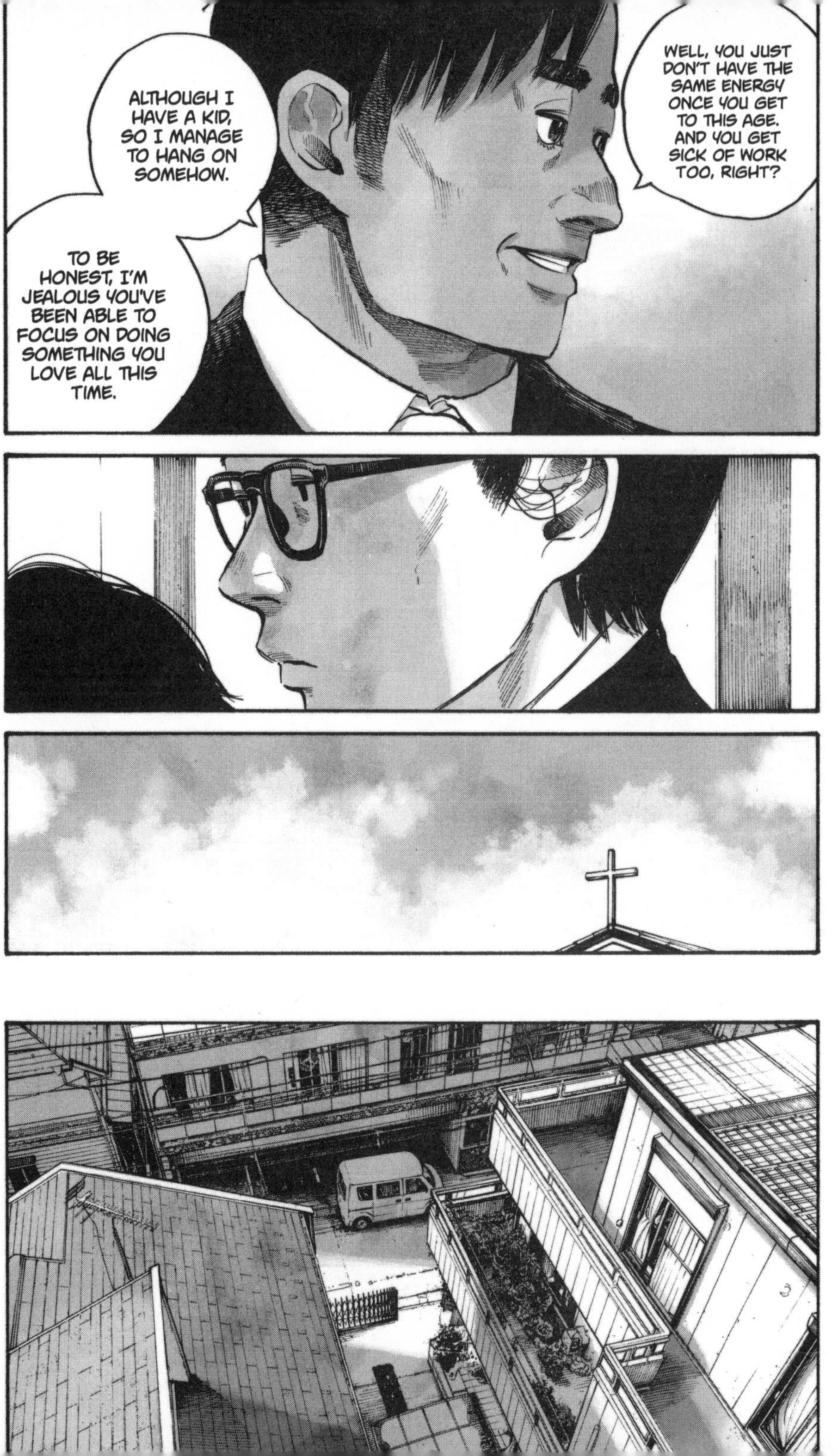
WELL, YOU JUST DON'T HAVE THE SAME ENERGY ONCE YOU GET TO THIS AGE. AND YOU GET SICK OF WORK TOO, RIGHT?
ALTHOUGH I HAVE A KID, SO I MANAGE TO HANG ON SOMEHOW.
TO BE HONEST, I'M JEALOUS YOU'VE BEEN ABLE TO FOCUS ON DOING SOMETHING YOU LOVE ALL THIS TIME.

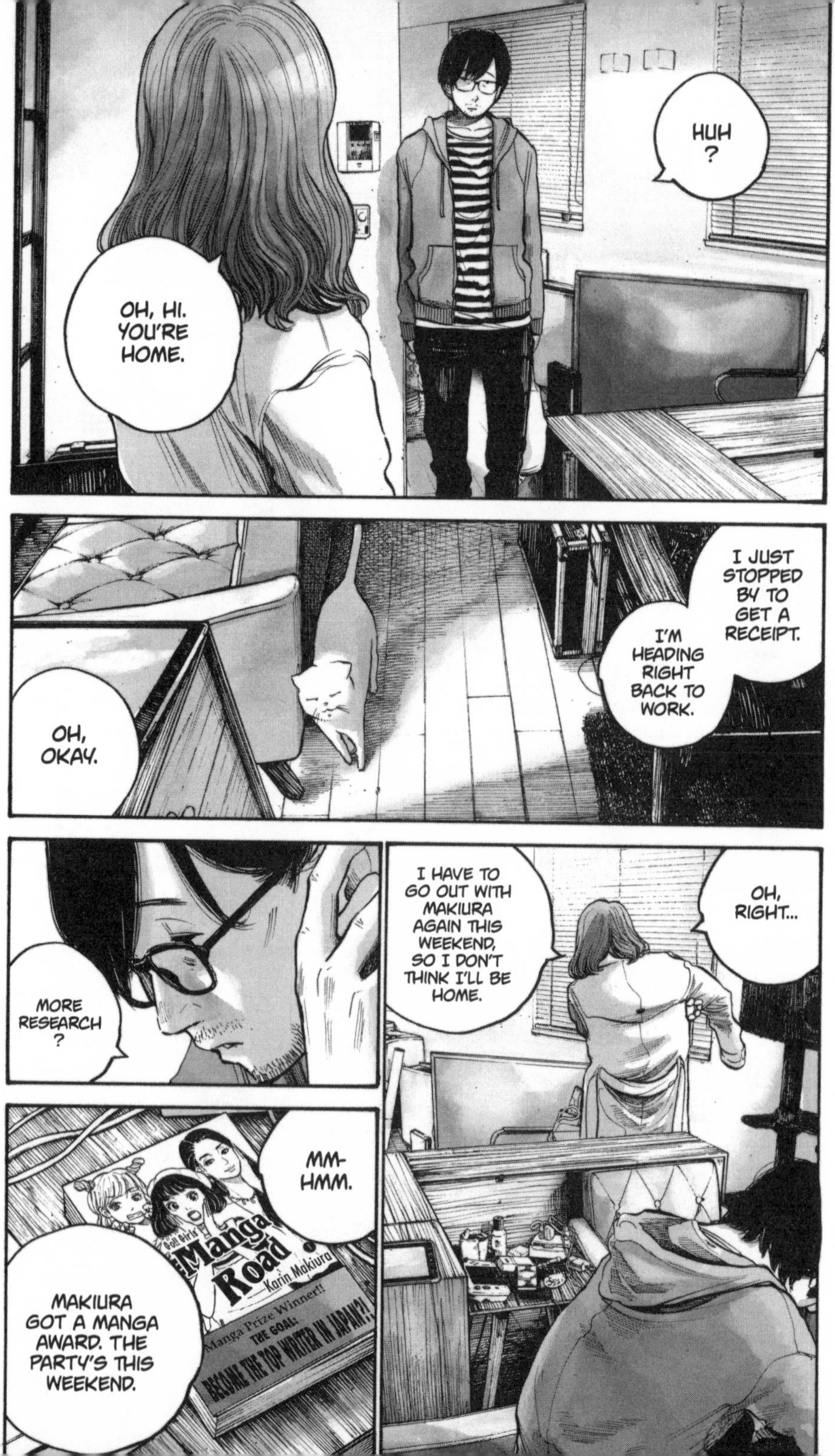
HUH?
OH, HI. YOU'RE HOME.
I JUST STOPPED BY TO GET A RECEIPT.
I'M HEADING RIGHT BACK TO WORK.
OH, OKAY.
OH, RIGHT...
I HAVE TO GO OUT WITH MAKIURA AGAIN THIS WEEKEND, SO I DON'T THINK I'LL BE HOME.
MORE RESEARCH?
MM-HMM.
Manga Road
Karin Makiura
Manga Prize Winner!!
THE GOAL: BECOME THE TOP WRITER IN JAPAN?!
MAKIURA GOT A MANGA AWARD. THE PARTY'S THIS WEEKEND.

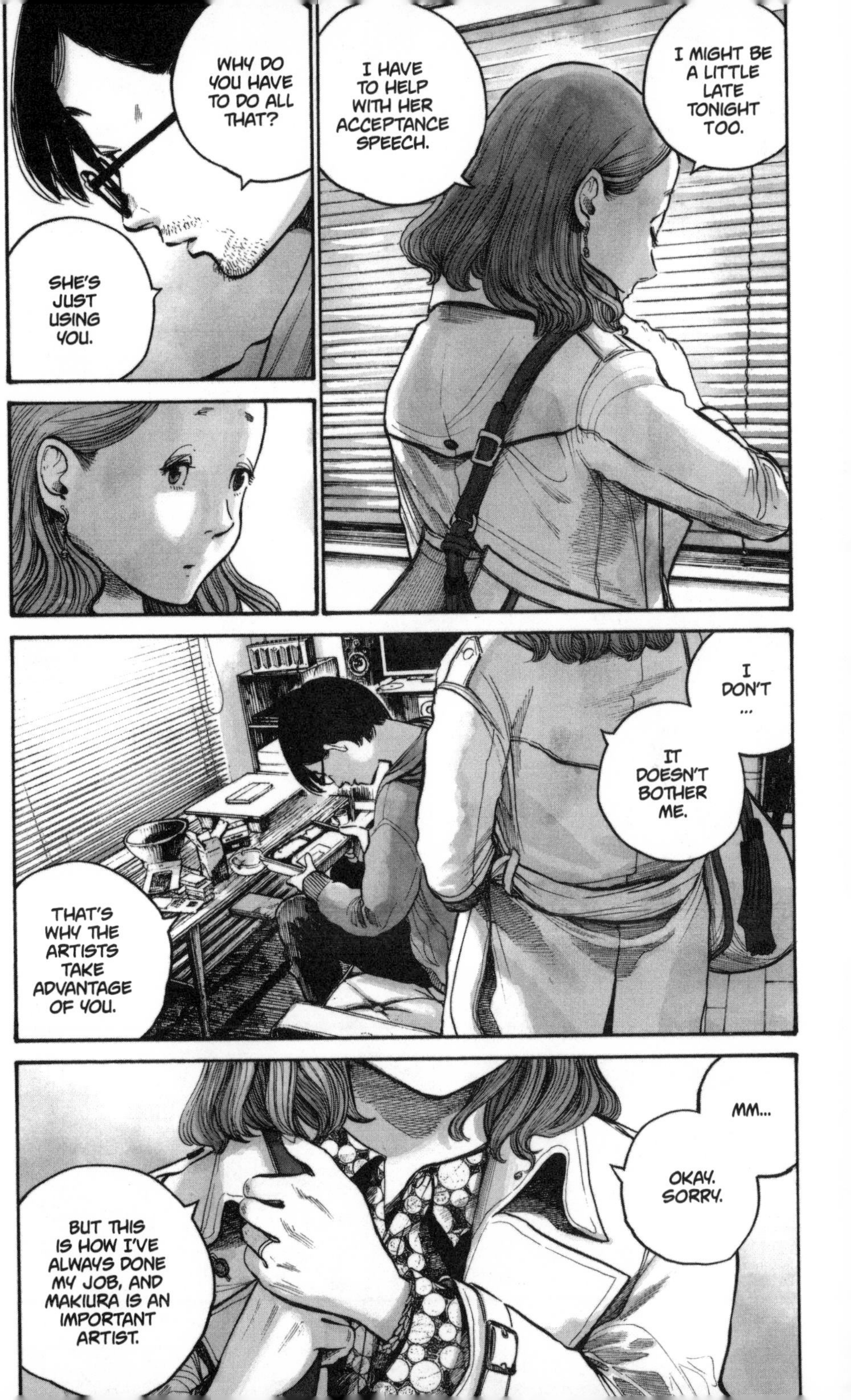
I MIGHT BE A LITTLE LATE TONIGHT TOO.
I HAVE TO HELP WITH HER ACCEPTANCE SPEECH.
WHY DO YOU HAVE TO DO ALL THAT?
SHE'S JUST USING YOU.
I DON'T ...
IT DOESN'T BOTHER ME.
THAT'S WHY THE ARTISTS TAKE ADVANTAGE OF YOU.
MM...
OKAY. SORRY.
BUT THIS IS HOW I'VE ALWAYS DONE MY JOB, AND MAKIURA IS AN IMPORTANT ARTIST.

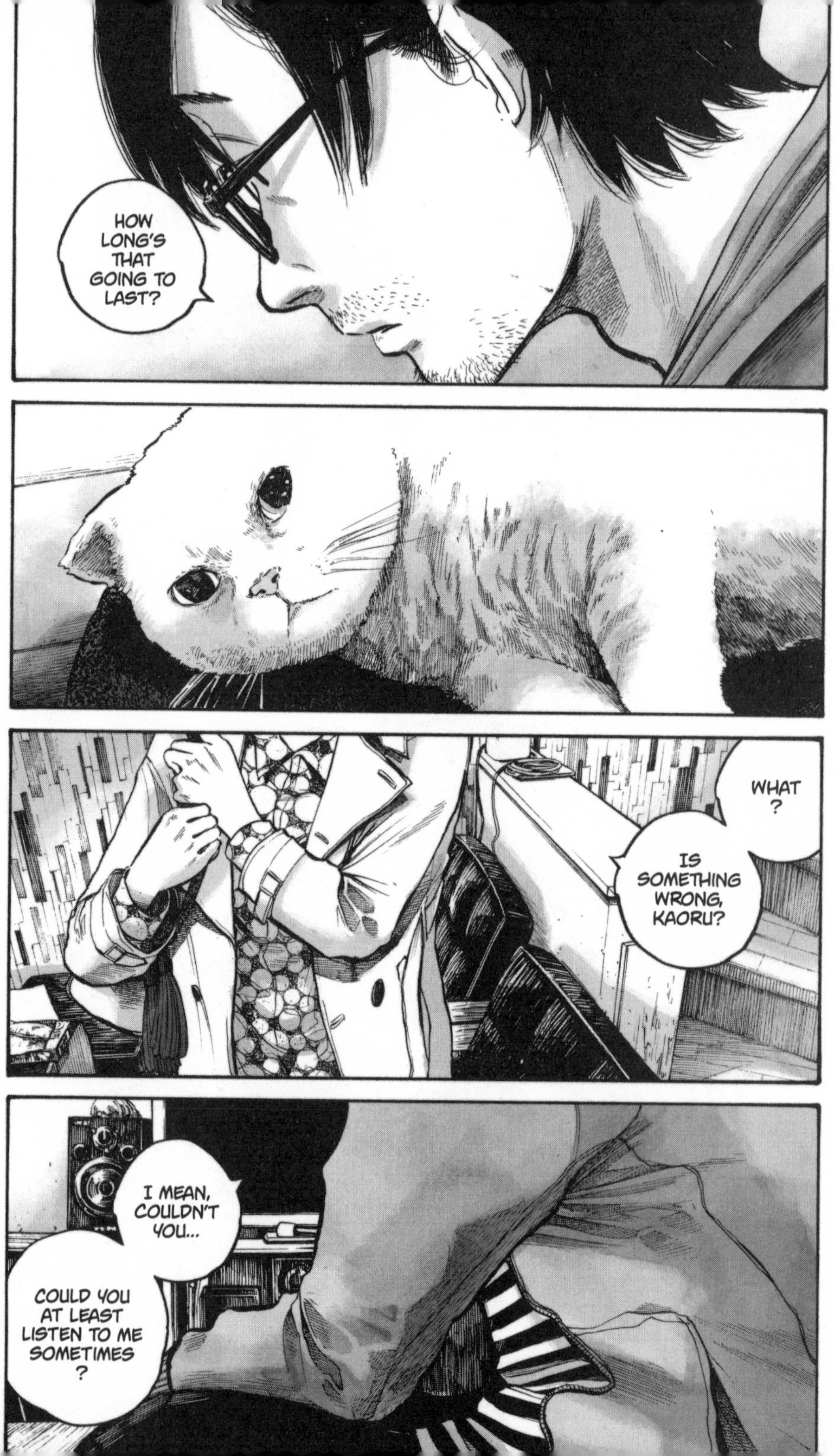
HOW LONG'S THAT GOING TO LAST?
WHAT?
IS SOMETHING WRONG, KAORU?
I MEAN, COULDN'T YOU...
COULD YOU AT LEAST LISTEN TO ME SOMETIMES?

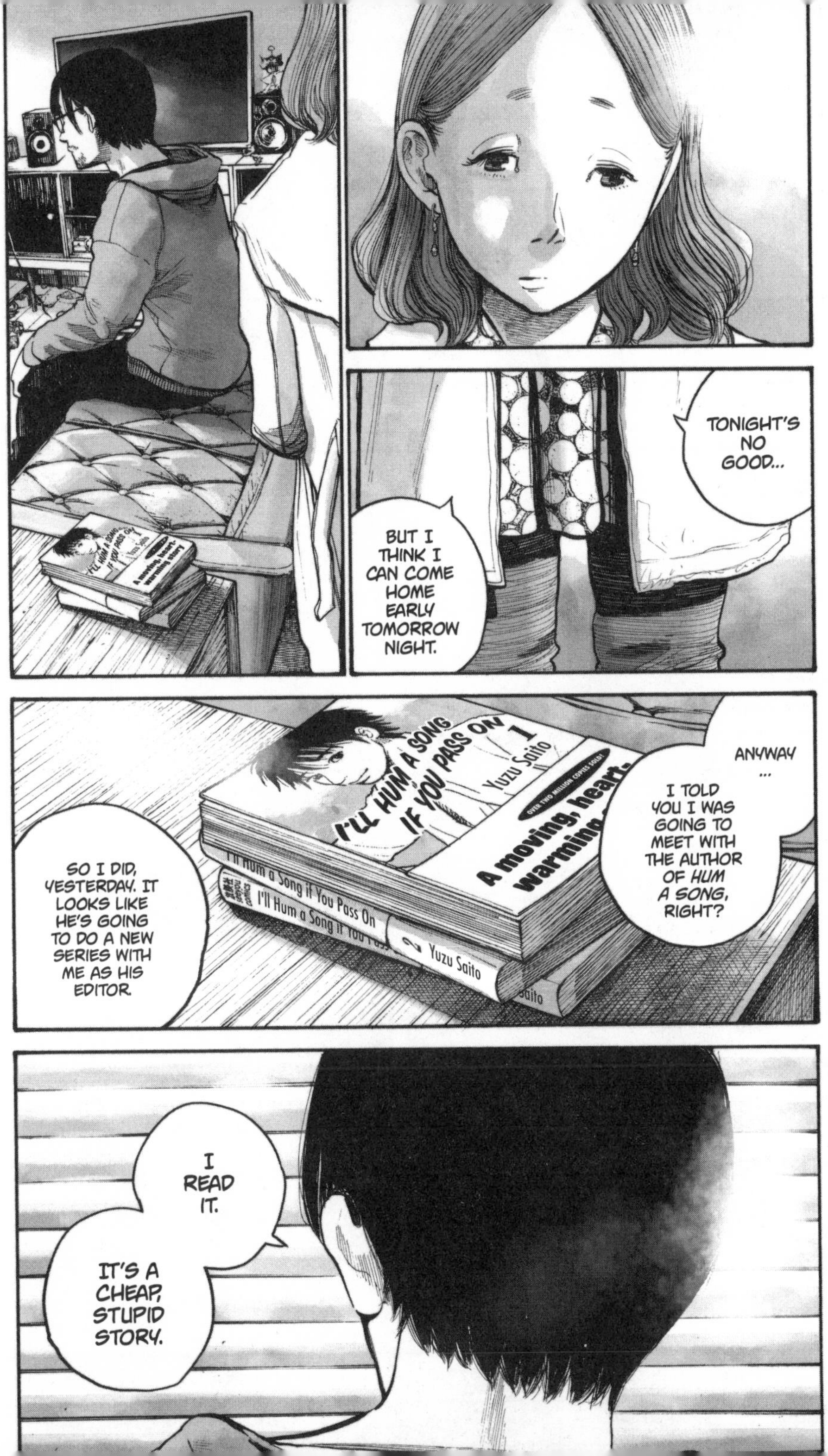
TONIGHT'S NO GOOD...
BUT I THINK I CAN COME HOME EARLY TOMORROW NIGHT.
ANYWAY ...
I TOLD YOU I WAS GOING TO MEET WITH THE AUTHOR OF *HUM A SONG*, RIGHT?
I'LL HUM A SONG IF YOU PASS ON 1
Yuzu Saito
OVER TWO MILLION COPIES SOLD
A moving, heart-
warming
I'll Hum a Song if You Pass On
2 Yuzu Saito
SO I DID, YESTERDAY. IT LOOKS LIKE HE'S GOING TO DO A NEW SERIES WITH ME AS HIS EDITOR.
I READ IT.
IT'S A CHEAP, STUPID STORY.

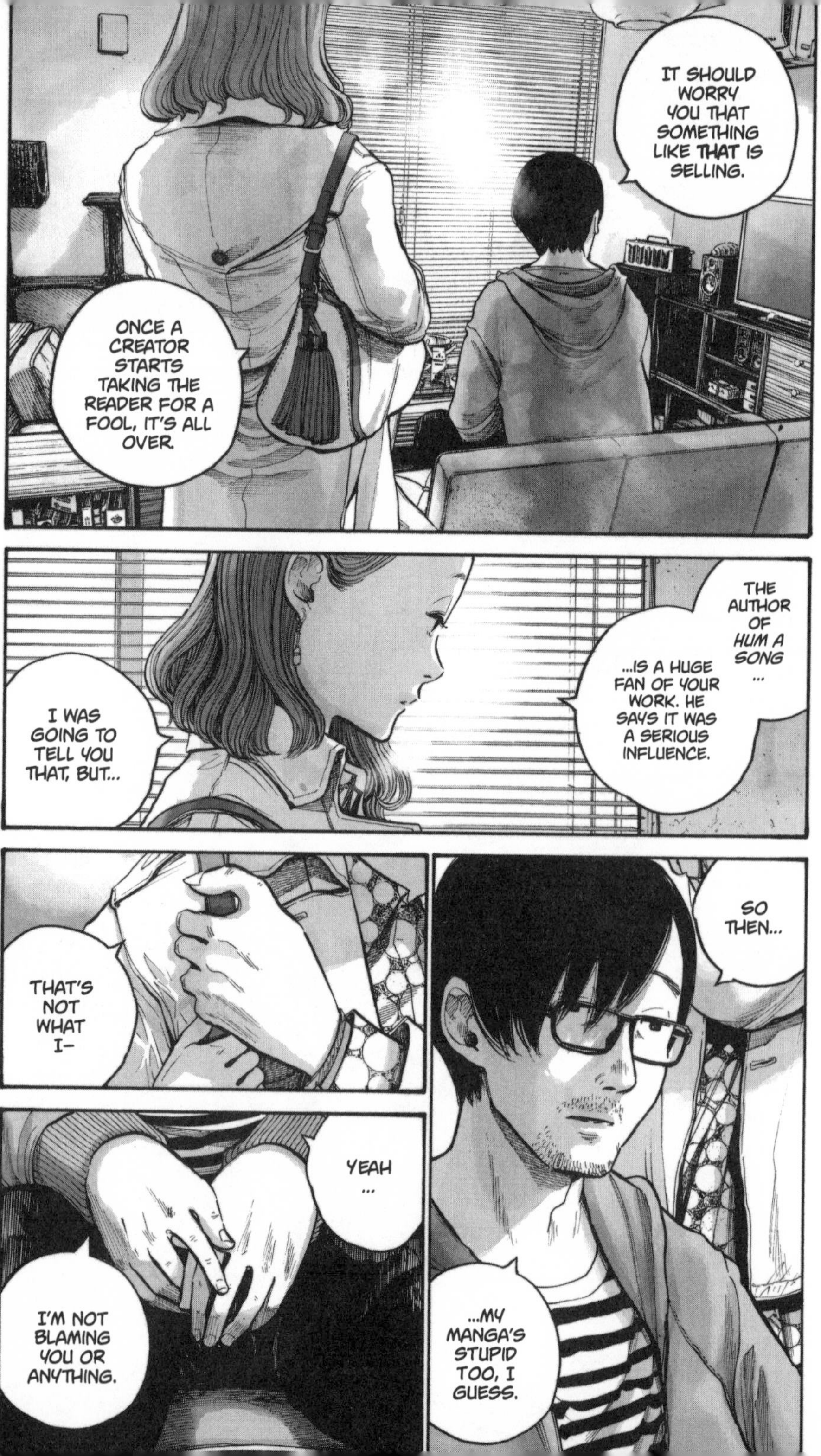
IT SHOULD WORRY YOU THAT SOMETHING LIKE THAT IS SELLING.
ONCE A CREATOR STARTS TAKING THE READER FOR A FOOL, IT'S ALL OVER.
THE AUTHOR OF *HUM A SONG*...
...IS A HUGE FAN OF YOUR WORK. HE SAYS IT WAS A SERIOUS INFLUENCE.
I WAS GOING TO TELL YOU THAT, BUT...
SO THEN...
...MY MANGA'S STUPID TOO, I GUESS.
THAT'S NOT WHAT I–
YEAH...
I'M NOT BLAMING YOU OR ANYTHING.

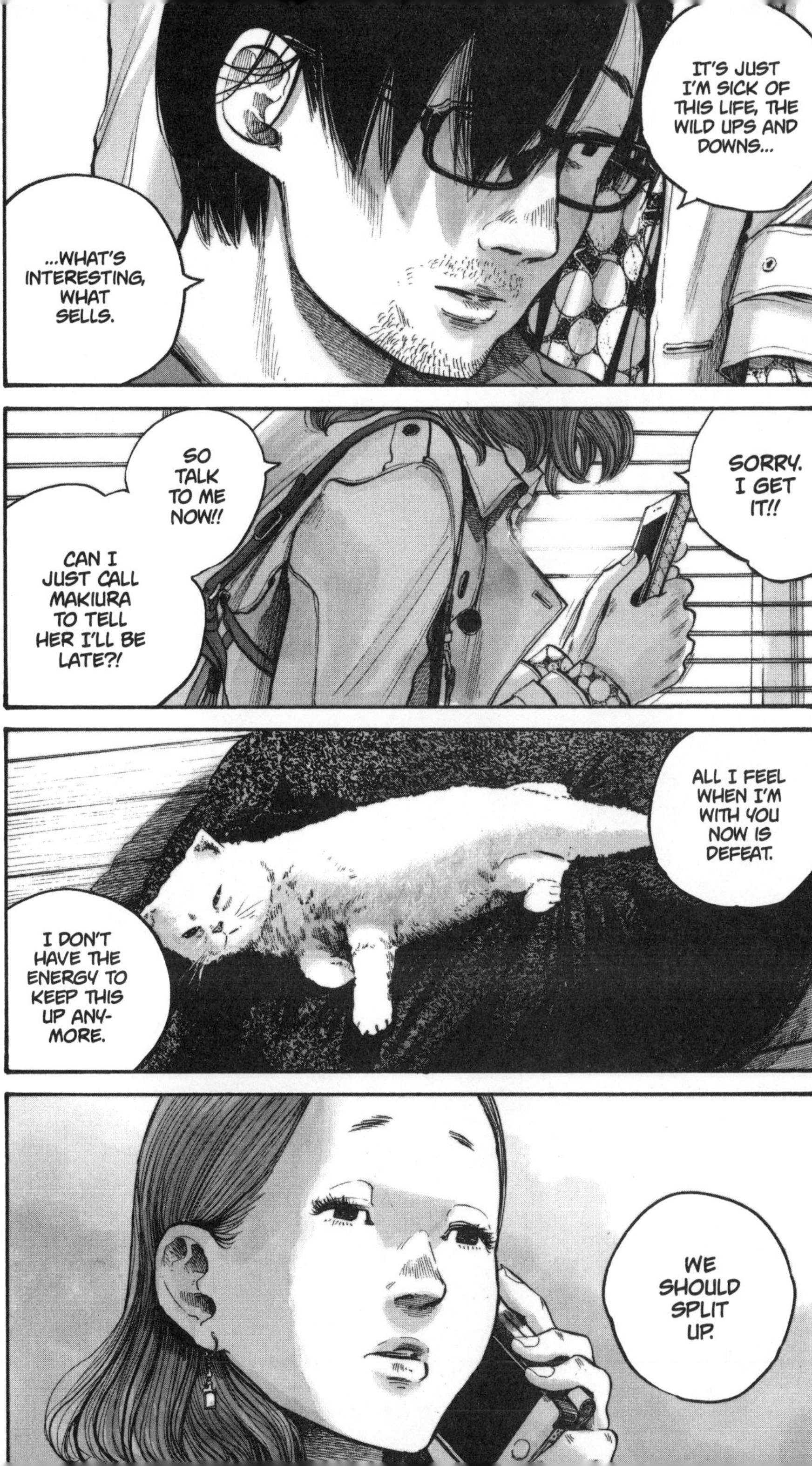
IT'S JUST I'M SICK OF THIS LIFE, THE WILD UPS AND DOWNS...
...WHAT'S INTERESTING, WHAT SELLS.
SORRY. I GET IT!!
SO TALK TO ME NOW!!
CAN I JUST CALL MAKIURA TO TELL HER I'LL BE LATE?!
ALL I FEEL WHEN I'M WITH YOU NOW IS DEFEAT.
I DON'T HAVE THE ENERGY TO KEEP THIS UP ANY-MORE.
WE SHOULD SPLIT UP.

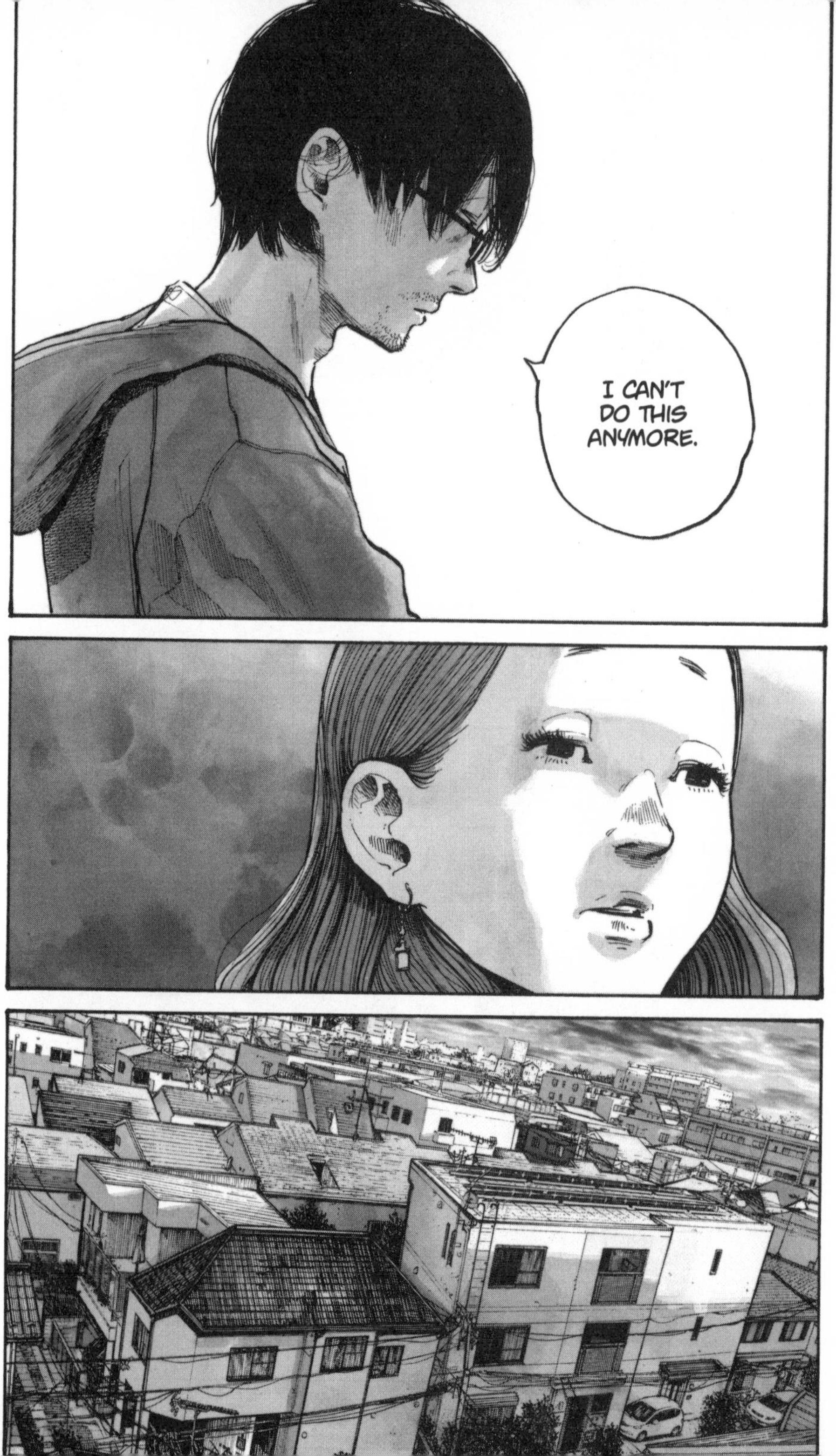
I CAN'T DO THIS ANYMORE.

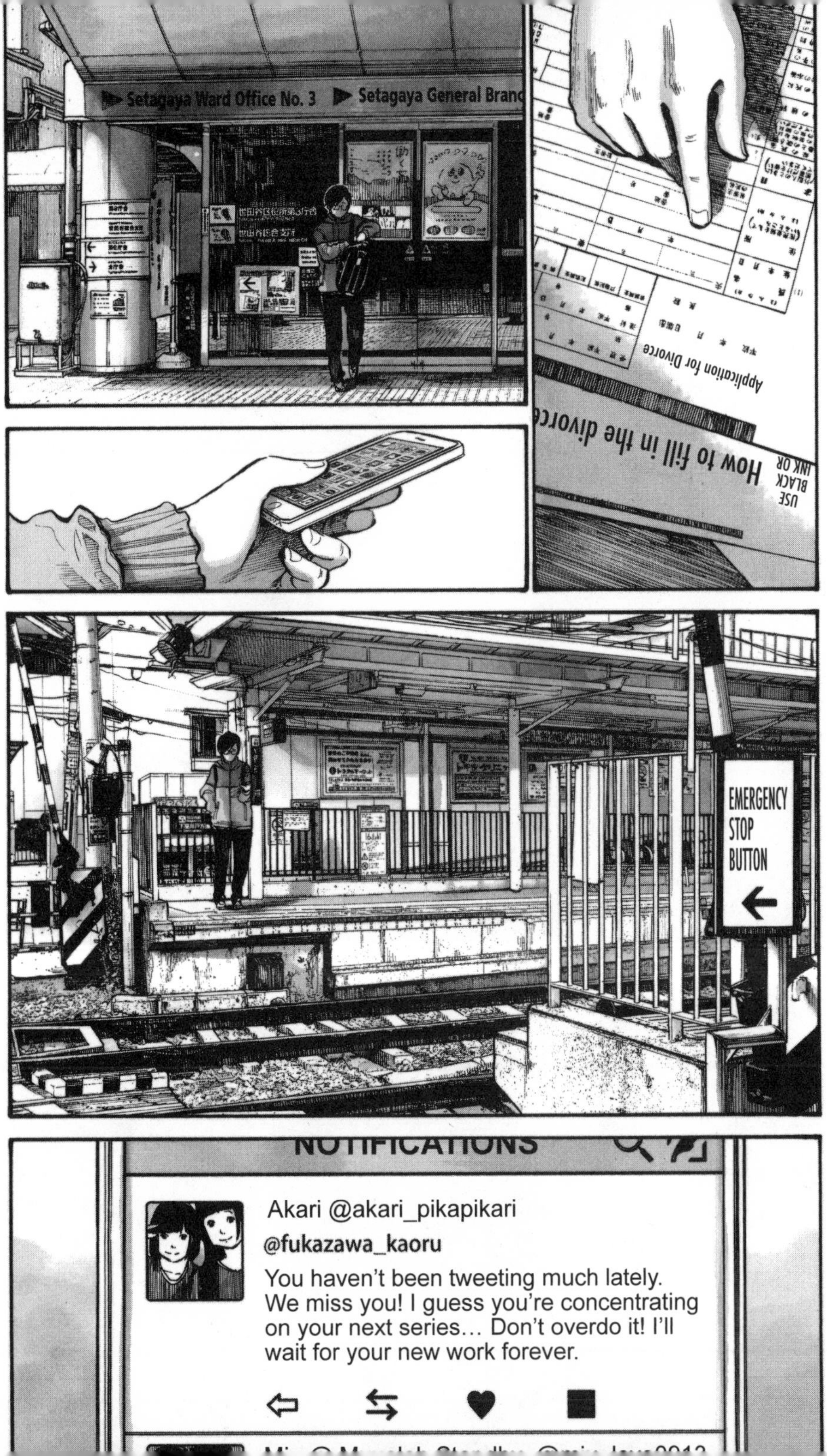
Application for Divorce
How to fill in the divorce
USE BLACK INK OR
Setagaya Ward Office No. 3
Setagaya General Branc
EMERGENCY STOP BUTTON
NOTIFICATIONS
Akari @akari_pikapikari
@fukazawa_kaoru
You haven't been tweeting much lately. We miss you! I guess you're concentrating on your next series… Don't overdo it! I'll wait for your new work forever.

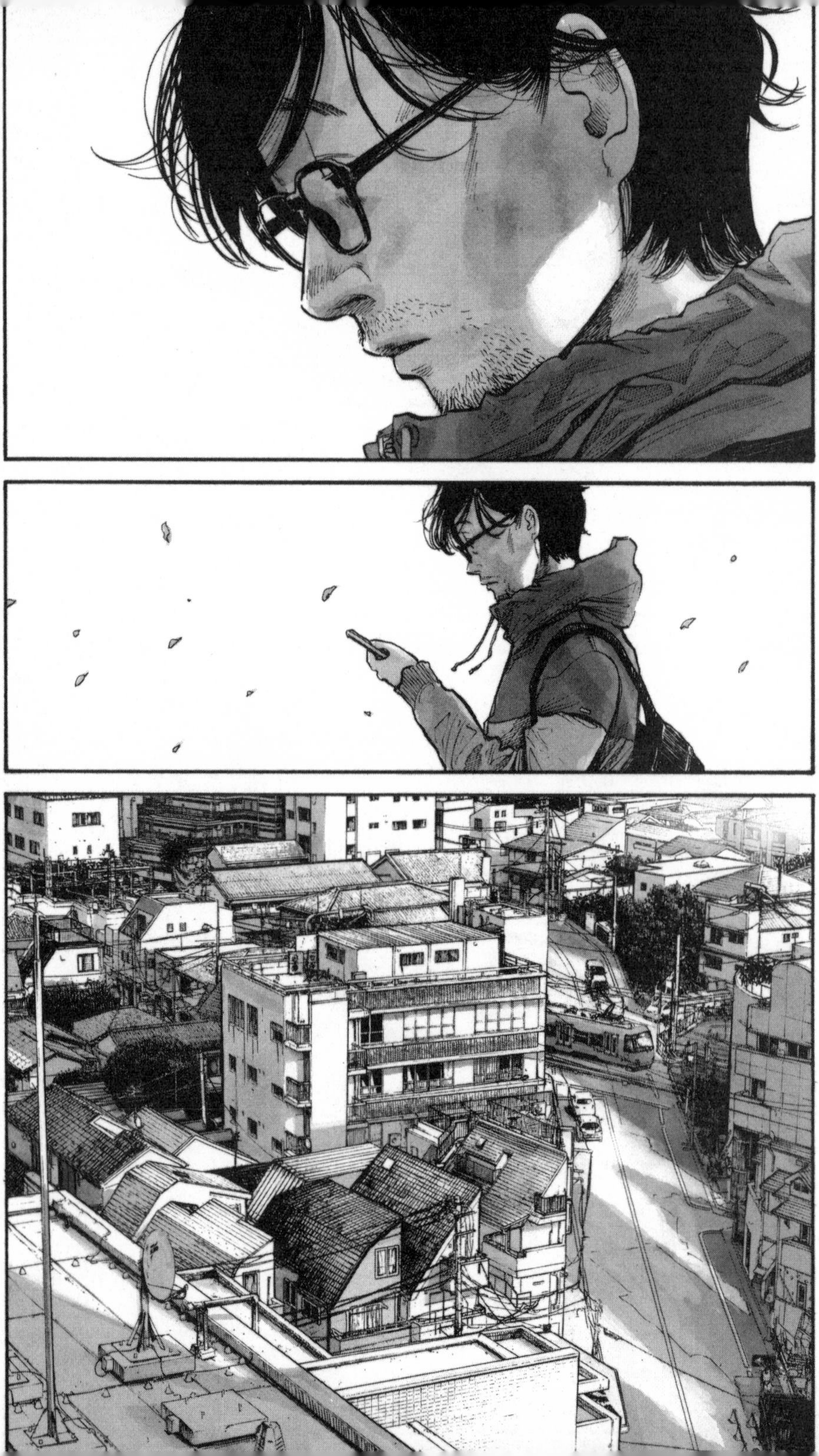

CHAPTER 2

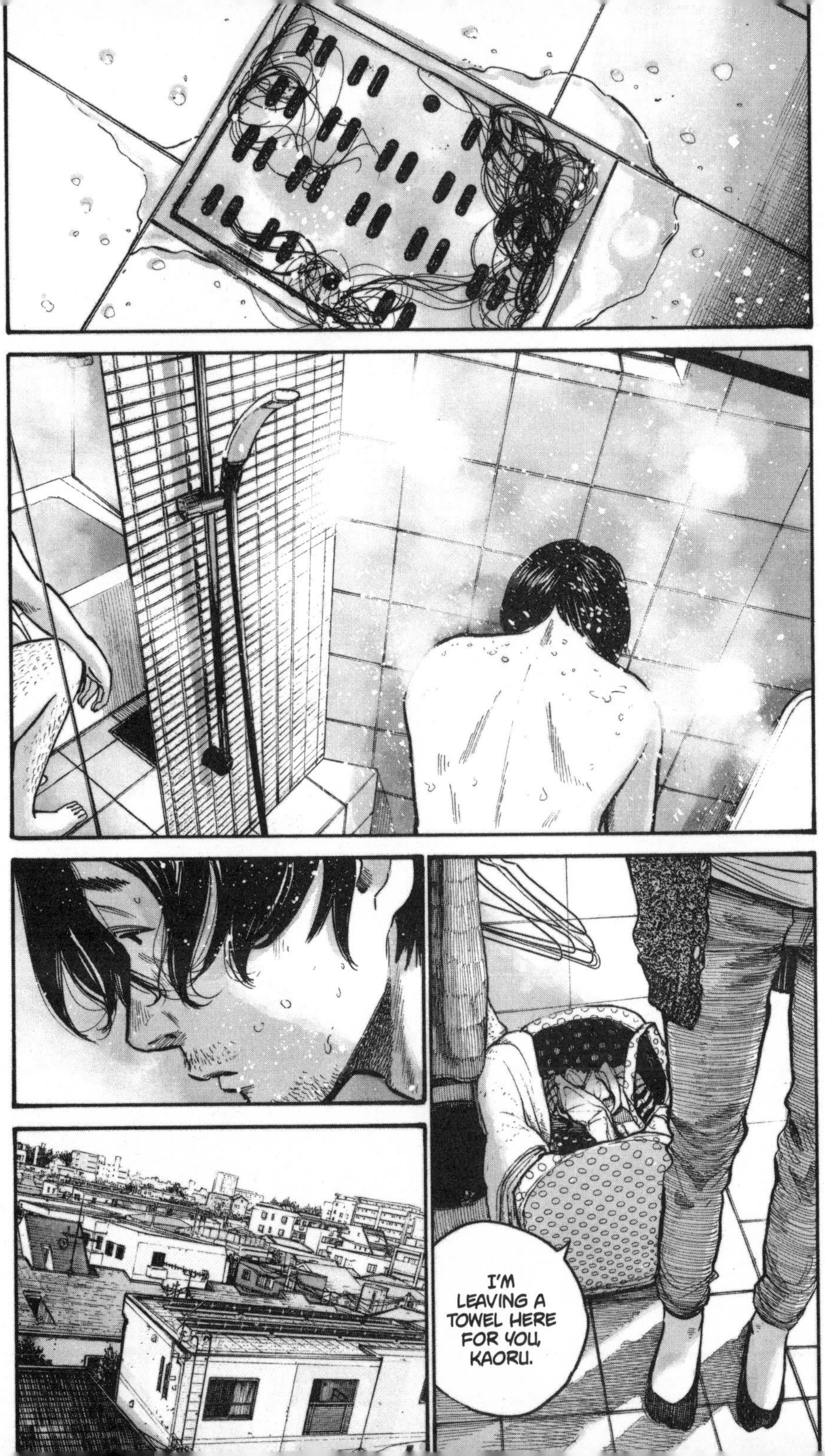
I'M LEAVING A TOWEL HERE FOR YOU, KAORU.

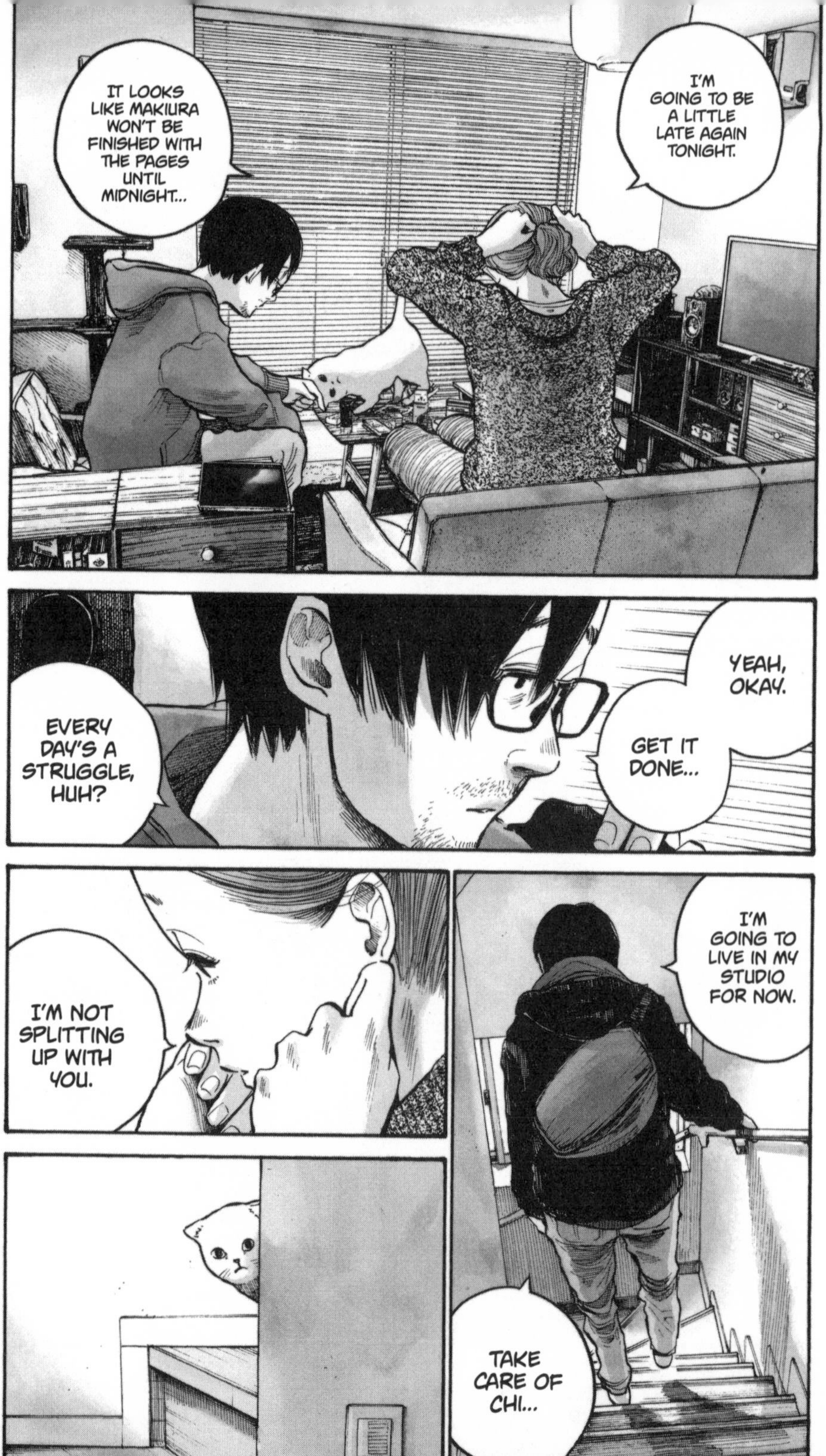
I'M GOING TO BE A LITTLE LATE AGAIN TONIGHT.
IT LOOKS LIKE MAKIURA WON'T BE FINISHED WITH THE PAGES UNTIL MIDNIGHT...
YEAH, OKAY.
GET IT DONE...
EVERY DAY'S A STRUGGLE, HUH?
I'M GOING TO LIVE IN MY STUDIO FOR NOW.
TAKE CARE OF CHI...
I'M NOT SPLITTING UP WITH YOU.

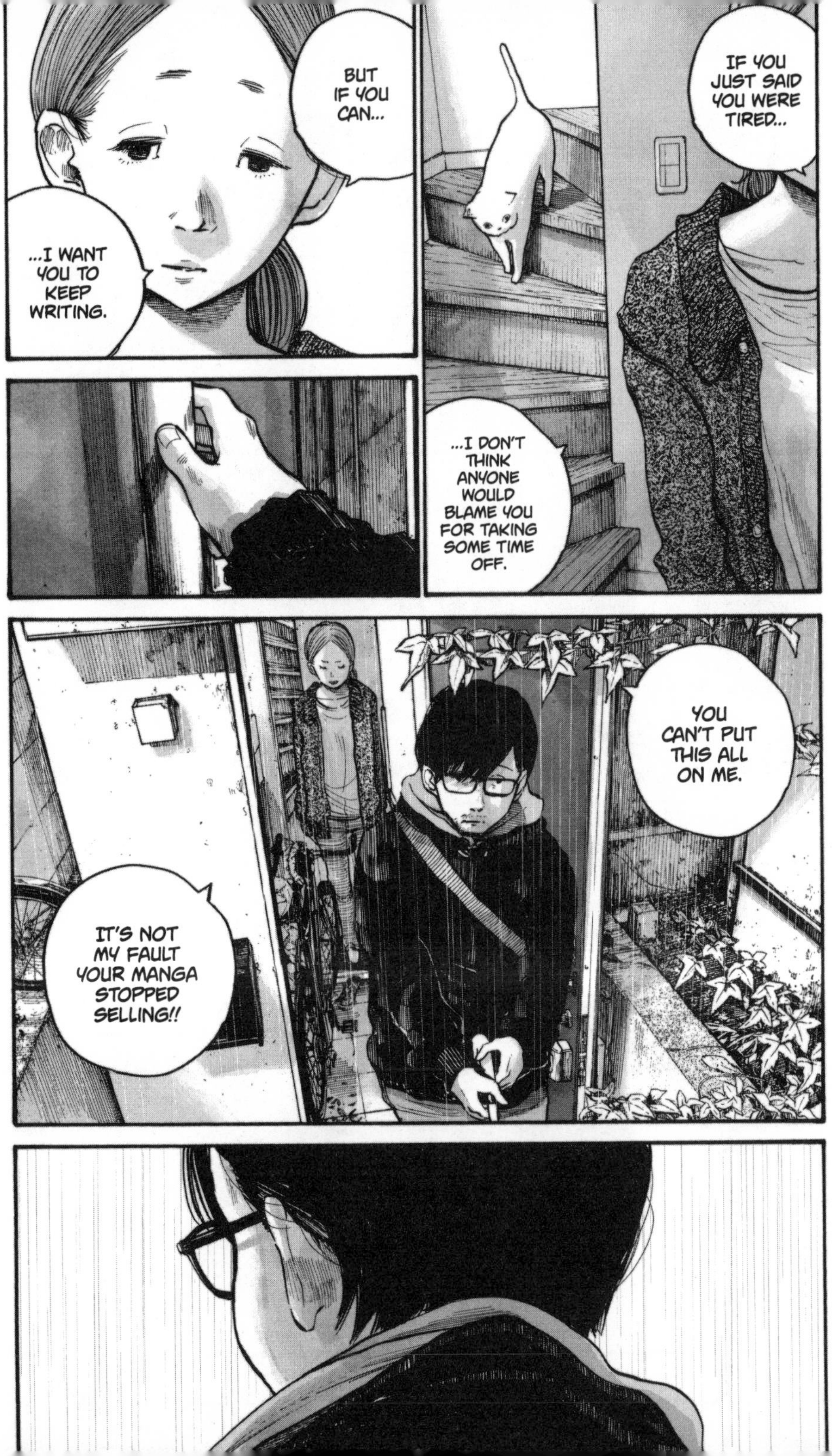

IF YOU JUST SAID YOU WERE TIRED...
...I DON'T THINK ANYONE WOULD BLAME YOU FOR TAKING SOME TIME OFF.
BUT IF YOU CAN...
...I WANT YOU TO KEEP WRITING.
YOU CAN'T PUT THIS ALL ON ME.
IT'S NOT MY FAULT YOUR MANGA STOPPED SELLING!!

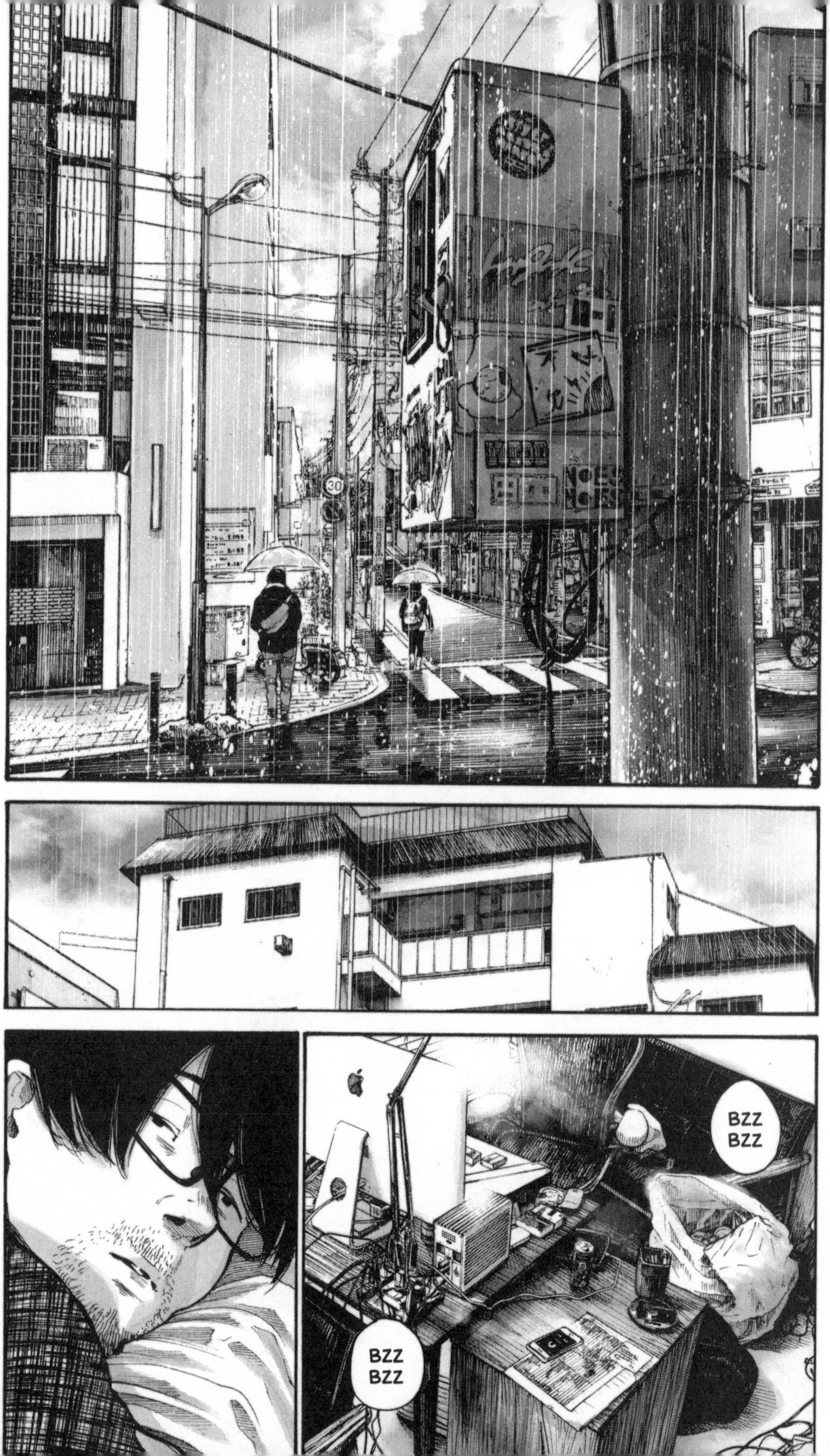
BZZ
BZZ
BZZ
BZZ

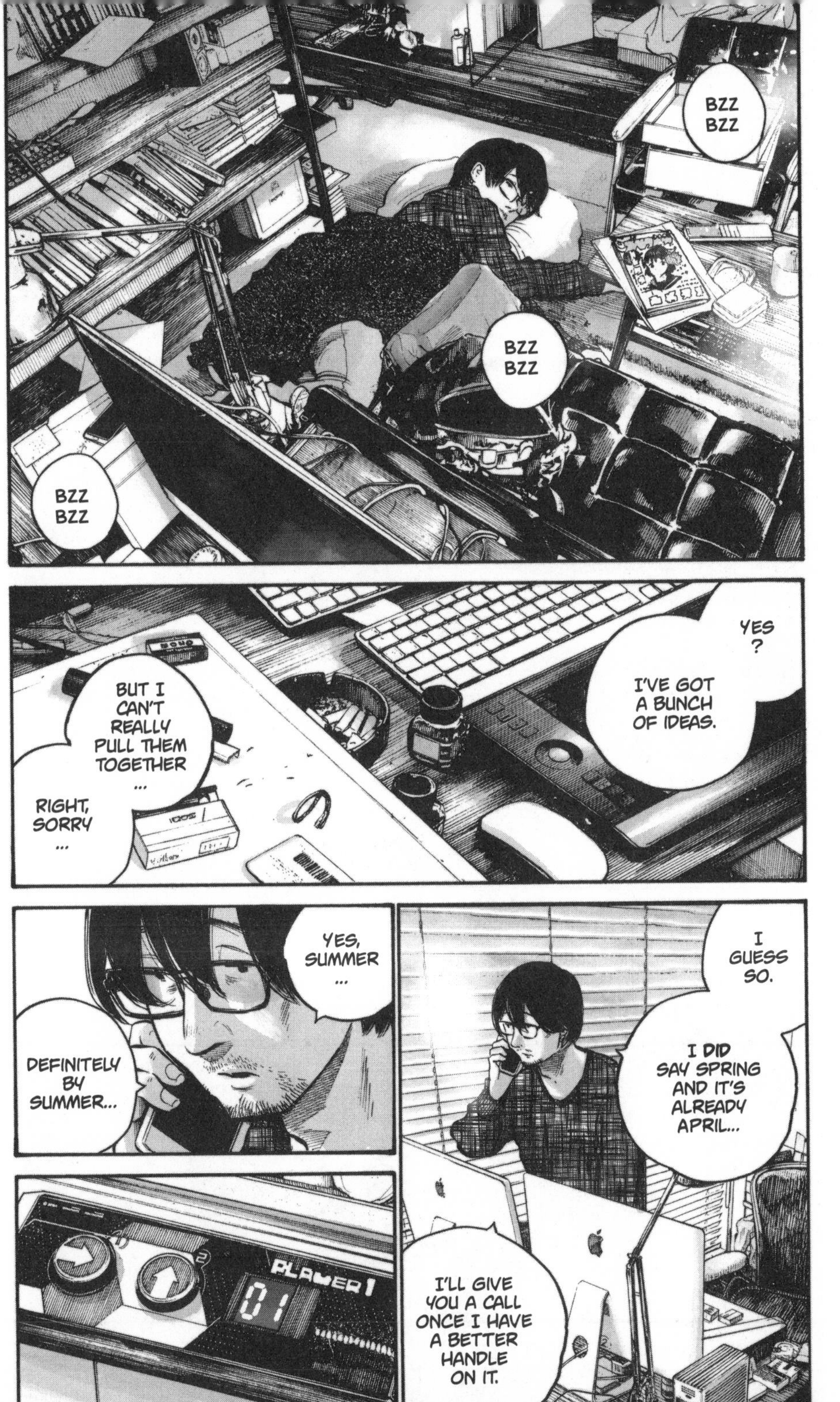
BZZ BZZ
BZZ BZZ
BZZ BZZ
YES ?
I'VE GOT A BUNCH OF IDEAS.
BUT I CAN'T REALLY PULL THEM TOGETHER ...
RIGHT, SORRY ...
I GUESS SO.
I DID SAY SPRING AND IT'S ALREADY APRIL...
YES, SUMMER ...
DEFINITELY BY SUMMER...
I'LL GIVE YOU A CALL ONCE I HAVE A BETTER HANDLE ON IT.
PLAYER1
01

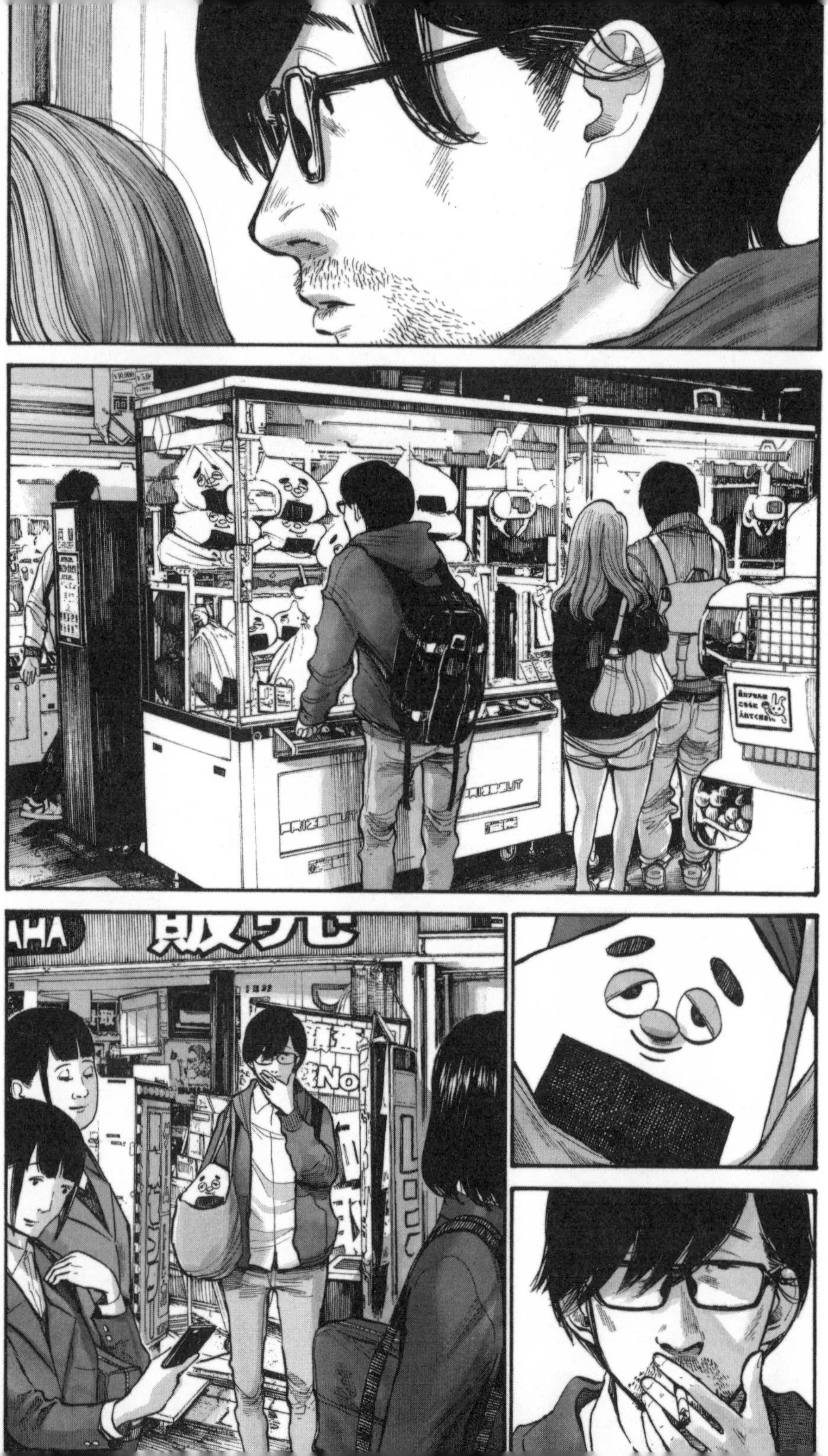

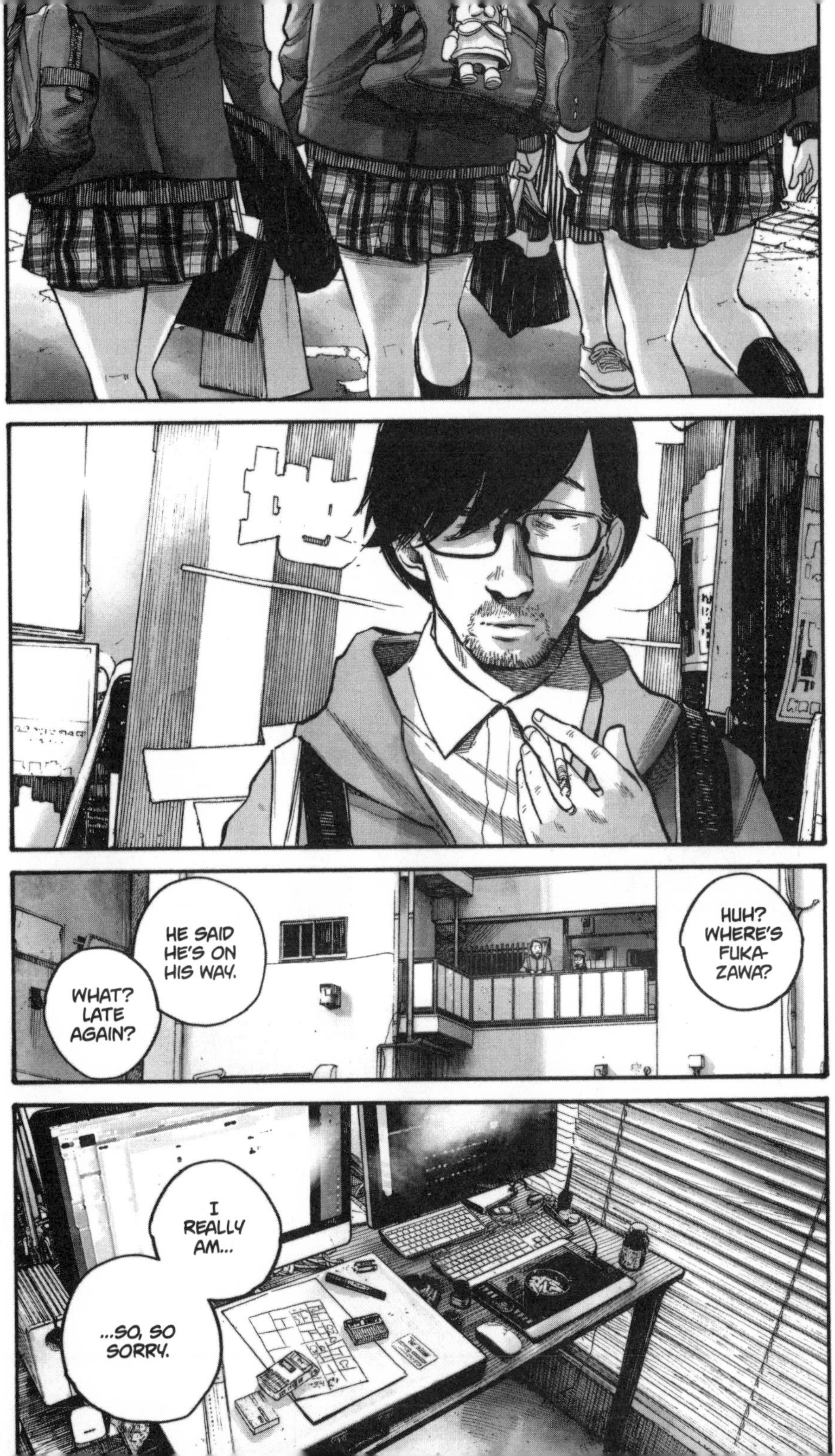
HUH? WHERE'S FUKA-ZAWA?
HE SAID HE'S ON HIS WAY.
WHAT? LATE AGAIN?
I REALLY AM...
...SO, SO SORRY.

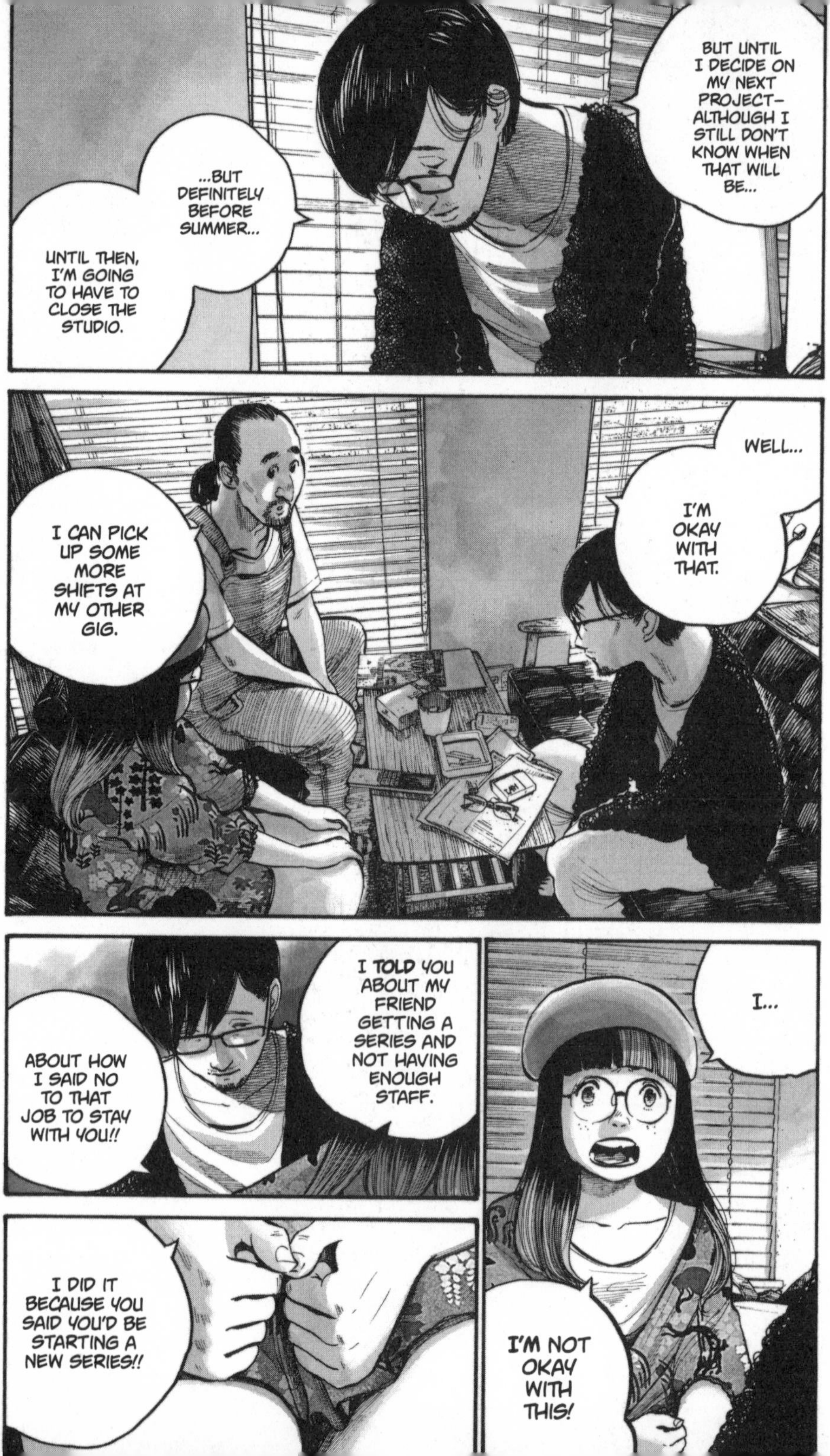

BUT UNTIL I DECIDE ON MY NEXT PROJECT— ALTHOUGH I STILL DON'T KNOW WHEN THAT WILL BE...
...BUT DEFINITELY BEFORE SUMMER...
UNTIL THEN, I'M GOING TO HAVE TO CLOSE THE STUDIO.
WELL...
I'M OKAY WITH THAT.
I CAN PICK UP SOME MORE SHIFTS AT MY OTHER GIG.
I...
I'M NOT OKAY WITH THIS!
I **TOLD** YOU ABOUT MY FRIEND GETTING A SERIES AND NOT HAVING ENOUGH STAFF.
ABOUT HOW I SAID NO TO THAT JOB TO STAY WITH YOU!!
I DID IT BECAUSE YOU SAID YOU'D BE STARTING A NEW SERIES!!

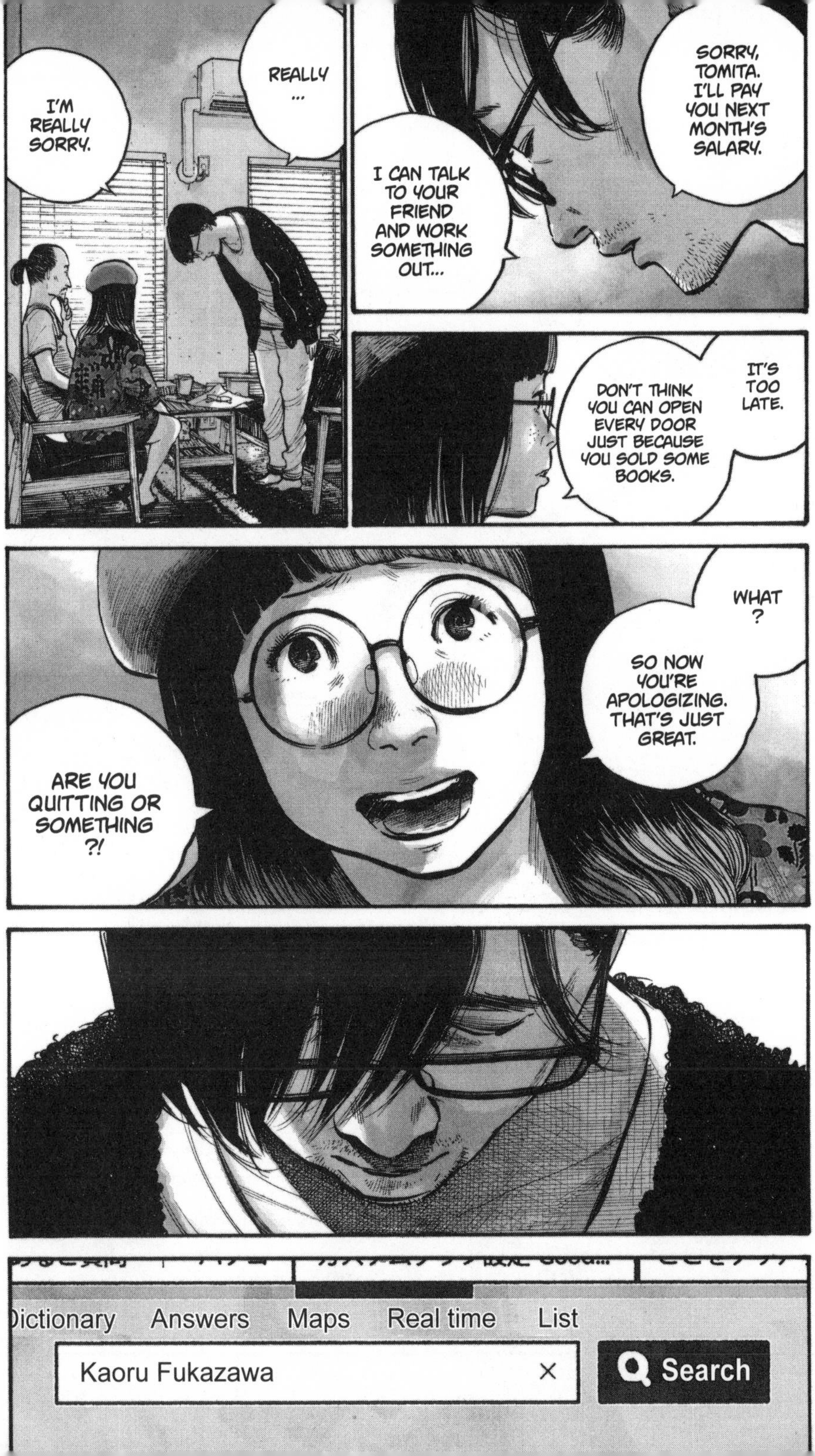
SORRY, TOMITA. I'LL PAY YOU NEXT MONTH'S SALARY.
I CAN TALK TO YOUR FRIEND AND WORK SOMETHING OUT...
IT'S TOO LATE.
DON'T THINK YOU CAN OPEN EVERY DOOR JUST BECAUSE YOU SOLD SOME BOOKS.
REALLY ...
I'M REALLY SORRY.
WHAT?
SO NOW YOU'RE APOLOGIZING. THAT'S JUST GREAT.
ARE YOU QUITTING OR SOMETHING ?!
Dictionary
Answers
Maps
Real time
List
Kaoru Fukazawa
Search

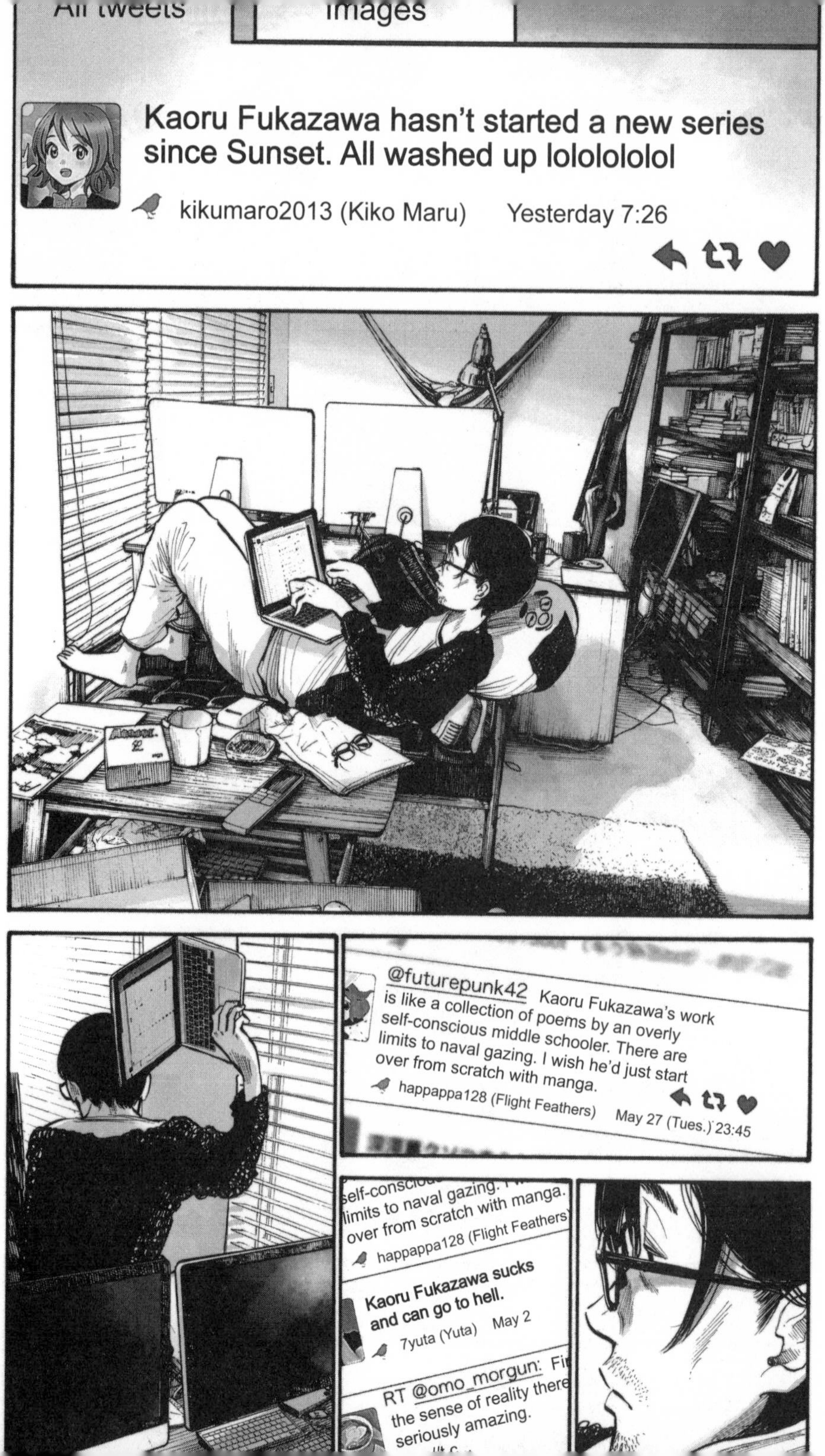
All tweets
Images
Kaoru Fukazawa hasn't started a new series since Sunset. All washed up lolololol
kikumaro2013 (Kiko Maru) Yesterday 7:26
@futurepunk42 Kaoru Fukazawa's work is like a collection of poems by an overly self-conscious middle schooler. There are limits to naval gazing. I wish he'd just start over from scratch with manga.
happappa128 (Flight Feathers) May 27 (Tues.) 23:45
limits to naval gazing.
over from scratch with manga.
happappa128 (Flight Feathers)
Kaoru Fukazawa sucks and can go to hell.
7yuta (Yuta) May 2
RT @omo_morgun:
the sense of reality there
seriously amazing.

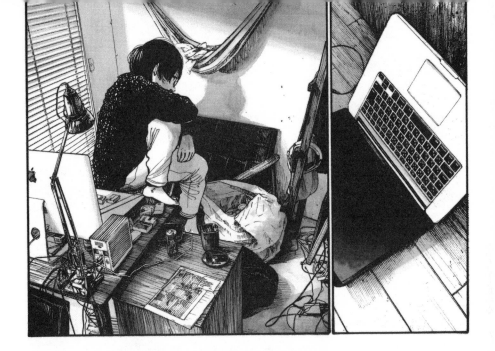

SORRY TO HAVE KEPT YOU WAITING.

SINCE THE COMPUTER WAS DAMAGED IN A FALL, IT'S CONSIDERED CUSTOMER ERROR AND ISN'T COVERED BY THE WARRANTY.

SO IT WOULD ACTUALLY BE CHEAPER TO BUY A NEW ONE...

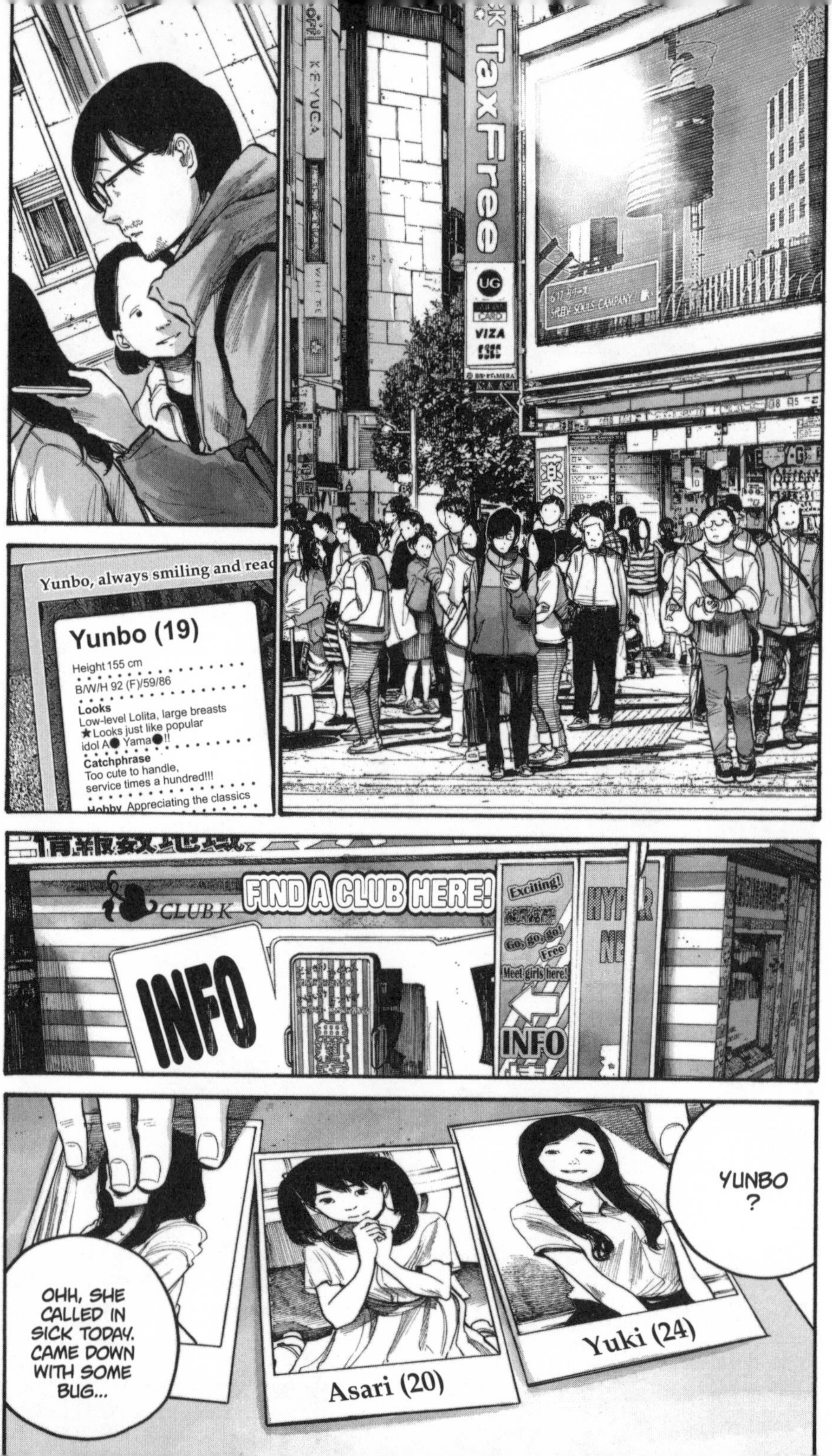

TaxFree
VIZA
KEYUCA
Yunbo, always smiling and read
Yunbo (19)
Height 155 cm
B/W/H 92 (F)/59/86
Looks
Low-level Lolita, large breasts
★Looks just like popular idol A● Yama●!!
Catchphrase
Too cute to handle, service times a hundred!!!
Hobby Appreciating the classics
FIND A CLUB HERE!
CLUB K
INFO
Exciting!
Go, go, go!
Free
Meet girls here!
INFO
YUNBO ?
OHH, SHE CALLED IN SICK TODAY. CAME DOWN WITH SOME BUG...
Yuki (24)
Asari (20)

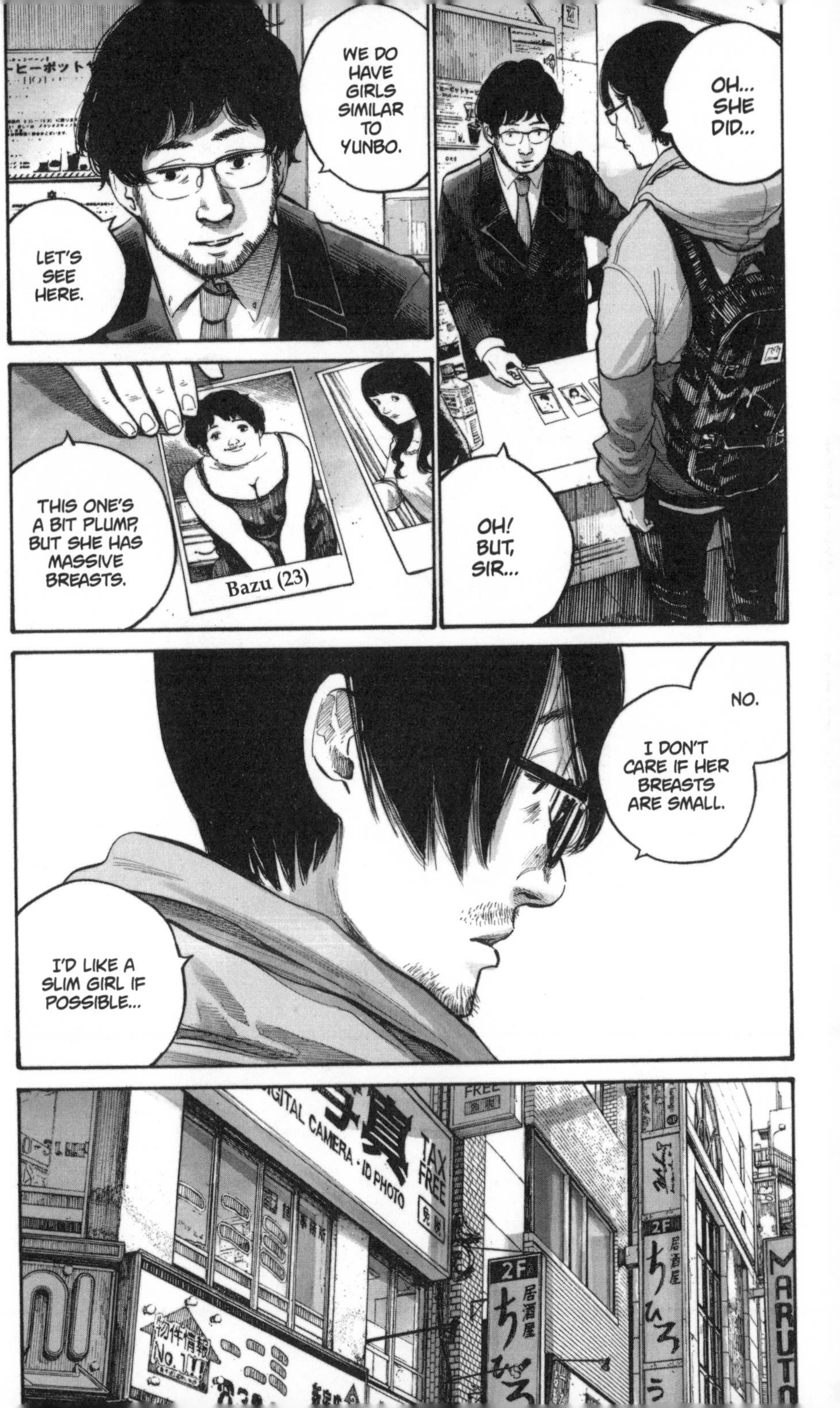
OH... SHE DID...
WE DO HAVE GIRLS SIMILAR TO YUNBO.
LET'S SEE HERE.
OH! BUT, SIR...
THIS ONE'S A BIT PLUMP, BUT SHE HAS MASSIVE BREASTS.
Bazu (23)
NO.
I DON'T CARE IF HER BREASTS ARE SMALL.
I'D LIKE A SLIM GIRL IF POSSIBLE...
CAMERA • ID PHOTO
TAX FREE
2F
居酒屋
物件情報 No.1!!

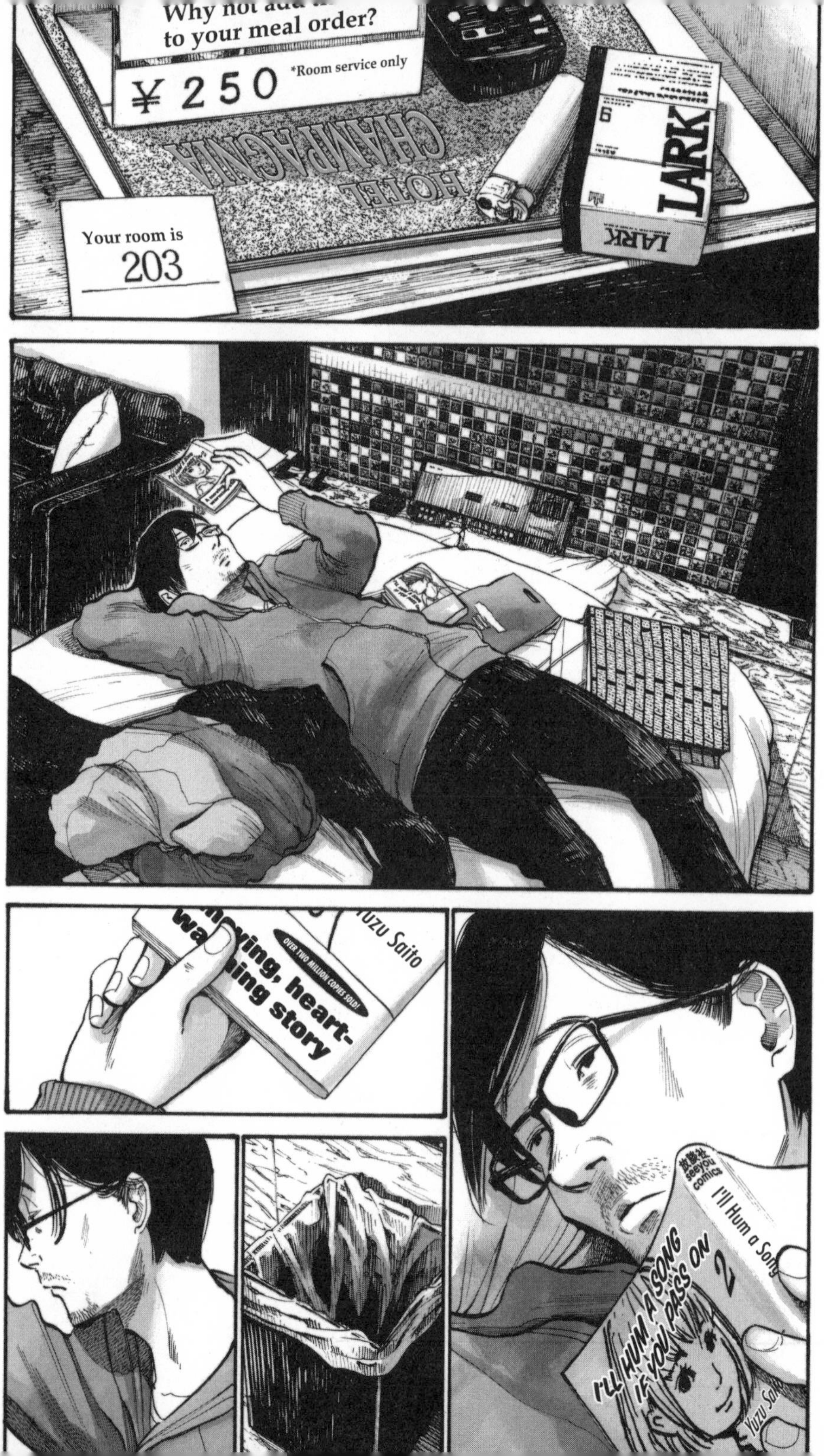
to your meal order?
¥250
*Room service only
HOTEL CHAMPAGNIA
Your room is
203
LARK
LARK
I'll Hum a Song
2
I'LL HUM A SONG IF YOU PASS ON
seeyou comics
Yuzu Saito
Yuzu Saito
OVER TWO MILLION COPIES SOLD!
story

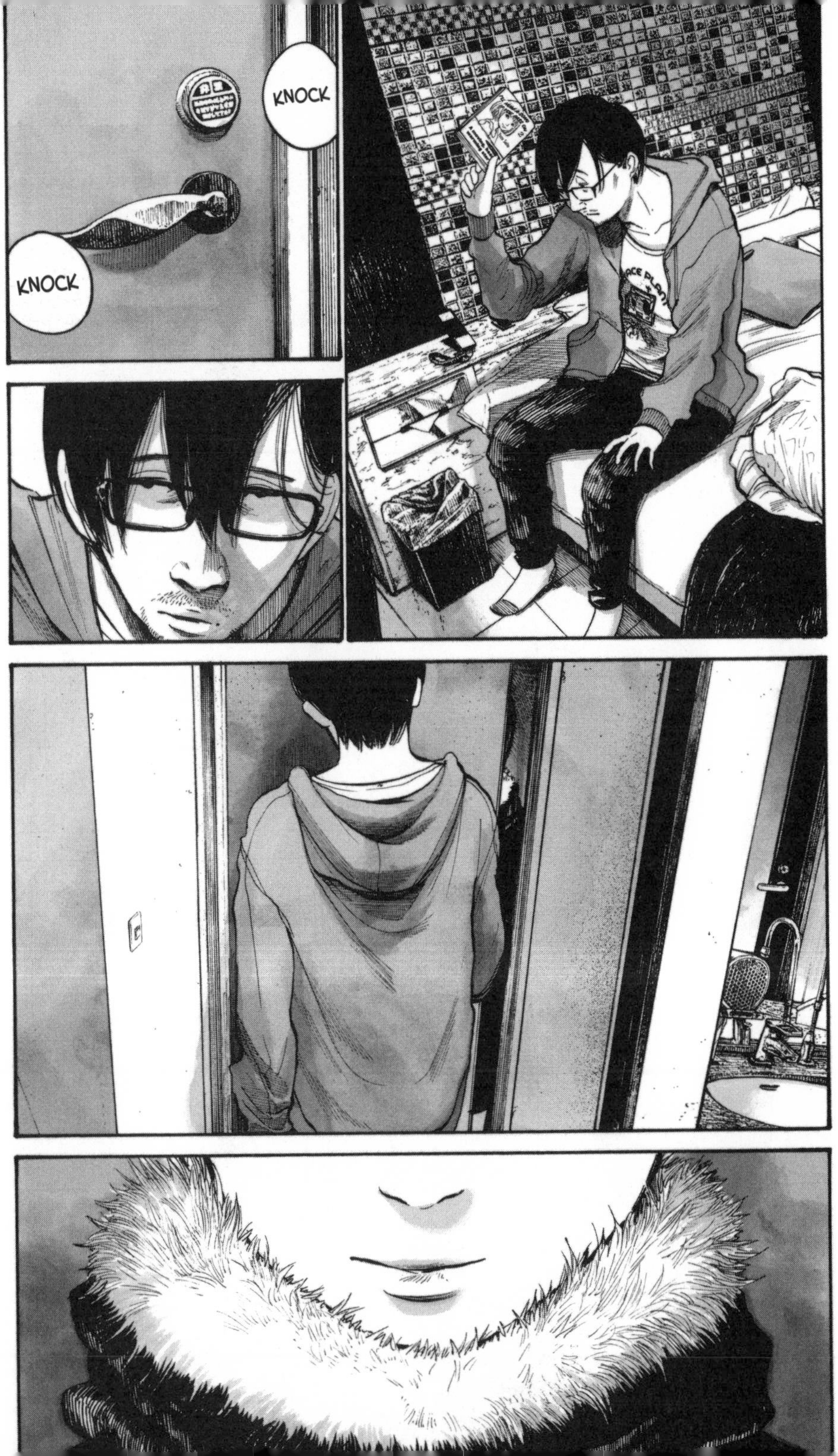
KNOCK
KNOCK

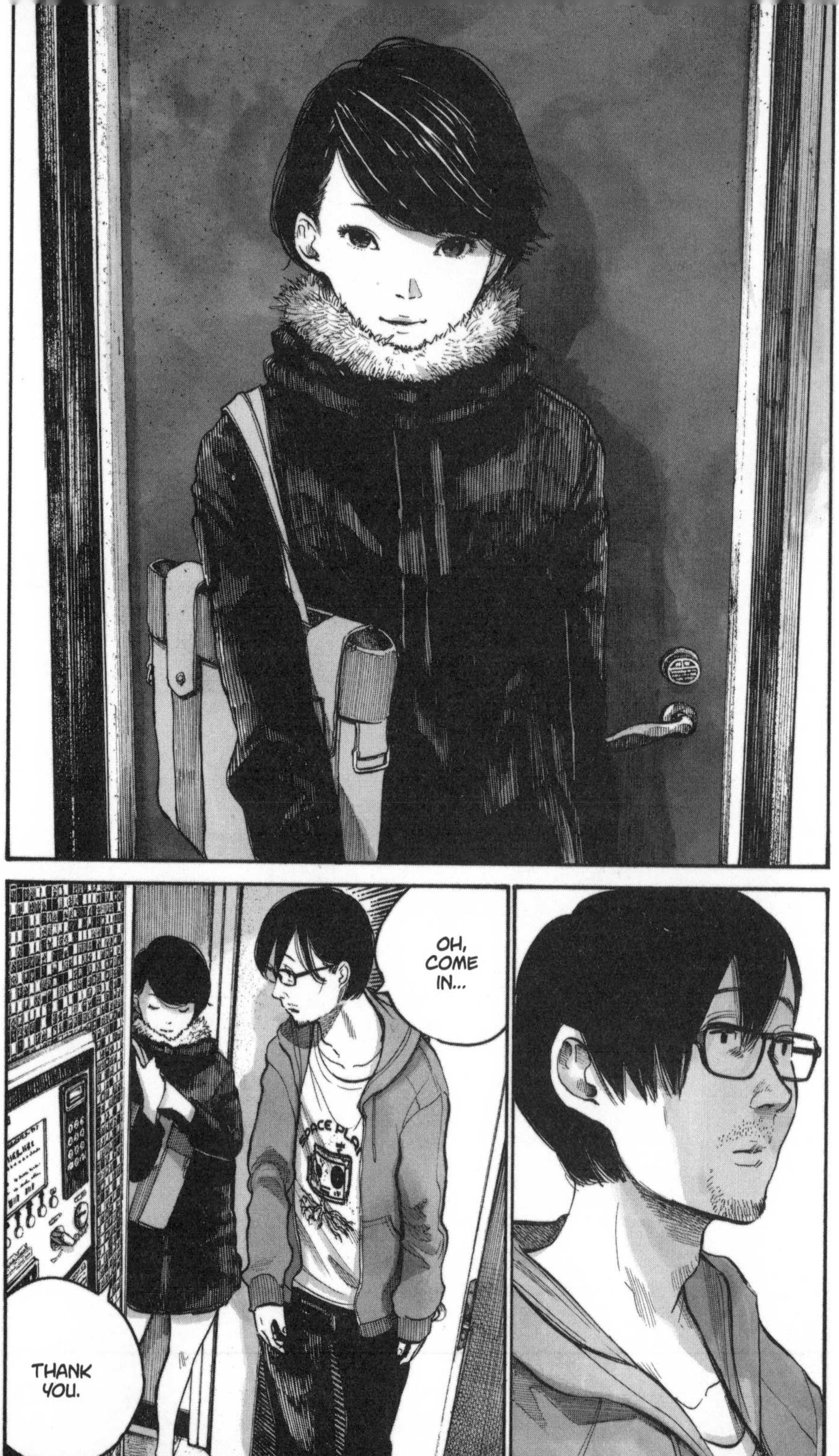
OH, COME IN...
THANK YOU.

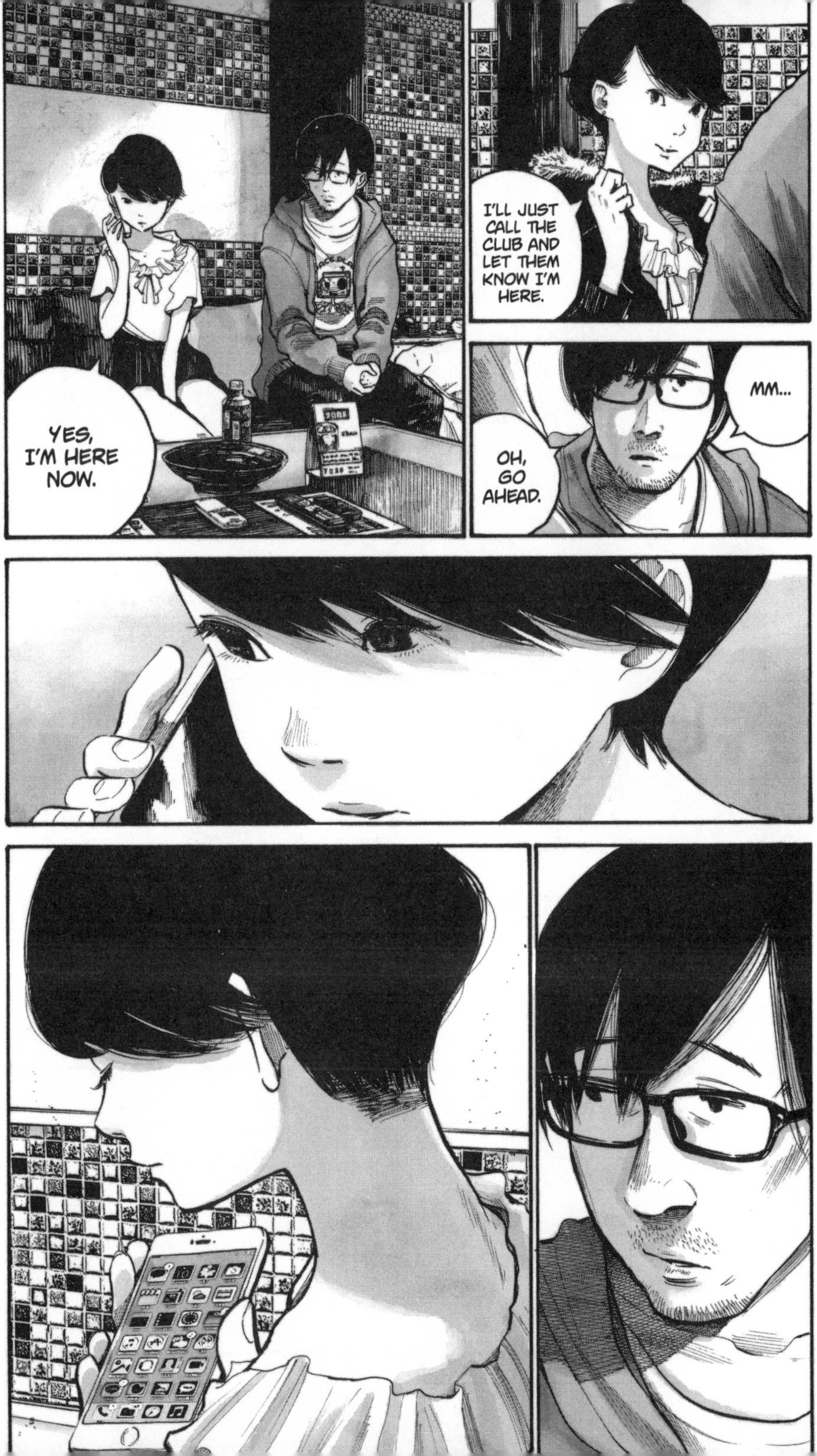
I'LL JUST CALL THE CLUB AND LET THEM KNOW I'M HERE.
MM...
OH, GO AHEAD.
YES, I'M HERE NOW.

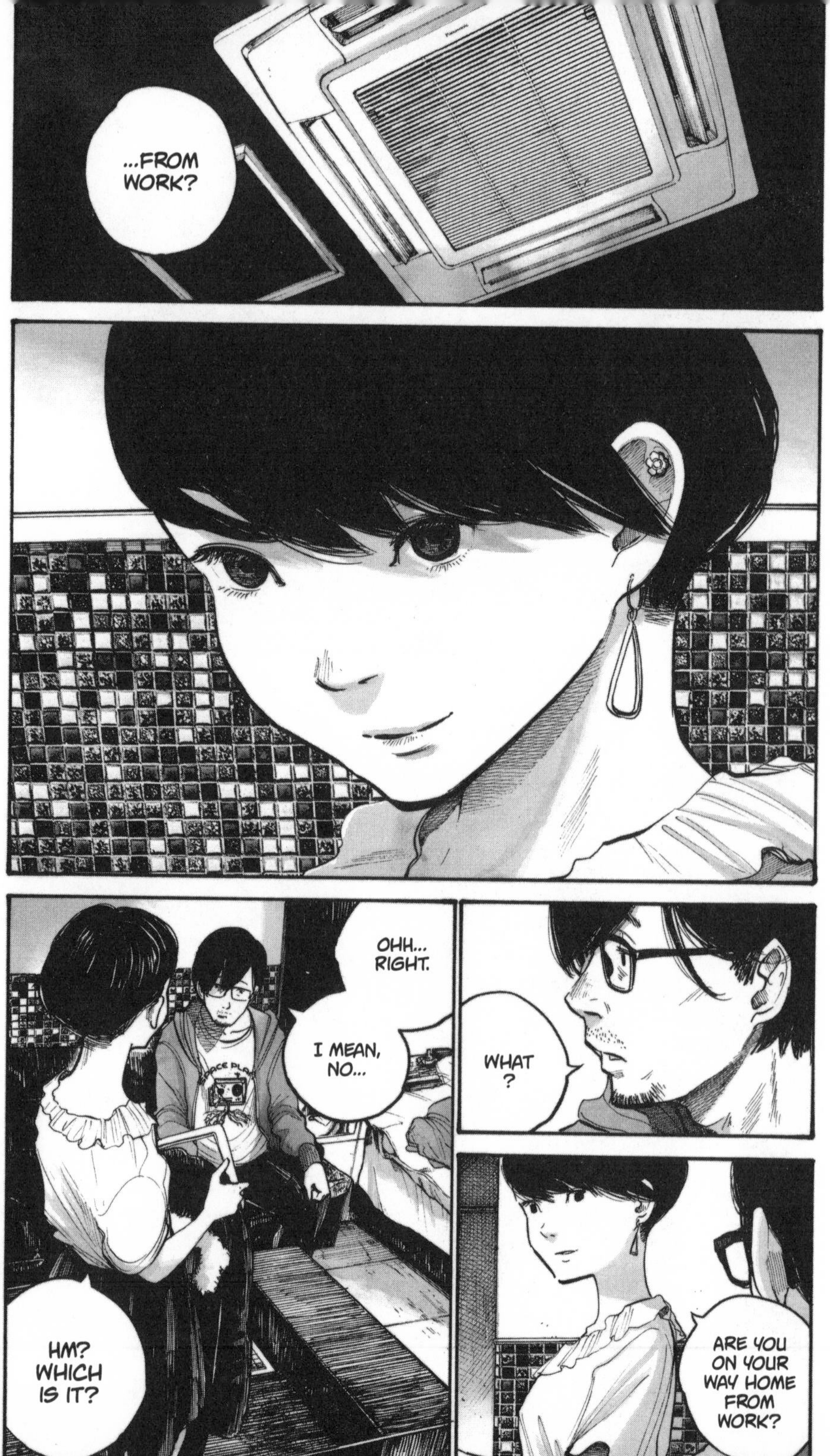
...FROM WORK?
WHAT?
ARE YOU ON YOUR WAY HOME FROM WORK?
OHH... RIGHT.
I MEAN, NO...
HM? WHICH IS IT?

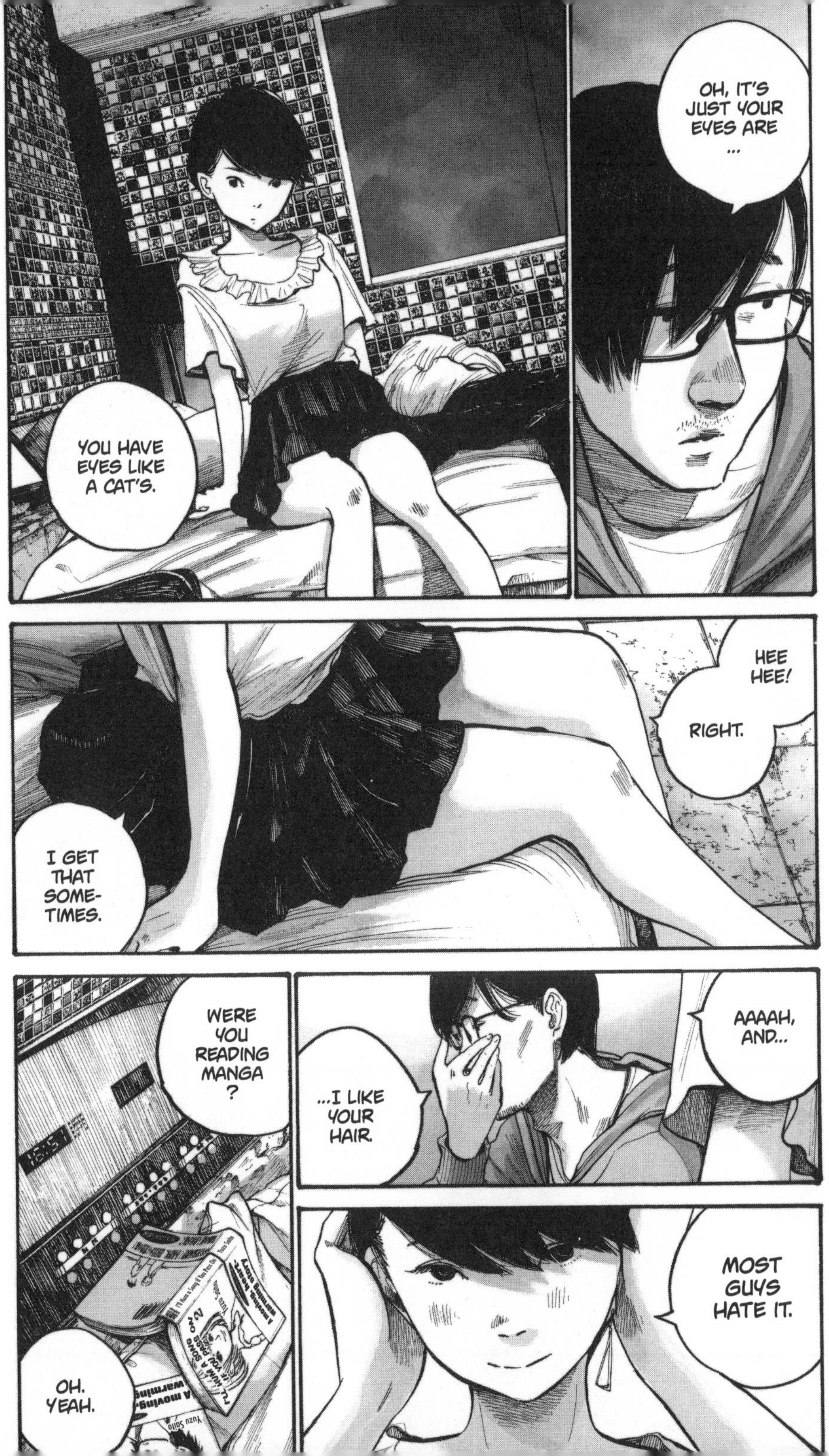
OH, IT'S JUST YOUR EYES ARE ...
YOU HAVE EYES LIKE A CAT'S.
HEE HEE!
RIGHT.
I GET THAT SOME-TIMES.
AAAAH, AND...
...I LIKE YOUR HAIR.
MOST GUYS HATE IT.
WERE YOU READING MANGA?
OH. YEAH.

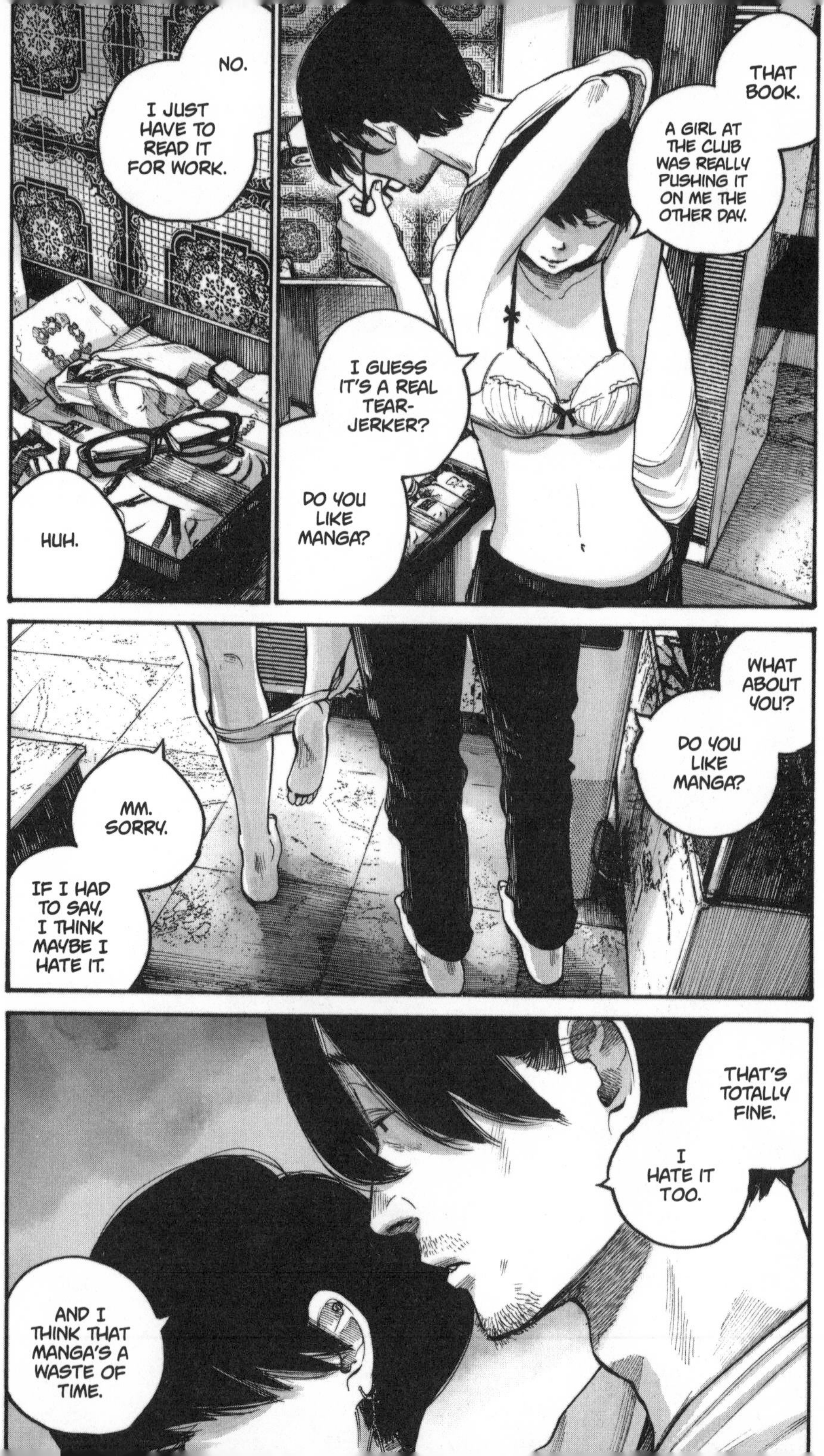
THAT BOOK.
A GIRL AT THE CLUB WAS REALLY PUSHING IT ON ME THE OTHER DAY.
I GUESS IT'S A REAL TEAR-JERKER?
DO YOU LIKE MANGA?
NO.
I JUST HAVE TO READ IT FOR WORK.
HUH.
WHAT ABOUT YOU?
DO YOU LIKE MANGA?
MM. SORRY.
IF I HAD TO SAY, I THINK MAYBE I HATE IT.
THAT'S TOTALLY FINE.
I HATE IT TOO.
AND I THINK THAT MANGA'S A WASTE OF TIME.

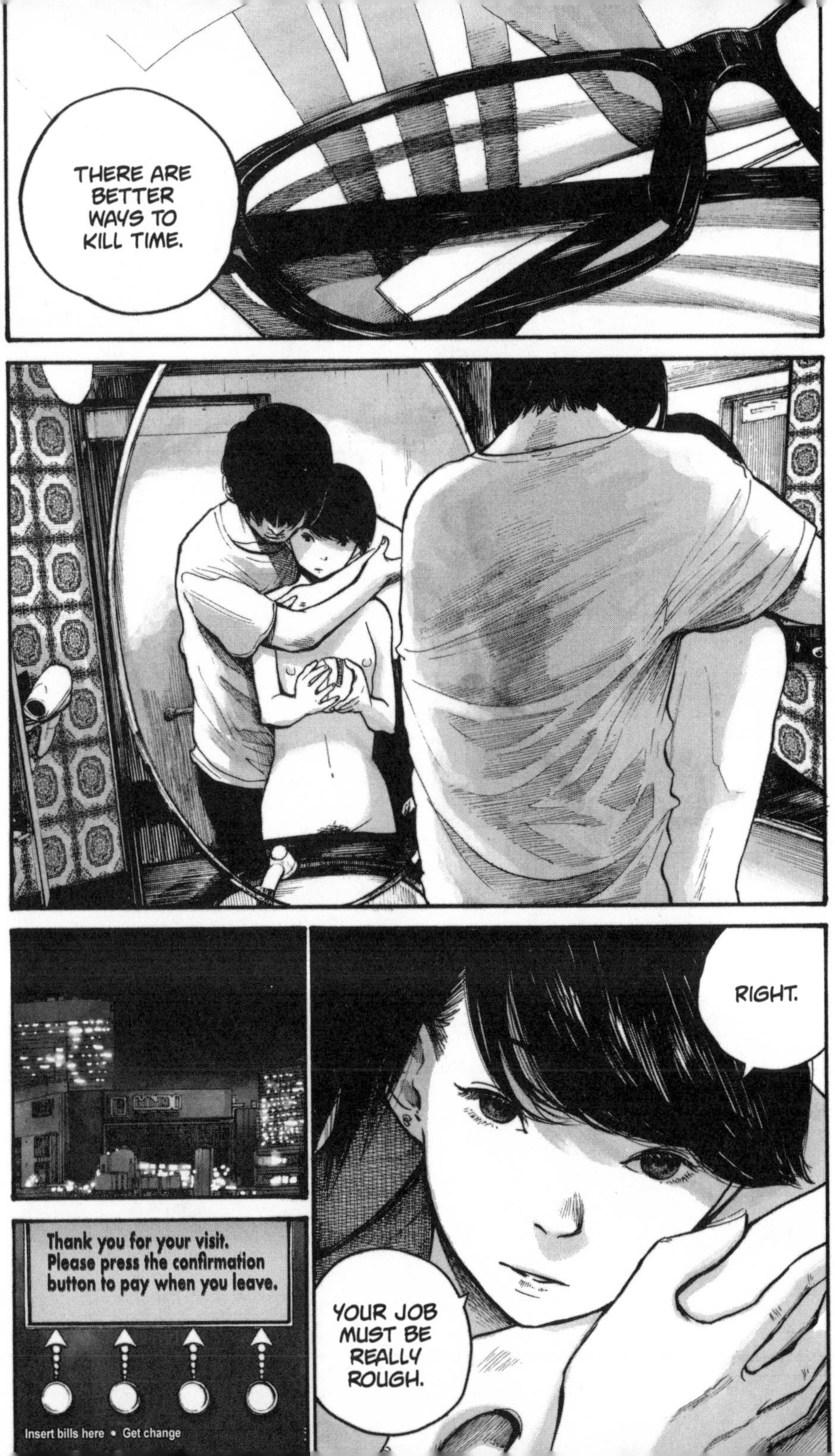
THERE ARE BETTER WAYS TO KILL TIME.
RIGHT.
YOUR JOB MUST BE REALLY ROUGH.
Thank you for your visit. Please press the confirmation button to pay when you leave.
Insert bills here • Get change

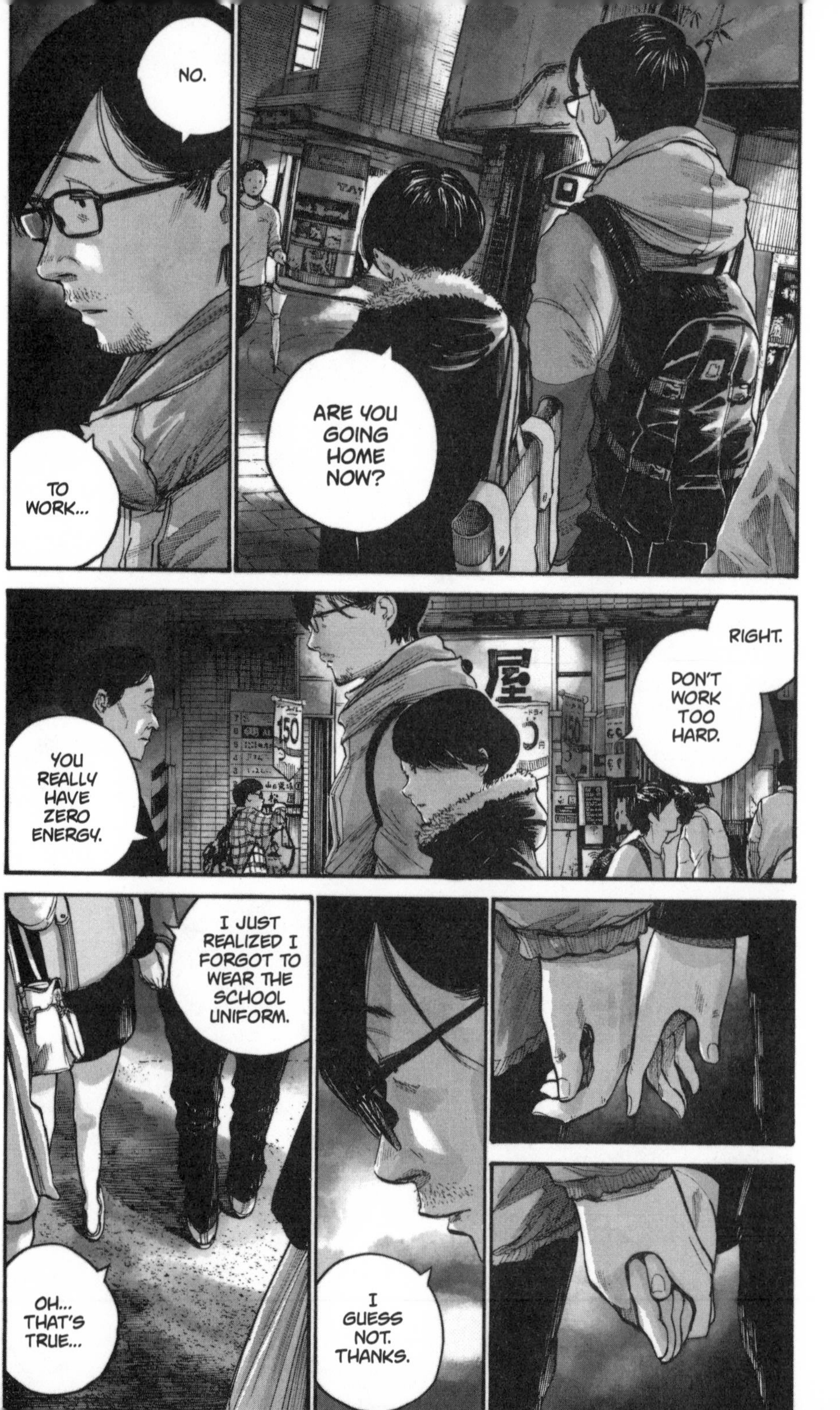
ARE YOU GOING HOME NOW?
NO.
TO WORK...
RIGHT.
DON'T WORK TOO HARD.
YOU REALLY HAVE ZERO ENERGY.
I GUESS NOT. THANKS.
I JUST REALIZED I FORGOT TO WEAR THE SCHOOL UNIFORM.
OH... THAT'S TRUE...

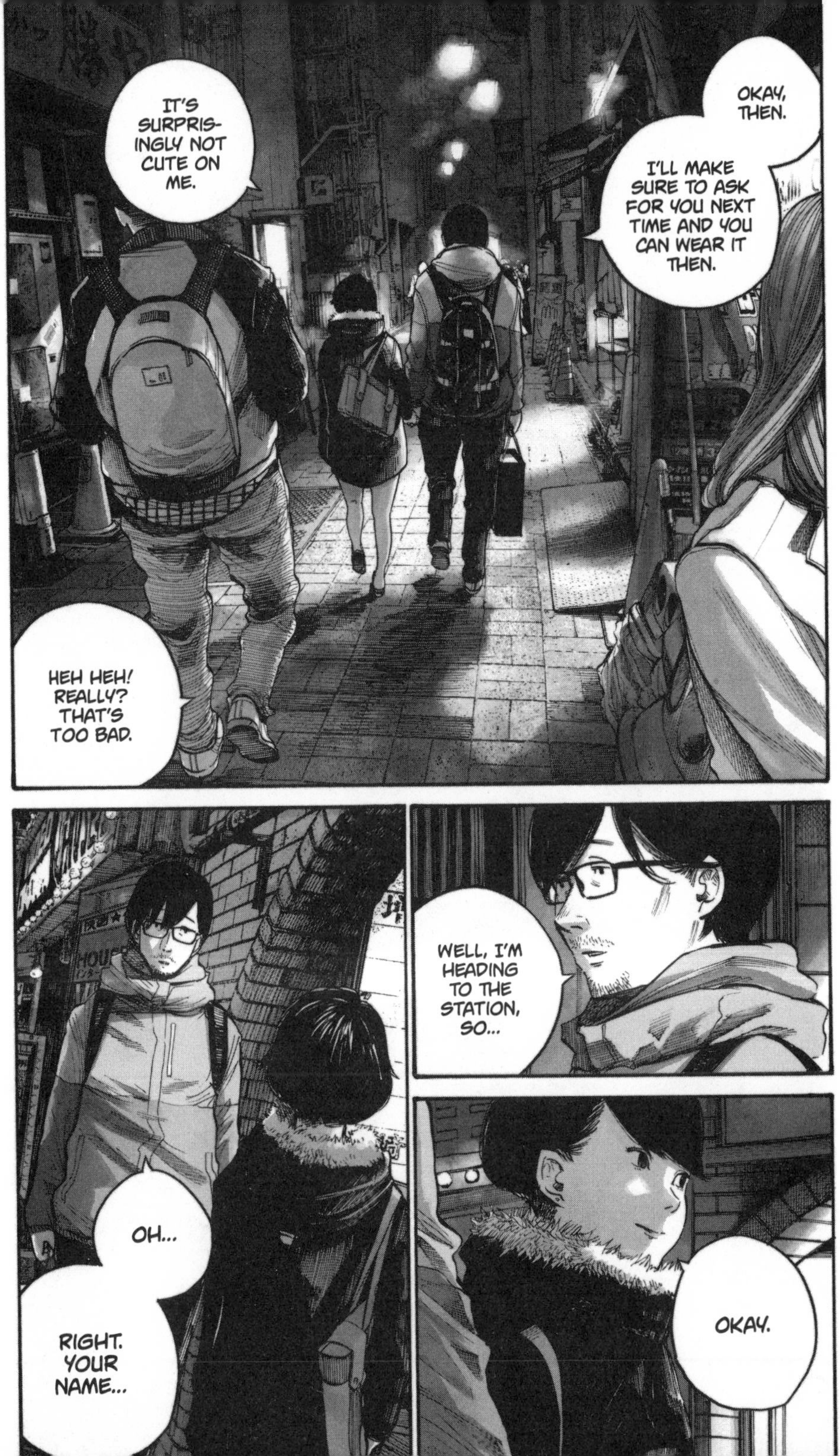
OKAY, THEN.
I'LL MAKE SURE TO ASK FOR YOU NEXT TIME AND YOU CAN WEAR IT THEN.
IT'S SURPRIS-INGLY NOT CUTE ON ME.
HEH HEH! REALLY? THAT'S TOO BAD.
WELL, I'M HEADING TO THE STATION, SO...
OKAY.
OH...
RIGHT. YOUR NAME...

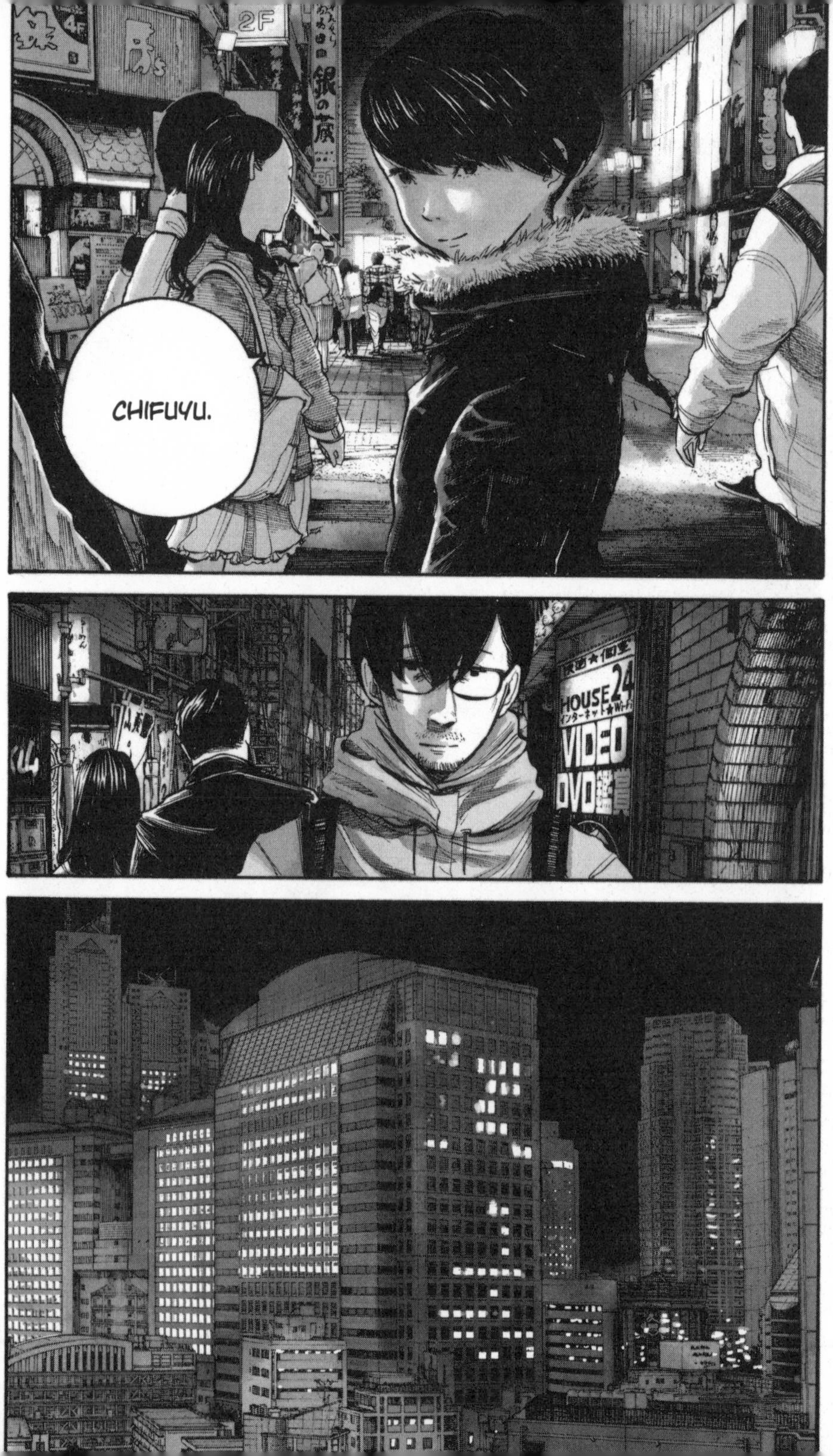
2F
銀の蔵
CHIFUYU.
HOUSE 24
インターネット★Wi-Fi
VIDEO
DVD

CHAPTER 3

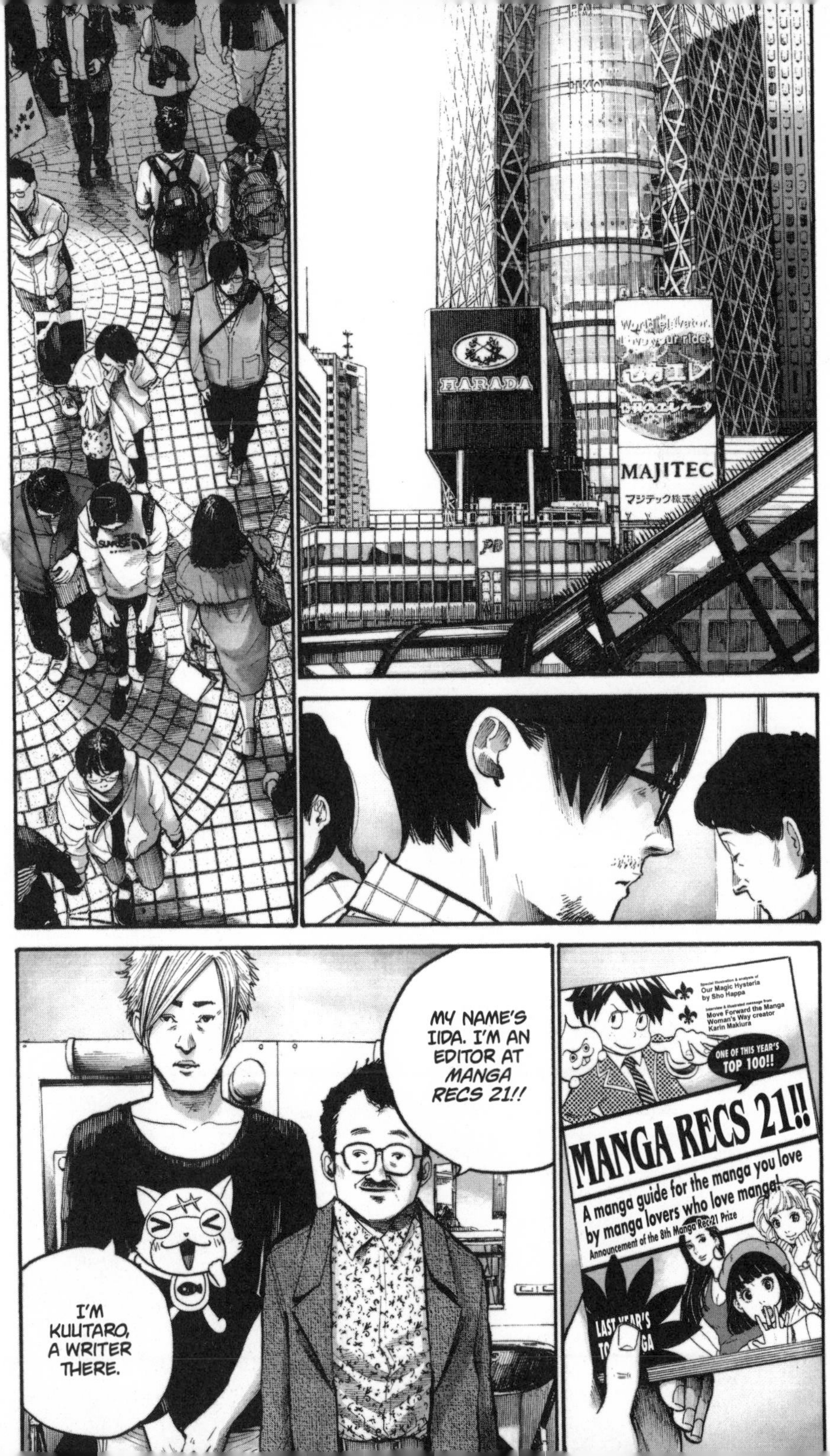
HARADA
MAJITEC
Special illustration & analysis of Our Magic Hysteria by Sho Happa
Interview & illustrated message from Move Forward the Manga Woman's Way creator Karin Makiura
ONE OF THIS YEAR'S TOP 100!!
MANGA RECS 21!!
A manga guide for the manga you love by manga lovers who love manga!
Announcement of the 8th Manga Rec 21 Prize
MY NAME'S IIDA. I'M AN EDITOR AT *MANGA RECS 21*!!
I'M KUUTARO, A WRITER THERE.

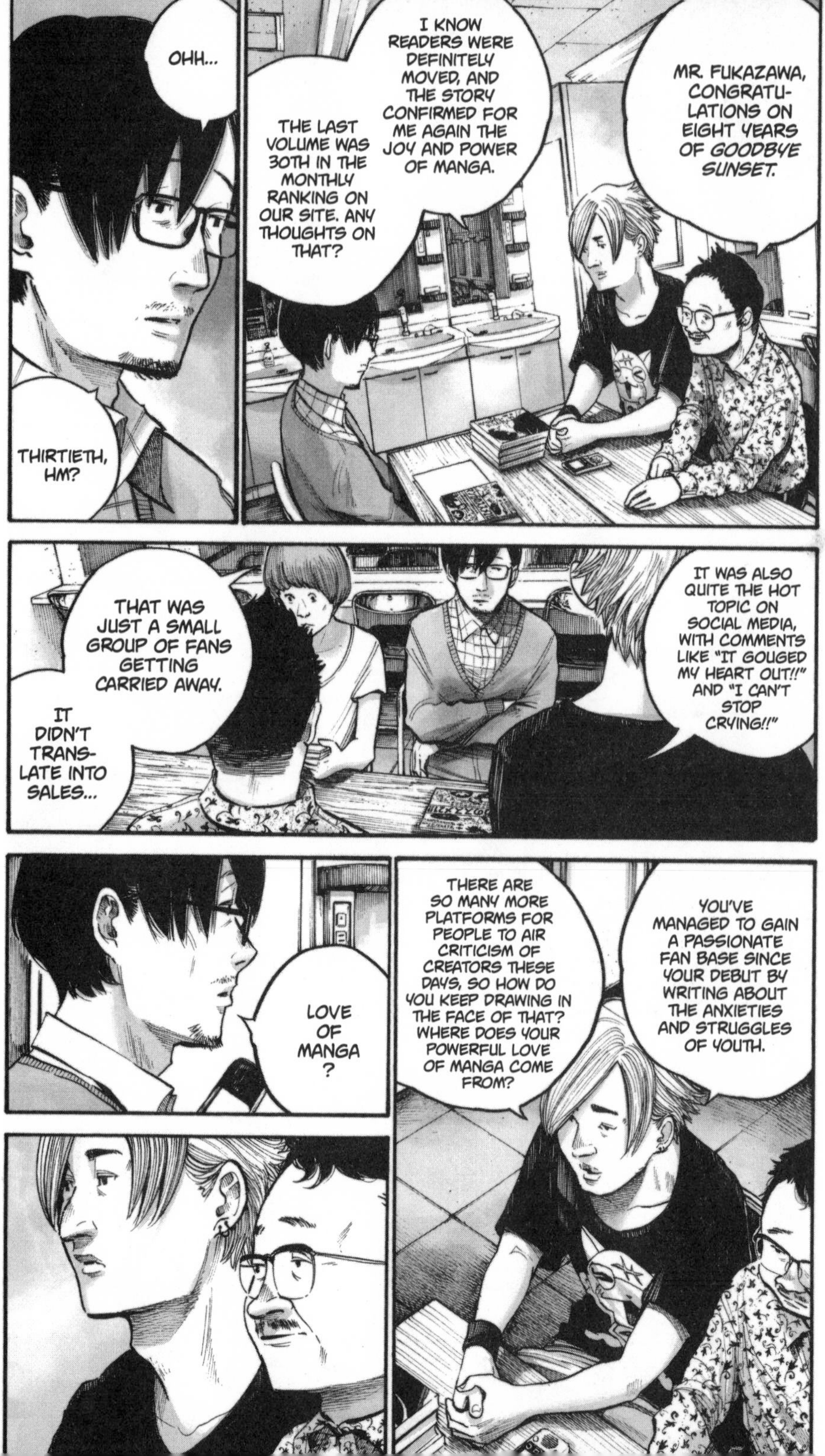
MR. FUKAZAWA, CONGRATULATIONS ON EIGHT YEARS OF *GOODBYE SUNSET.*
I KNOW READERS WERE DEFINITELY MOVED, AND THE STORY CONFIRMED FOR ME AGAIN THE JOY AND POWER OF MANGA.
THE LAST VOLUME WAS 30TH IN THE MONTHLY RANKING ON OUR SITE. ANY THOUGHTS ON THAT?
OHH...
THIRTIETH, HM?
IT WAS ALSO QUITE THE HOT TOPIC ON SOCIAL MEDIA, WITH COMMENTS LIKE "IT GOUGED MY HEART OUT!!" AND "I CAN'T STOP CRYING!!"
THAT WAS JUST A SMALL GROUP OF FANS GETTING CARRIED AWAY.
IT DIDN'T TRANSLATE INTO SALES...
YOU'VE MANAGED TO GAIN A PASSIONATE FAN BASE SINCE YOUR DEBUT BY WRITING ABOUT THE ANXIETIES AND STRUGGLES OF YOUTH.
THERE ARE SO MANY MORE PLATFORMS FOR PEOPLE TO AIR CRITICISM OF CREATORS THESE DAYS, SO HOW DO YOU KEEP DRAWING IN THE FACE OF THAT? WHERE DOES YOUR POWERFUL LOVE OF MANGA COME FROM?
LOVE OF MANGA?

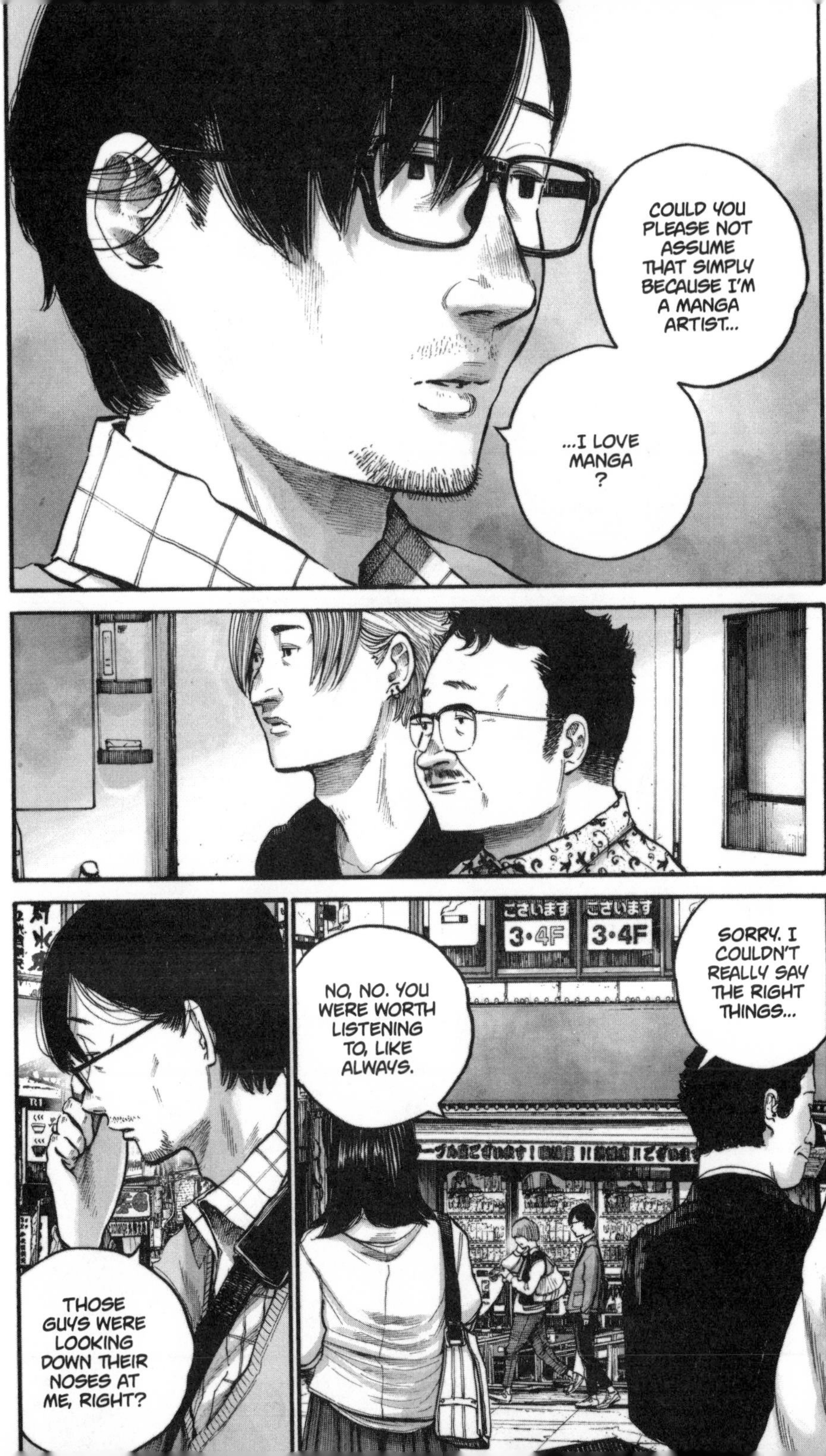
COULD YOU PLEASE NOT ASSUME THAT SIMPLY BECAUSE I'M A MANGA ARTIST...
...I LOVE MANGA ?
3·4F
3·4F
SORRY. I COULDN'T REALLY SAY THE RIGHT THINGS...
NO, NO. YOU WERE WORTH LISTENING TO, LIKE ALWAYS.
THOSE GUYS WERE LOOKING DOWN THEIR NOSES AT ME, RIGHT?

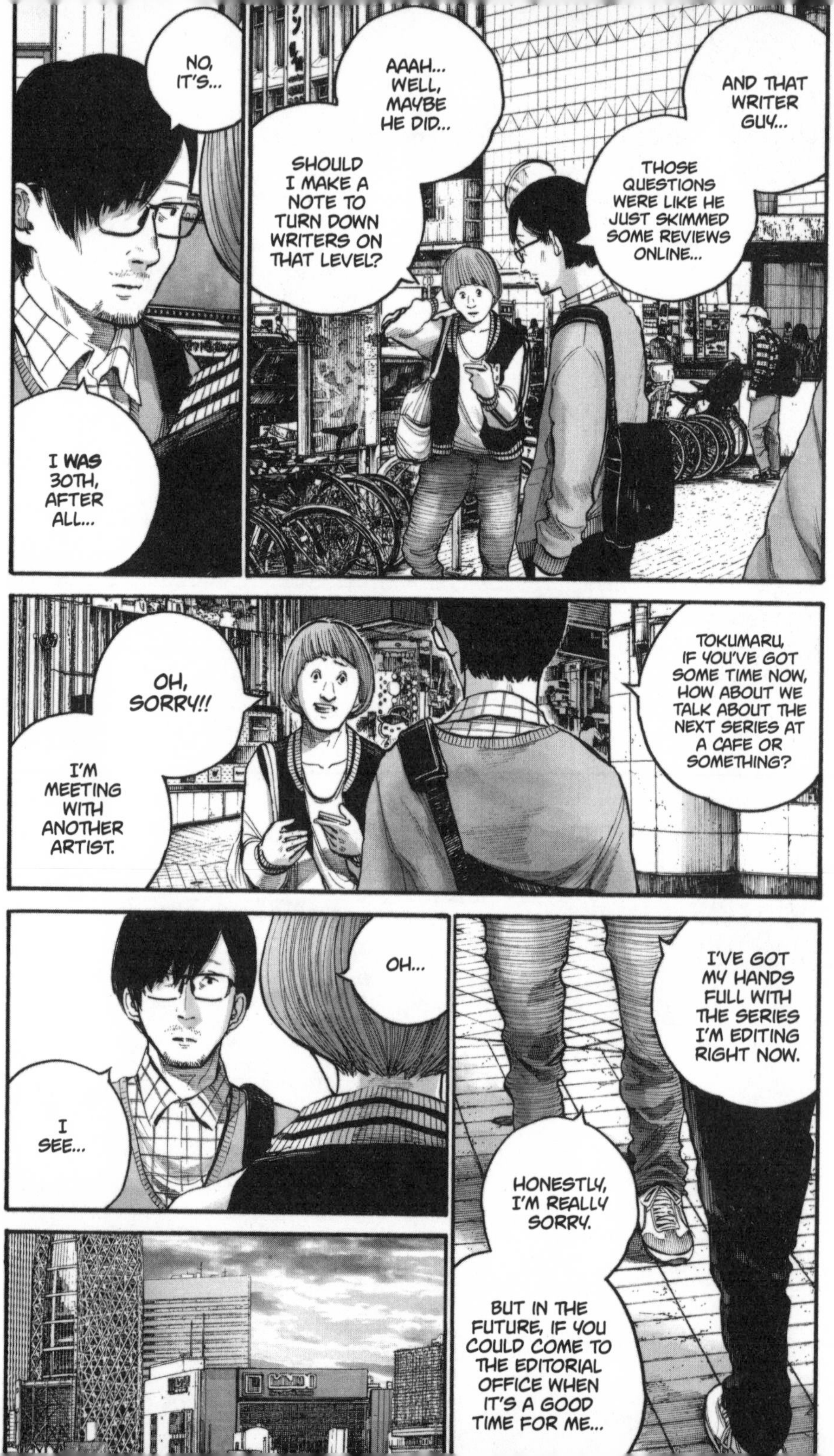
AND THAT WRITER GUY...
THOSE QUESTIONS WERE LIKE HE JUST SKIMMED SOME REVIEWS ONLINE...
AAAH... WELL, MAYBE HE DID...
SHOULD I MAKE A NOTE TO TURN DOWN WRITERS ON THAT LEVEL?
NO, IT'S...
I WAS 30TH, AFTER ALL...
TOKUMARU, IF YOU'VE GOT SOME TIME NOW, HOW ABOUT WE TALK ABOUT THE NEXT SERIES AT A CAFE OR SOMETHING?
OH, SORRY!!
I'M MEETING WITH ANOTHER ARTIST.
I'VE GOT MY HANDS FULL WITH THE SERIES I'M EDITING RIGHT NOW.
HONESTLY, I'M REALLY SORRY.
BUT IN THE FUTURE, IF YOU COULD COME TO THE EDITORIAL OFFICE WHEN IT'S A GOOD TIME FOR ME...
OH...
I SEE...

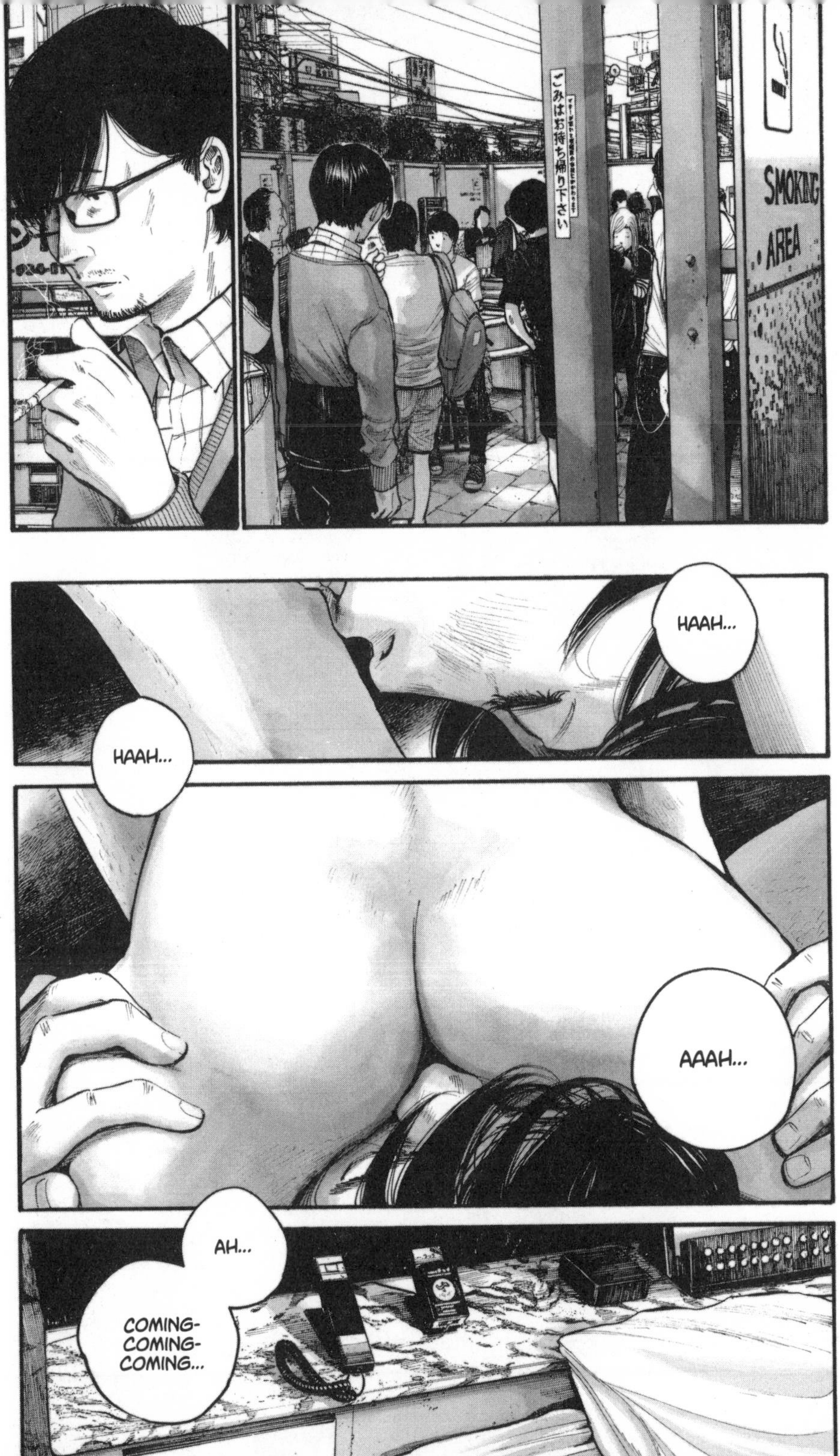
SMOKING AREA
ごみはお持ち帰り下さい
HAAH...
HAAH...
AAAH...
AH...
COMING-
COMING-
COMING...

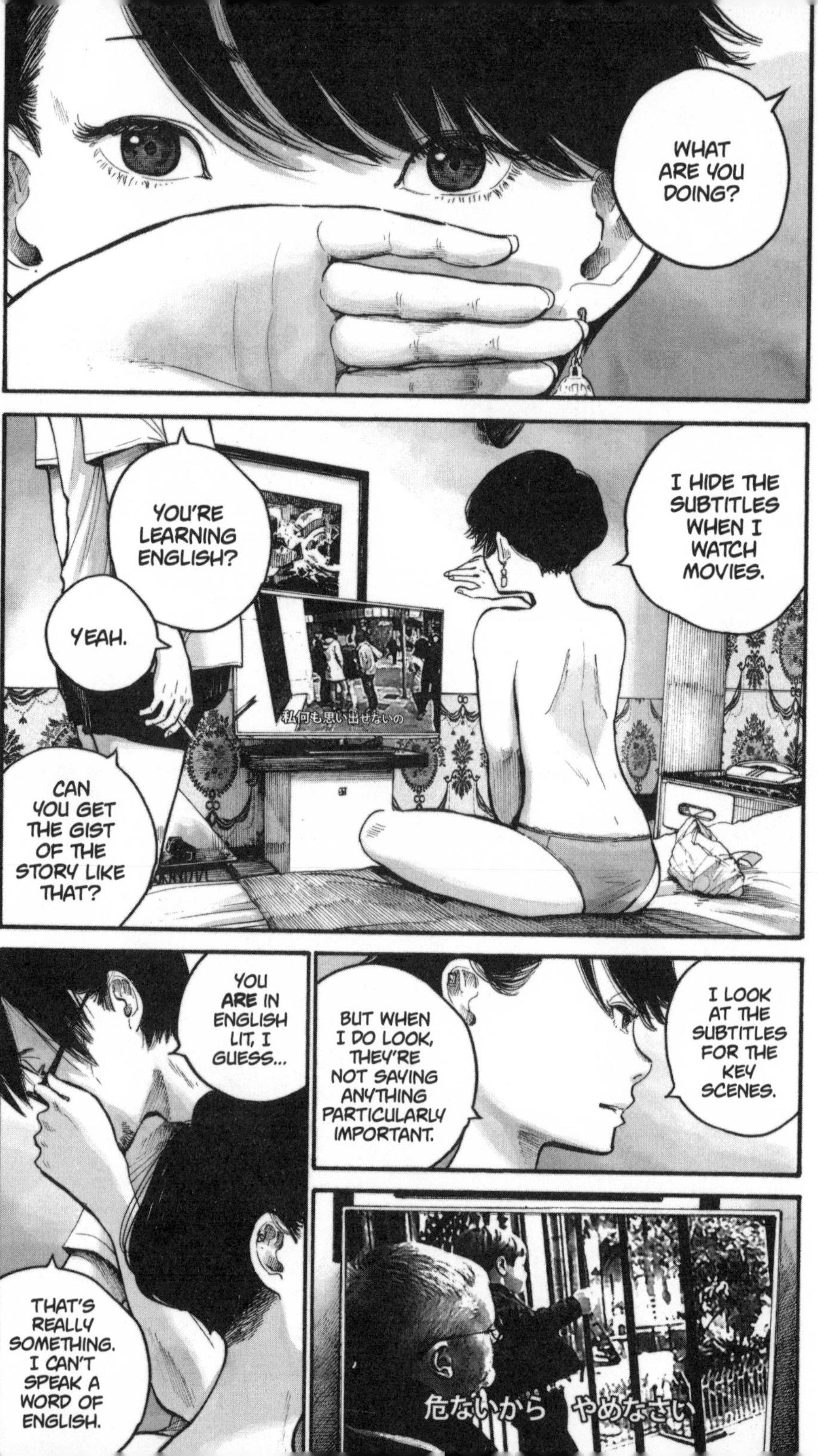
WHAT ARE YOU DOING?
I HIDE THE SUBTITLES WHEN I WATCH MOVIES.
YOU'RE LEARNING ENGLISH?
YEAH.
私何も思い出せないの
CAN YOU GET THE GIST OF THE STORY LIKE THAT?
I LOOK AT THE SUBTITLES FOR THE KEY SCENES.
BUT WHEN I DO LOOK, THEY'RE NOT SAYING ANYTHING PARTICULARLY IMPORTANT.
危ないから やめなさい
YOU **ARE** IN ENGLISH LIT, I GUESS...
THAT'S REALLY SOMETHING. I CAN'T SPEAK A WORD OF ENGLISH.

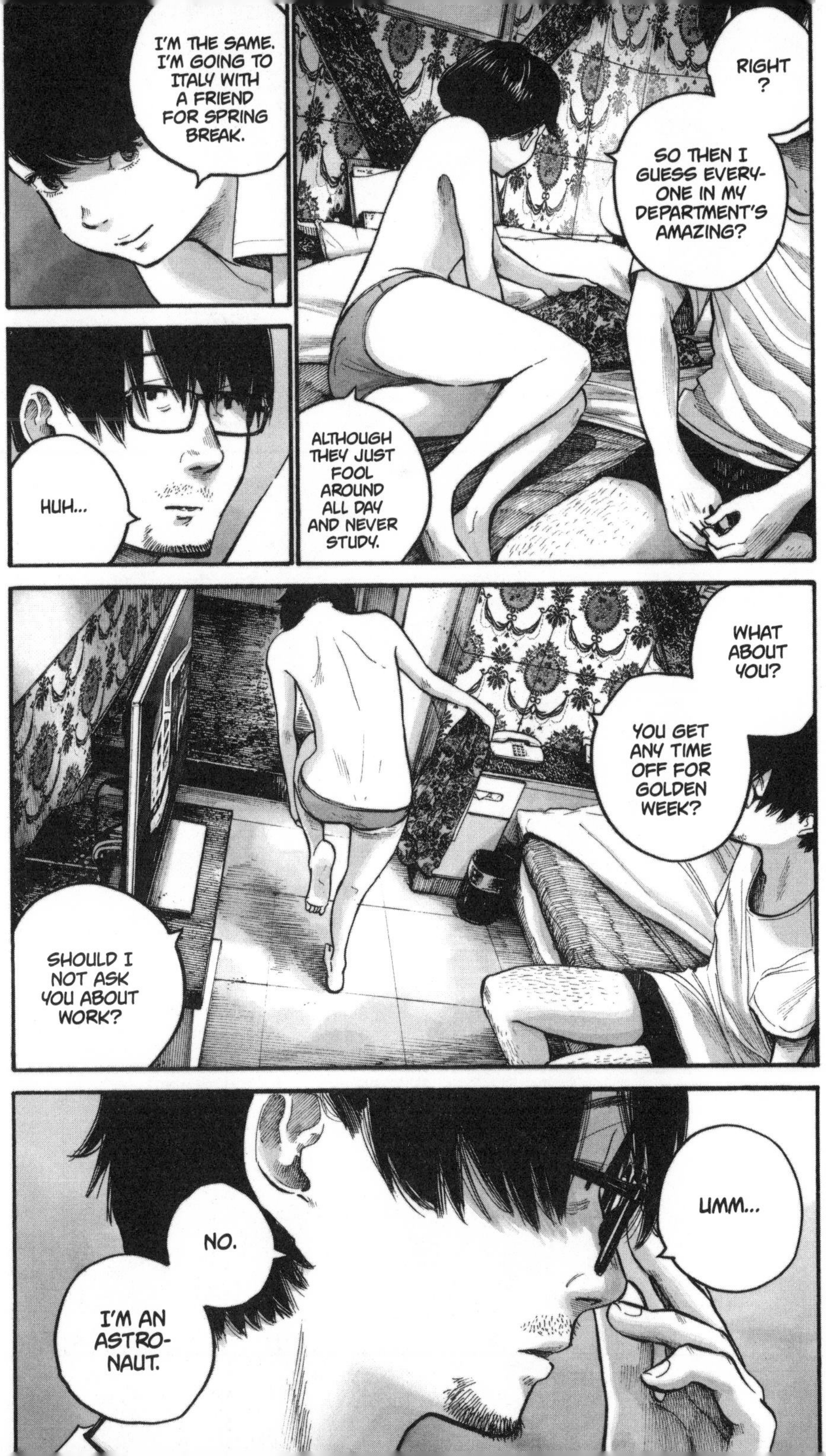

RIGHT?
SO THEN I GUESS EVERY-ONE IN MY DEPARTMENT'S AMAZING?
ALTHOUGH THEY JUST FOOL AROUND ALL DAY AND NEVER STUDY.
I'M THE SAME. I'M GOING TO ITALY WITH A FRIEND FOR SPRING BREAK.
HUH...
WHAT ABOUT YOU?
YOU GET ANY TIME OFF FOR GOLDEN WEEK?
SHOULD I NOT ASK YOU ABOUT WORK?
UMM...
NO.
I'M AN ASTRO-NAUT.

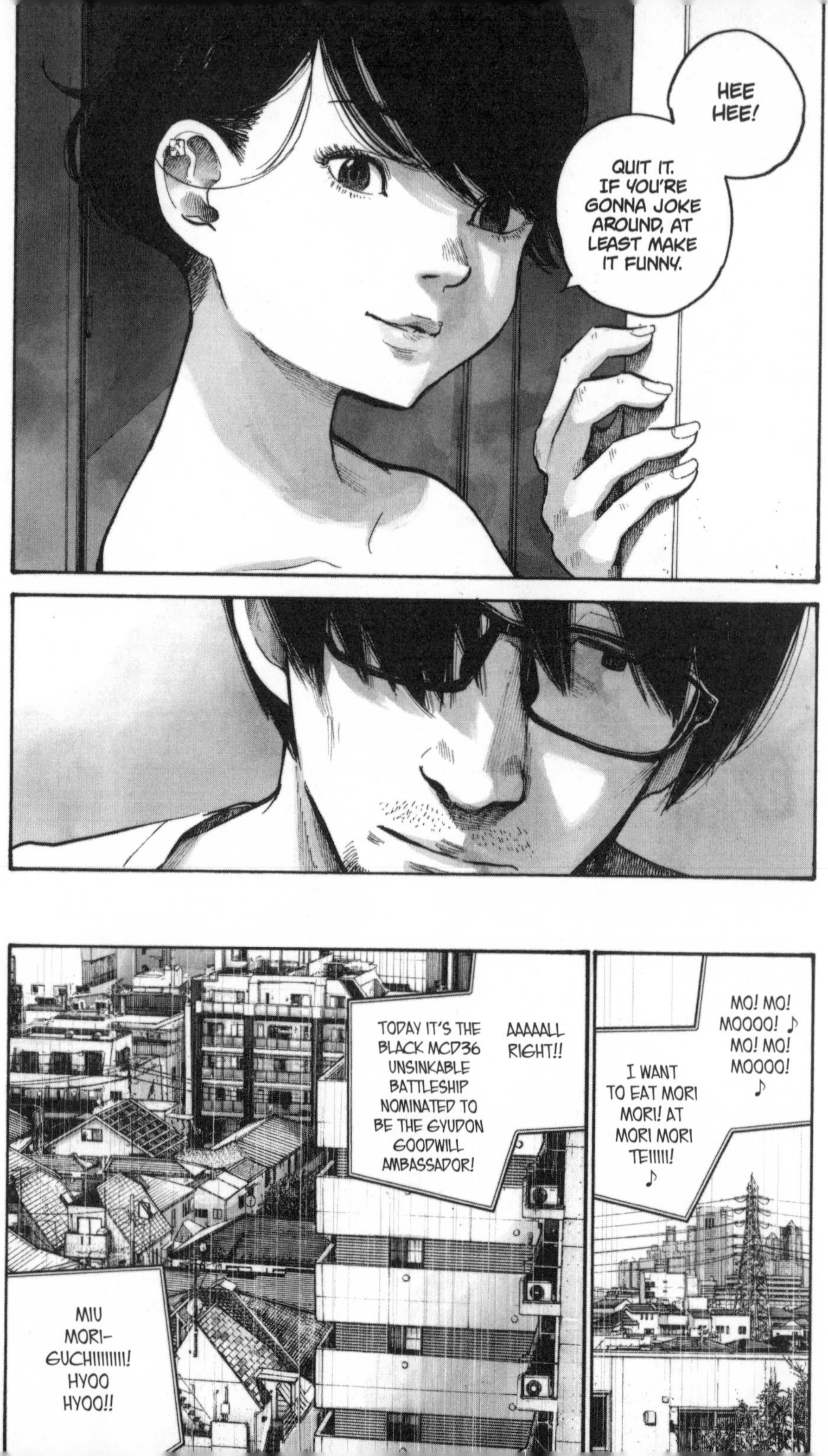
HEE HEE!
QUIT IT. IF YOU'RE GONNA JOKE AROUND, AT LEAST MAKE IT FUNNY.
MO! MO! MOOOO! ♪ MO! MO! MOOOO! ♪
I WANT TO EAT MORI MORI! AT MORI MORI TEIIIII! ♪
AAAAALL RIGHT!!
TODAY IT'S THE BLACK MCD36 UNSINKABLE BATTLESHIP NOMINATED TO BE THE GYUDON GOODWILL AMBASSADOR!
MIU MORI-GUCHIIIIIIIII! HYOO HYOO!!

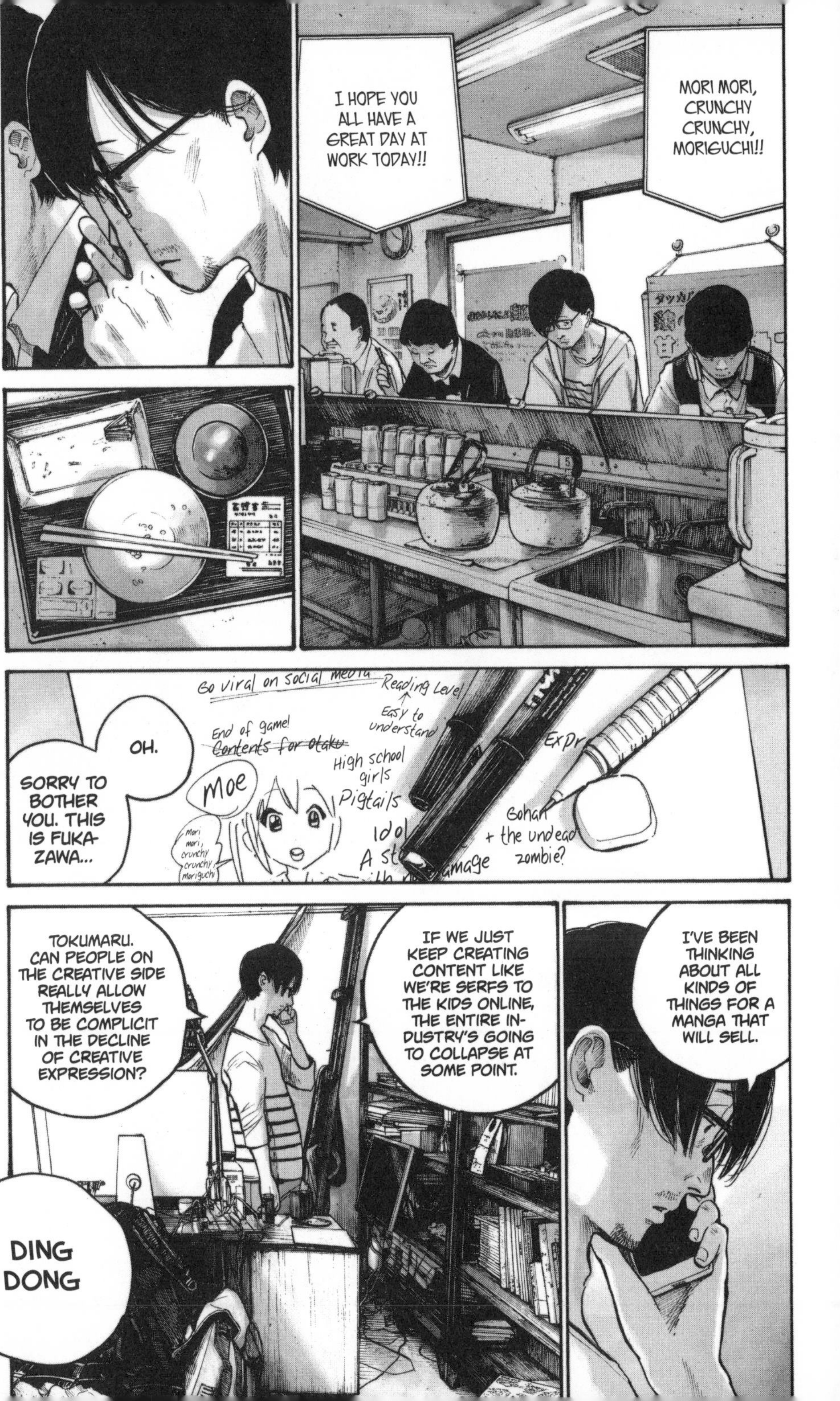
MORI MORI, CRUNCHY CRUNCHY, MORIGUCHI!!
I HOPE YOU ALL HAVE A GREAT DAY AT WORK TODAY!!
Go viral on social media
Reading Level
Easy to understand
End of game!
Contents for otaku
High school girls
Pigtails
Moe
Mori mori, crunchy crunchy, moriguchi
Idol
Expr
Gohan + the undead zombie?
OH.
SORRY TO BOTHER YOU. THIS IS FUKA-ZAWA...
I'VE BEEN THINKING ABOUT ALL KINDS OF THINGS FOR A MANGA THAT WILL SELL.
IF WE JUST KEEP CREATING CONTENT LIKE WE'RE SERFS TO THE KIDS ONLINE, THE ENTIRE IN-DUSTRY'S GOING TO COLLAPSE AT SOME POINT.
TOKUMARU. CAN PEOPLE ON THE CREATIVE SIDE REALLY ALLOW THEMSELVES TO BE COMPLICIT IN THE DECLINE OF CREATIVE EXPRESSION?
DING DONG

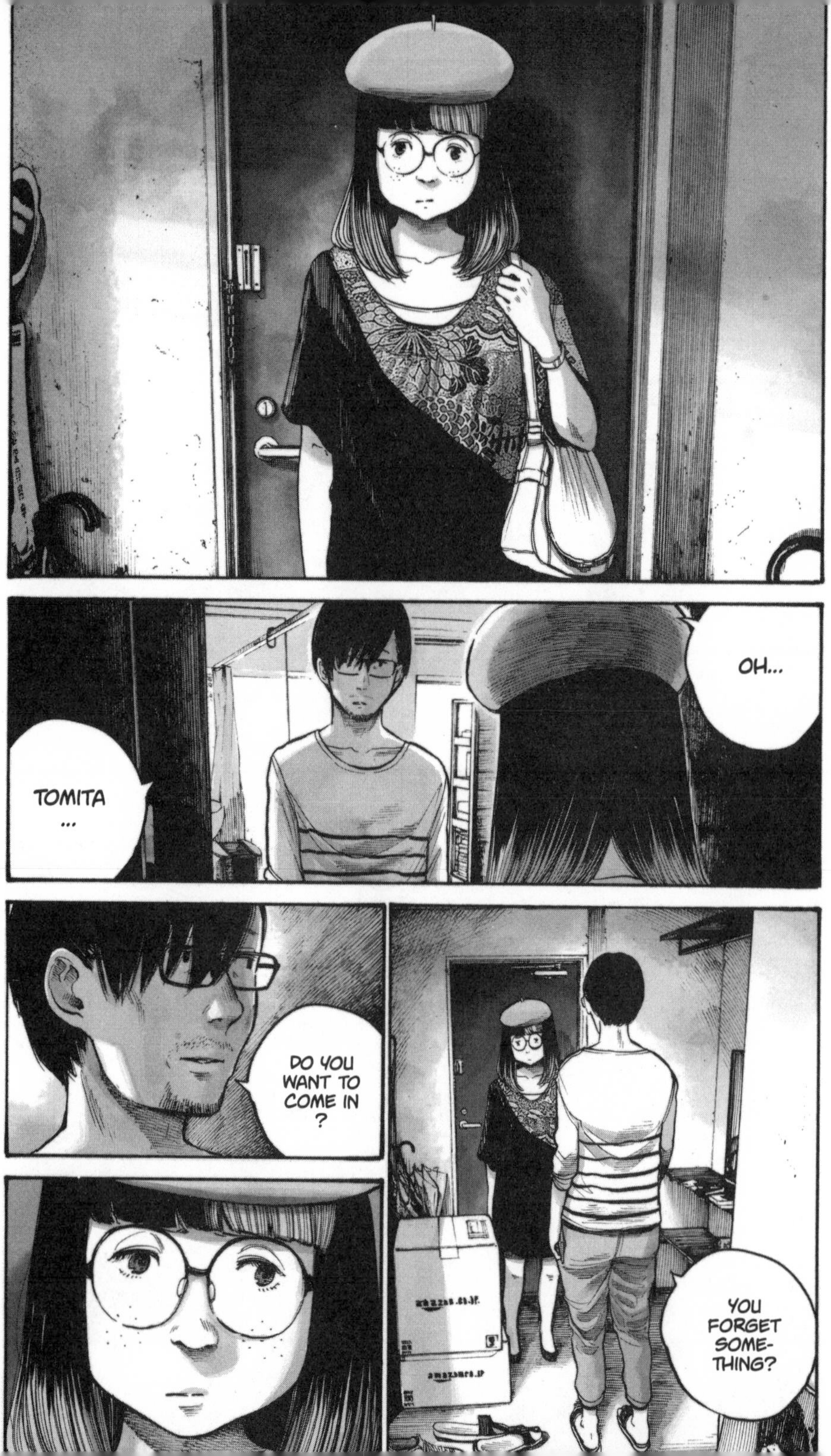
OH...
TOMITA ...
YOU FORGET SOME-THING?
DO YOU WANT TO COME IN ?

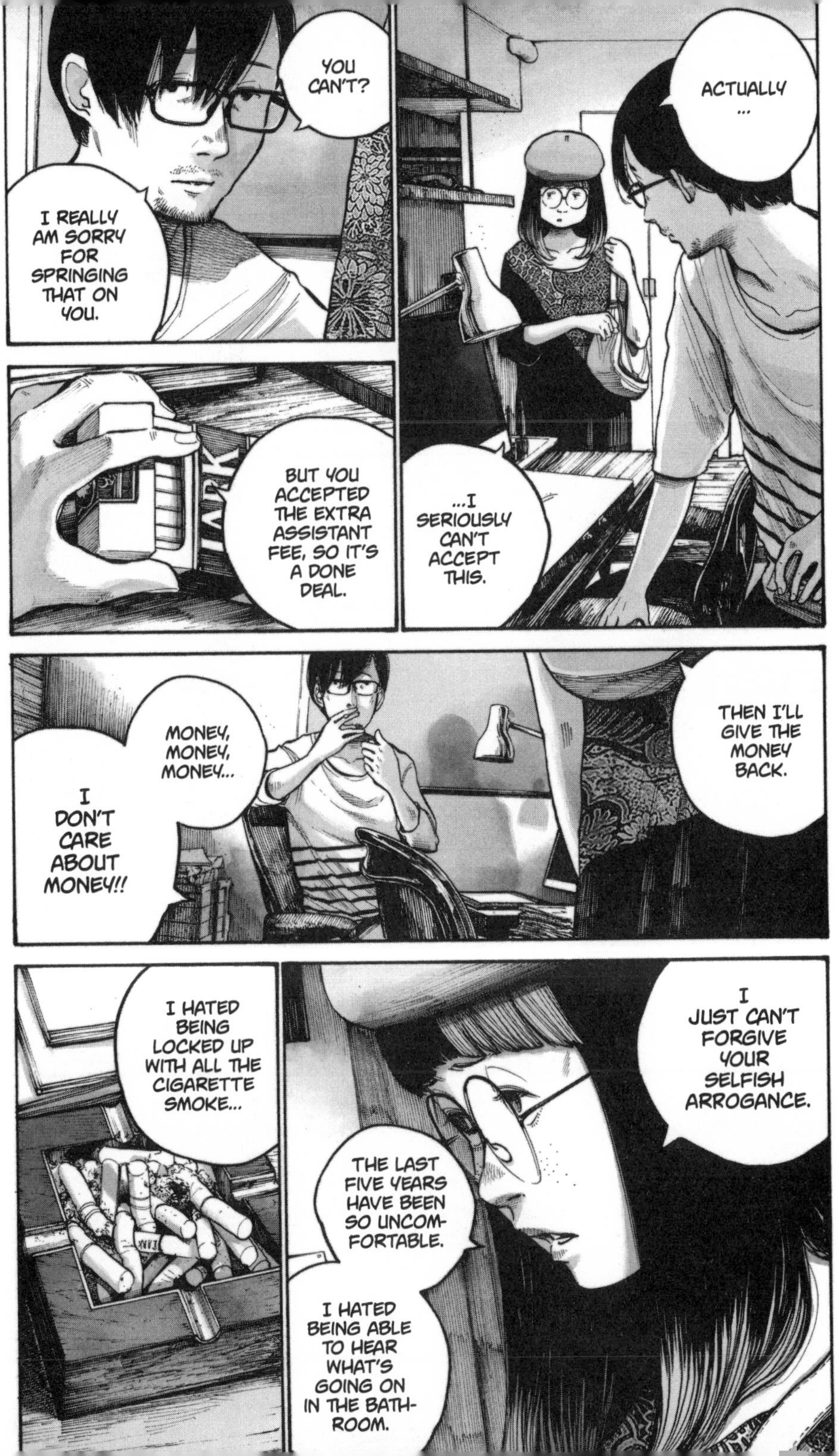
ACTUALLY ...
...I SERIOUSLY CAN'T ACCEPT THIS.
YOU CAN'T?
I REALLY AM SORRY FOR SPRINGING THAT ON YOU.
BUT YOU ACCEPTED THE EXTRA ASSISTANT FEE, SO IT'S A DONE DEAL.
THEN I'LL GIVE THE MONEY BACK.
MONEY, MONEY, MONEY...
I DON'T CARE ABOUT MONEY!!
I JUST CAN'T FORGIVE YOUR SELFISH ARROGANCE.
THE LAST FIVE YEARS HAVE BEEN SO UNCOM-FORTABLE.
I HATED BEING ABLE TO HEAR WHAT'S GOING ON IN THE BATH-ROOM.
I HATED BEING LOCKED UP WITH ALL THE CIGARETTE SMOKE...

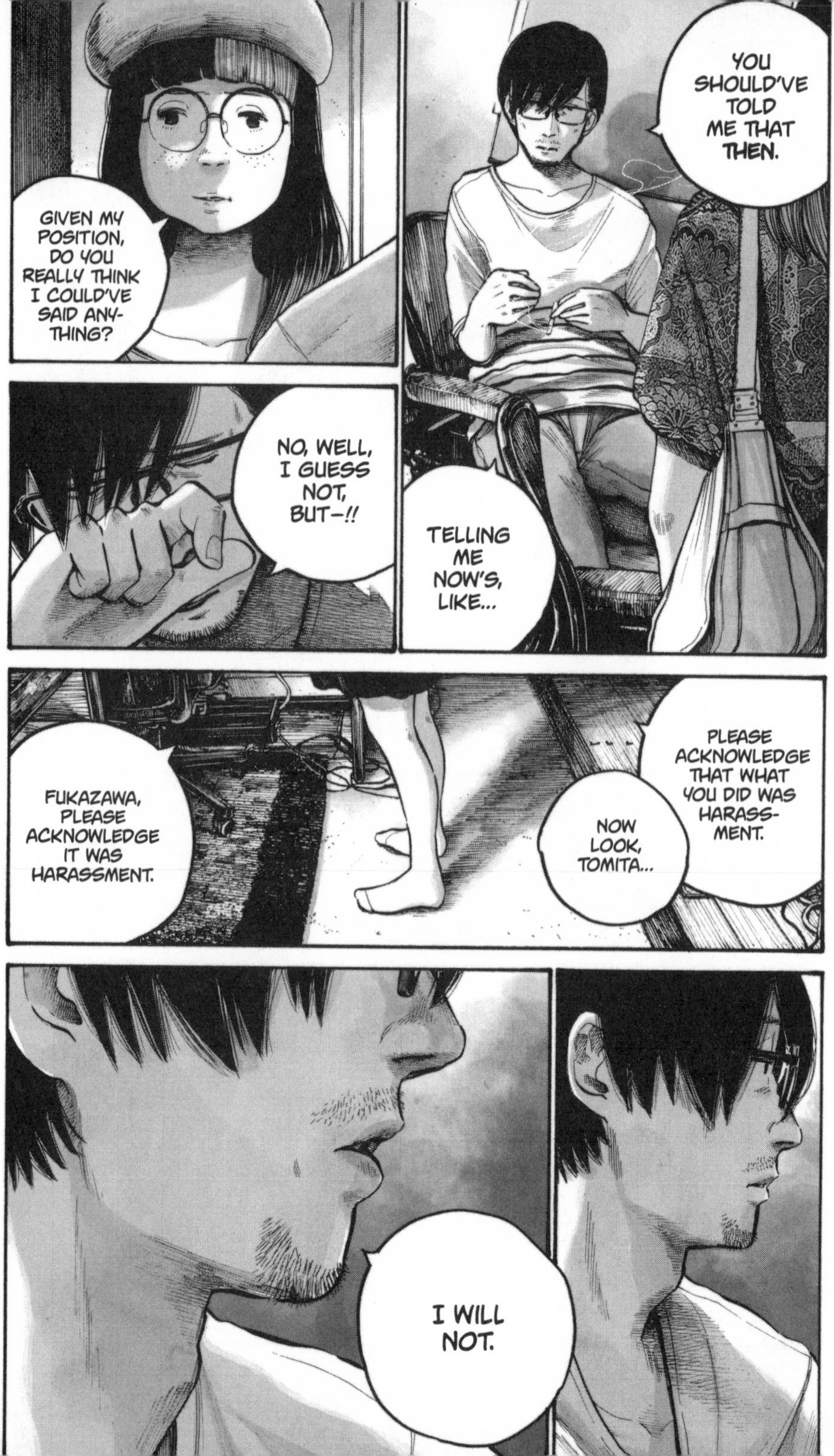
YOU SHOULD'VE TOLD ME THAT THEN.
GIVEN MY POSITION, DO YOU REALLY THINK I COULD'VE SAID ANY-THING?
NO, WELL, I GUESS NOT, BUT—!!
TELLING ME NOW'S, LIKE...
...
PLEASE ACKNOWLEDGE THAT WHAT YOU DID WAS HARASS-MENT.
NOW LOOK, TOMITA...
FUKAZAWA, PLEASE ACKNOWLEDGE IT WAS HARASSMENT.
I WILL NOT.

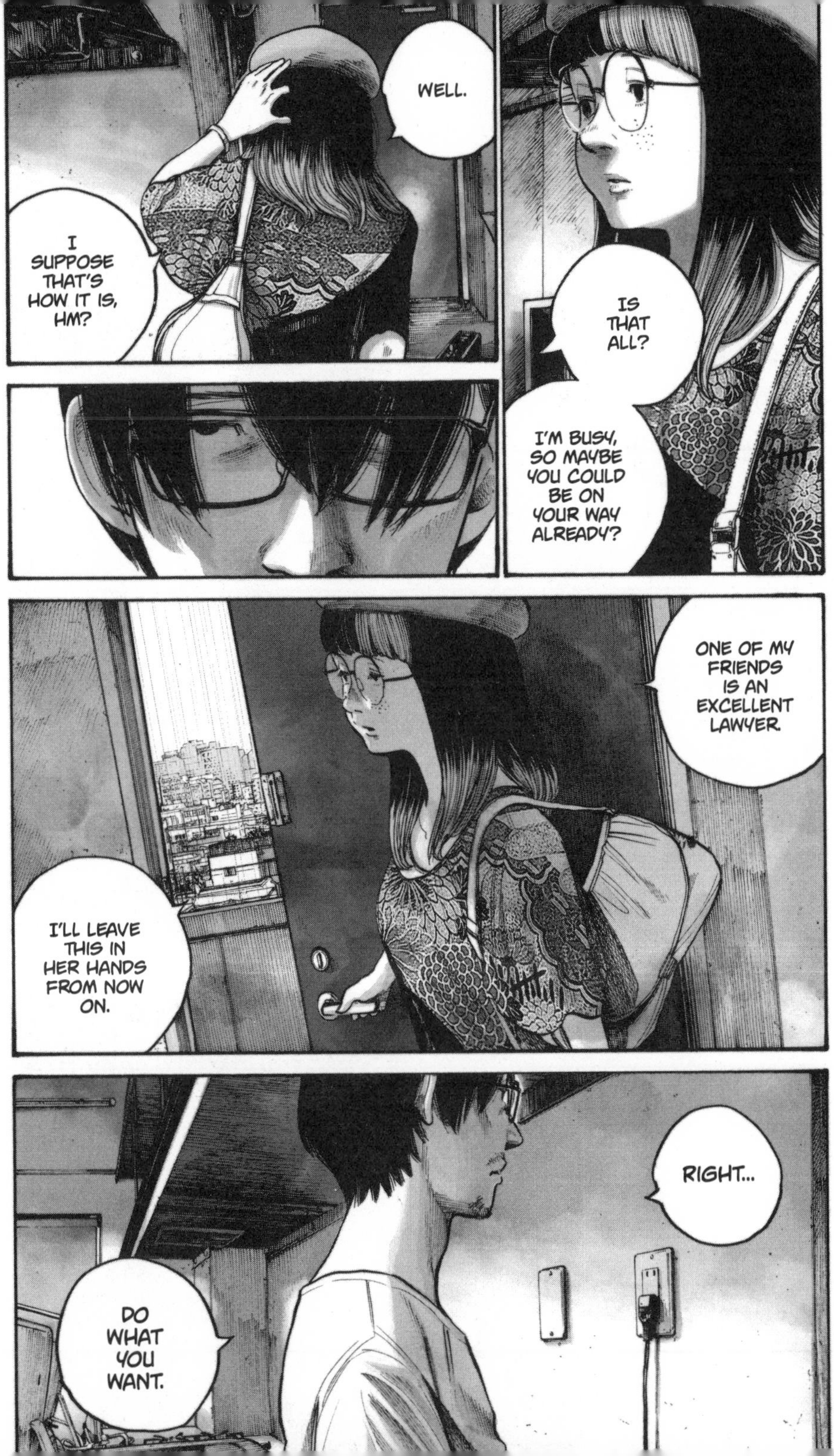
IS THAT ALL?
I'M BUSY, SO MAYBE YOU COULD BE ON YOUR WAY ALREADY?
WELL.
I SUPPOSE THAT'S HOW IT IS, HM?
ONE OF MY FRIENDS IS AN EXCELLENT LAWYER.
I'LL LEAVE THIS IN HER HANDS FROM NOW ON.
RIGHT...
DO WHAT YOU WANT.

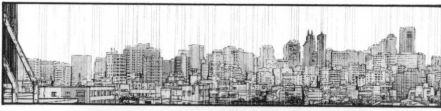

KSSSSH

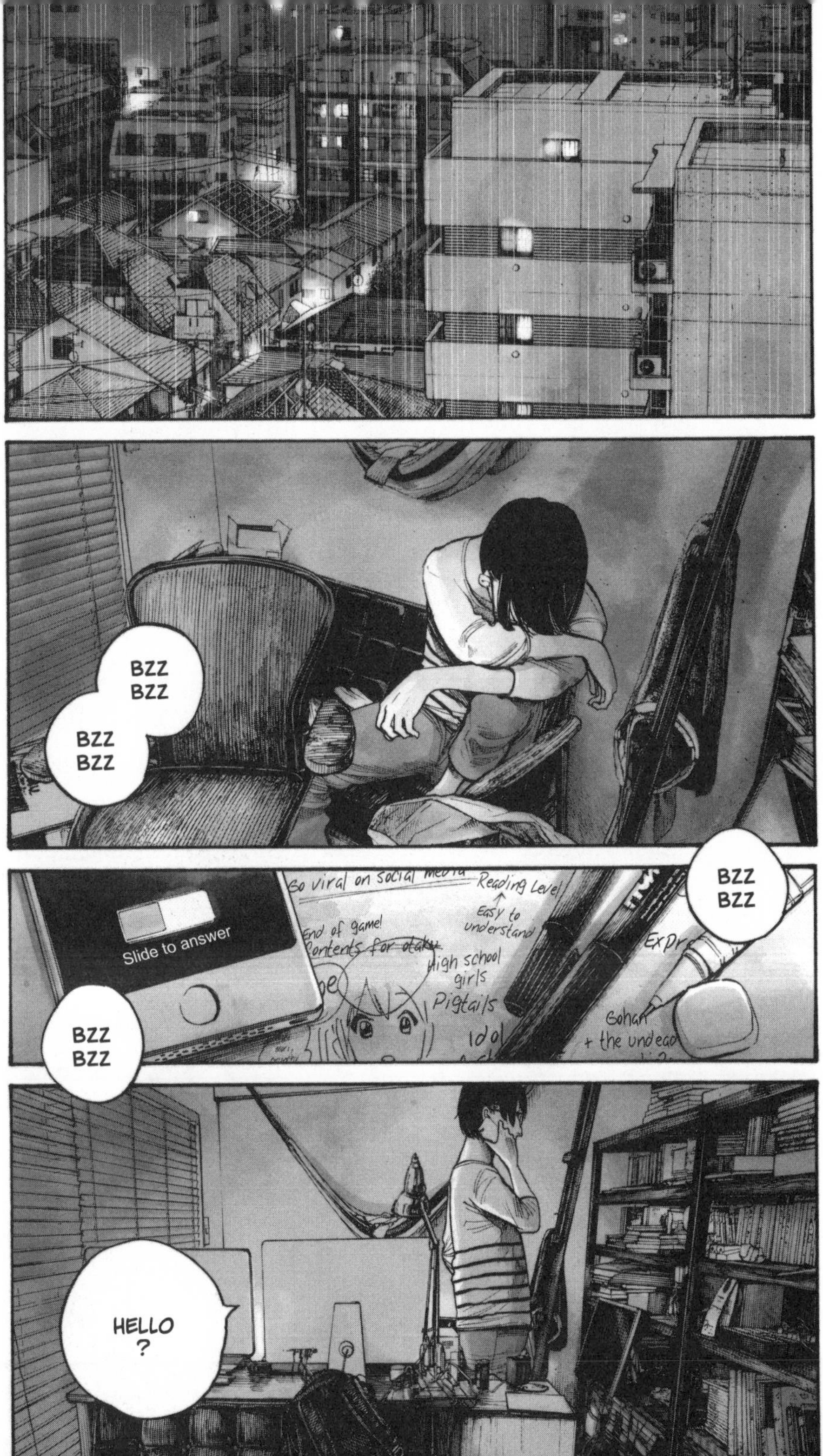
BZZ BZZ
BZZ BZZ
BZZ BZZ
Expr
So viral on social media
Reading Level
Easy to understand
End of game!
Contents for otaku
High school girls
Pigtails
idol
Gohan + the undead
Slide to answer
BZZ BZZ
HELLO ?

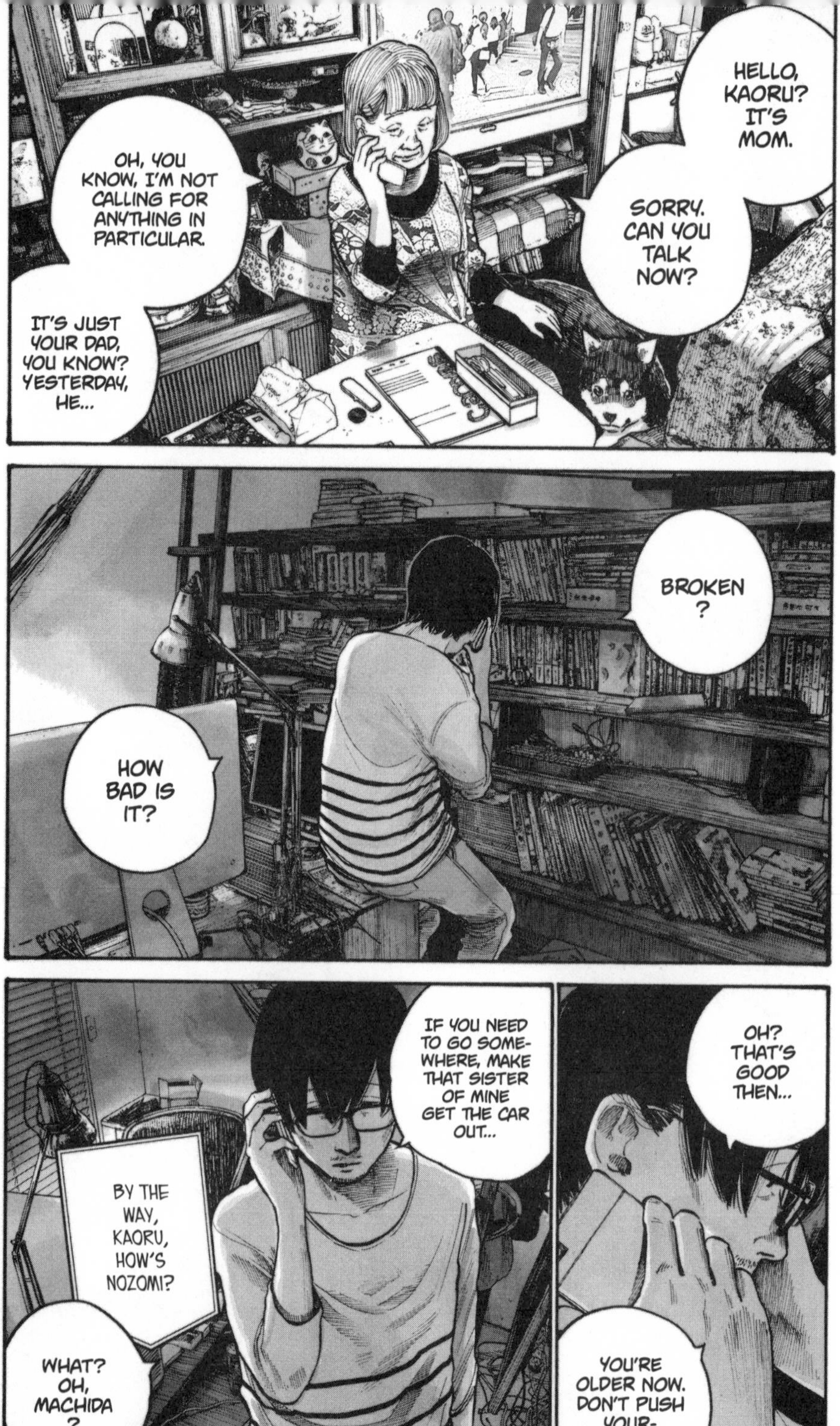
HELLO, KAORU? IT'S MOM.
SORRY. CAN YOU TALK NOW?
OH, YOU KNOW, I'M NOT CALLING FOR ANYTHING IN PARTICULAR.
IT'S JUST YOUR DAD, YOU KNOW? YESTERDAY, HE...
BROKEN?
HOW BAD IS IT?
OH? THAT'S GOOD THEN...
YOU'RE OLDER NOW. DON'T PUSH YOUR-SELVES.
IF YOU NEED TO GO SOME-WHERE, MAKE THAT SISTER OF MINE GET THE CAR OUT...
BY THE WAY, KAORU, HOW'S NOZOMI?
WHAT? OH, MACHIDA?

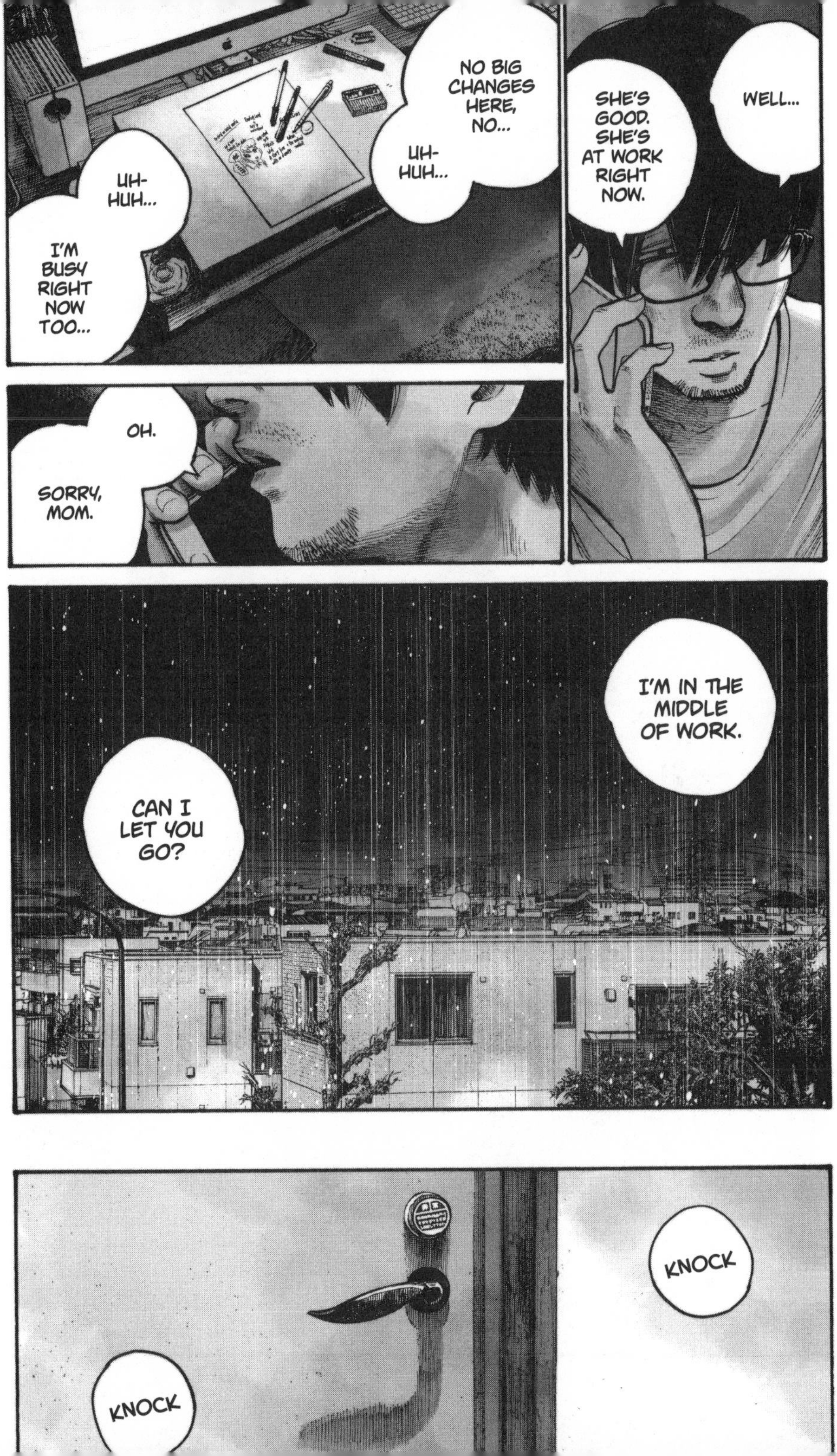
WELL...
SHE'S GOOD. SHE'S AT WORK RIGHT NOW.
NO BIG CHANGES HERE, NO...
UH-HUH...
UH-HUH...
I'M BUSY RIGHT NOW TOO...
OH.
SORRY, MOM.
I'M IN THE MIDDLE OF WORK.
CAN I LET YOU GO?
KNOCK
KNOCK

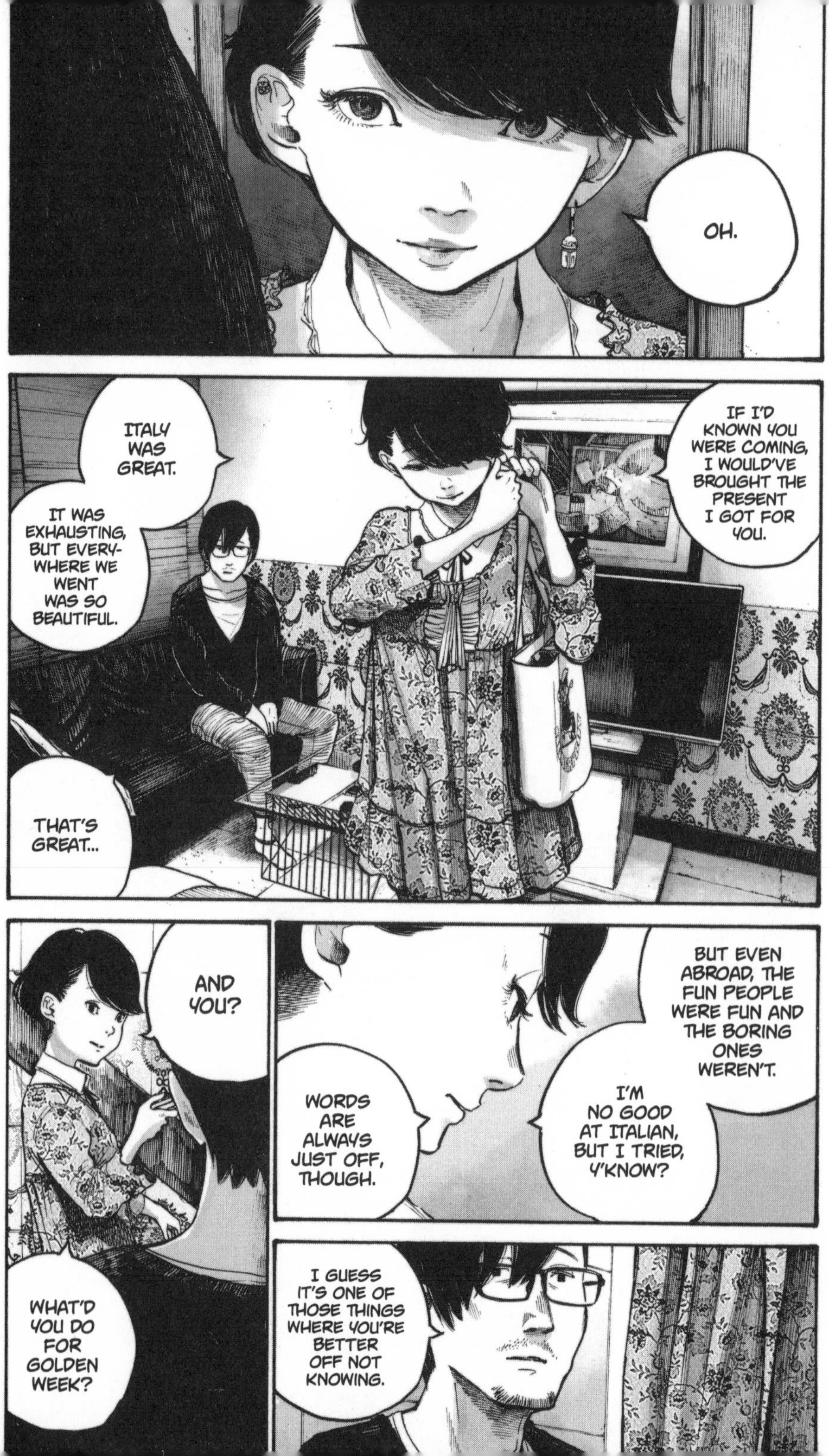
OH.
IF I'D KNOWN YOU WERE COMING, I WOULD'VE BROUGHT THE PRESENT I GOT FOR YOU.
ITALY WAS GREAT.
IT WAS EXHAUSTING, BUT EVERY-WHERE WE WENT WAS SO BEAUTIFUL.
THAT'S GREAT...
BUT EVEN ABROAD, THE FUN PEOPLE WERE FUN AND THE BORING ONES WEREN'T.
I'M NO GOOD AT ITALIAN, BUT I TRIED, Y'KNOW?
WORDS ARE ALWAYS JUST OFF, THOUGH.
I GUESS IT'S ONE OF THOSE THINGS WHERE YOU'RE BETTER OFF NOT KNOWING.
AND YOU?
WHAT'D YOU DO FOR GOLDEN WEEK?

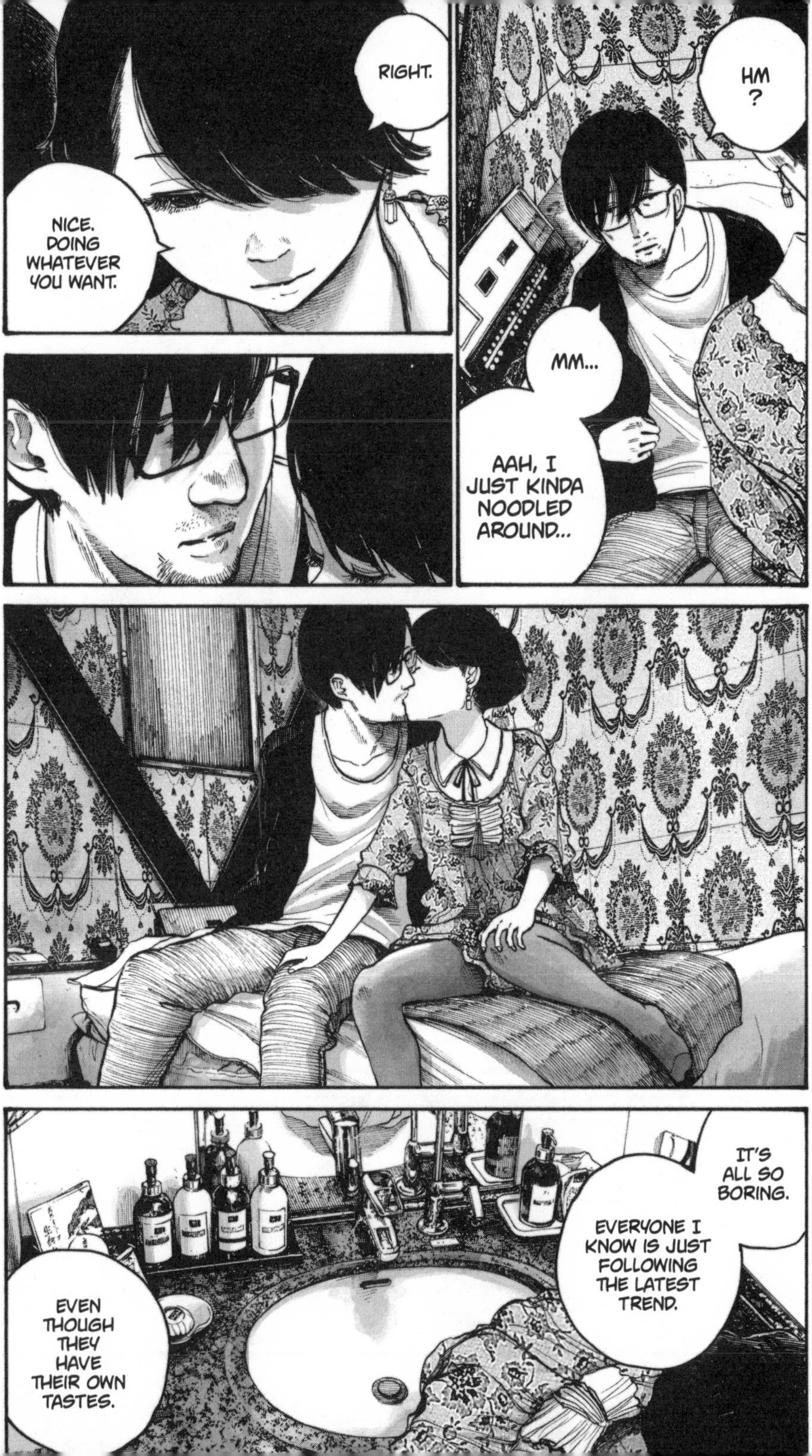
HM ?
MM...
AAH, I JUST KINDA NOODLED AROUND...
RIGHT.
NICE. DOING WHATEVER YOU WANT.
IT'S ALL SO BORING.
EVERYONE I KNOW IS JUST FOLLOWING THE LATEST TREND.
EVEN THOUGH THEY HAVE THEIR OWN TASTES.

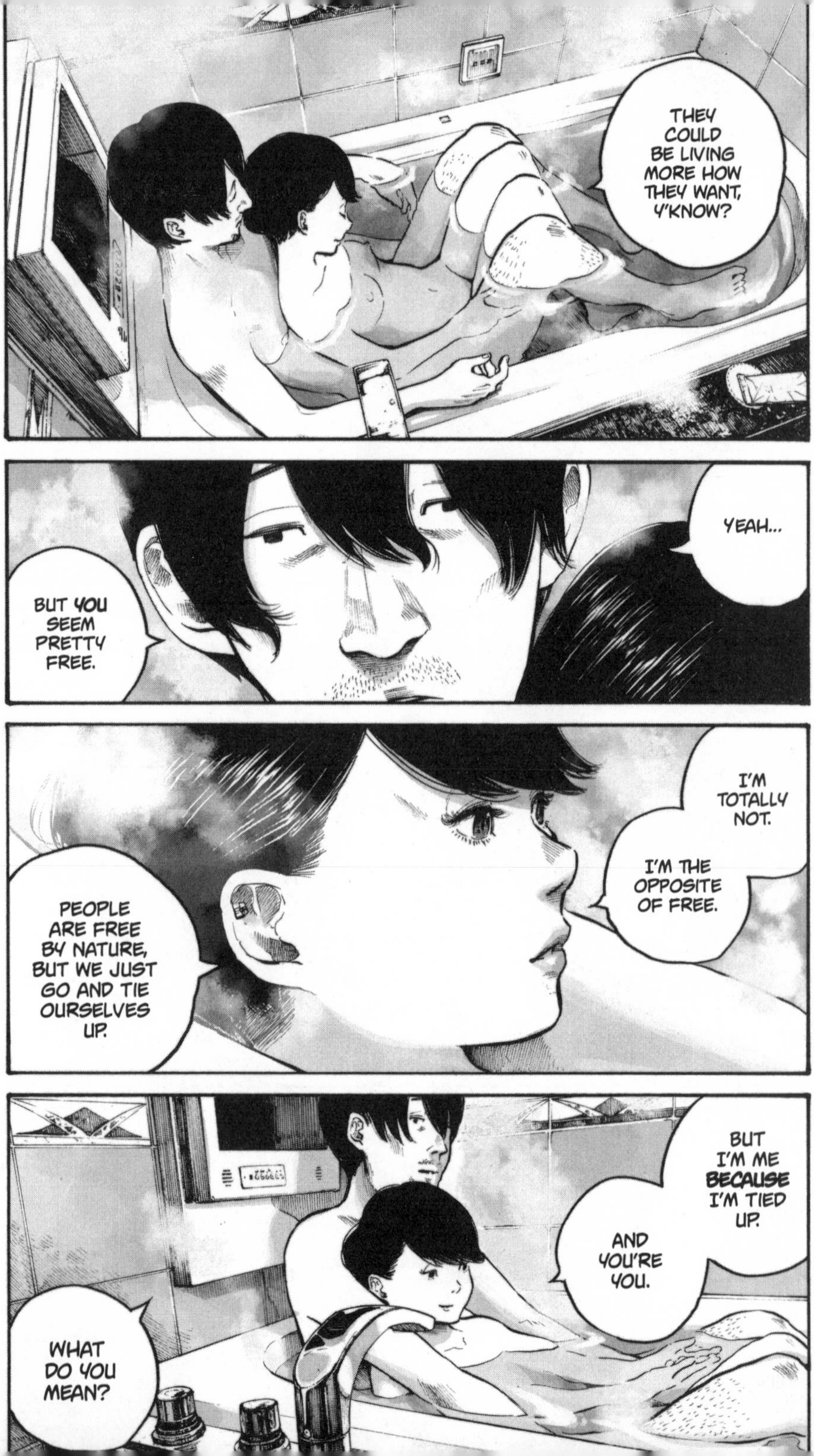
THEY COULD BE LIVING MORE HOW THEY WANT, Y'KNOW?
YEAH...
BUT YOU SEEM PRETTY FREE.
I'M TOTALLY NOT.
I'M THE OPPOSITE OF FREE.
PEOPLE ARE FREE BY NATURE, BUT WE JUST GO AND TIE OURSELVES UP.
BUT I'M ME BECAUSE I'M TIED UP.
AND YOU'RE YOU.
WHAT DO YOU MEAN?

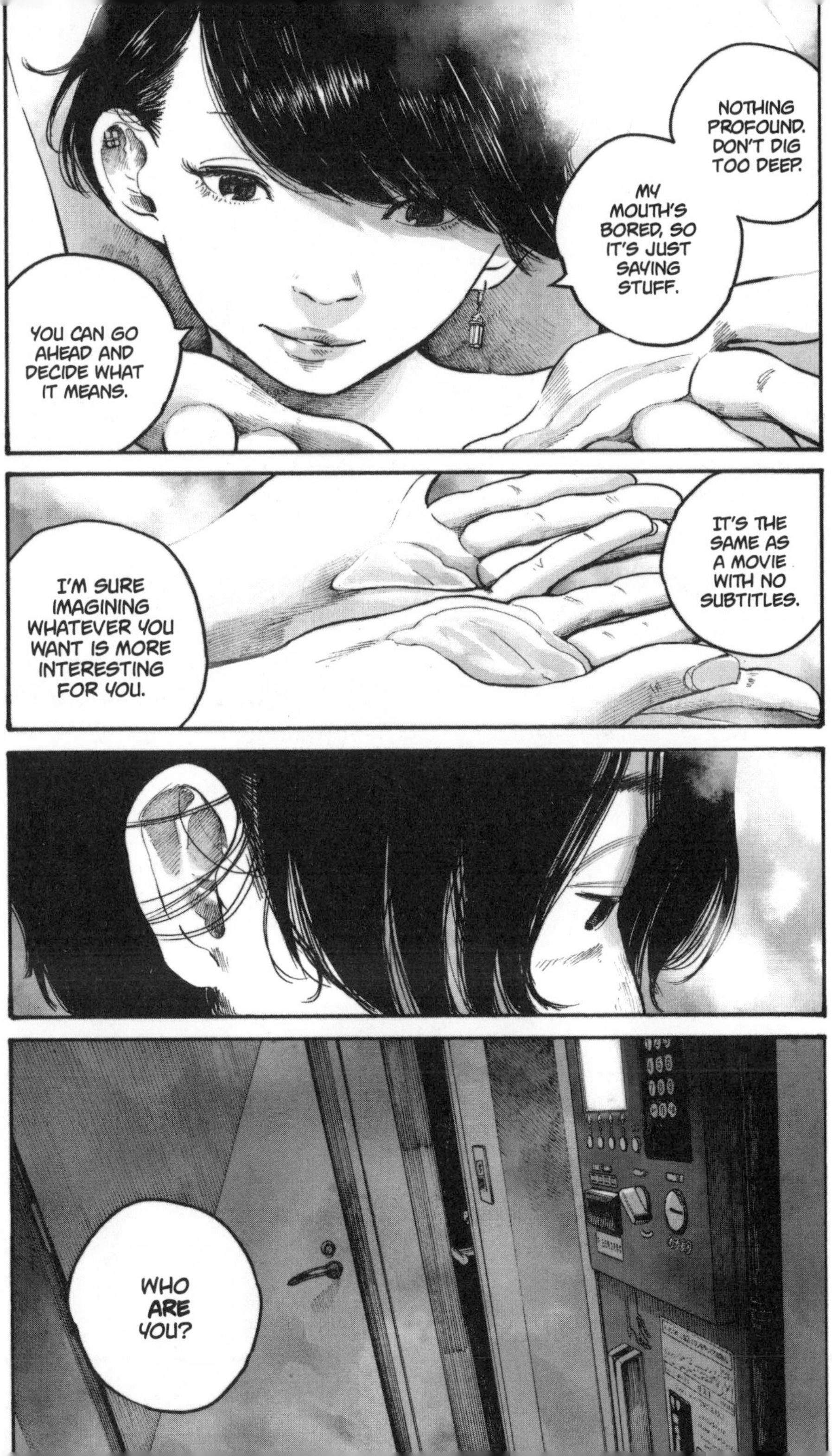
NOTHING PROFOUND. DON'T DIG TOO DEEP.
MY MOUTH'S BORED, SO IT'S JUST SAYING STUFF.
YOU CAN GO AHEAD AND DECIDE WHAT IT MEANS.
IT'S THE SAME AS A MOVIE WITH NO SUBTITLES.
I'M SURE IMAGINING WHATEVER YOU WANT IS MORE INTERESTING FOR YOU.
WHO **ARE** YOU?

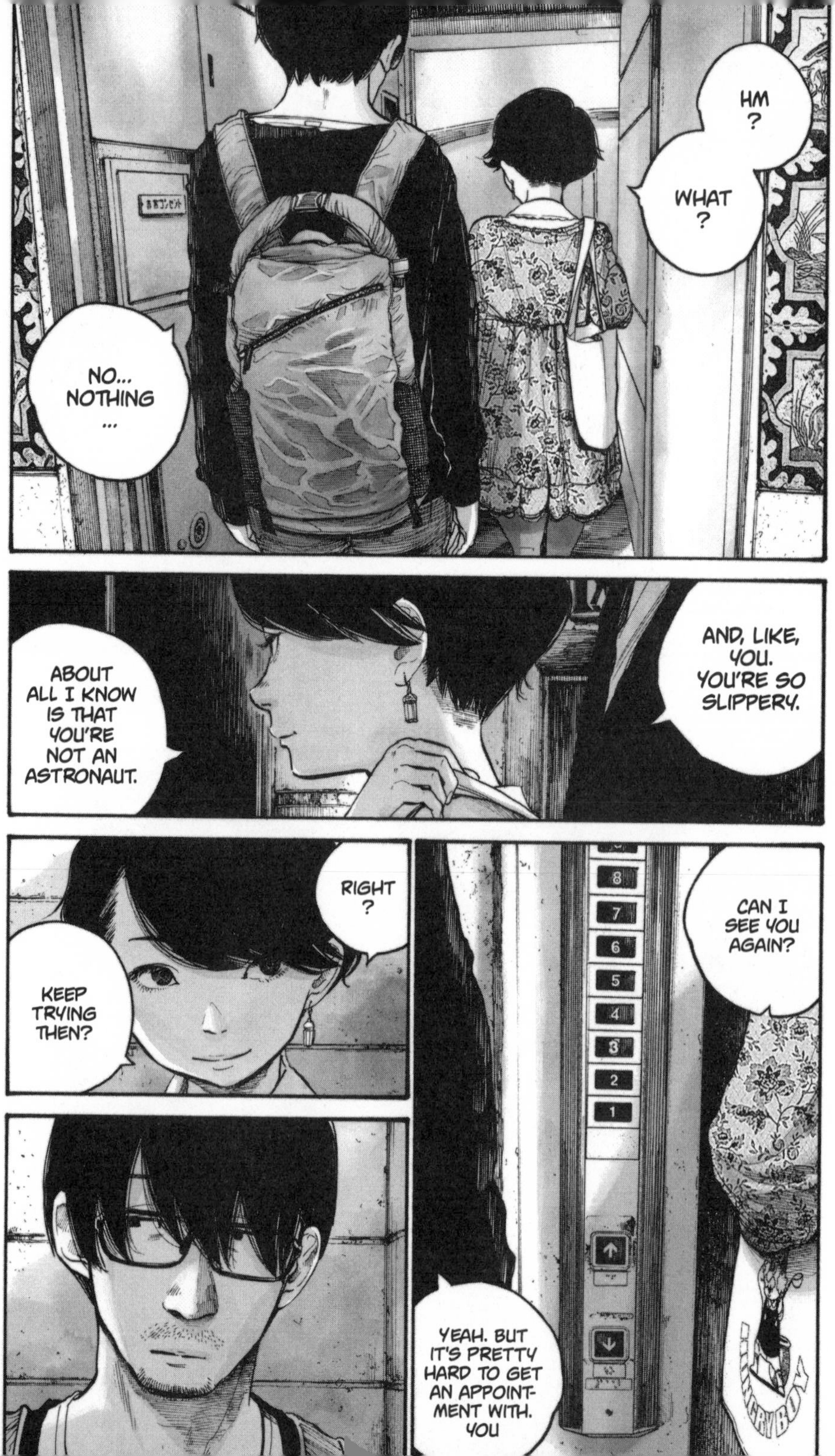
HM?
WHAT?
NO... NOTHING ...
AND, LIKE, YOU. YOU'RE SO SLIPPERY.
ABOUT ALL I KNOW IS THAT YOU'RE NOT AN ASTRONAUT.
CAN I SEE YOU AGAIN?
YEAH. BUT IT'S PRETTY HARD TO GET AN APPOINTMENT WITH. YOU
RIGHT?
KEEP TRYING THEN?

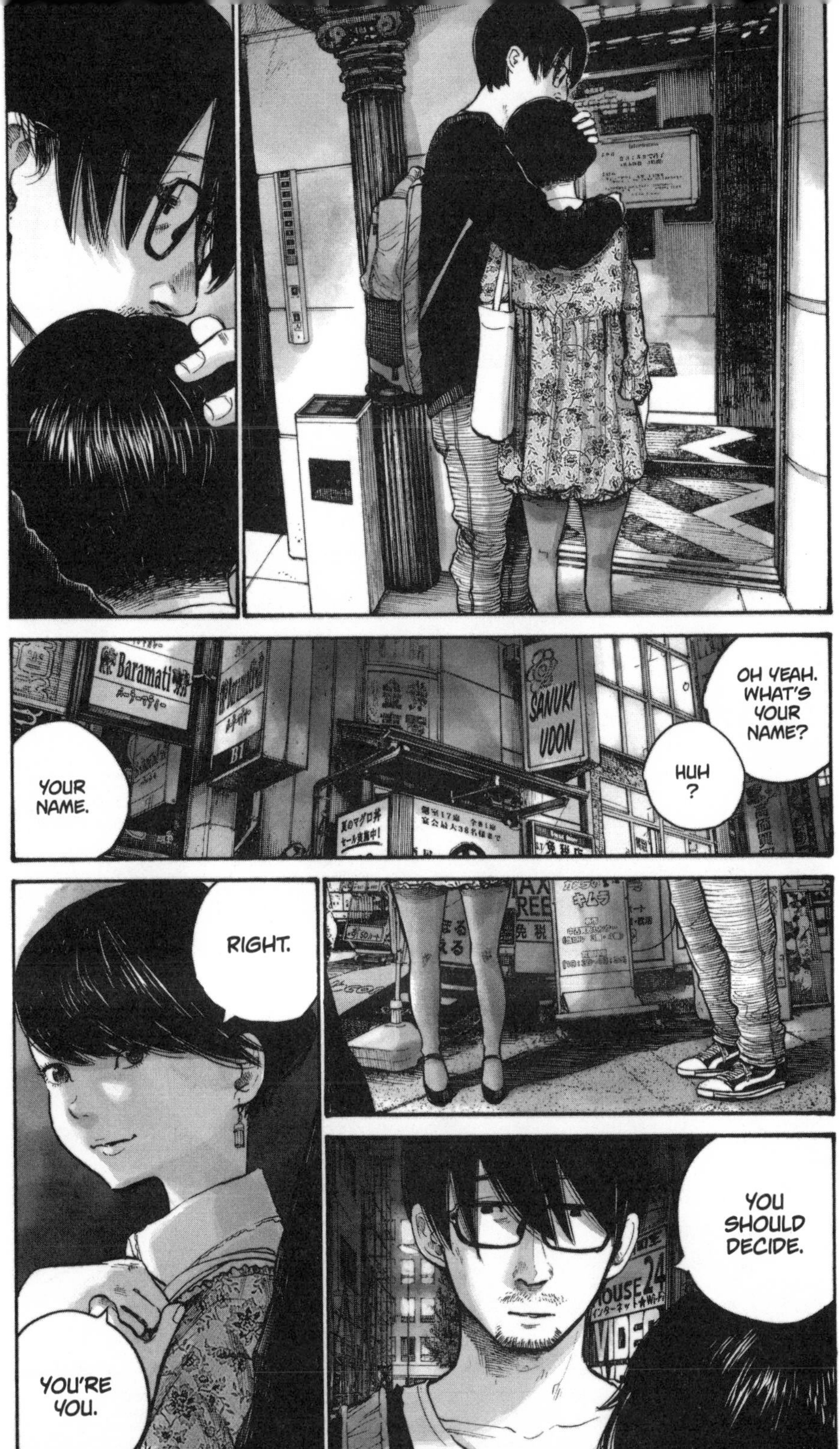
OH YEAH. WHAT'S YOUR NAME?
HUH?
YOUR NAME.
SANUKI UDON
Baramati
YOU SHOULD DECIDE.
HOUSE 24
RIGHT.
YOU'RE YOU.

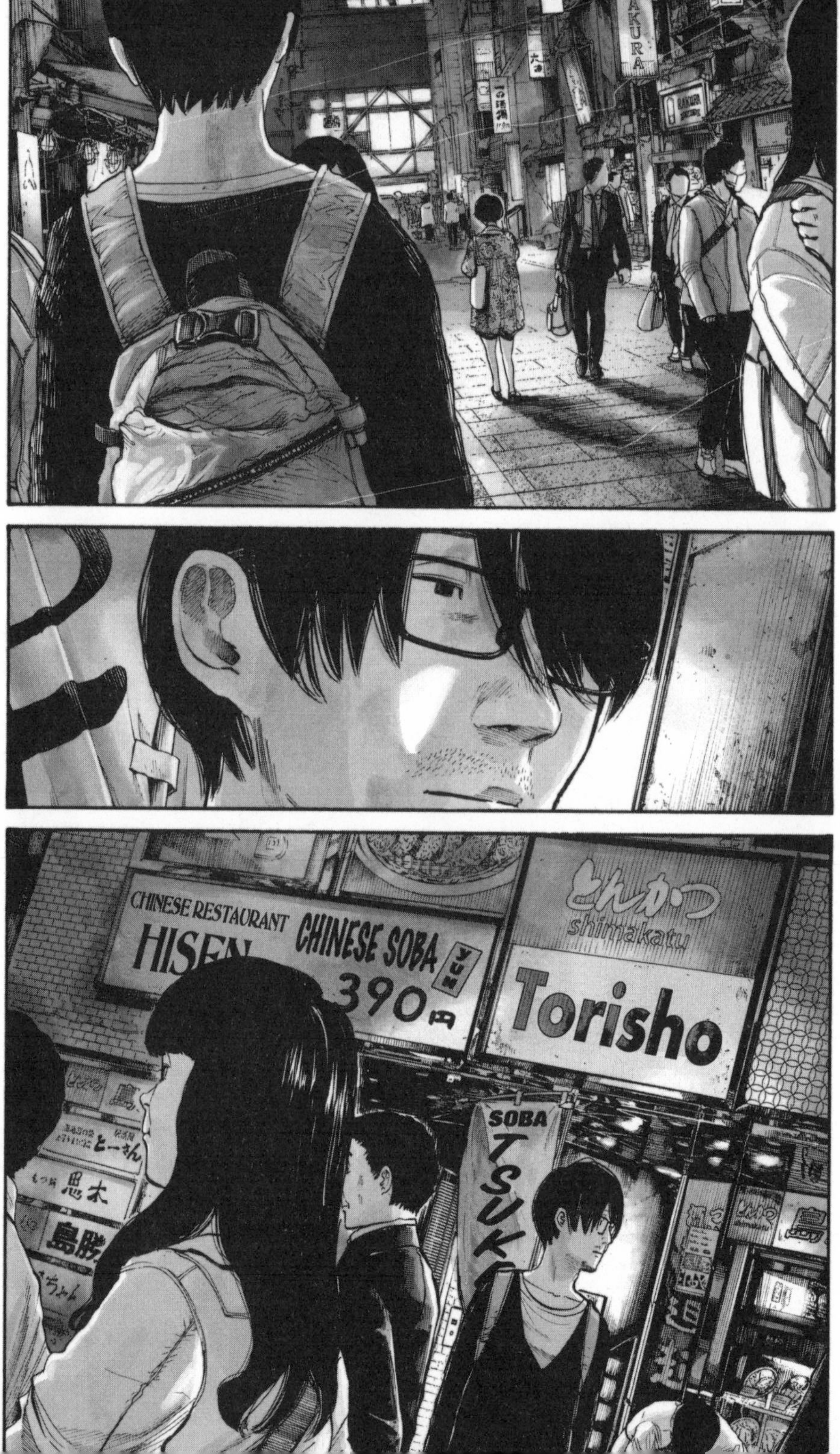
RAKURA
CHINESE RESTAURANT
HISEN
CHINESE SOBA
JUN
390円
とんかつ
shimakatu
Torisho
SOBA
TSUK
とーさん
鳥勝

CHAPTER 4

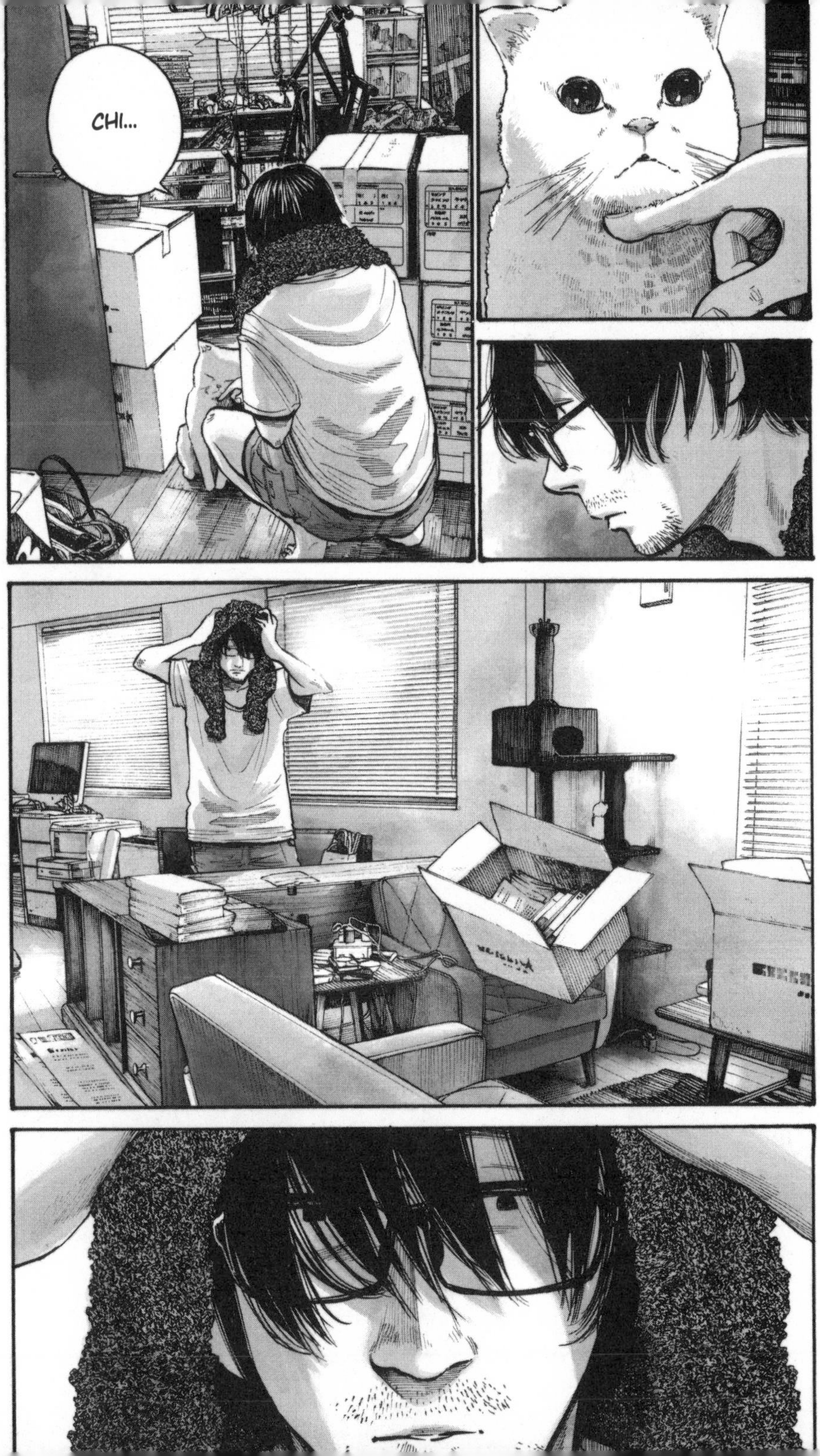
CHI...

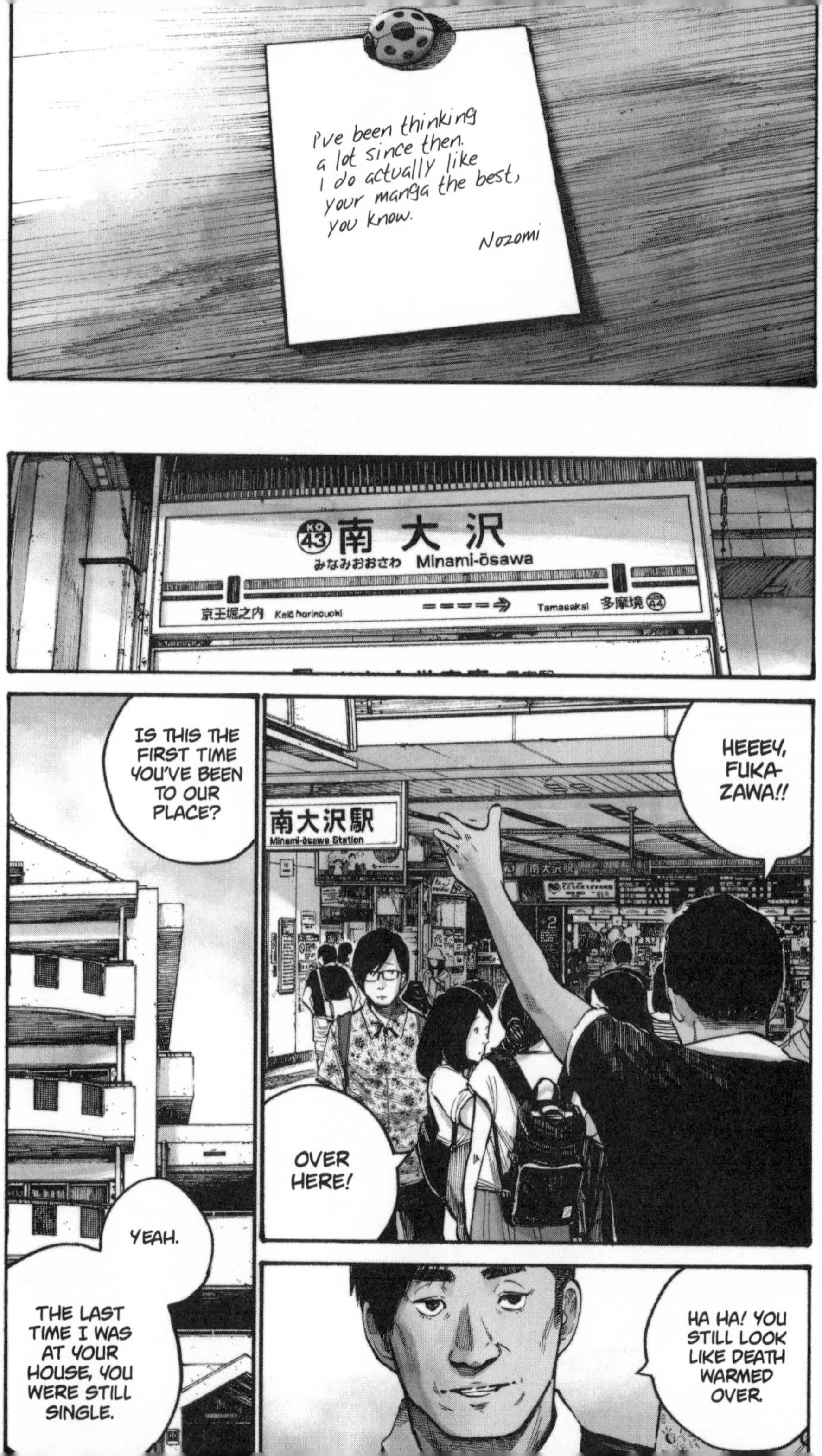
I've been thinking a lot since then. I do actually like your manga the best, you know.
Nozomi
南大沢
KO 43
みなみおおさわ Minami-ōsawa
京王堀之内 Keiō horinouchi
Tamasakai 多摩境 KO 44
南大沢駅
Minami-ōsawa Station
HEEEY, FUKA-ZAWA!!
OVER HERE!
HA HA! YOU STILL LOOK LIKE DEATH WARMED OVER.
IS THIS THE FIRST TIME YOU'VE BEEN TO OUR PLACE?
YEAH.
THE LAST TIME I WAS AT YOUR HOUSE, YOU WERE STILL SINGLE.

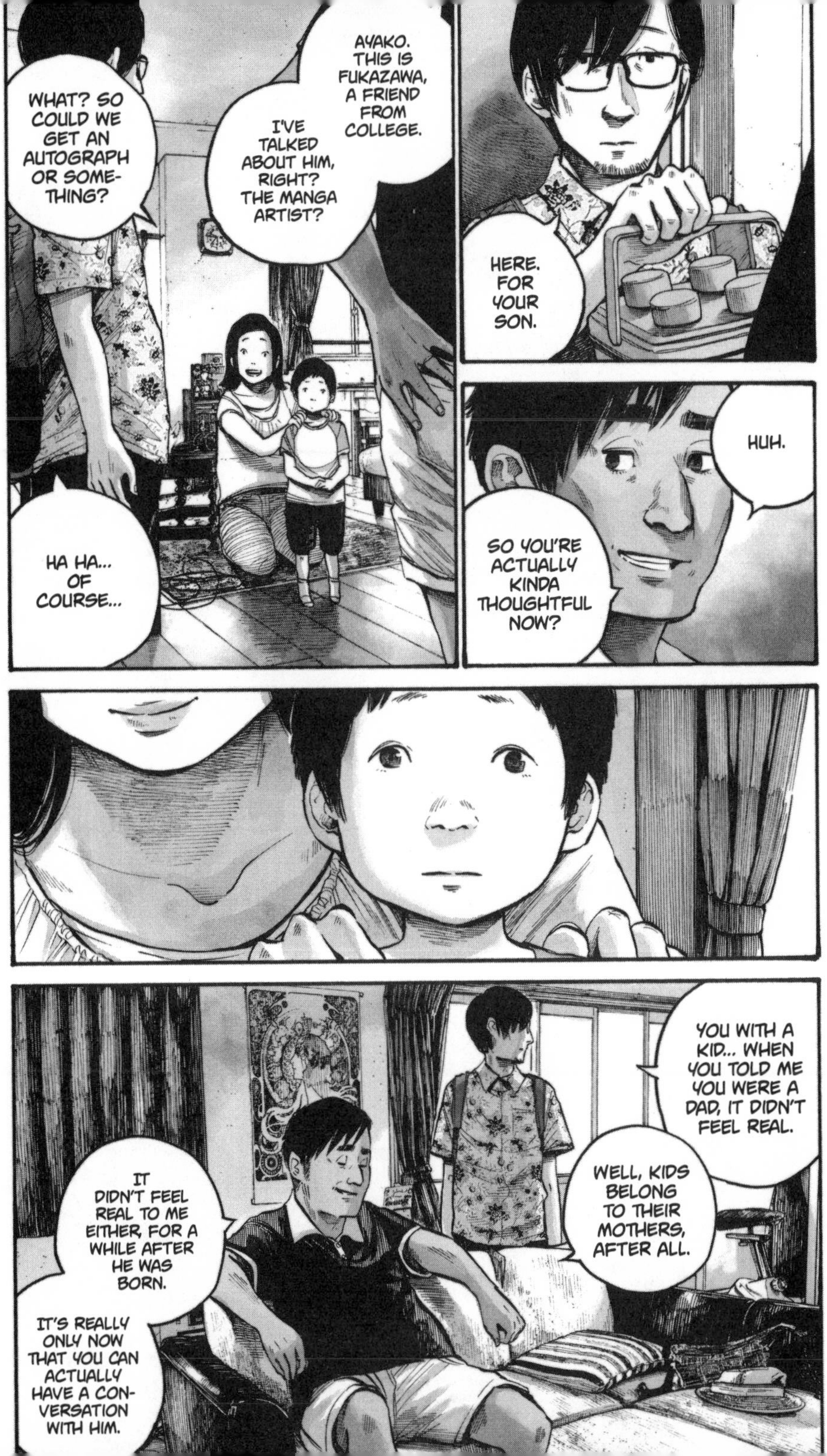
HERE. FOR YOUR SON.
HUH.
SO YOU'RE ACTUALLY KINDA THOUGHTFUL NOW?
AYAKO. THIS IS FUKAZAWA, A FRIEND FROM COLLEGE.
I'VE TALKED ABOUT HIM, RIGHT? THE MANGA ARTIST?
WHAT? SO COULD WE GET AN AUTOGRAPH OR SOME-THING?
HA HA... OF COURSE...
YOU WITH A KID... WHEN YOU TOLD ME YOU WERE A DAD, IT DIDN'T FEEL REAL.
WELL, KIDS BELONG TO THEIR MOTHERS, AFTER ALL.
IT DIDN'T FEEL REAL TO ME EITHER, FOR A WHILE AFTER HE WAS BORN.
IT'S REALLY ONLY NOW THAT YOU CAN ACTUALLY HAVE A CON-VERSATION WITH HIM.

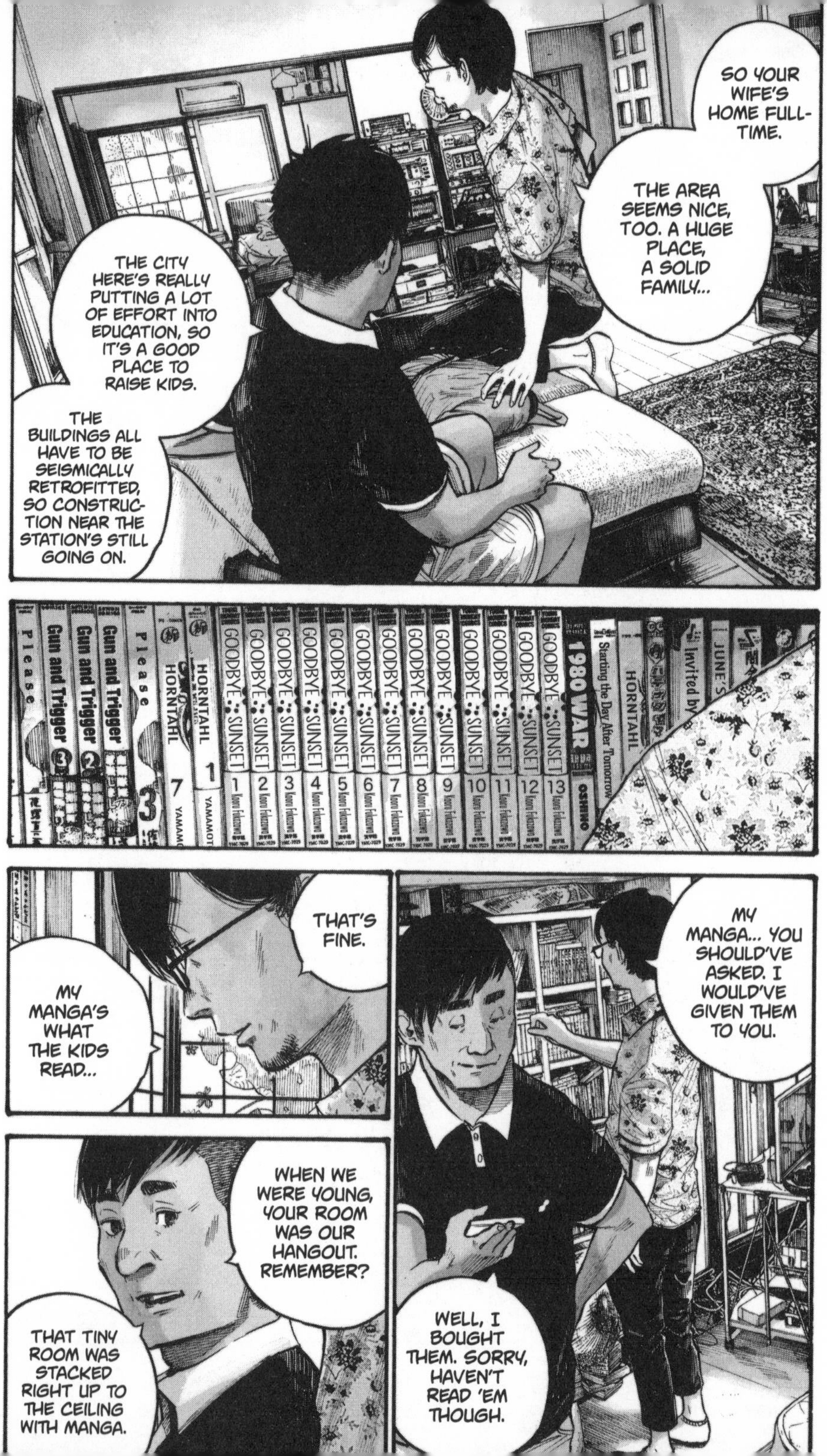
SO YOUR WIFE'S HOME FULL-TIME.
THE AREA SEEMS NICE, TOO. A HUGE PLACE, A SOLID FAMILY...
THE CITY HERE'S REALLY PUTTING A LOT OF EFFORT INTO EDUCATION, SO IT'S A GOOD PLACE TO RAISE KIDS.
THE BUILDINGS ALL HAVE TO BE SEISMICALLY RETROFITTED, SO CONSTRUCTION NEAR THE STATION'S STILL GOING ON.
JUNE'S
Invited by
HORNTAHL
Starting the Day After Tomorrow
1980 WAR OSHINO
GOODBYE SUNSET 13 Kaoru Fukuzawa
GOODBYE SUNSET 12 Kaoru Fukuzawa
GOODBYE SUNSET 11 Kaoru Fukuzawa
GOODBYE SUNSET 10 Kaoru Fukuzawa
GOODBYE SUNSET 9 Kaoru Fukuzawa
GOODBYE SUNSET 8 Kaoru Fukuzawa
GOODBYE SUNSET 7 Kaoru Fukuzawa
GOODBYE SUNSET 6 Kaoru Fukuzawa
GOODBYE SUNSET 5 Kaoru Fukuzawa
GOODBYE SUNSET 4 Kaoru Fukuzawa
GOODBYE SUNSET 3 Kaoru Fukuzawa
GOODBYE SUNSET 2 Kaoru Fukuzawa
GOODBYE SUNSET 1 Kaoru Fukuzawa
HORNTAHL 1 YAMAMOTO
HORNTAHL 7
Please 3
Gun and Trigger
Gun and Trigger 2
Gun and Trigger 3
Please
MY MANGA... YOU SHOULD'VE ASKED. I WOULD'VE GIVEN THEM TO YOU.
WELL, I BOUGHT THEM. SORRY, HAVEN'T READ 'EM THOUGH.
THAT'S FINE.
MY MANGA'S WHAT THE KIDS READ...
WHEN WE WERE YOUNG, YOUR ROOM WAS OUR HANGOUT. REMEMBER?
THAT TINY ROOM WAS STACKED RIGHT UP TO THE CEILING WITH MANGA.

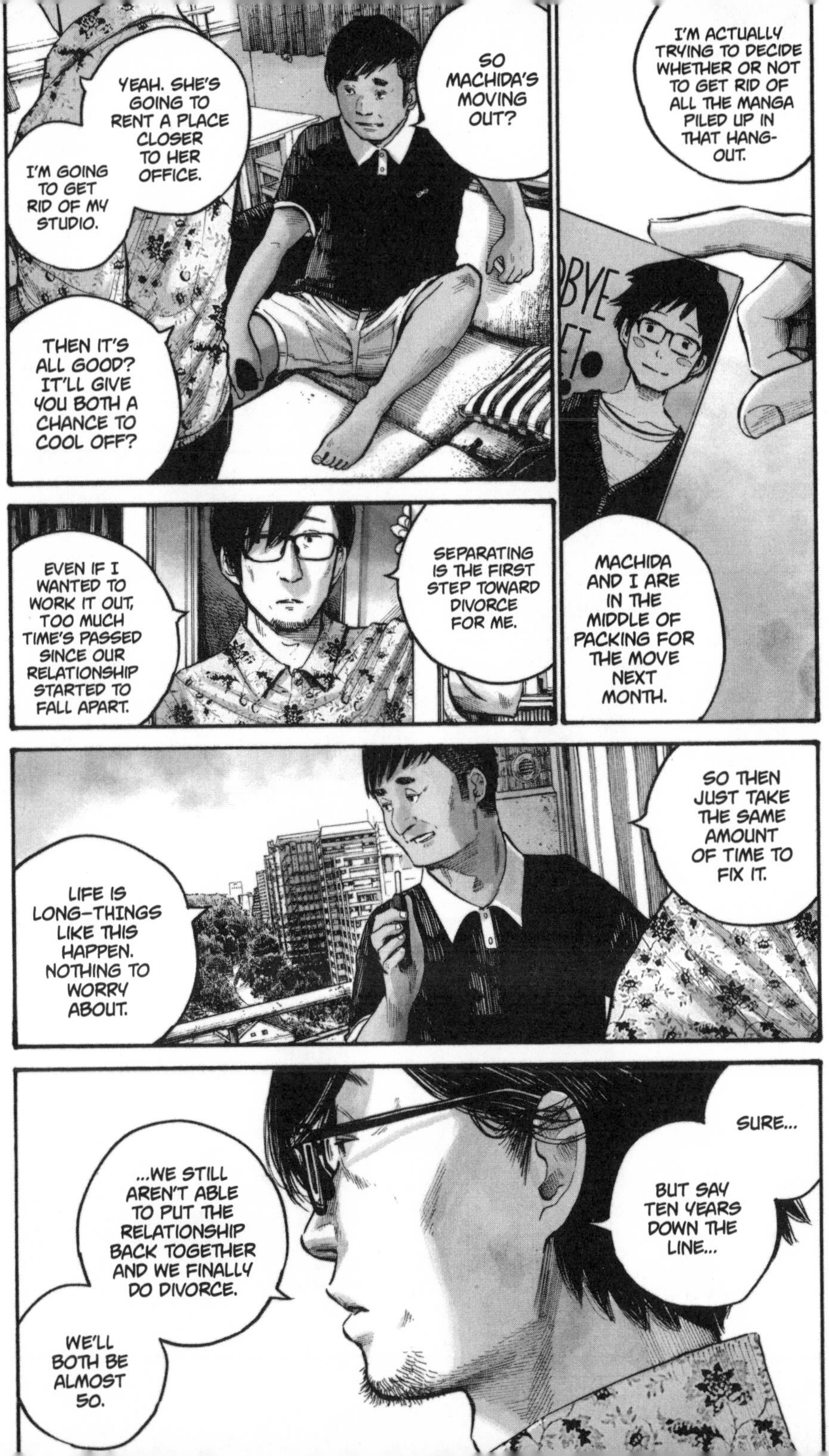

I'M ACTUALLY TRYING TO DECIDE WHETHER OR NOT TO GET RID OF ALL THE MANGA PILED UP IN THAT HANG-OUT.
MACHIDA AND I ARE IN THE MIDDLE OF PACKING FOR THE MOVE NEXT MONTH.
SO MACHIDA'S MOVING OUT?
YEAH. SHE'S GOING TO RENT A PLACE CLOSER TO HER OFFICE.
I'M GOING TO GET RID OF MY STUDIO.
THEN IT'S ALL GOOD? IT'LL GIVE YOU BOTH A CHANCE TO COOL OFF?
SEPARATING IS THE FIRST STEP TOWARD DIVORCE FOR ME.
EVEN IF I WANTED TO WORK IT OUT, TOO MUCH TIME'S PASSED SINCE OUR RELATIONSHIP STARTED TO FALL APART.
SO THEN JUST TAKE THE SAME AMOUNT OF TIME TO FIX IT.
LIFE IS LONG–THINGS LIKE THIS HAPPEN. NOTHING TO WORRY ABOUT.
SURE...
BUT SAY TEN YEARS DOWN THE LINE...
...WE STILL AREN'T ABLE TO PUT THE RELATIONSHIP BACK TOGETHER AND WE FINALLY DO DIVORCE.
WE'LL BOTH BE ALMOST 50.

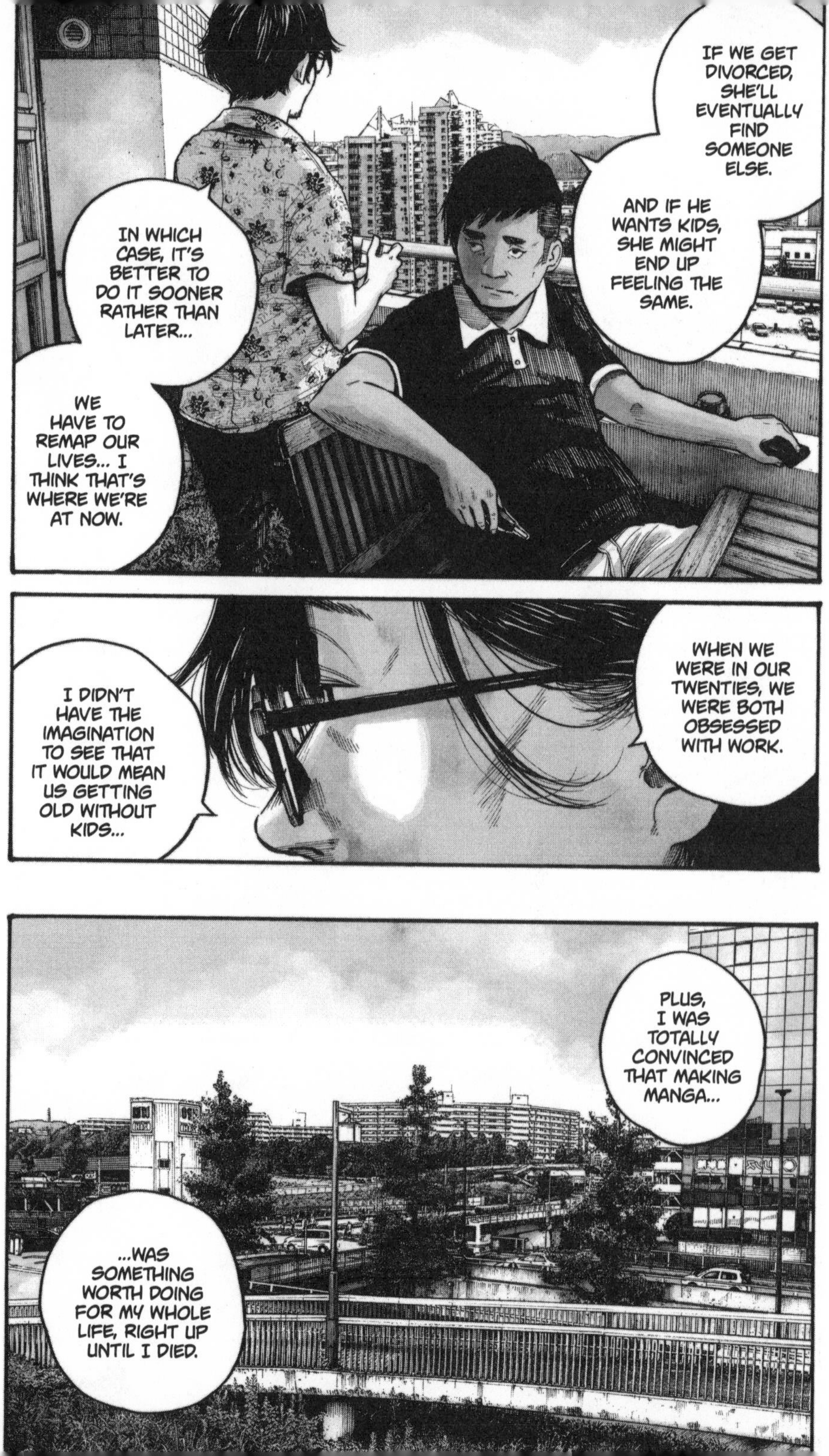
IF WE GET DIVORCED, SHE'LL EVENTUALLY FIND SOMEONE ELSE.
AND IF HE WANTS KIDS, SHE MIGHT END UP FEELING THE SAME.
IN WHICH CASE, IT'S BETTER TO DO IT SOONER RATHER THAN LATER...
WE HAVE TO REMAP OUR LIVES... I THINK THAT'S WHERE WE'RE AT NOW.
WHEN WE WERE IN OUR TWENTIES, WE WERE BOTH OBSESSED WITH WORK.
I DIDN'T HAVE THE IMAGINATION TO SEE THAT IT WOULD MEAN US GETTING OLD WITHOUT KIDS...
PLUS, I WAS TOTALLY CONVINCED THAT MAKING MANGA...
...WAS SOMETHING WORTH DOING FOR MY WHOLE LIFE, RIGHT UP UNTIL I DIED.

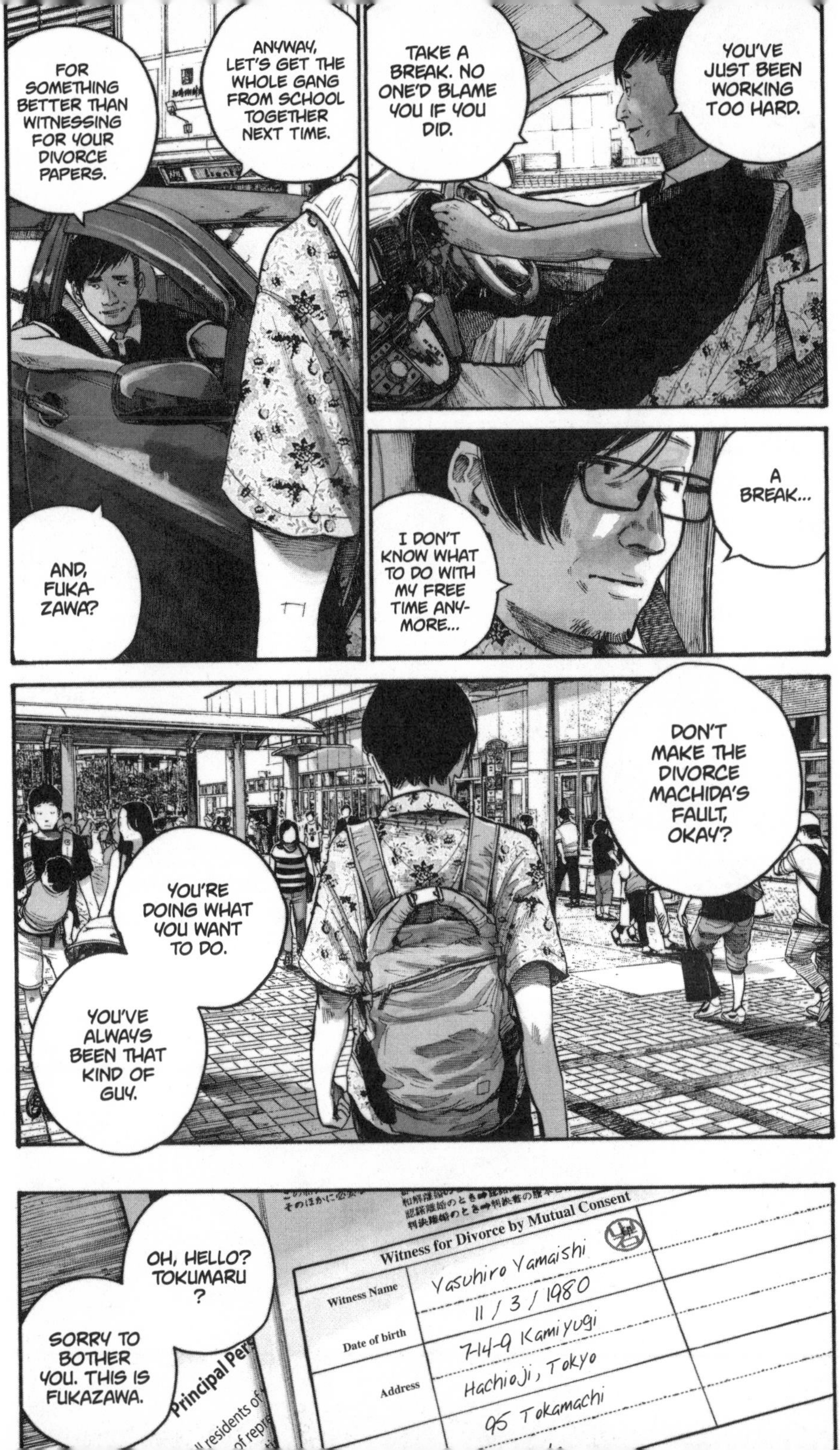
YOU'VE JUST BEEN WORKING TOO HARD.
TAKE A BREAK. NO ONE'D BLAME YOU IF YOU DID.
A BREAK...
I DON'T KNOW WHAT TO DO WITH MY FREE TIME ANYMORE...
ANYWAY, LET'S GET THE WHOLE GANG FROM SCHOOL TOGETHER NEXT TIME.
FOR SOMETHING BETTER THAN WITNESSING FOR YOUR DIVORCE PAPERS.
AND, FUKAZAWA?
DON'T MAKE THE DIVORCE MACHIDA'S FAULT, OKAY?
YOU'RE DOING WHAT YOU WANT TO DO.
YOU'VE ALWAYS BEEN THAT KIND OF GUY.
Witness for Divorce by Mutual Consent
Witness Name
Yasuhiro Yamaishi
Date of birth
11 / 3 / 1980
Address
7-14-9 Kamiyugi
Hachioji, Tokyo
95 Tokamachi
OH, HELLO? TOKUMARU ?
SORRY TO BOTHER YOU. THIS IS FUKAZAWA.

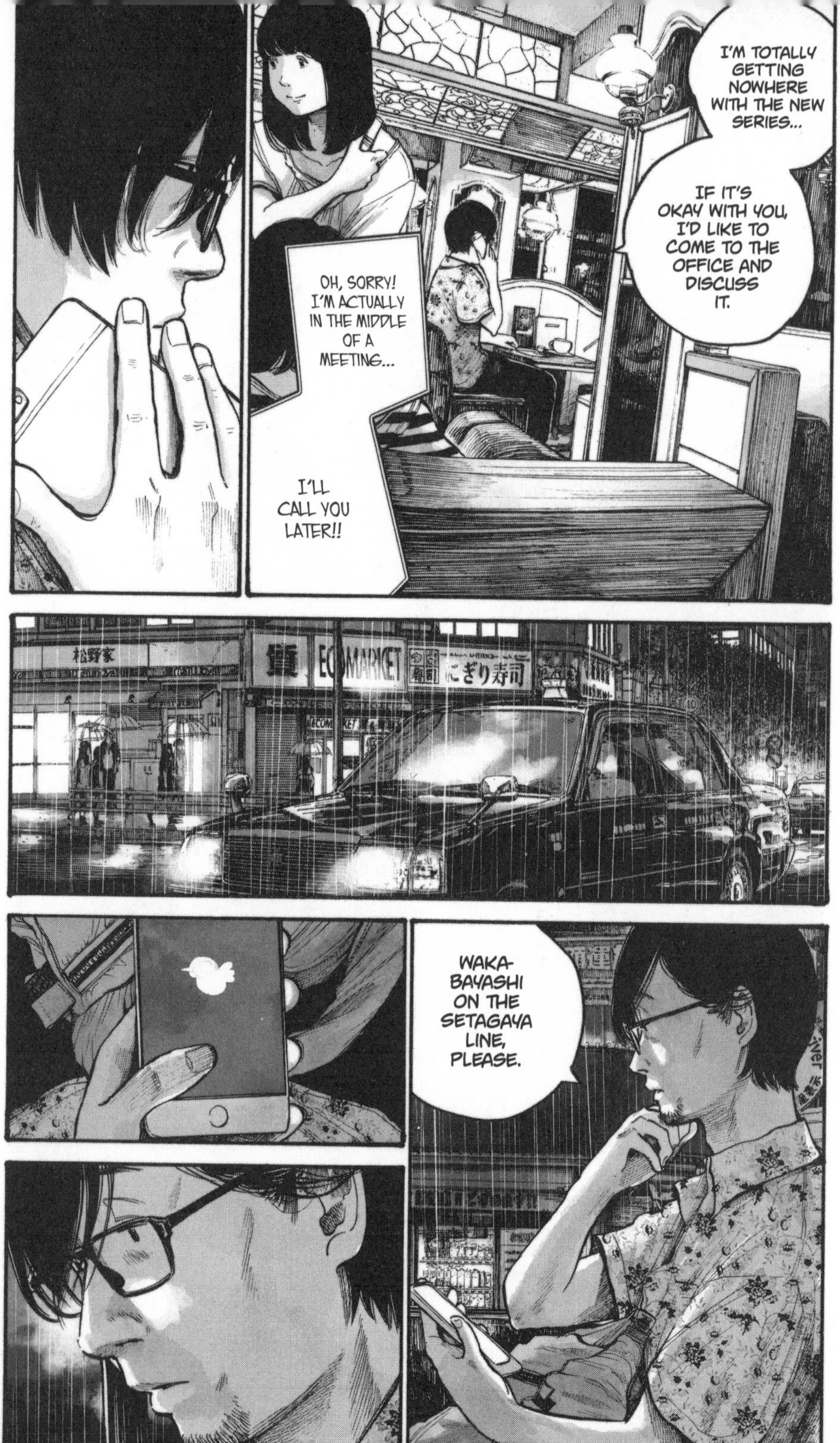
I'M TOTALLY GETTING NOWHERE WITH THE NEW SERIES...
IF IT'S OKAY WITH YOU, I'D LIKE TO COME TO THE OFFICE AND DISCUSS IT.
OH, SORRY! I'M ACTUALLY IN THE MIDDLE OF A MEETING...
I'LL CALL YOU LATER!!
松野家
ECOMARKET
にぎり寿司
WAKA-BAYASHI ON THE SETAGAYA LINE, PLEASE.

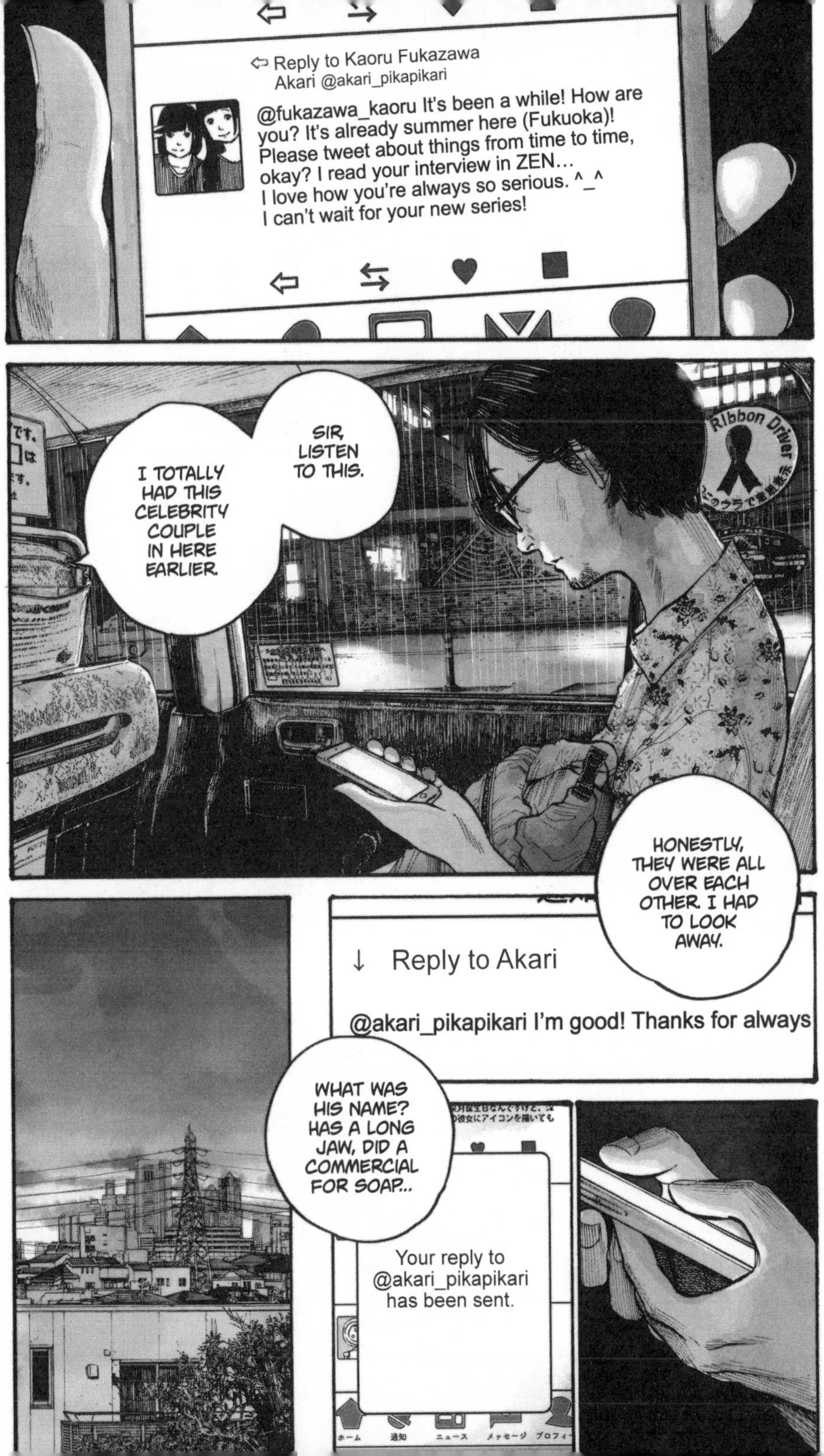
⇦ Reply to Kaoru Fukazawa
Akari @akari_pikapikari
@fukazawa_kaoru It's been a while! How are you? It's already summer here (Fukuoka)! Please tweet about things from time to time, okay? I read your interview in ZEN... I love how you're always so serious. ^_^ I can't wait for your new series!
Ribbon Driver
SIR, LISTEN TO THIS.
I TOTALLY HAD THIS CELEBRITY COUPLE IN HERE EARLIER.
HONESTLY, THEY WERE ALL OVER EACH OTHER. I HAD TO LOOK AWAY.
↓ Reply to Akari
@akari_pikapikari I'm good! Thanks for always
WHAT WAS HIS NAME? HAS A LONG JAW, DID A COMMERCIAL FOR SOAP...
Your reply to @akari_pikapikari has been sent.
ホーム
通知
ニュース
メッセージ

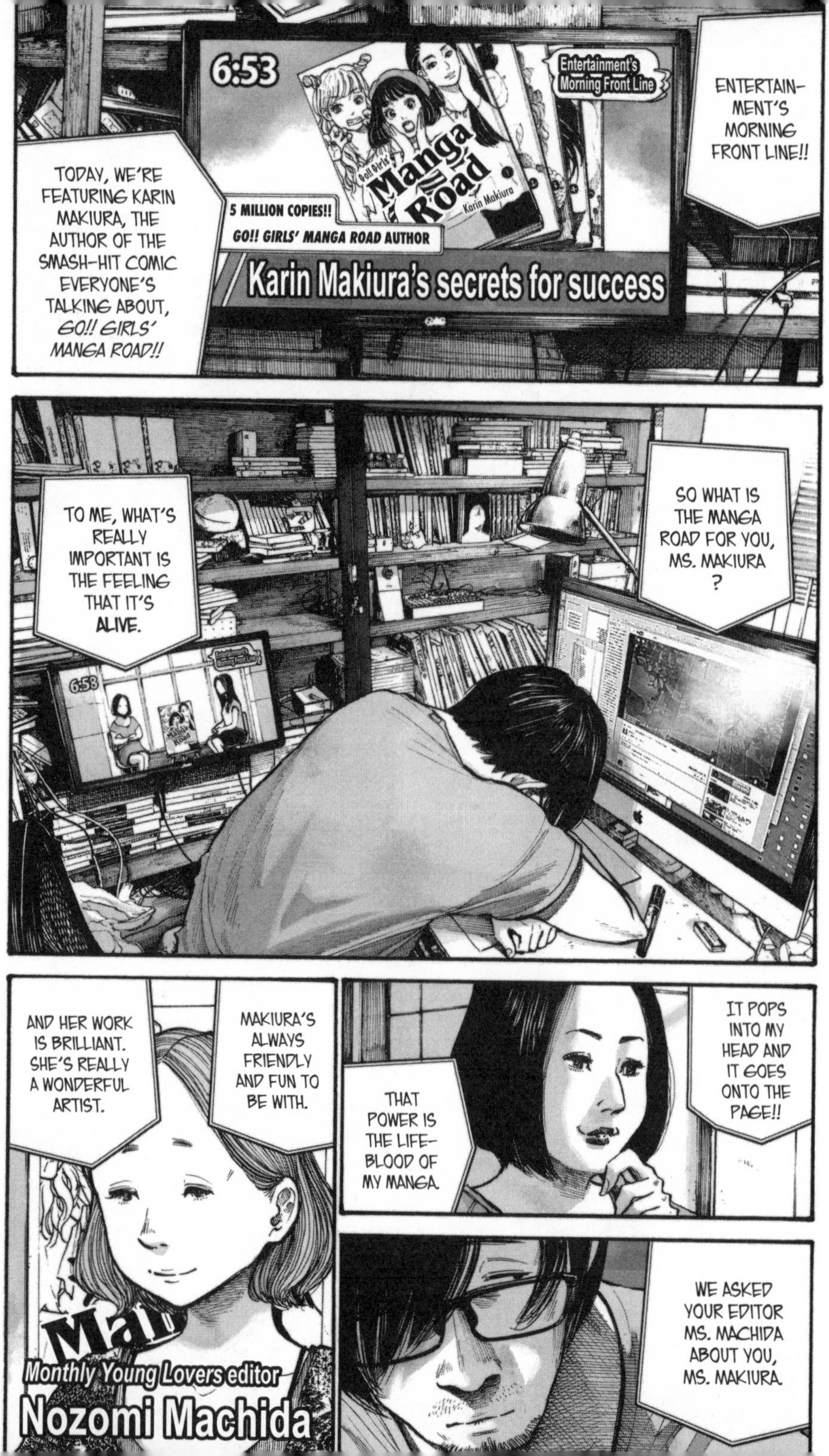
ENTERTAINMENT'S MORNING FRONT LINE!!
6:53
Entertainment's Morning Front Line
Go!! Girls' Manga Road
Karin Makiura
5 MILLION COPIES!!
GO!! GIRLS' MANGA ROAD AUTHOR
Karin Makiura's secrets for success
TODAY, WE'RE FEATURING KARIN MAKIURA, THE AUTHOR OF THE SMASH-HIT COMIC EVERYONE'S TALKING ABOUT, GO!! GIRLS' MANGA ROAD!!
SO WHAT IS THE MANGA ROAD FOR YOU, MS. MAKIURA ?
TO ME, WHAT'S REALLY IMPORTANT IS THE FEELING THAT IT'S ALIVE.
6:58
IT POPS INTO MY HEAD AND IT GOES ONTO THE PAGE!!
THAT POWER IS THE LIFE-BLOOD OF MY MANGA.
WE ASKED YOUR EDITOR MS. MACHIDA ABOUT YOU, MS. MAKIURA.
MAKIURA'S ALWAYS FRIENDLY AND FUN TO BE WITH.
AND HER WORK IS BRILLIANT. SHE'S REALLY A WONDERFUL ARTIST.
Monthly Young Lovers editor
Nozomi Machida

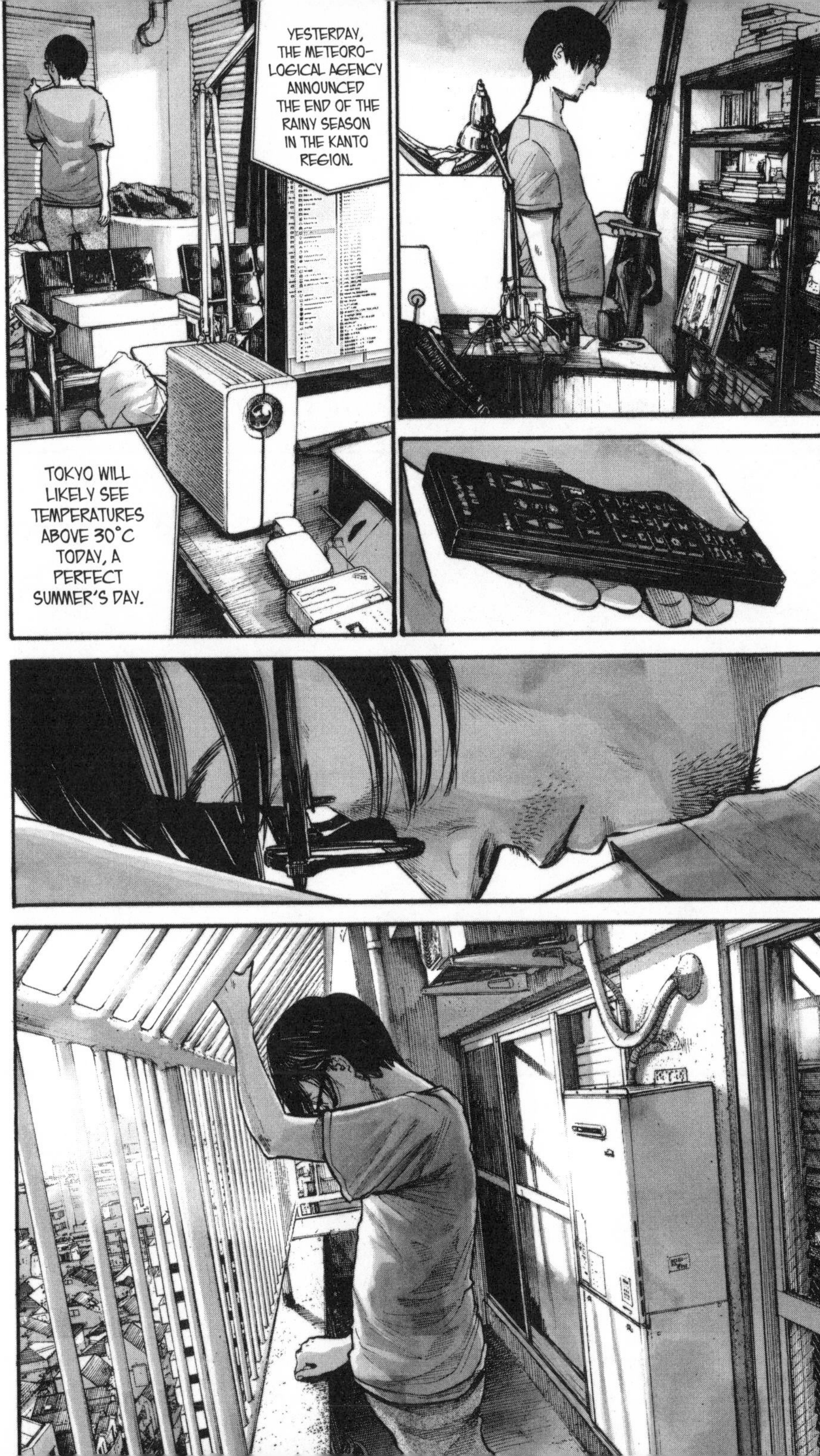
YESTERDAY, THE METEORO-LOGICAL AGENCY ANNOUNCED THE END OF THE RAINY SEASON IN THE KANTO REGION.
TOKYO WILL LIKELY SEE TEMPERATURES ABOVE 30°C TODAY, A PERFECT SUMMER'S DAY.

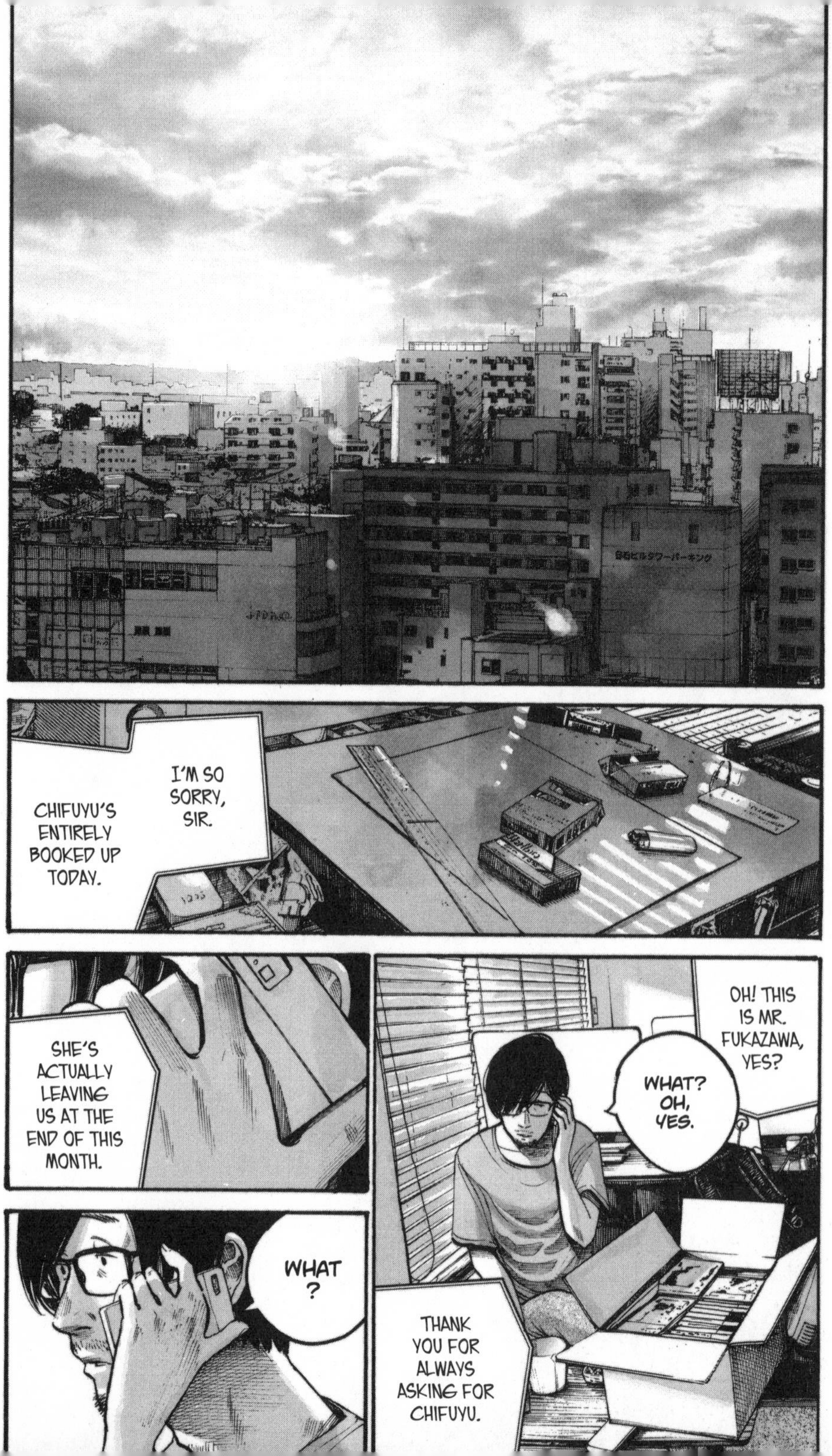
I'M SO SORRY, SIR.
CHIFUYU'S ENTIRELY BOOKED UP TODAY.
OH! THIS IS MR. FUKAZAWA, YES?
WHAT? OH, YES.
THANK YOU FOR ALWAYS ASKING FOR CHIFUYU.
SHE'S ACTUALLY LEAVING US AT THE END OF THIS MONTH.
WHAT?

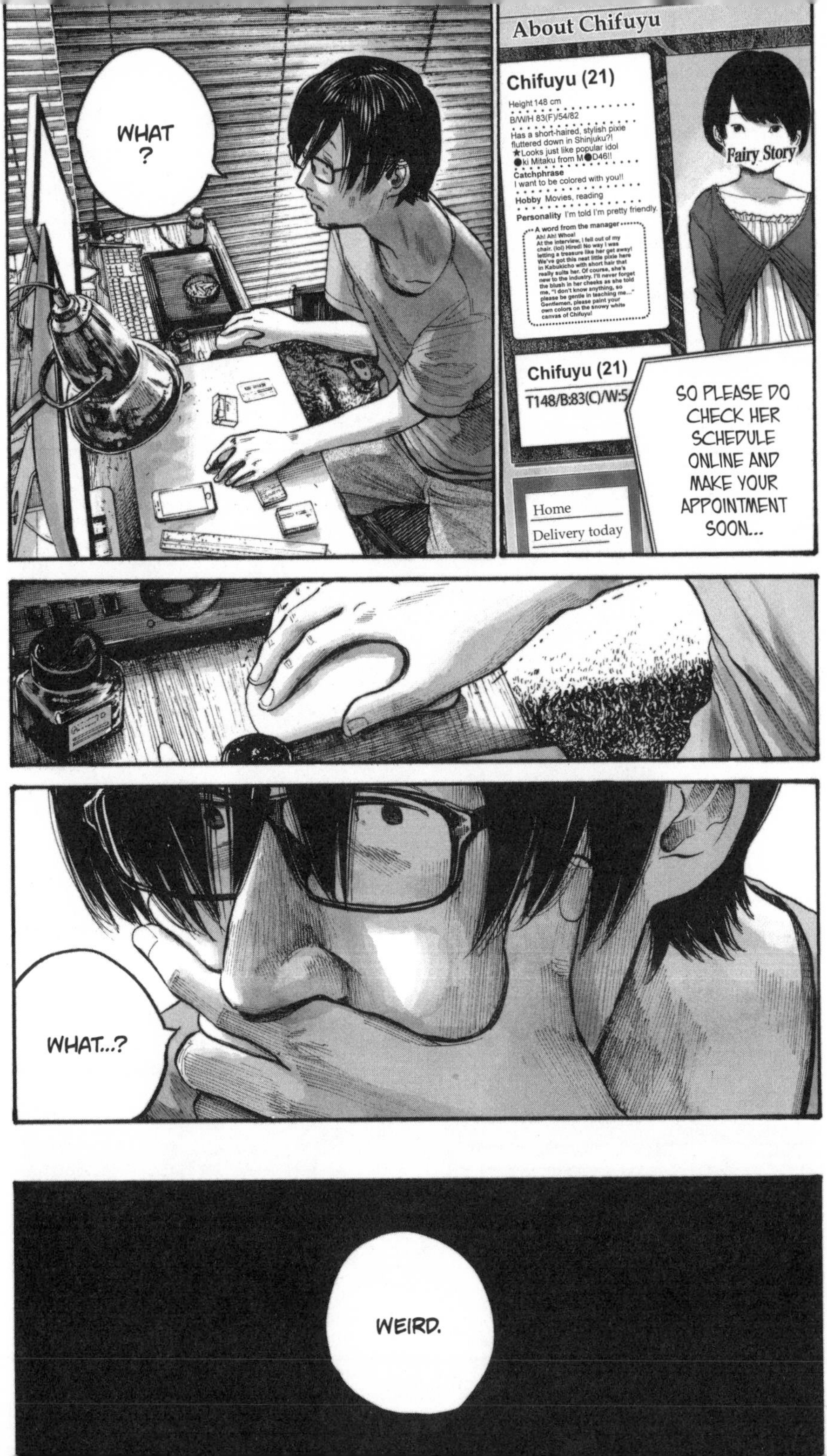
About Chifuyu
Chifuyu (21)
Height 148 cm
B/W/H 83(F)/54/82
Has a short-haired, stylish pixie fluttered down in Shinjuku?! ★Looks just like popular idol ●ki Mitaku from M●D46!!
Catchphrase
I want to be colored with you!!
Hobby Movies, reading
Personality I'm told I'm pretty friendly.
A word from the manager
Ah! Ah! Whoa! At the interview, I fell out of my chair. (lol) Hired! No way I was letting a treasure like her get away! We've got this neat little pixie here in Kabukicho with short hair that really suits her. Of course, she's new to the industry. I'll never forget the blush in her cheeks as she told me, "I don't know anything, so please be gentle in teaching me..." Gentlemen, please paint your own colors on the snowy white canvas of Chifuyu!
Fairy Story
Chifuyu (21)
T148/B:83(C)/W:5
Home
Delivery today
SO PLEASE DO CHECK HER SCHEDULE ONLINE AND MAKE YOUR APPOINTMENT SOON...
WHAT ?
WHAT...?
WEIRD.

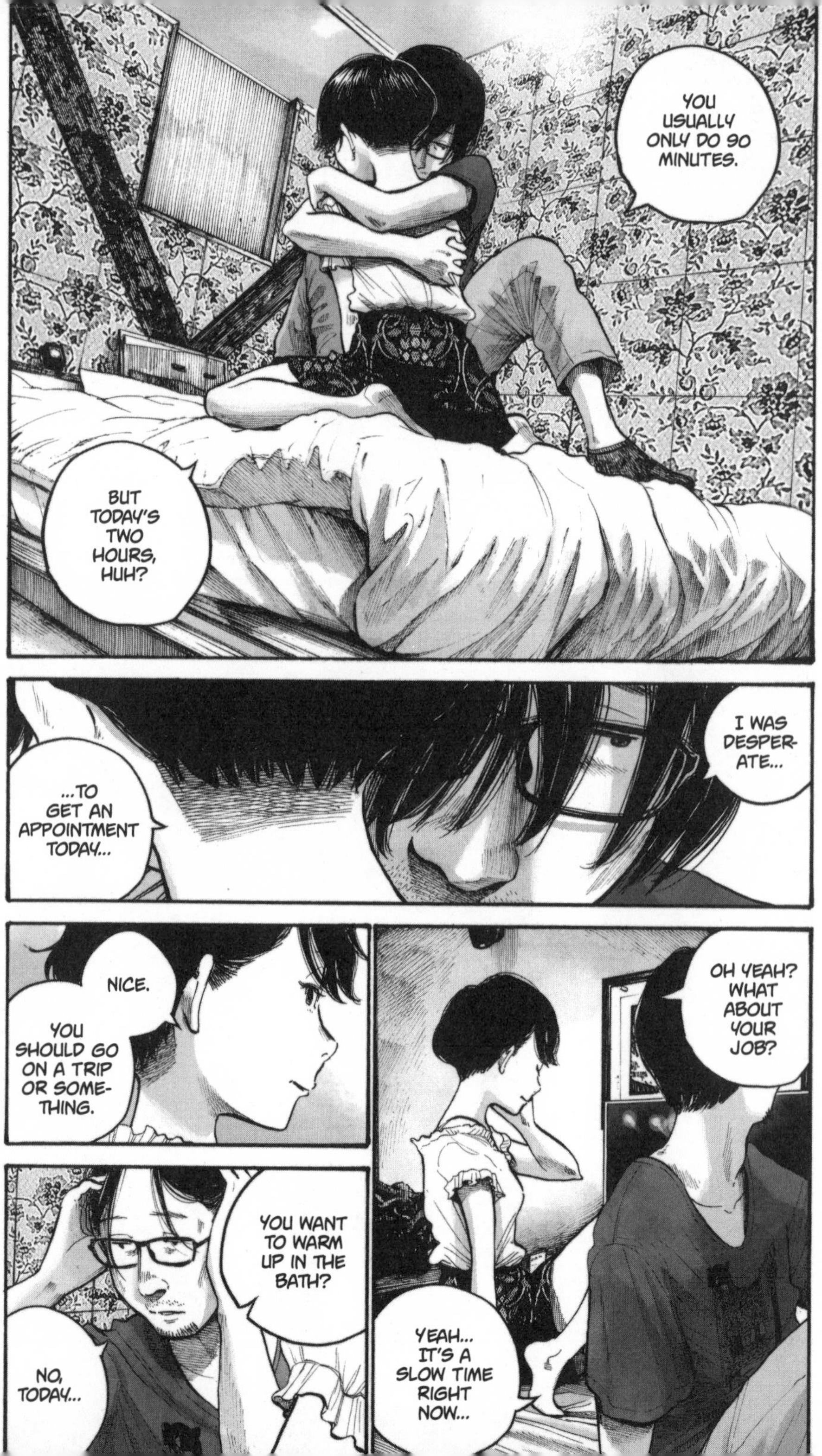
YOU USUALLY ONLY DO 90 MINUTES.
BUT TODAY'S TWO HOURS, HUH?
I WAS DESPERATE...
...TO GET AN APPOINTMENT TODAY...
OH YEAH? WHAT ABOUT YOUR JOB?
YEAH... IT'S A SLOW TIME RIGHT NOW...
NICE.
YOU SHOULD GO ON A TRIP OR SOMETHING.
YOU WANT TO WARM UP IN THE BATH?
NO, TODAY...

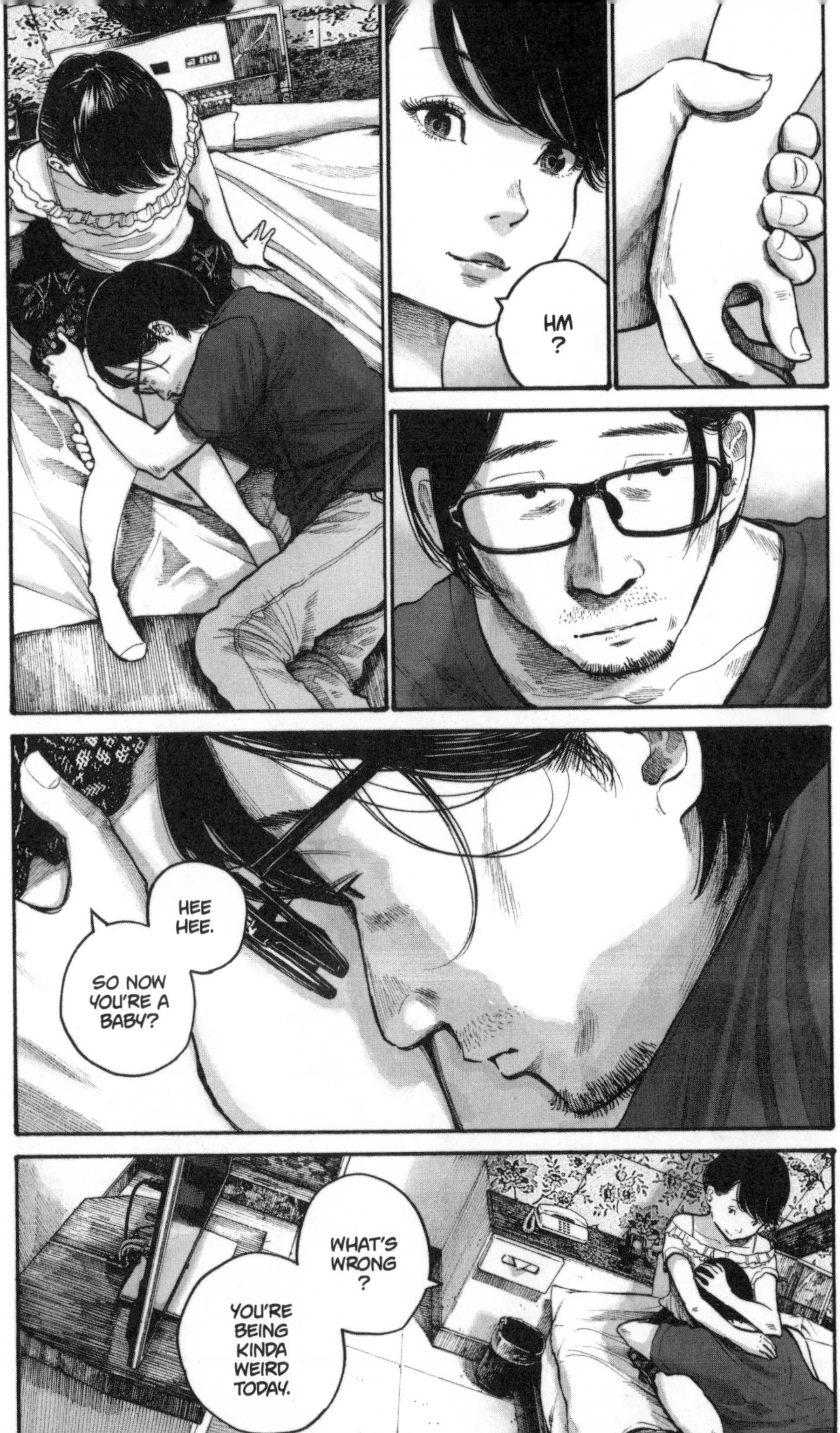
HM?
HEE HEE.
SO NOW YOU'RE A BABY?
WHAT'S WRONG?
YOU'RE BEING KINDA WEIRD TODAY.

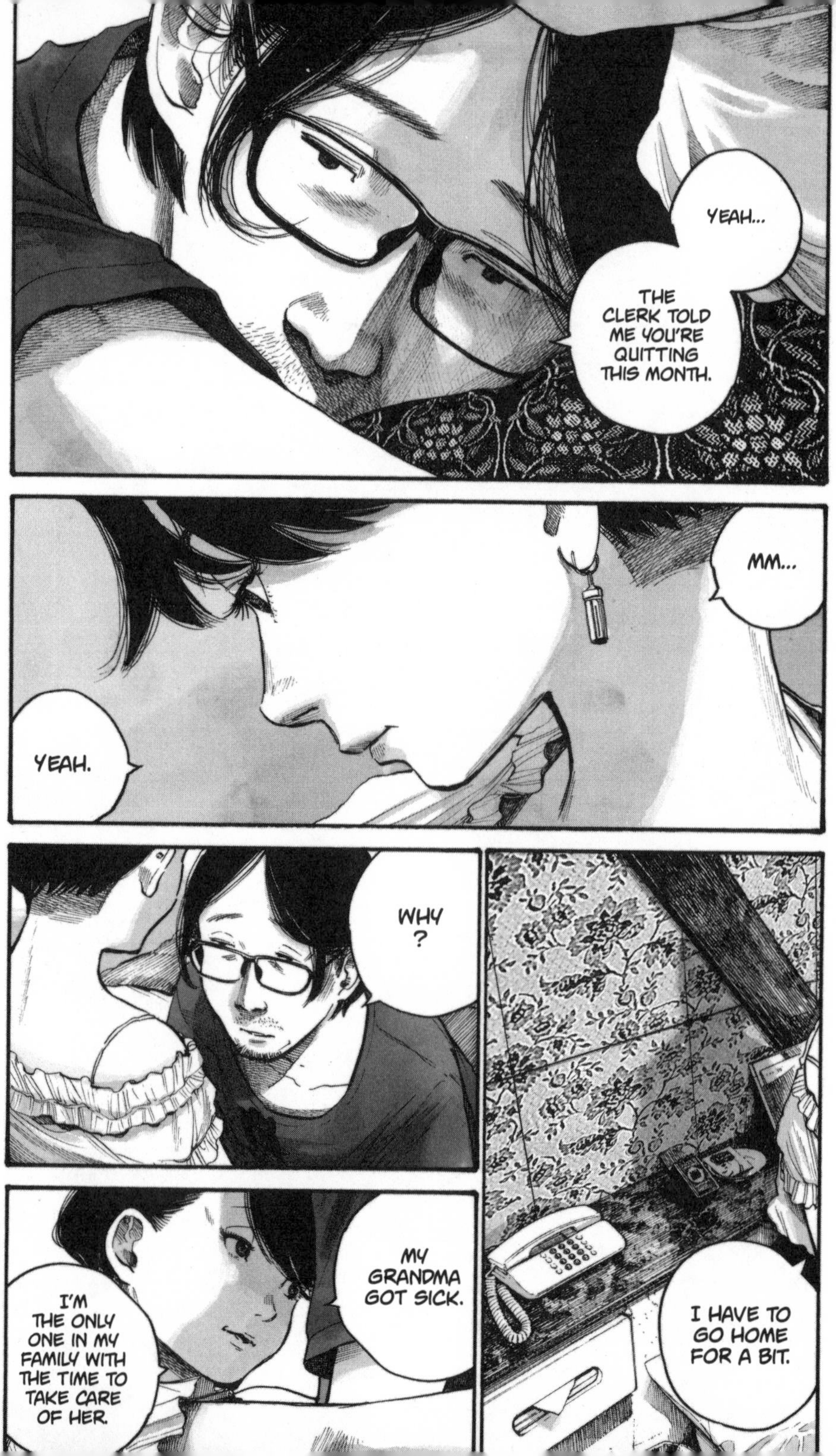
YEAH...
THE CLERK TOLD ME YOU'RE QUITTING THIS MONTH.
MM...
YEAH.
I HAVE TO GO HOME FOR A BIT.
WHY?
MY GRANDMA GOT SICK.
I'M THE ONLY ONE IN MY FAMILY WITH THE TIME TO TAKE CARE OF HER.

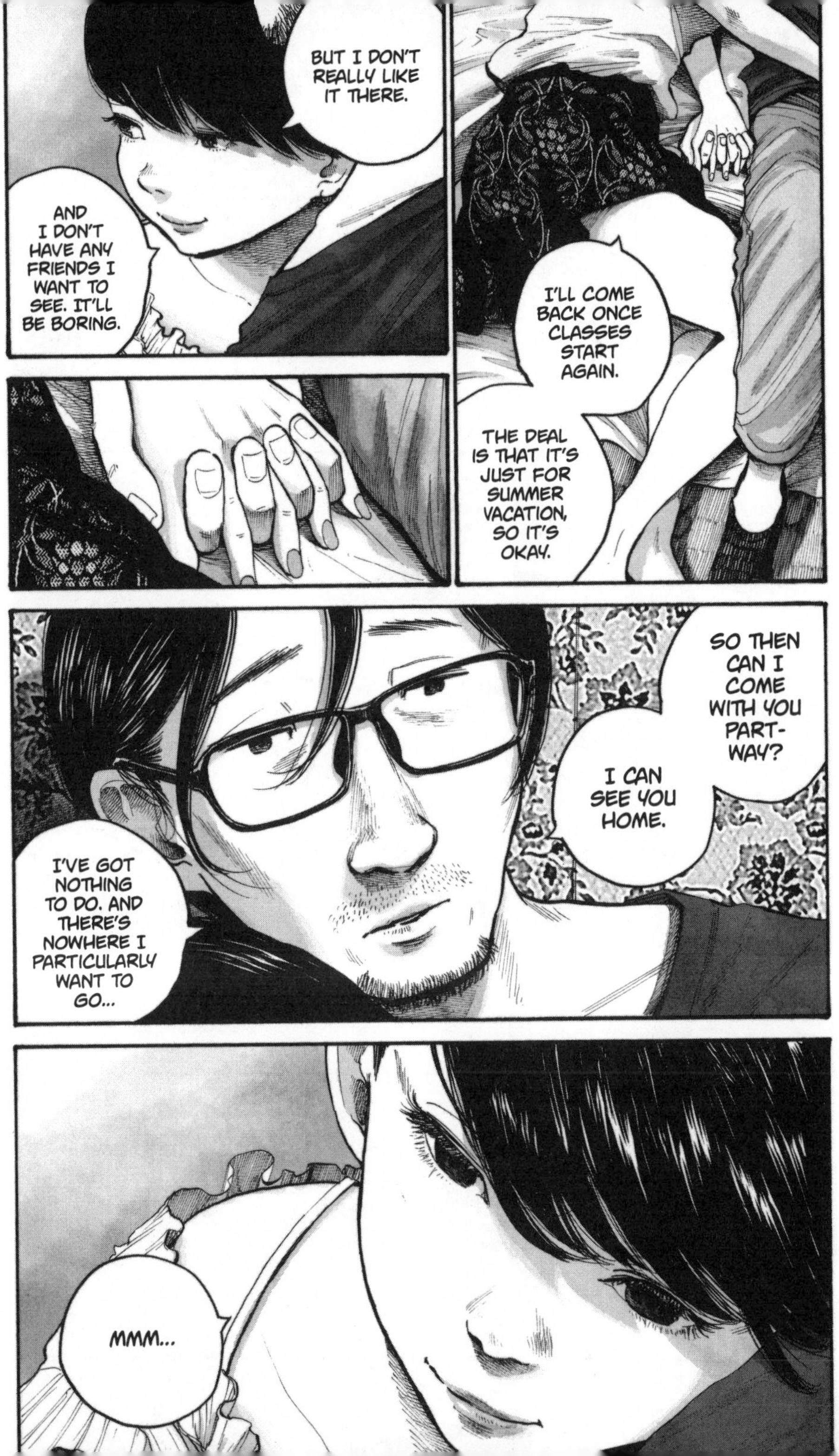
I'LL COME BACK ONCE CLASSES START AGAIN.
THE DEAL IS THAT IT'S JUST FOR SUMMER VACATION, SO IT'S OKAY.
BUT I DON'T REALLY LIKE IT THERE.
AND I DON'T HAVE ANY FRIENDS I WANT TO SEE. IT'LL BE BORING.
SO THEN CAN I COME WITH YOU PART-WAY?
I CAN SEE YOU HOME.
I'VE GOT NOTHING TO DO. AND THERE'S NOWHERE I PARTICULARLY WANT TO GO...
MMM...

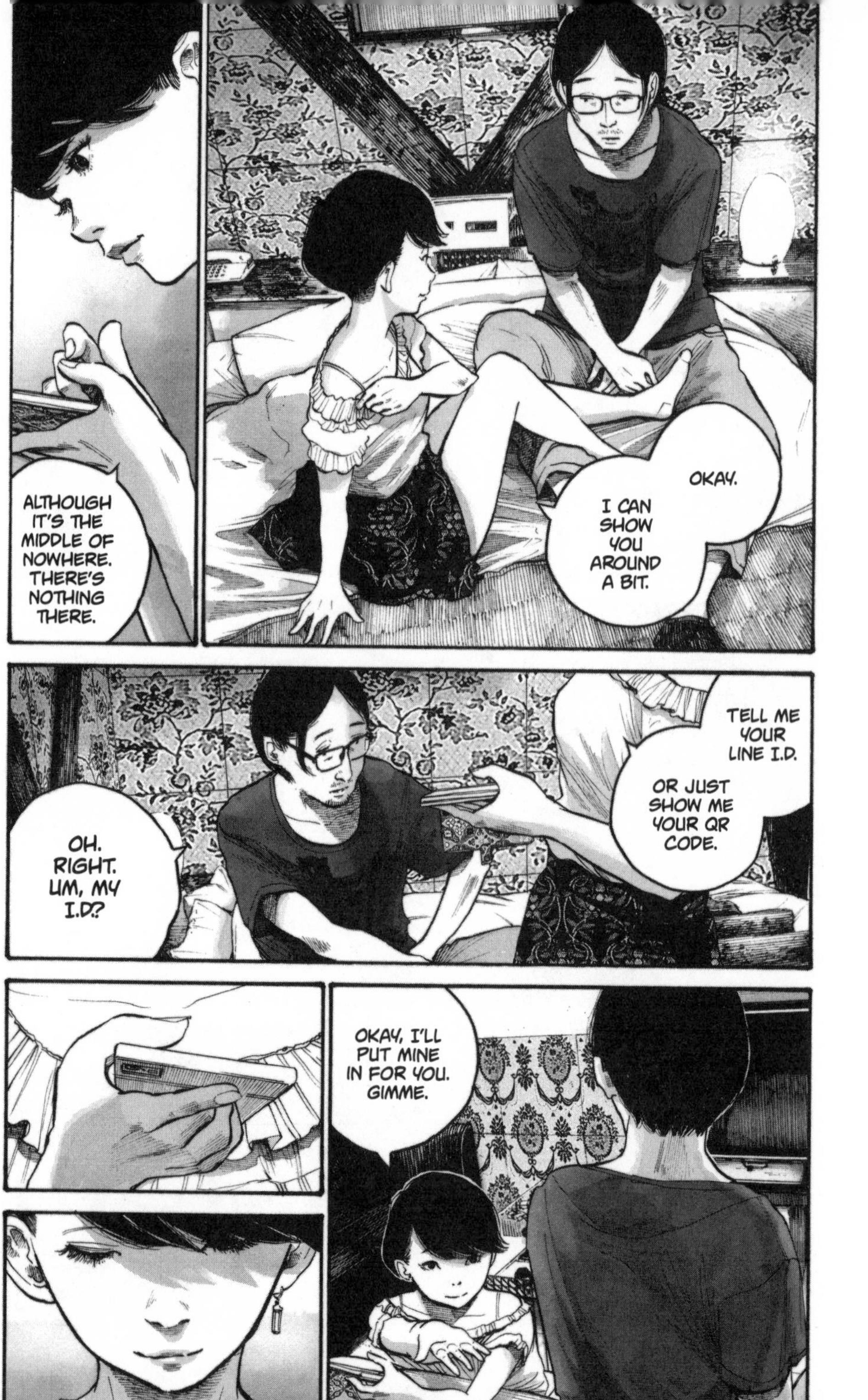
OKAY.
I CAN SHOW YOU AROUND A BIT.
ALTHOUGH IT'S THE MIDDLE OF NOWHERE. THERE'S NOTHING THERE.
TELL ME YOUR LINE I.D.
OR JUST SHOW ME YOUR QR CODE.
OH. RIGHT. UM, MY I.D.?
OKAY, I'LL PUT MINE IN FOR YOU. GIMME.

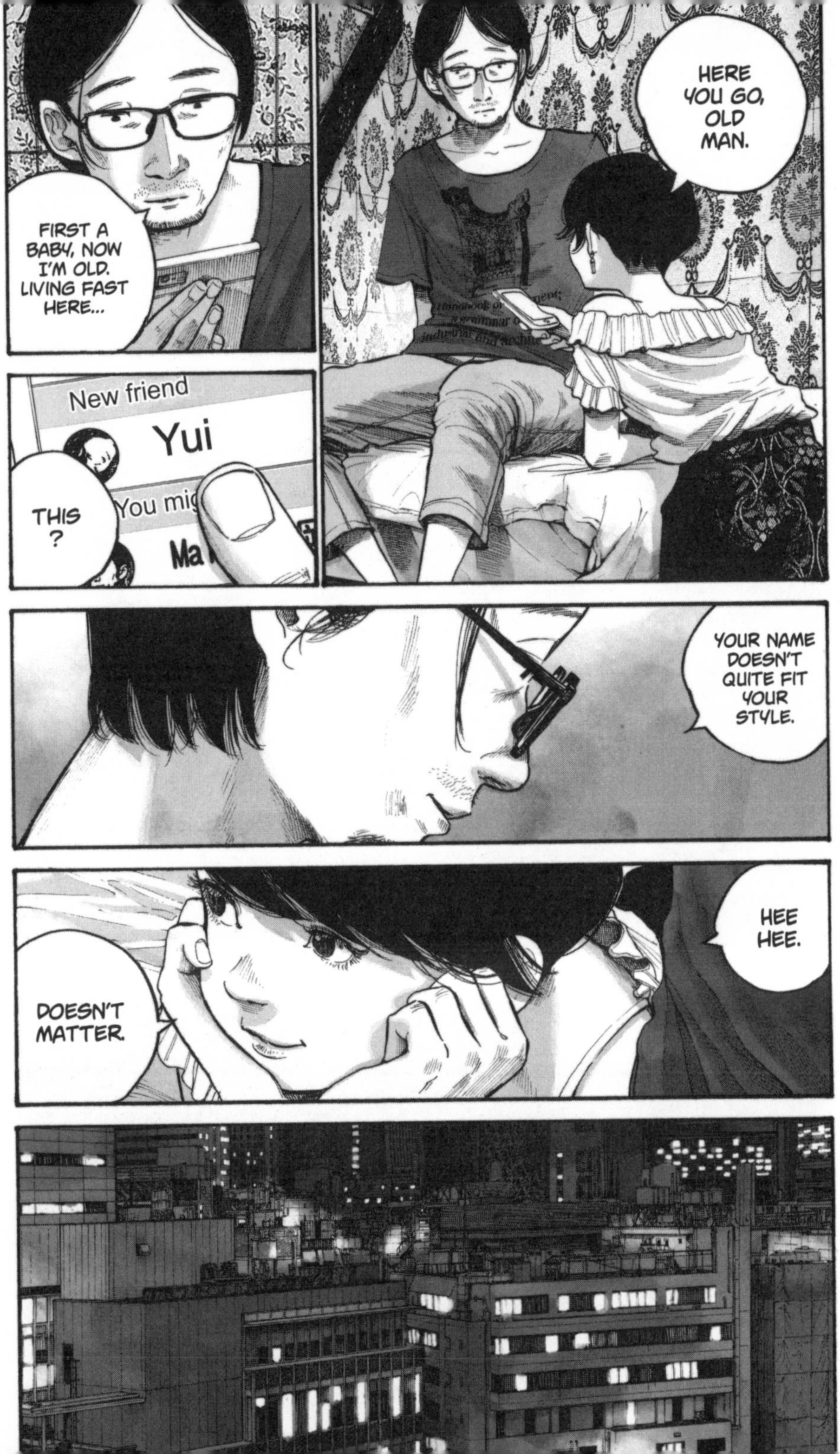
HERE YOU GO, OLD MAN.
FIRST A BABY, NOW I'M OLD. LIVING FAST HERE...
New friend
Yui
THIS ?
YOUR NAME DOESN'T QUITE FIT YOUR STYLE.
HEE HEE.
DOESN'T MATTER.

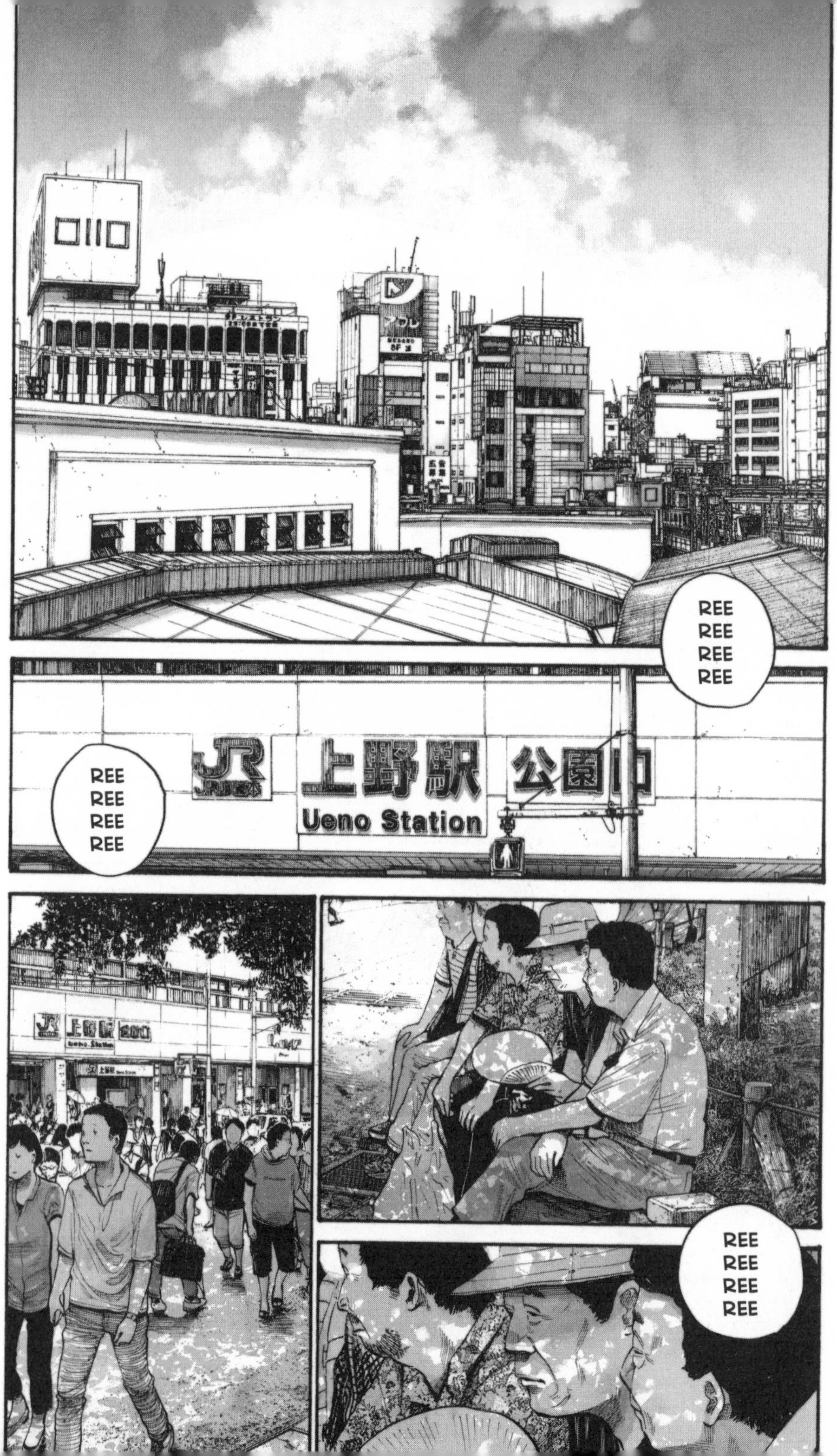
REE
REE
REE
REE
上野駅
公園口
Ueno Station
REE
REE
REE
REE
REE
REE
REE
REE

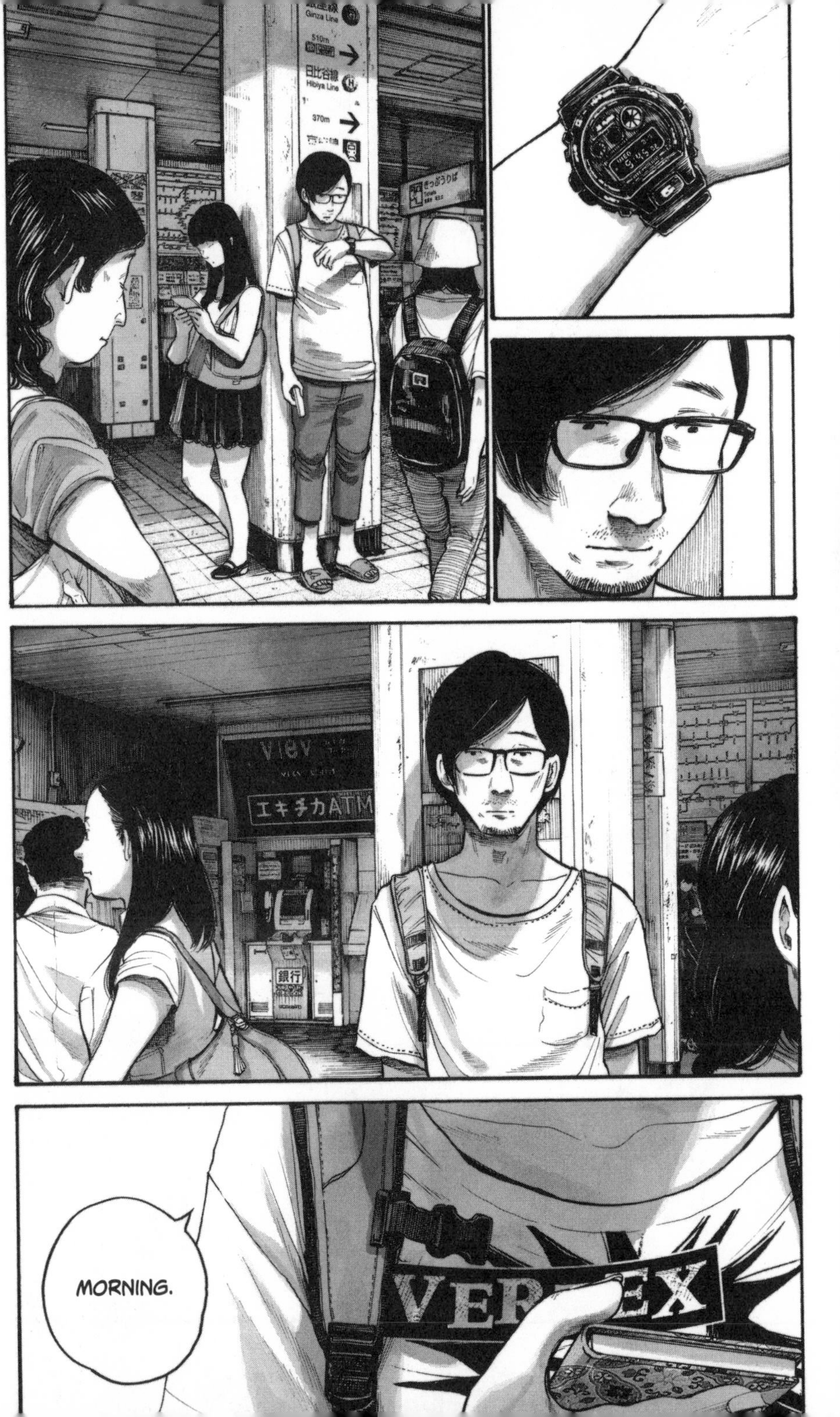
Ginza Line
510m
日比谷線
Hibiya Line
370m
エキチカATM
銀行
MORNING.

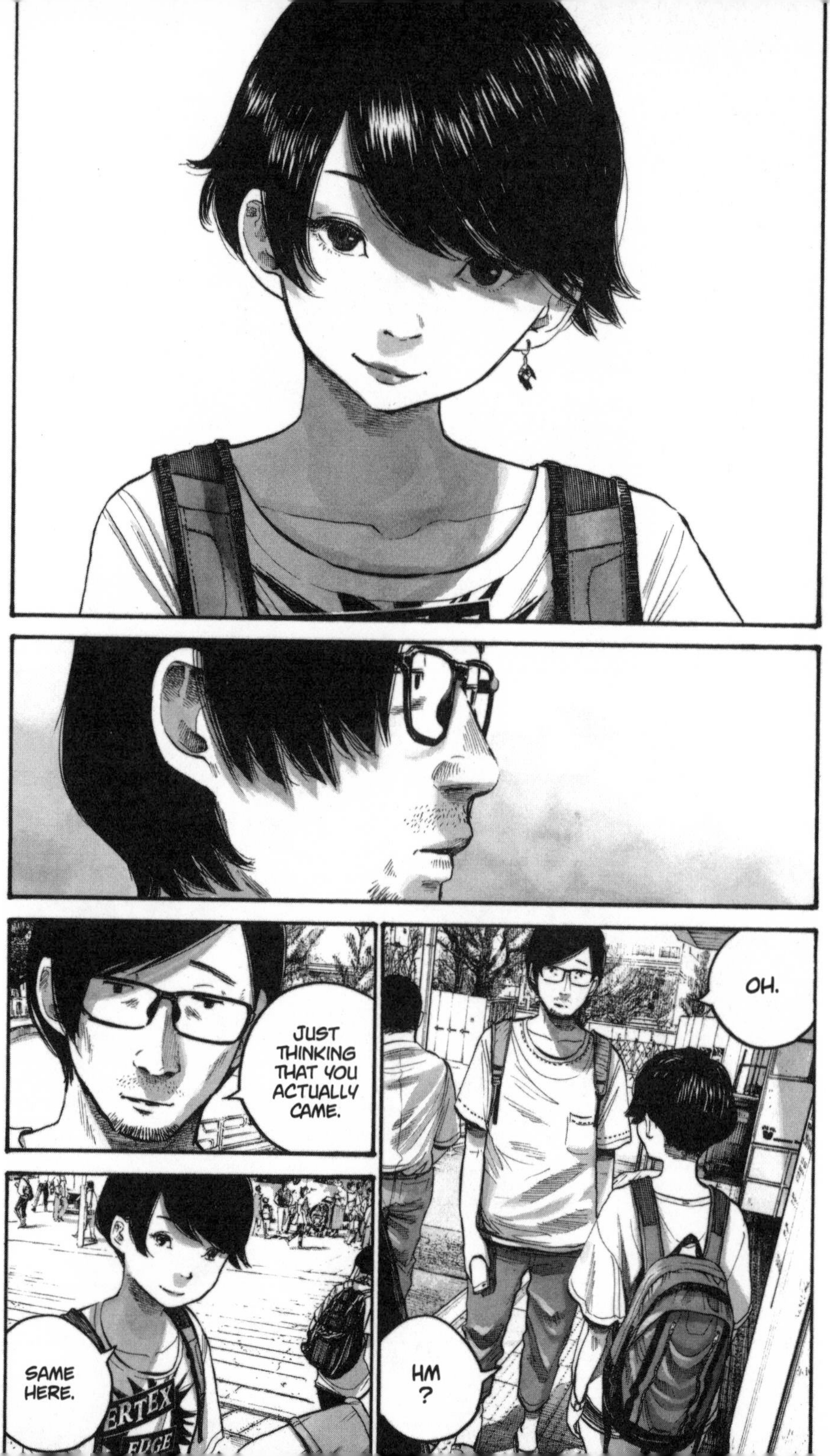
OH.
HM ?
JUST THINKING THAT YOU ACTUALLY CAME.
SAME HERE.

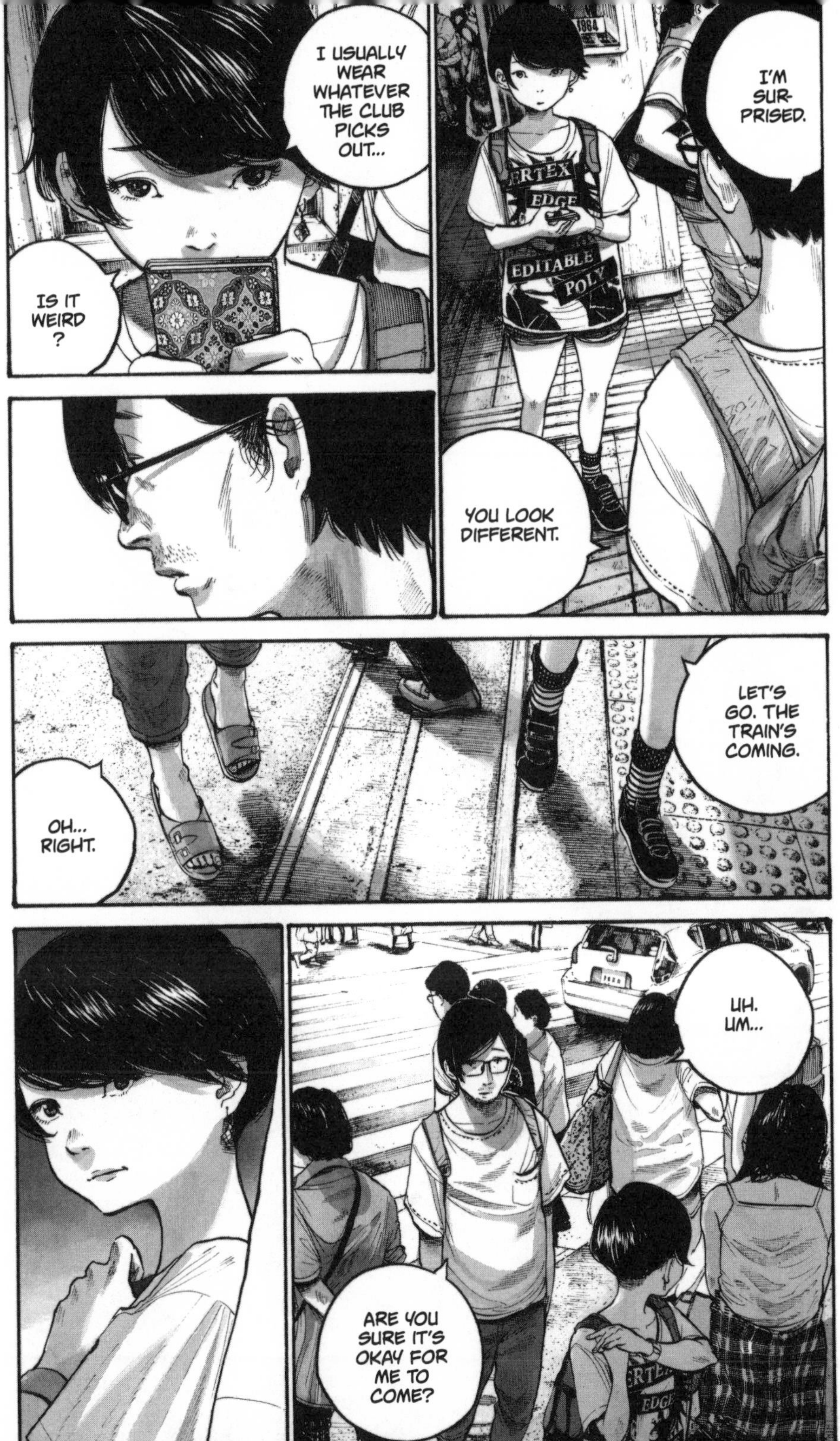
I'M SUR-PRISED.
EDGE
EDITABLE
POLY
YOU LOOK DIFFERENT.
I USUALLY WEAR WHATEVER THE CLUB PICKS OUT...
IS IT WEIRD ?
LET'S GO. THE TRAIN'S COMING.
OH... RIGHT.
UH. UM...
ARE YOU SURE IT'S OKAY FOR ME TO COME?

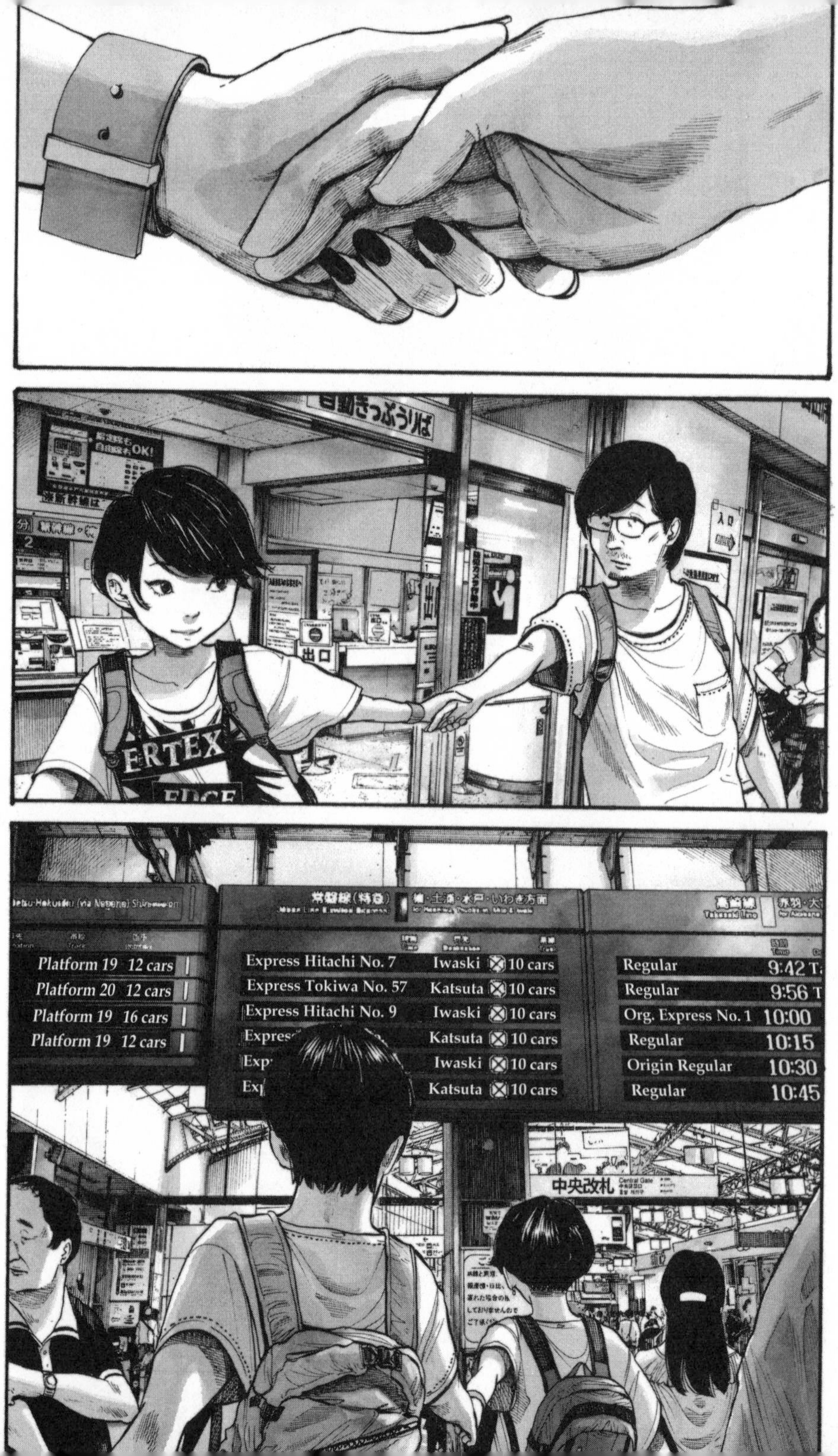
自動きっぷうりば
出口
入口
ERTEX
常磐線(特急)
高崎線
Platform 19 12 cars
Platform 20 12 cars
Platform 19 16 cars
Platform 19 12 cars
Express Hitachi No. 7 Iwaski 10 cars
Express Tokiwa No. 57 Katsuta 10 cars
Express Hitachi No. 9 Iwaski 10 cars
Katsuta 10 cars
Iwaski 10 cars
Katsuta 10 cars
Regular 9:42
Regular 9:56
Org. Express No. 1 10:00
Regular 10:15
Origin Regular 10:30
Regular 10:45
中央改札

CHAPTER 5

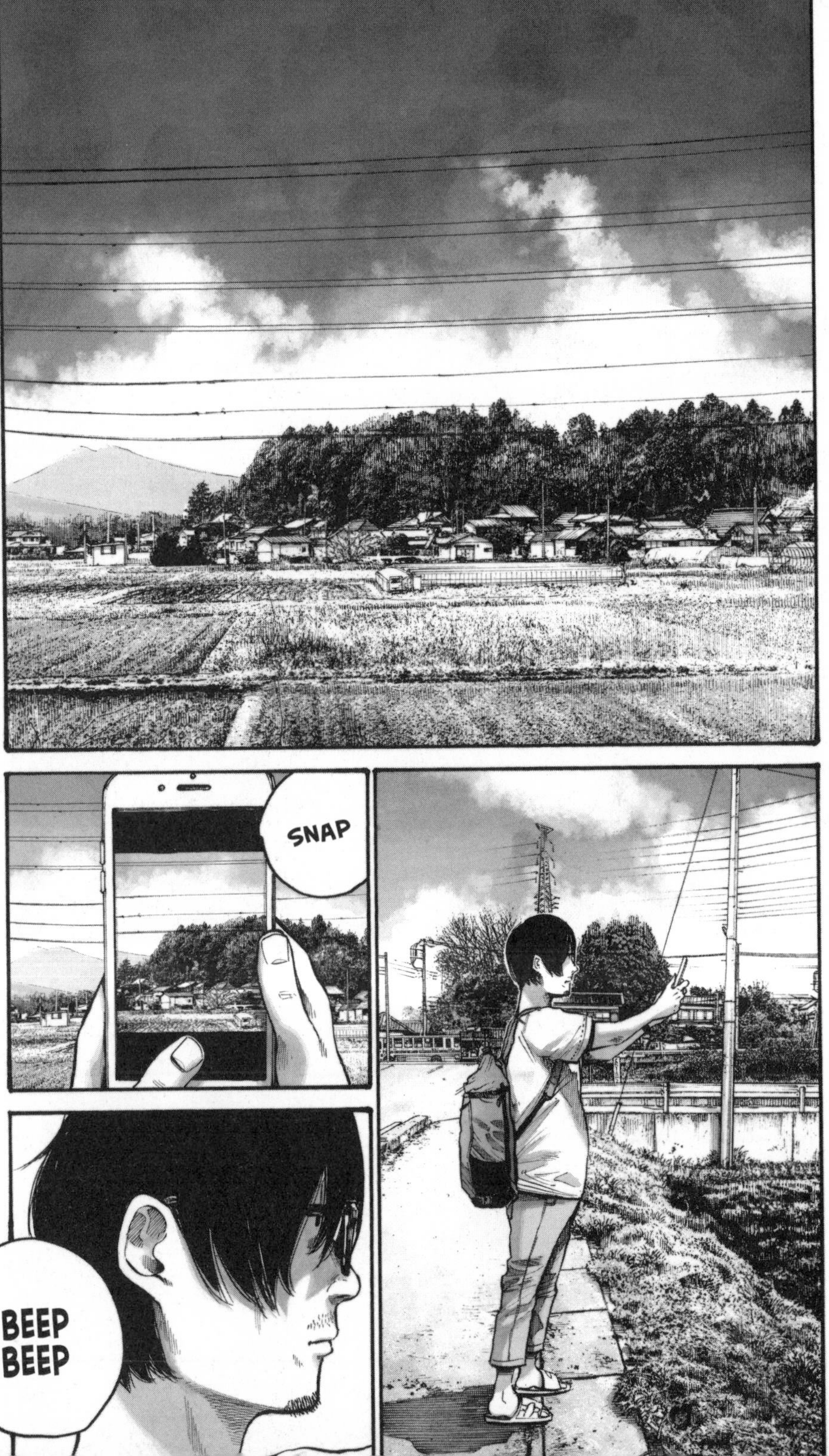
SNAP
BEEP BEEP

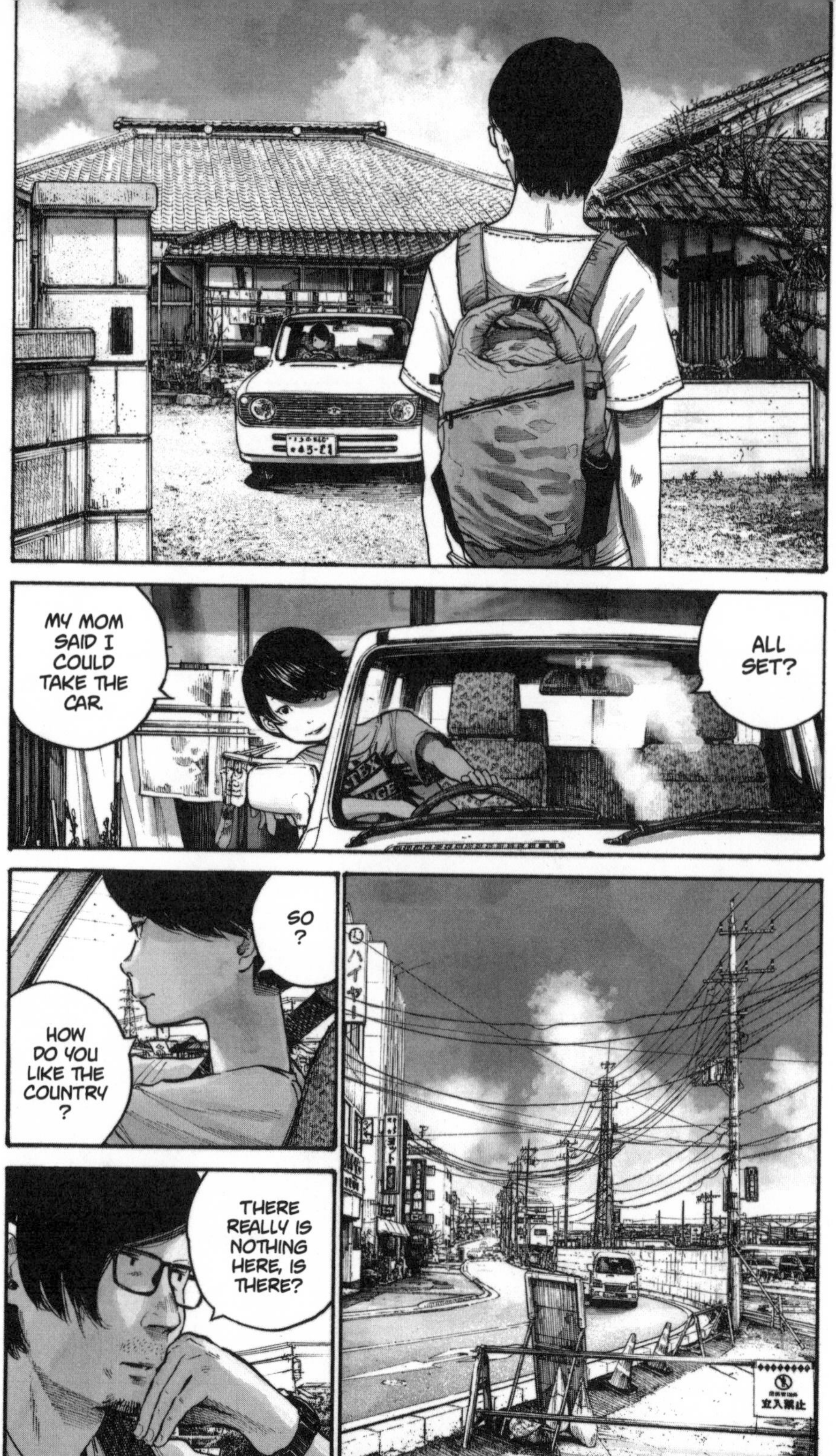
ALL SET?
MY MOM SAID I COULD TAKE THE CAR.
ハイヤー
立入禁止
SO?
HOW DO YOU LIKE THE COUNTRY?
THERE REALLY IS NOTHING HERE, IS THERE?

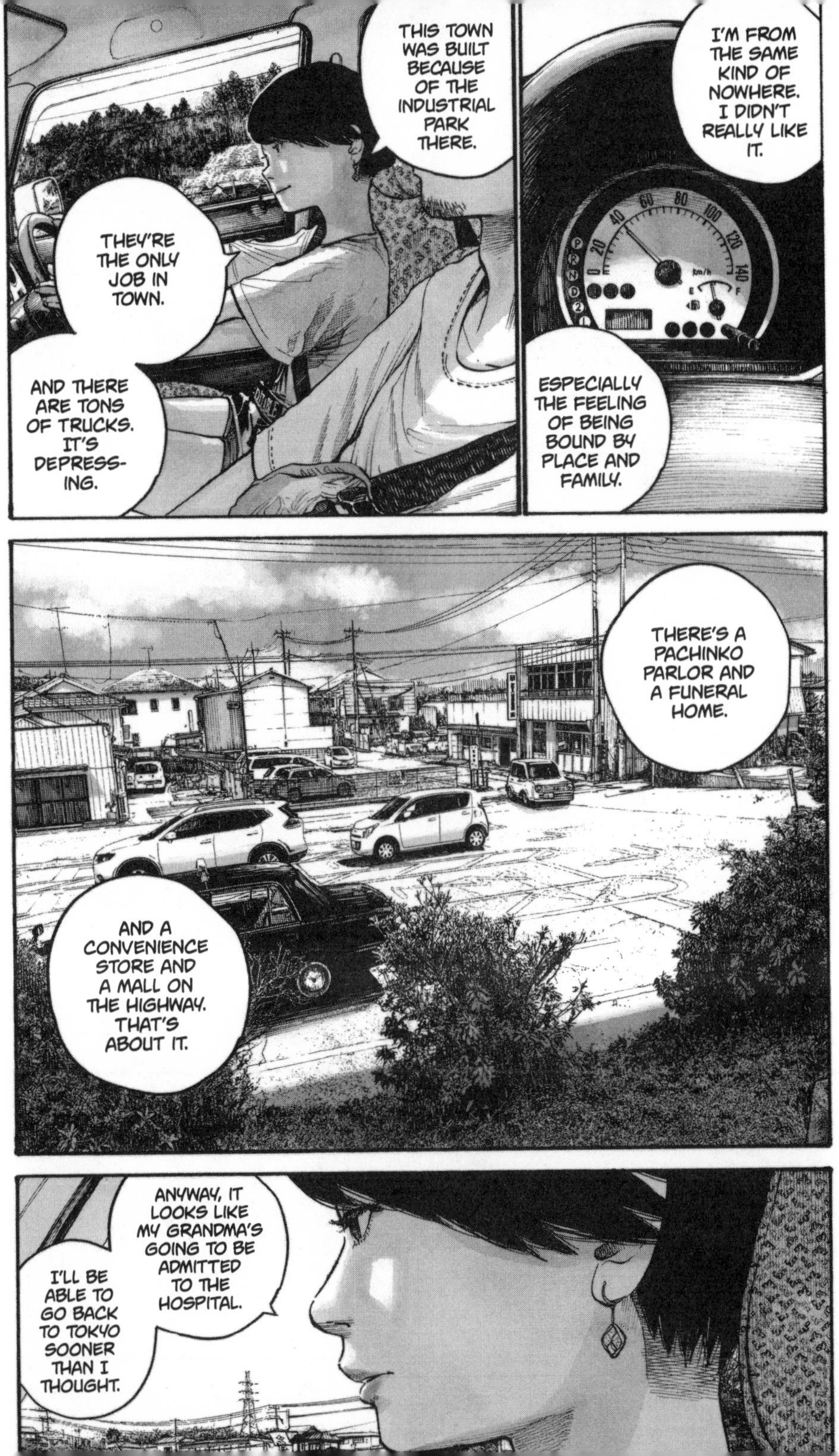
I'M FROM THE SAME KIND OF NOWHERE. I DIDN'T REALLY LIKE IT.
ESPECIALLY THE FEELING OF BEING BOUND BY PLACE AND FAMILY.
THIS TOWN WAS BUILT BECAUSE OF THE INDUSTRIAL PARK THERE.
THEY'RE THE ONLY JOB IN TOWN.
AND THERE ARE TONS OF TRUCKS. IT'S DEPRESS-ING.
THERE'S A PACHINKO PARLOR AND A FUNERAL HOME.
AND A CONVENIENCE STORE AND A MALL ON THE HIGHWAY. THAT'S ABOUT IT.
ANYWAY, IT LOOKS LIKE MY GRANDMA'S GOING TO BE ADMITTED TO THE HOSPITAL.
I'LL BE ABLE TO GO BACK TO TOKYO SOONER THAN I THOUGHT.

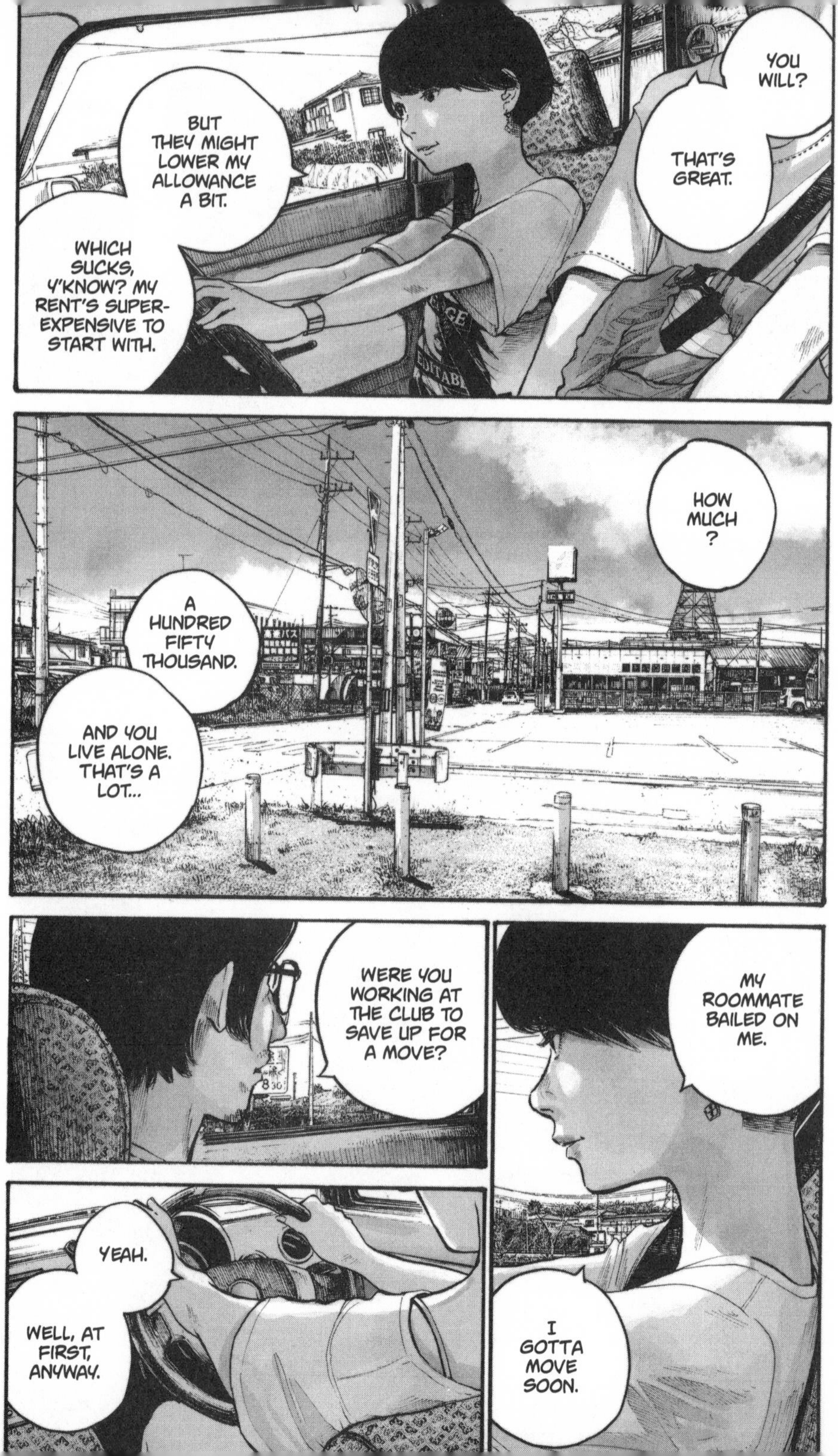
YOU WILL?
THAT'S GREAT.
BUT THEY MIGHT LOWER MY ALLOWANCE A BIT.
WHICH SUCKS, Y'KNOW? MY RENT'S SUPER-EXPENSIVE TO START WITH.
HOW MUCH?
A HUNDRED FIFTY THOUSAND.
AND YOU LIVE ALONE. THAT'S A LOT...
MY ROOMMATE BAILED ON ME.
I GOTTA MOVE SOON.
WERE YOU WORKING AT THE CLUB TO SAVE UP FOR A MOVE?
YEAH.
WELL, AT FIRST, ANYWAY.

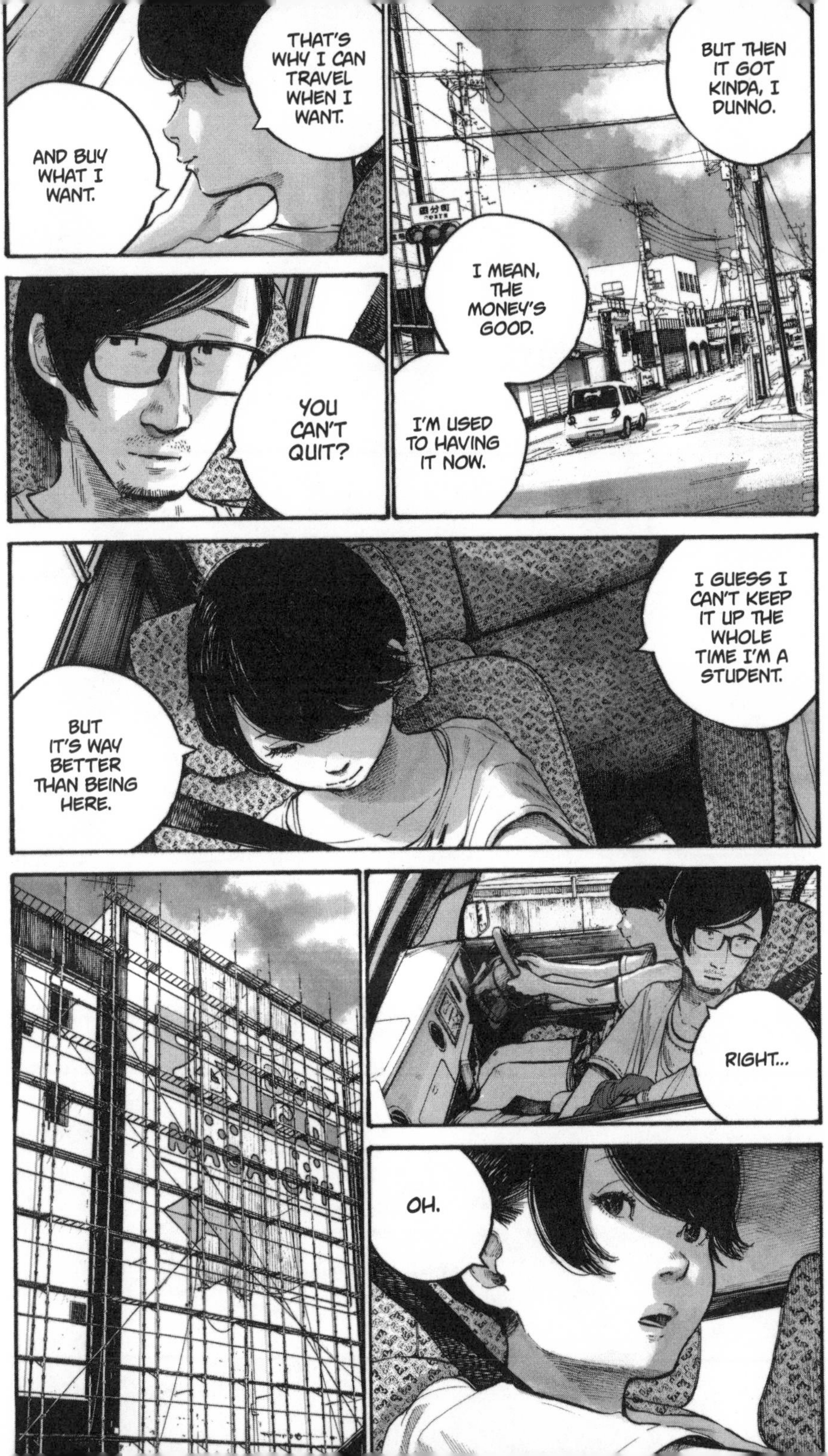
BUT THEN IT GOT KINDA, I DUNNO.
I MEAN, THE MONEY'S GOOD.
I'M USED TO HAVING IT NOW.
THAT'S WHY I CAN TRAVEL WHEN I WANT.
AND BUY WHAT I WANT.
YOU CAN'T QUIT?
I GUESS I CAN'T KEEP IT UP THE WHOLE TIME I'M A STUDENT.
BUT IT'S WAY BETTER THAN BEING HERE.
RIGHT...
OH.

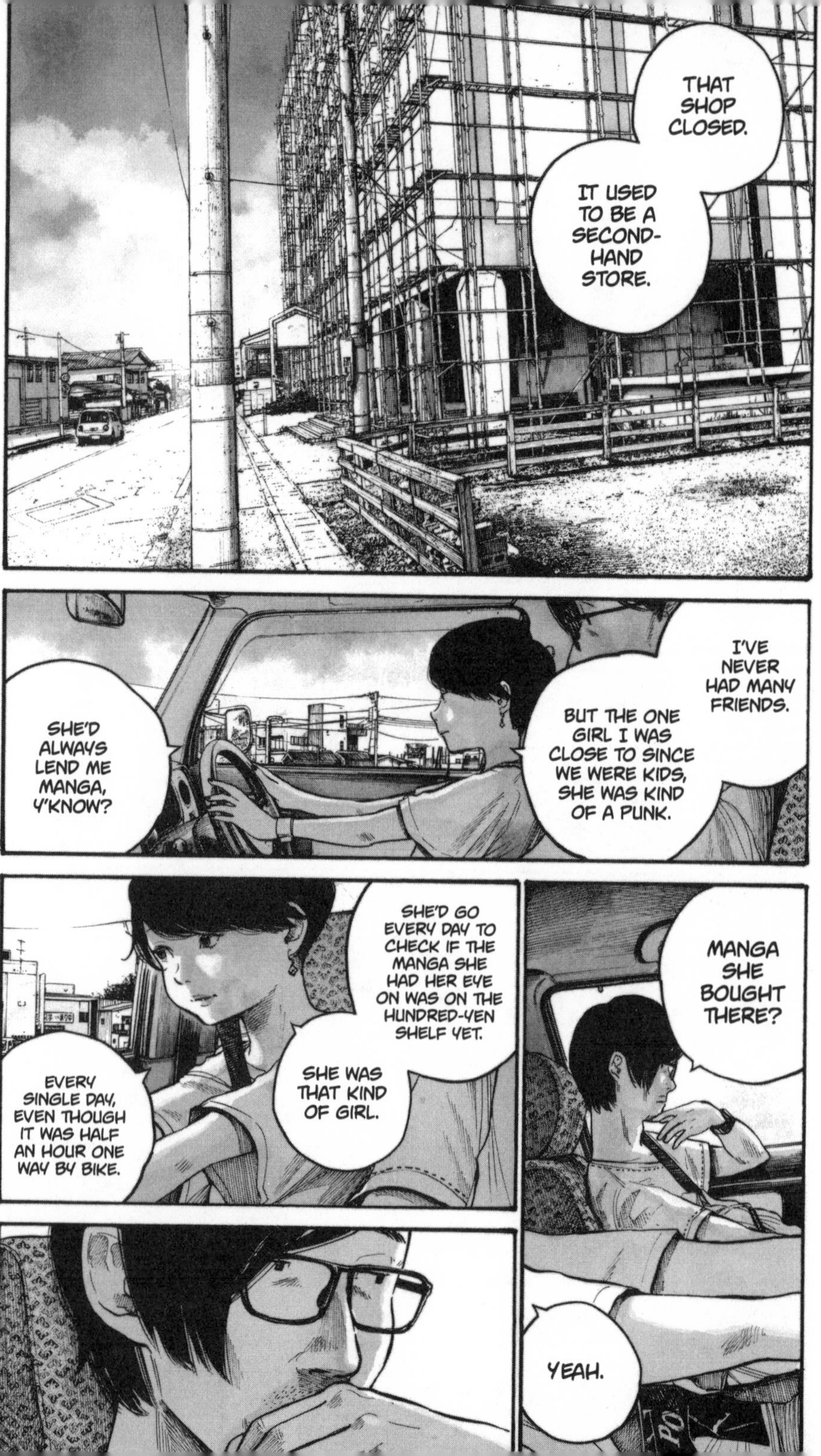
THAT SHOP CLOSED.
IT USED TO BE A SECOND-HAND STORE.
I'VE NEVER HAD MANY FRIENDS.
BUT THE ONE GIRL I WAS CLOSE TO SINCE WE WERE KIDS, SHE WAS KIND OF A PUNK.
SHE'D ALWAYS LEND ME MANGA, Y'KNOW?
MANGA SHE BOUGHT THERE?
SHE'D GO EVERY DAY TO CHECK IF THE MANGA SHE HAD HER EYE ON WAS ON THE HUNDRED-YEN SHELF YET.
SHE WAS THAT KIND OF GIRL.
EVERY SINGLE DAY, EVEN THOUGH IT WAS HALF AN HOUR ONE WAY BY BIKE.
YEAH.

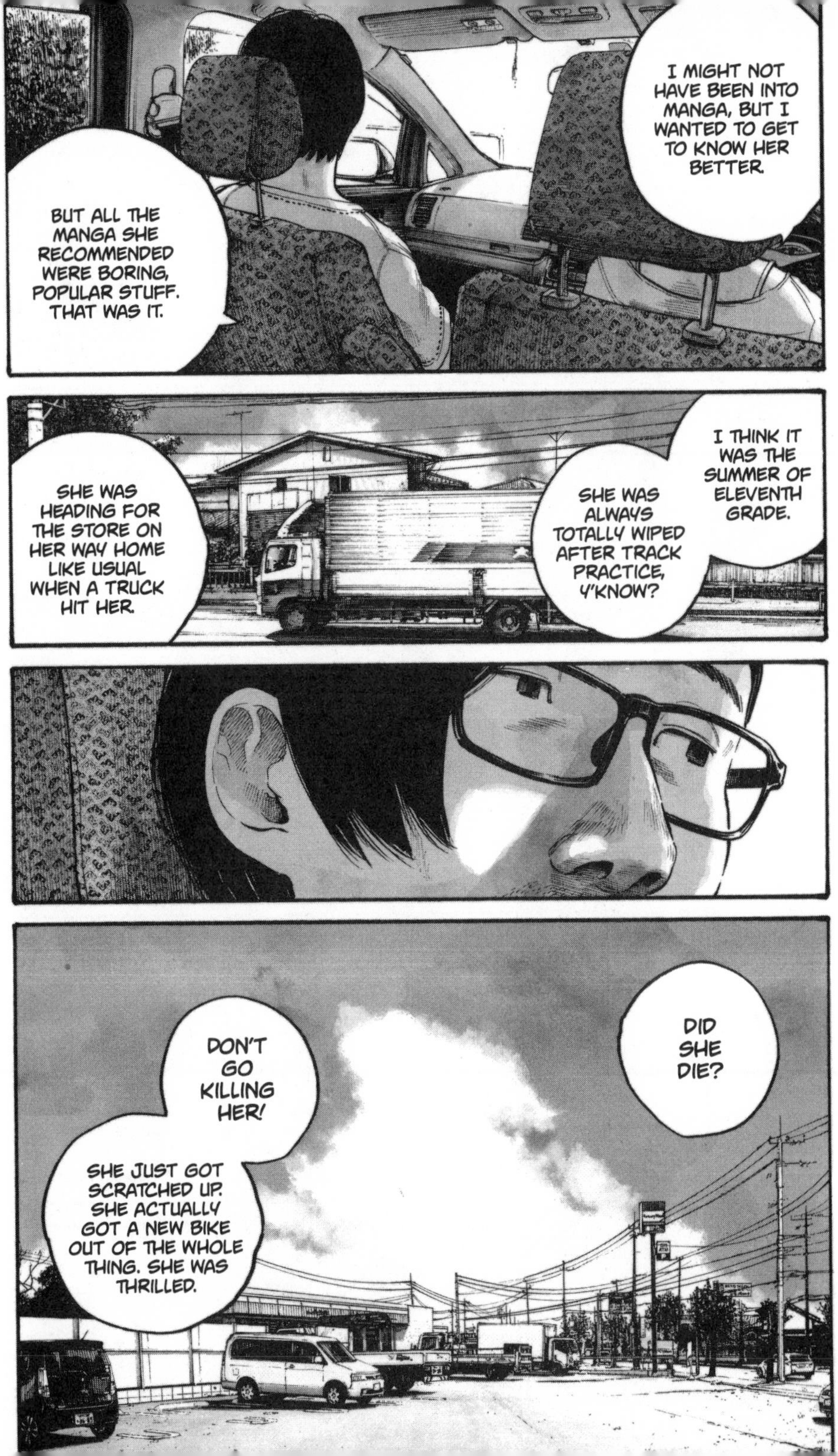
I MIGHT NOT HAVE BEEN INTO MANGA, BUT I WANTED TO GET TO KNOW HER BETTER.
BUT ALL THE MANGA SHE RECOMMENDED WERE BORING, POPULAR STUFF. THAT WAS IT.
I THINK IT WAS THE SUMMER OF ELEVENTH GRADE.
SHE WAS ALWAYS TOTALLY WIPED AFTER TRACK PRACTICE, Y'KNOW?
SHE WAS HEADING FOR THE STORE ON HER WAY HOME LIKE USUAL WHEN A TRUCK HIT HER.
DID SHE DIE?
DON'T GO KILLING HER!
SHE JUST GOT SCRATCHED UP. SHE ACTUALLY GOT A NEW BIKE OUT OF THE WHOLE THING. SHE WAS THRILLED.

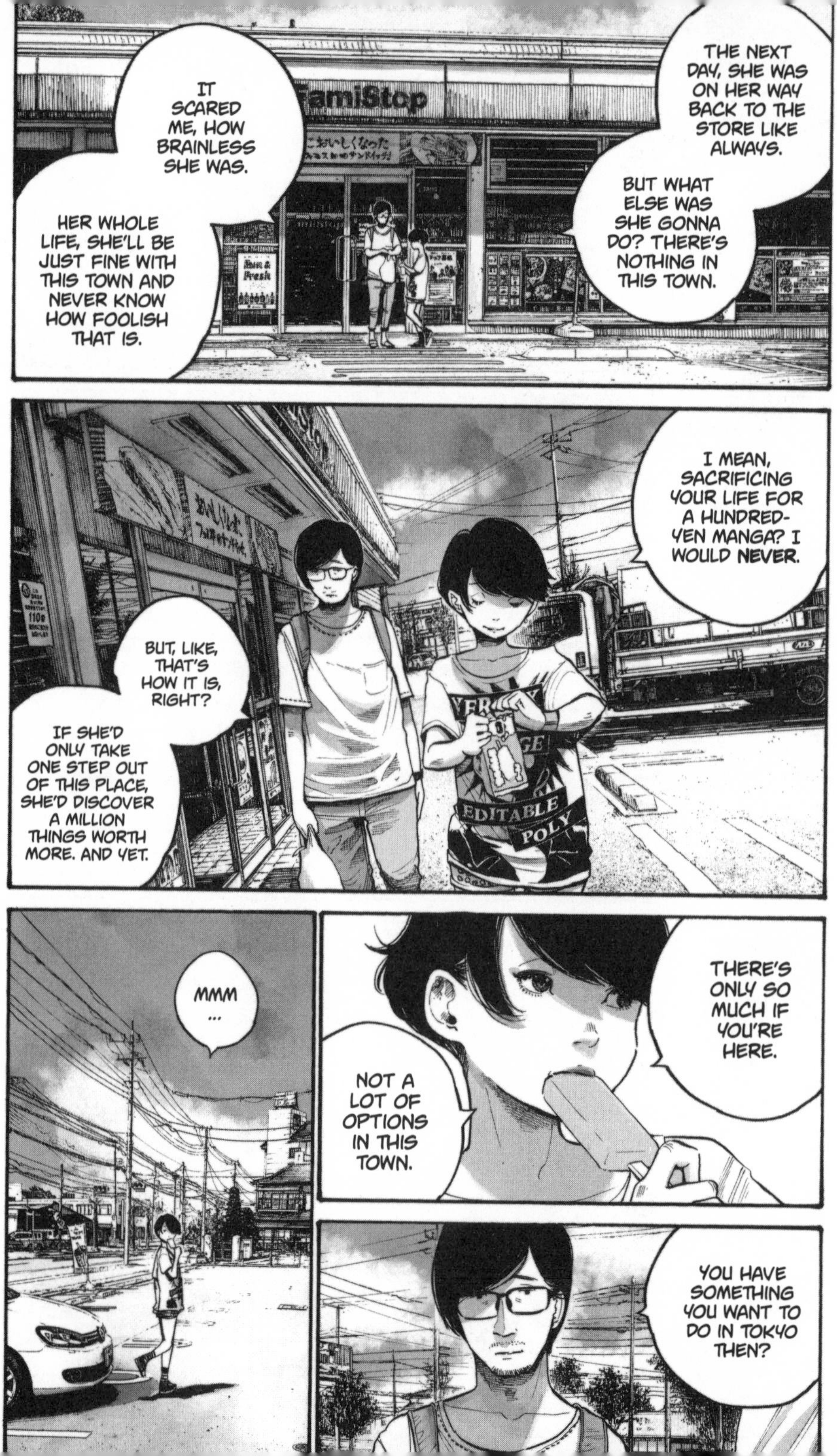
THE NEXT DAY, SHE WAS ON HER WAY BACK TO THE STORE LIKE ALWAYS.
BUT WHAT ELSE WAS SHE GONNA DO? THERE'S NOTHING IN THIS TOWN.
IT SCARED ME, HOW BRAINLESS SHE WAS.
HER WHOLE LIFE, SHE'LL BE JUST FINE WITH THIS TOWN AND NEVER KNOW HOW FOOLISH THAT IS.
I MEAN, SACRIFICING YOUR LIFE FOR A HUNDRED-YEN MANGA? I WOULD **NEVER**.
BUT, LIKE, THAT'S HOW IT IS, RIGHT?
IF SHE'D ONLY TAKE ONE STEP OUT OF THIS PLACE, SHE'D DISCOVER A MILLION THINGS WORTH MORE. AND YET.
THERE'S ONLY SO MUCH IF YOU'RE HERE.
NOT A LOT OF OPTIONS IN THIS TOWN.
YOU HAVE SOMETHING YOU WANT TO DO IN TOKYO THEN?
MMM ...

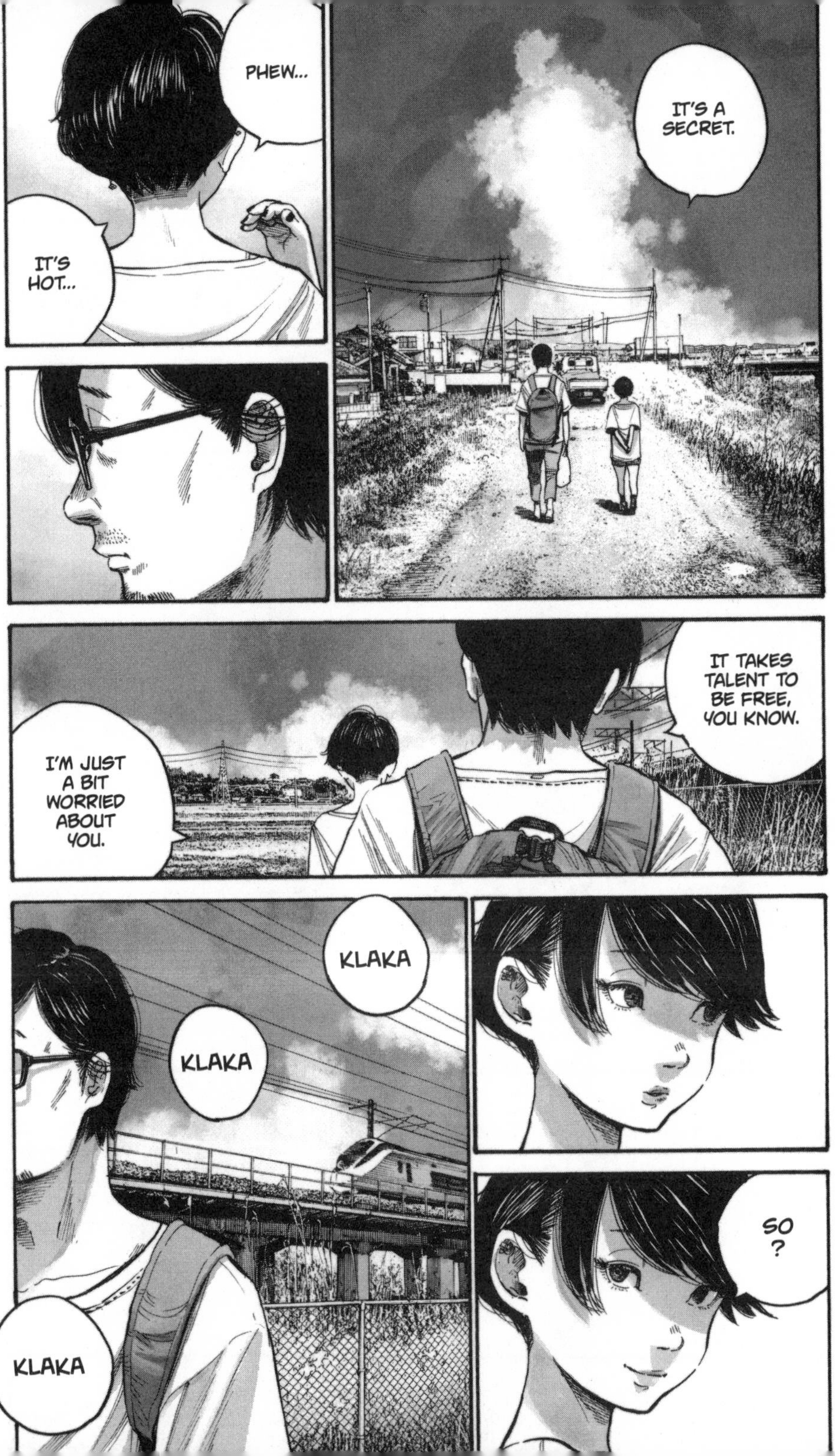
IT'S A SECRET.
PHEW...
IT'S HOT...
IT TAKES TALENT TO BE FREE, YOU KNOW.
I'M JUST A BIT WORRIED ABOUT YOU.
SO ?
KLAKA
KLAKA
KLAKA

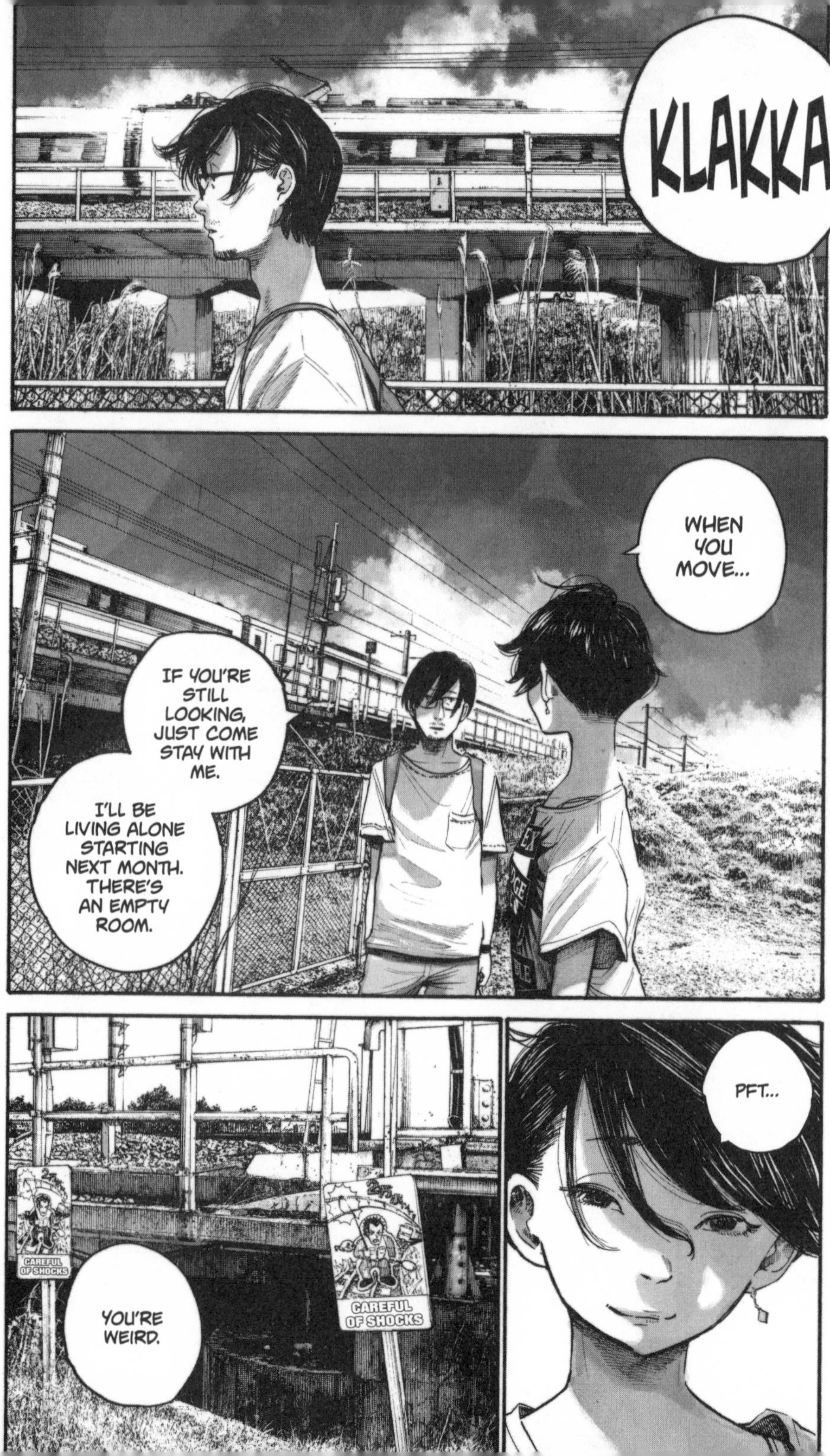
KLAKKA
WHEN YOU MOVE...
IF YOU'RE STILL LOOKING, JUST COME STAY WITH ME.
I'LL BE LIVING ALONE STARTING NEXT MONTH. THERE'S AN EMPTY ROOM.
PFT...
CAREFUL OF SHOCKS
CAREFUL OF SHOCKS
YOU'RE WEIRD.

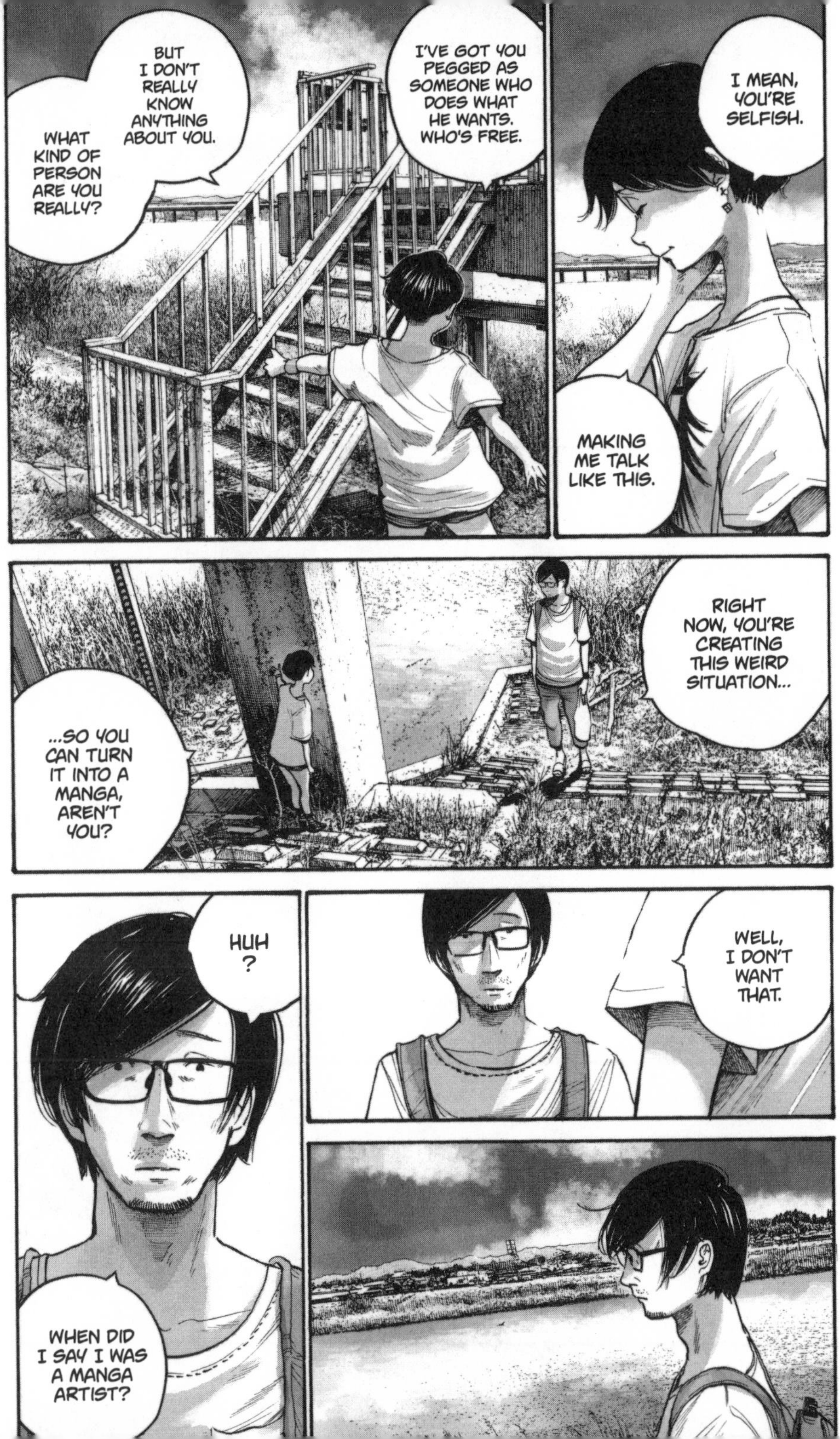
I MEAN, YOU'RE SELFISH.
MAKING ME TALK LIKE THIS.
I'VE GOT YOU PEGGED AS SOMEONE WHO DOES WHAT HE WANTS. WHO'S FREE.
BUT I DON'T REALLY KNOW ANYTHING ABOUT YOU.
WHAT KIND OF PERSON ARE YOU REALLY?
RIGHT NOW, YOU'RE CREATING THIS WEIRD SITUATION...
...SO YOU CAN TURN IT INTO A MANGA, AREN'T YOU?
WELL, I DON'T WANT THAT.
HUH?
WHEN DID I SAY I WAS A MANGA ARTIST?

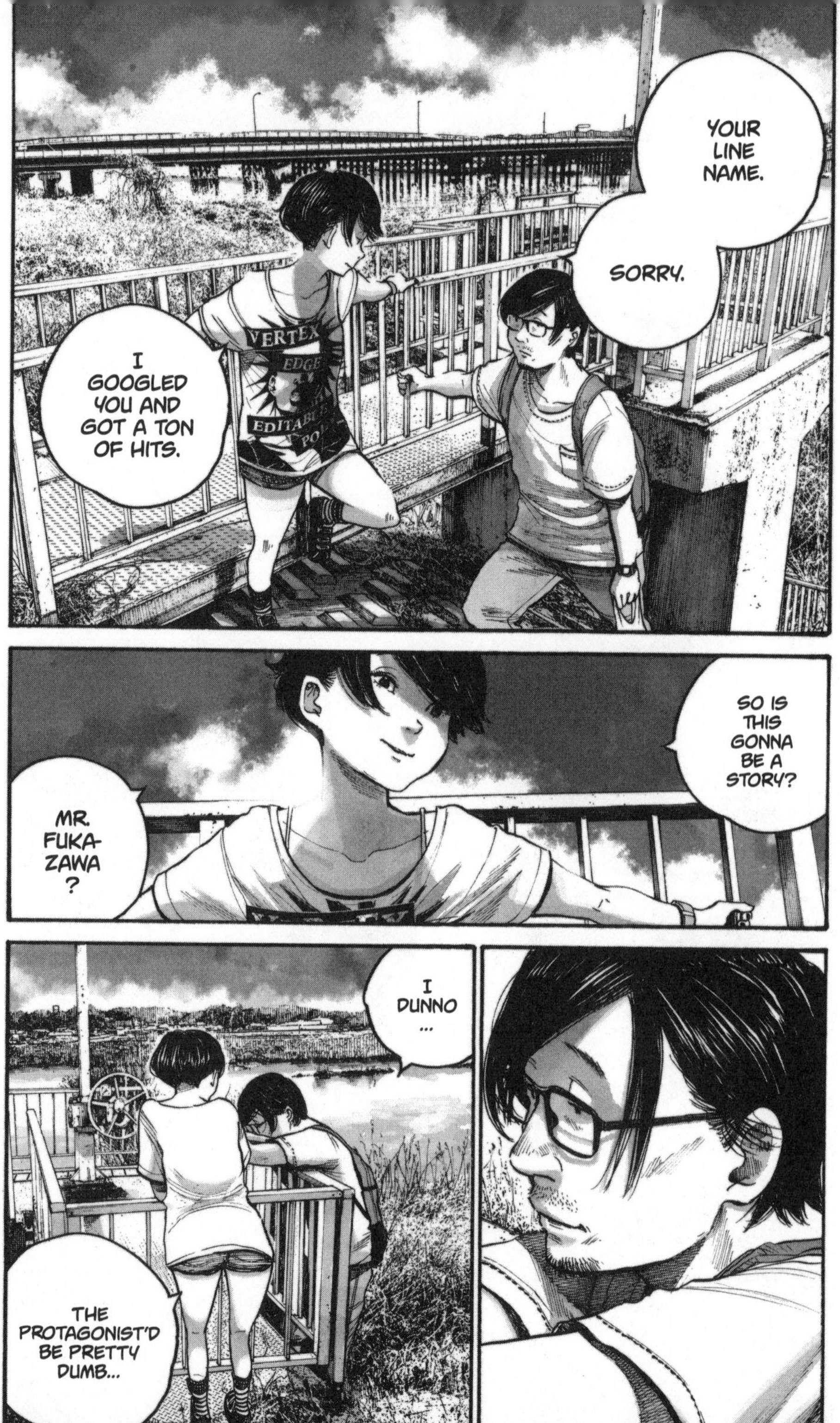
YOUR LINE NAME.
SORRY.
I GOOGLED YOU AND GOT A TON OF HITS.
SO IS THIS GONNA BE A STORY?
MR. FUKAZAWA?
I DUNNO...
THE PROTAGONIST'D BE PRETTY DUMB...

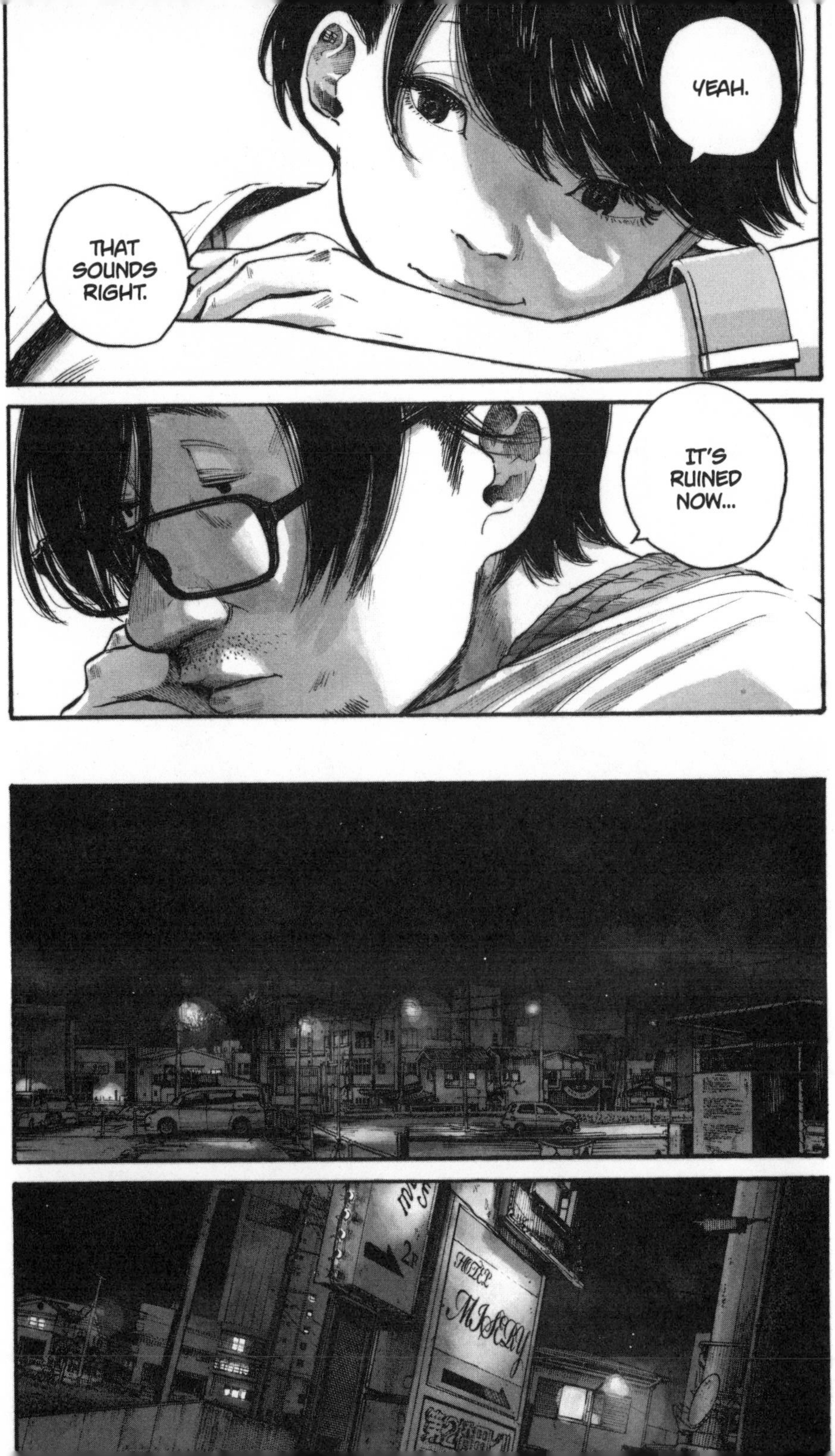
YEAH.
THAT SOUNDS RIGHT.
IT'S RUINED NOW...

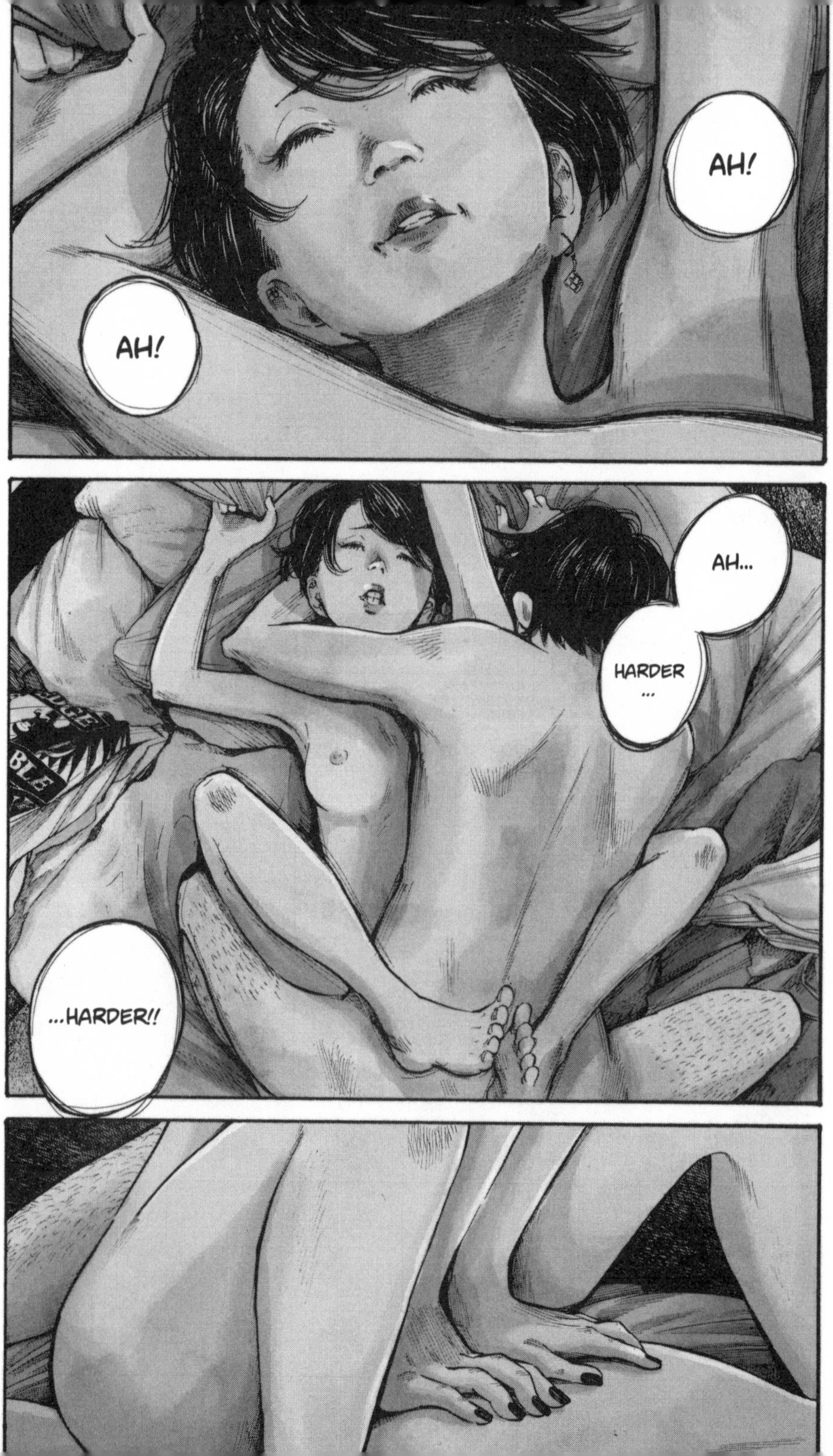
AH!
AH!
AH...
HARDER ...
...HARDER!!

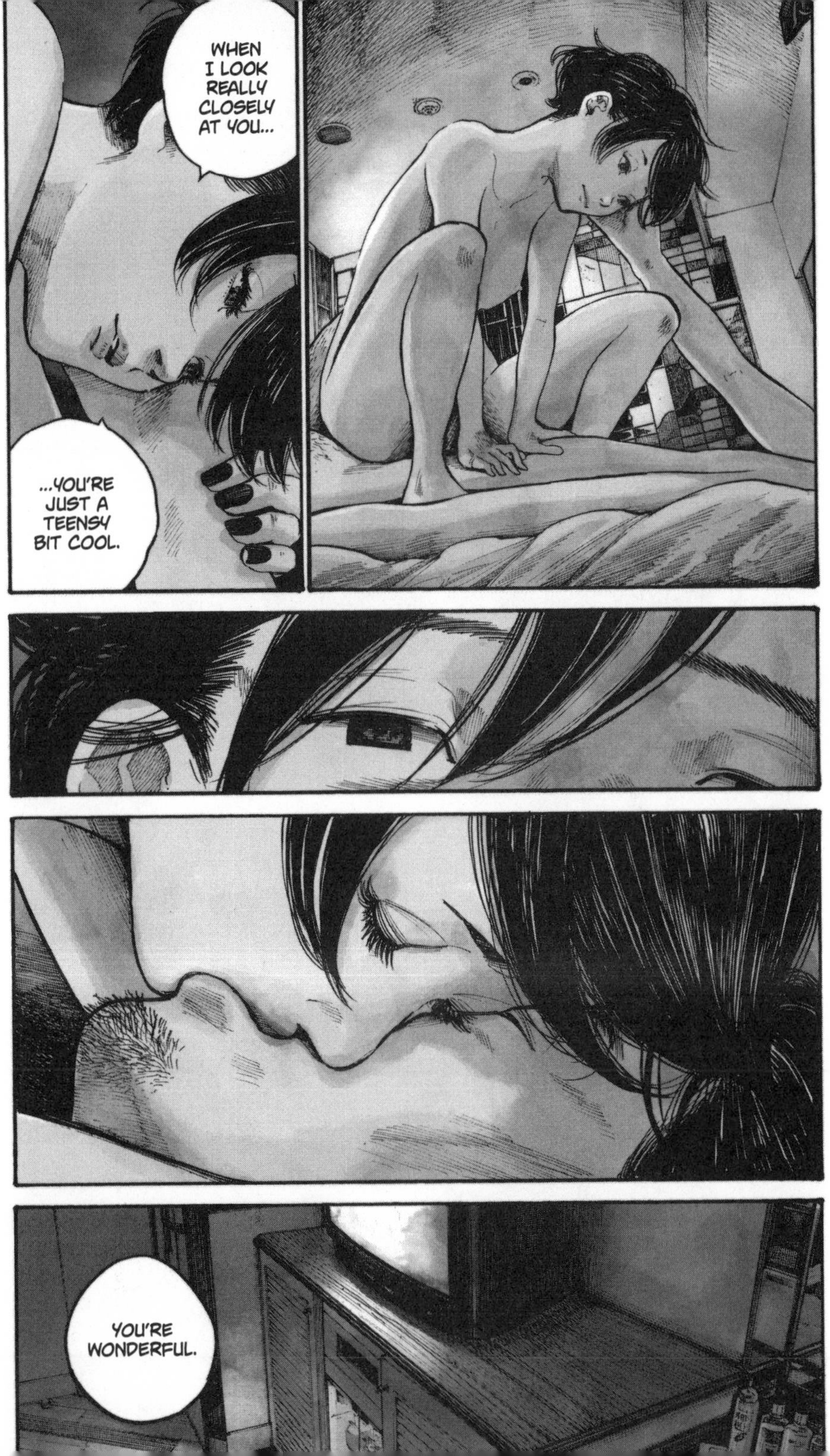
WHEN I LOOK REALLY CLOSELY AT YOU...
...YOU'RE JUST A TEENSY BIT COOL.
YOU'RE WONDERFUL.

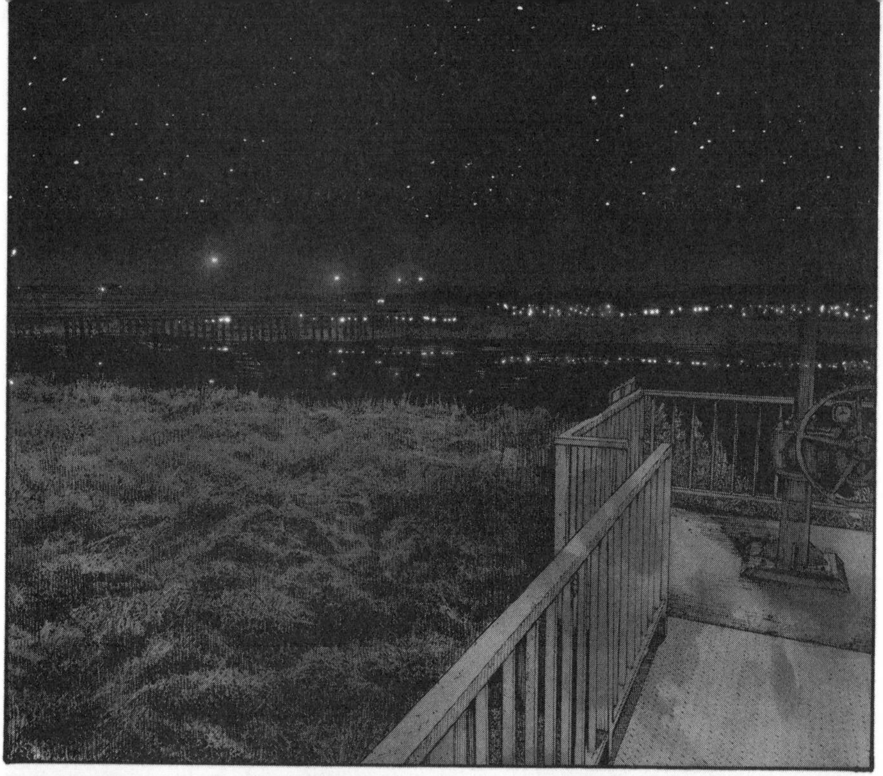

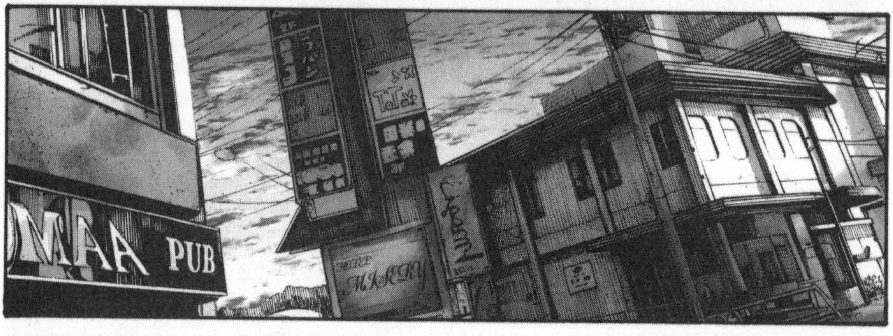
MAA PUB

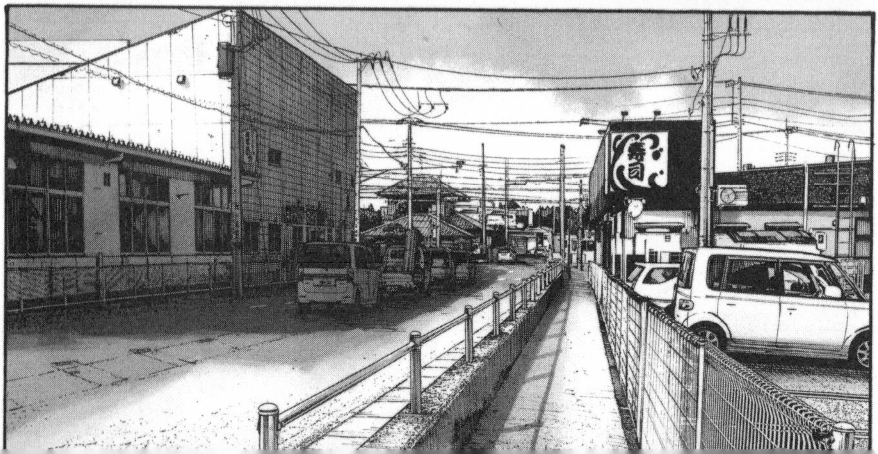
寿司

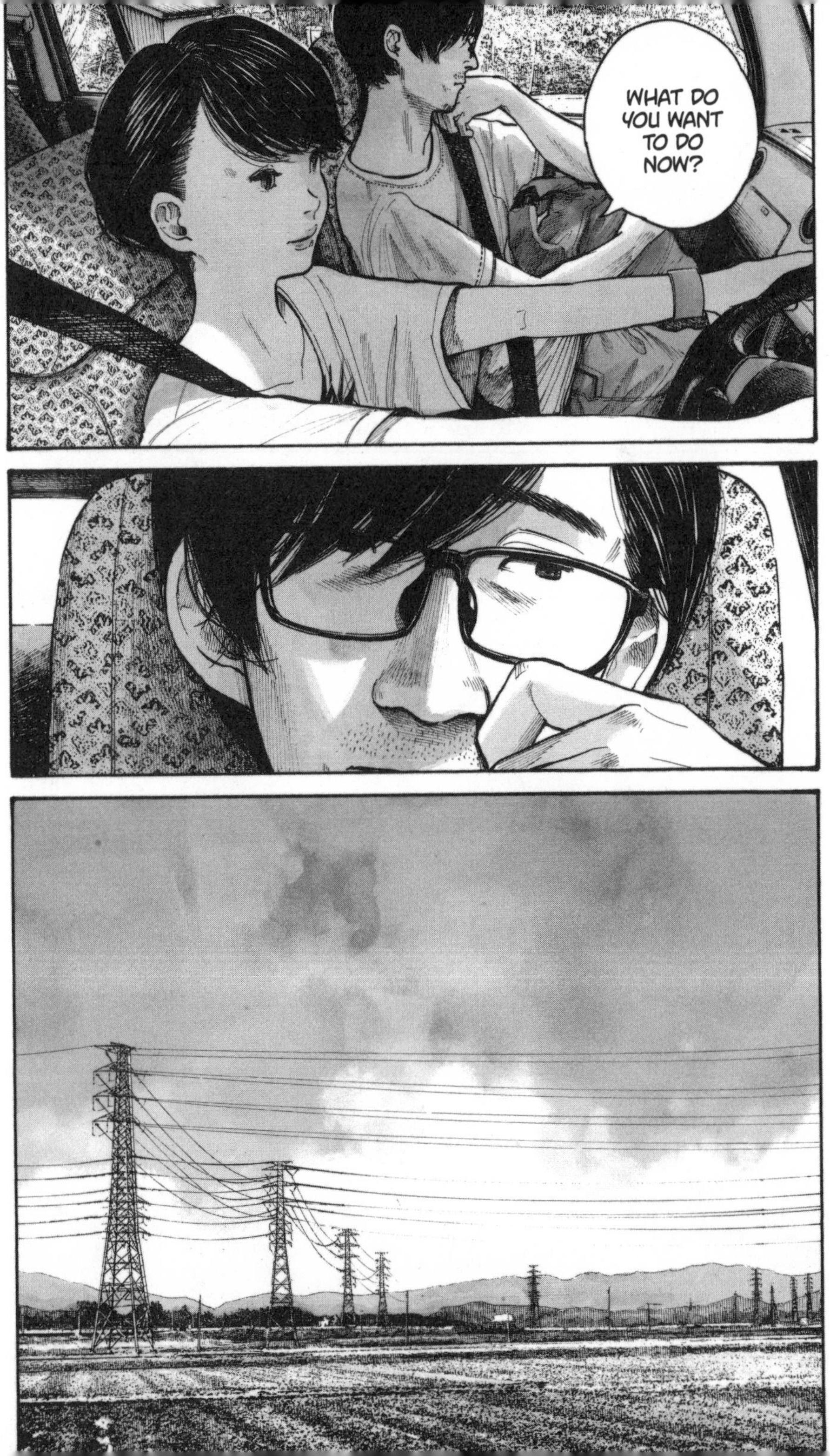
WHAT DO YOU WANT TO DO NOW?

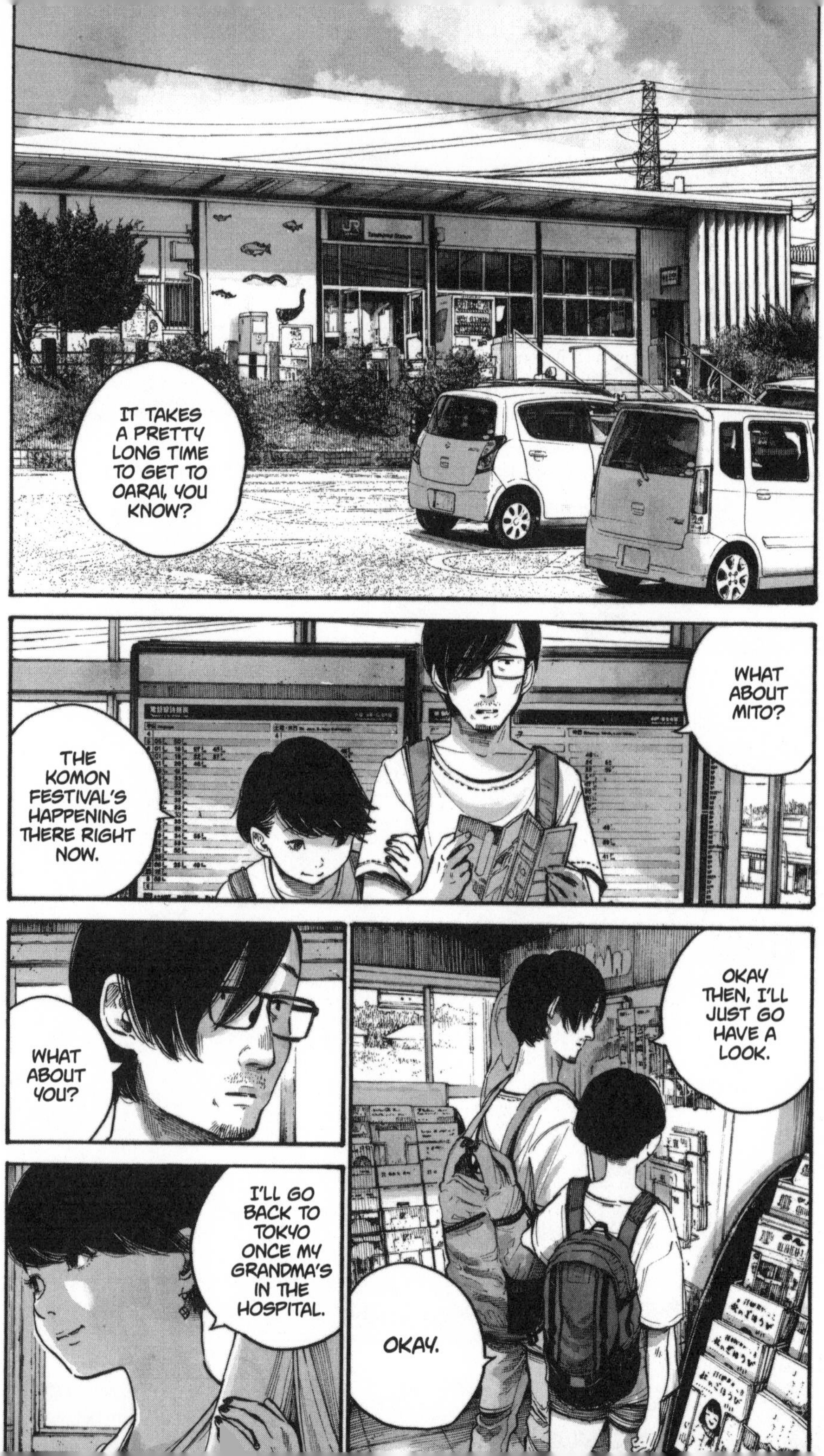
IT TAKES A PRETTY LONG TIME TO GET TO OARAI, YOU KNOW?
WHAT ABOUT MITO?
THE KOMON FESTIVAL'S HAPPENING THERE RIGHT NOW.
OKAY THEN, I'LL JUST GO HAVE A LOOK.
OKAY.
WHAT ABOUT YOU?
I'LL GO BACK TO TOKYO ONCE MY GRANDMA'S IN THE HOSPITAL.

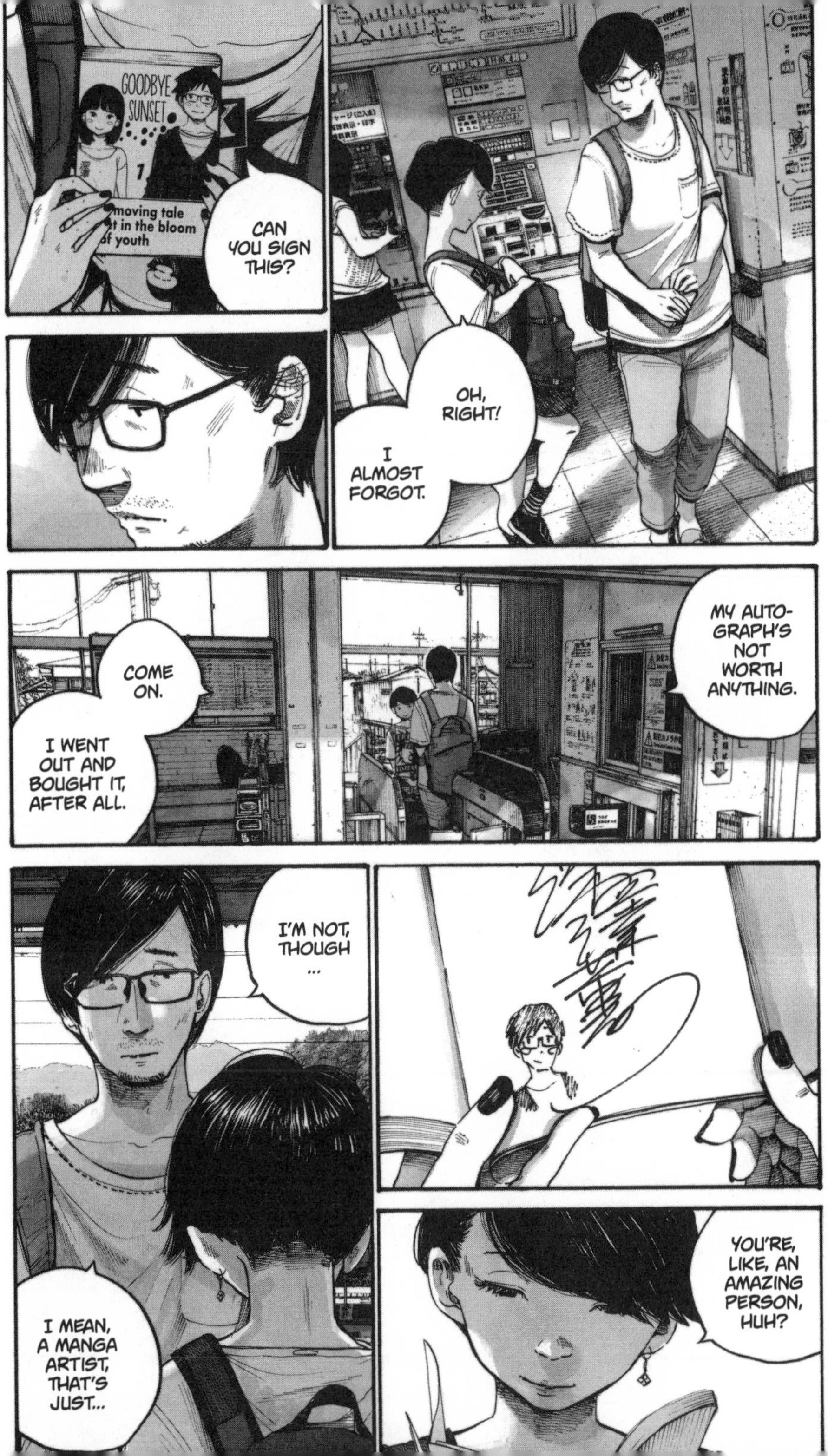
OH, RIGHT!
I ALMOST FORGOT.
GOODBYE SUNSET
1
moving tale
t in the bloom
of youth
CAN YOU SIGN THIS?
MY AUTO-GRAPH'S NOT WORTH ANYTHING.
COME ON.
I WENT OUT AND BOUGHT IT, AFTER ALL.
YOU'RE, LIKE, AN AMAZING PERSON, HUH?
I'M NOT, THOUGH ...
I MEAN, A MANGA ARTIST, THAT'S JUST...

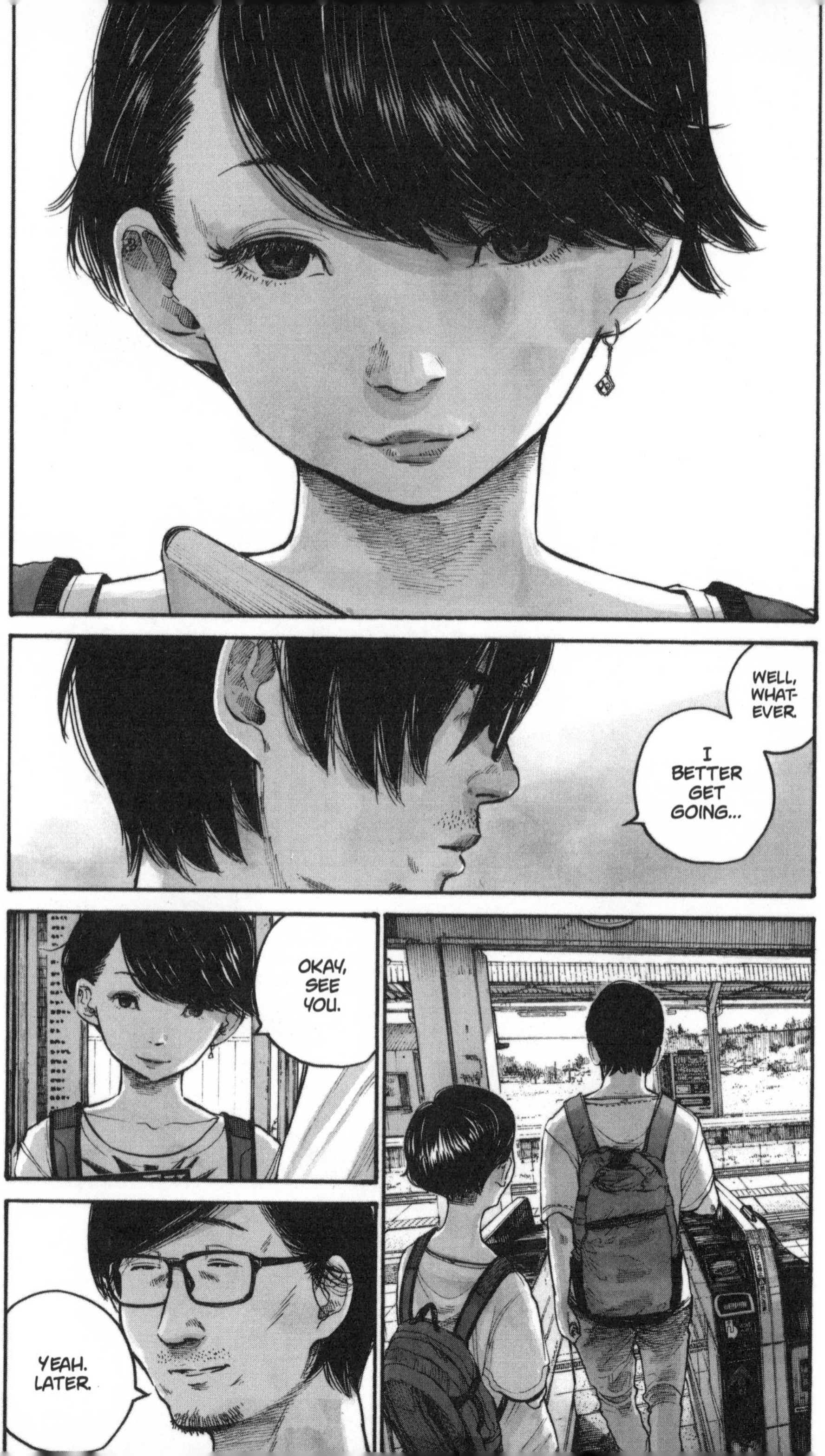
WELL, WHAT-EVER.
I BETTER GET GOING...
OKAY, SEE YOU.
YEAH. LATER.

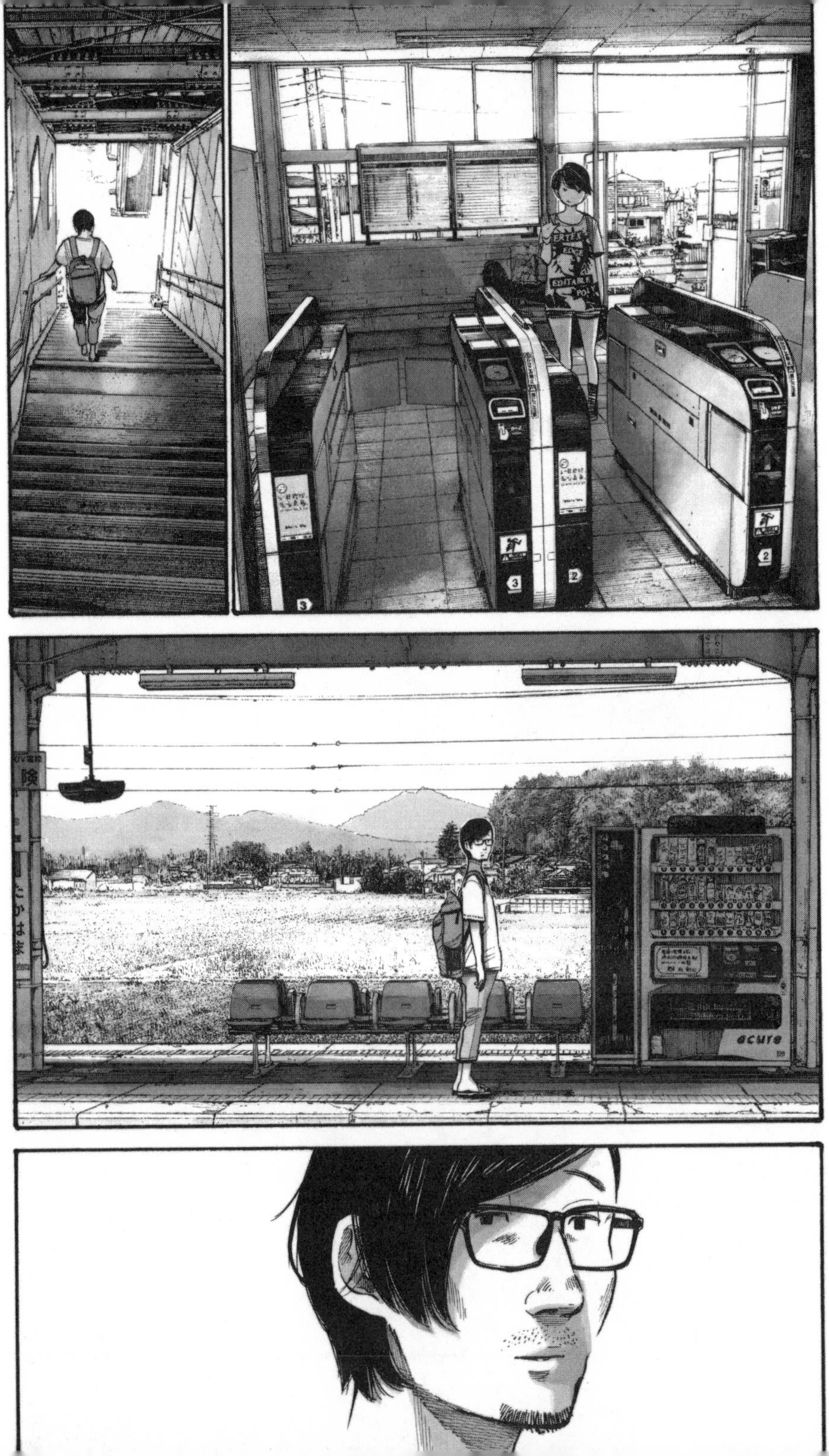
たかはま
acure

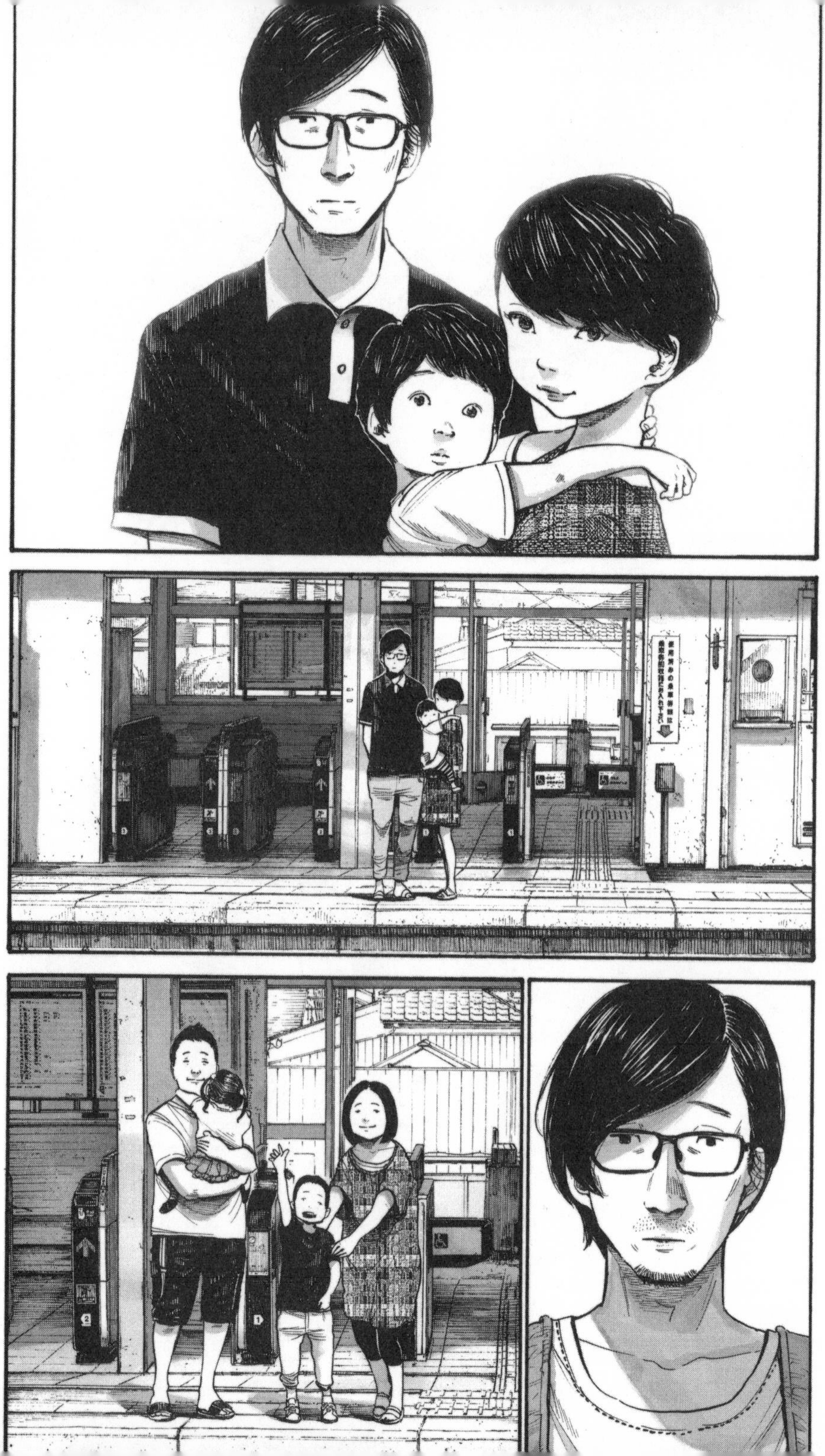

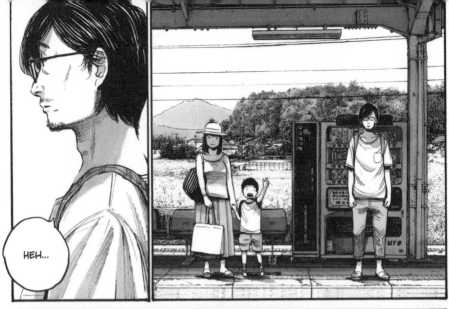

HEH...

THE TRAIN WILL ARRIVE SHORTLY.

PLEASE STAY BEHIND THE WHITE LINE.

WHAT AM I DOING...?

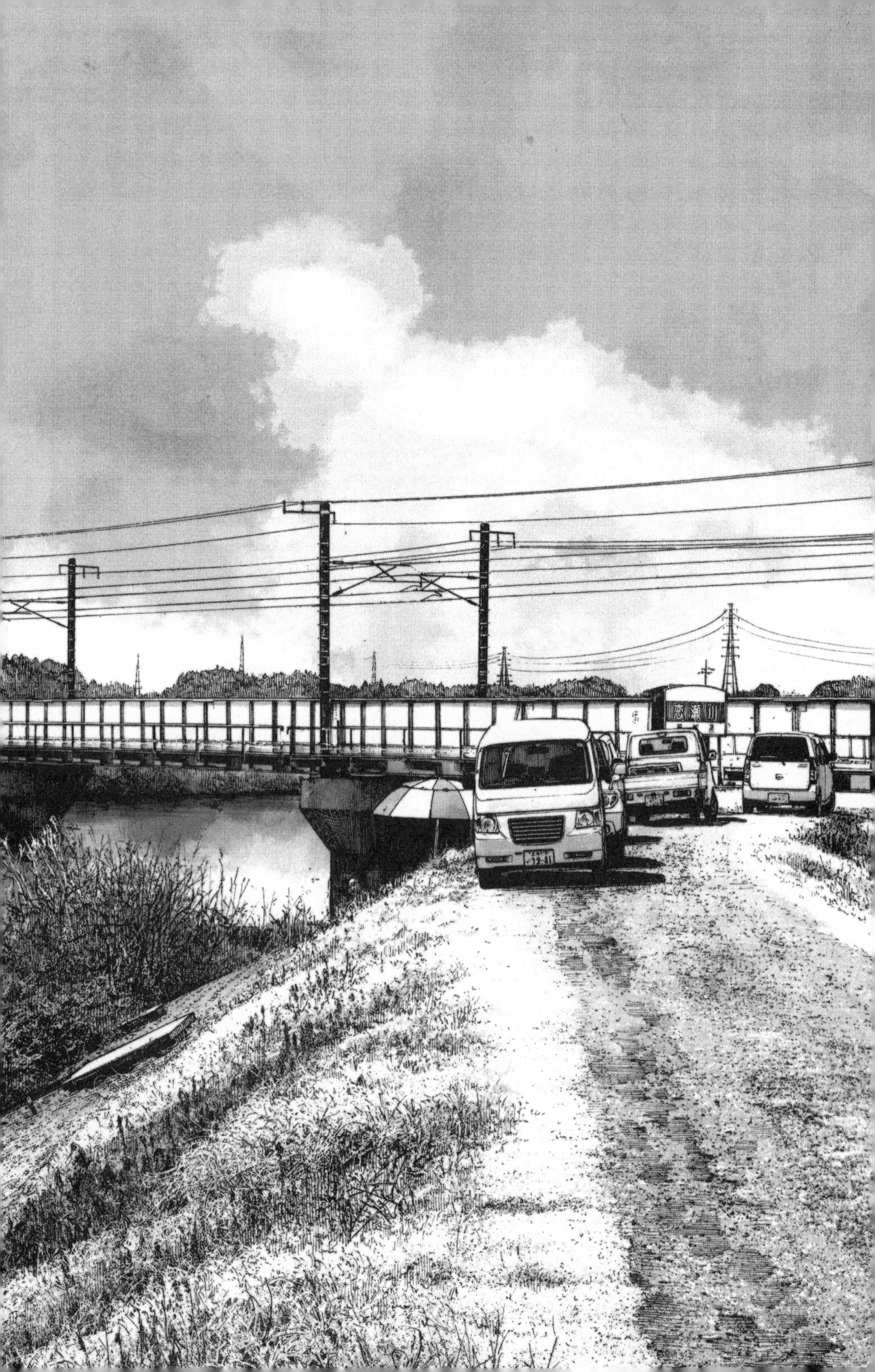
恋瀬川

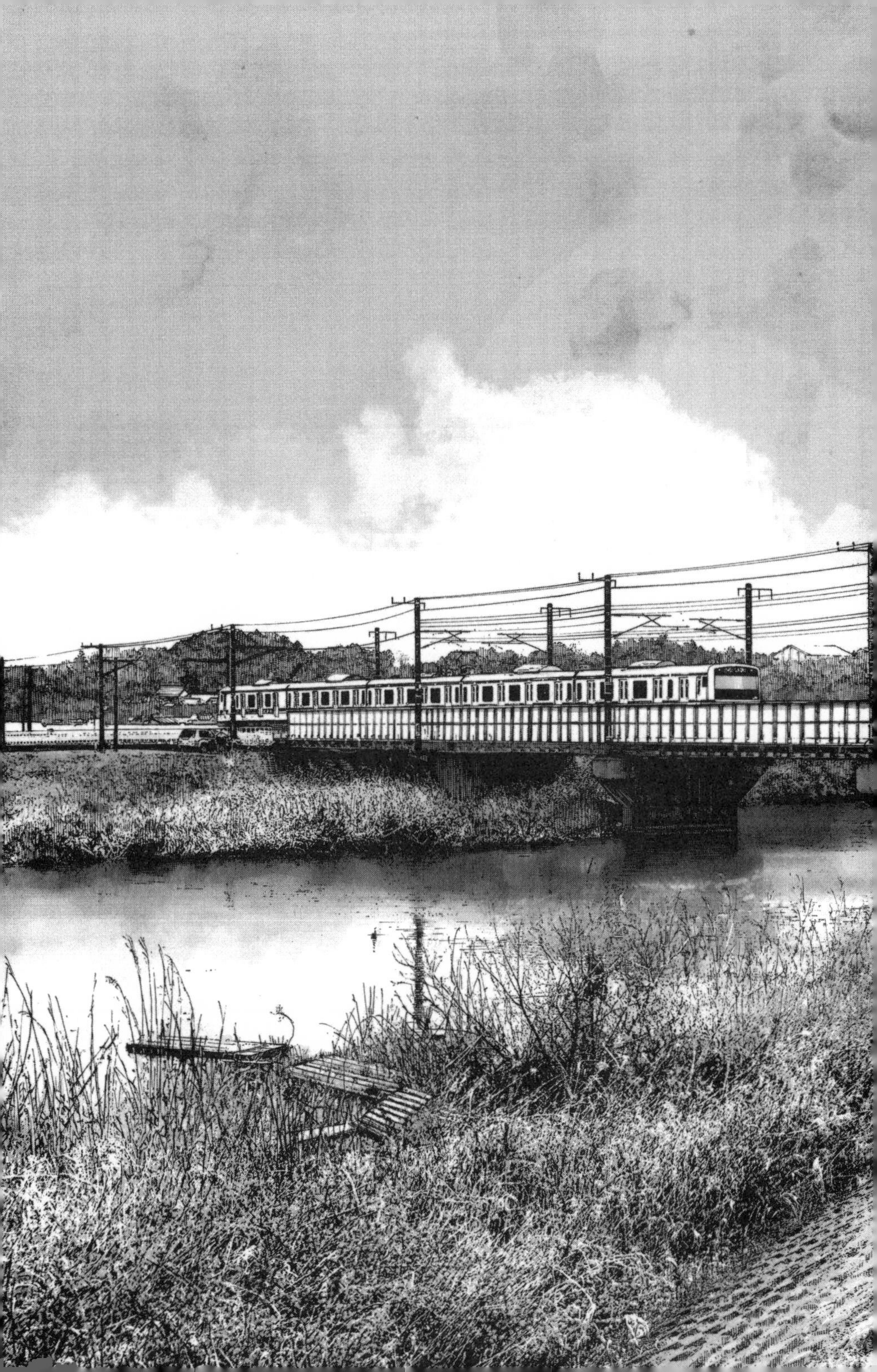

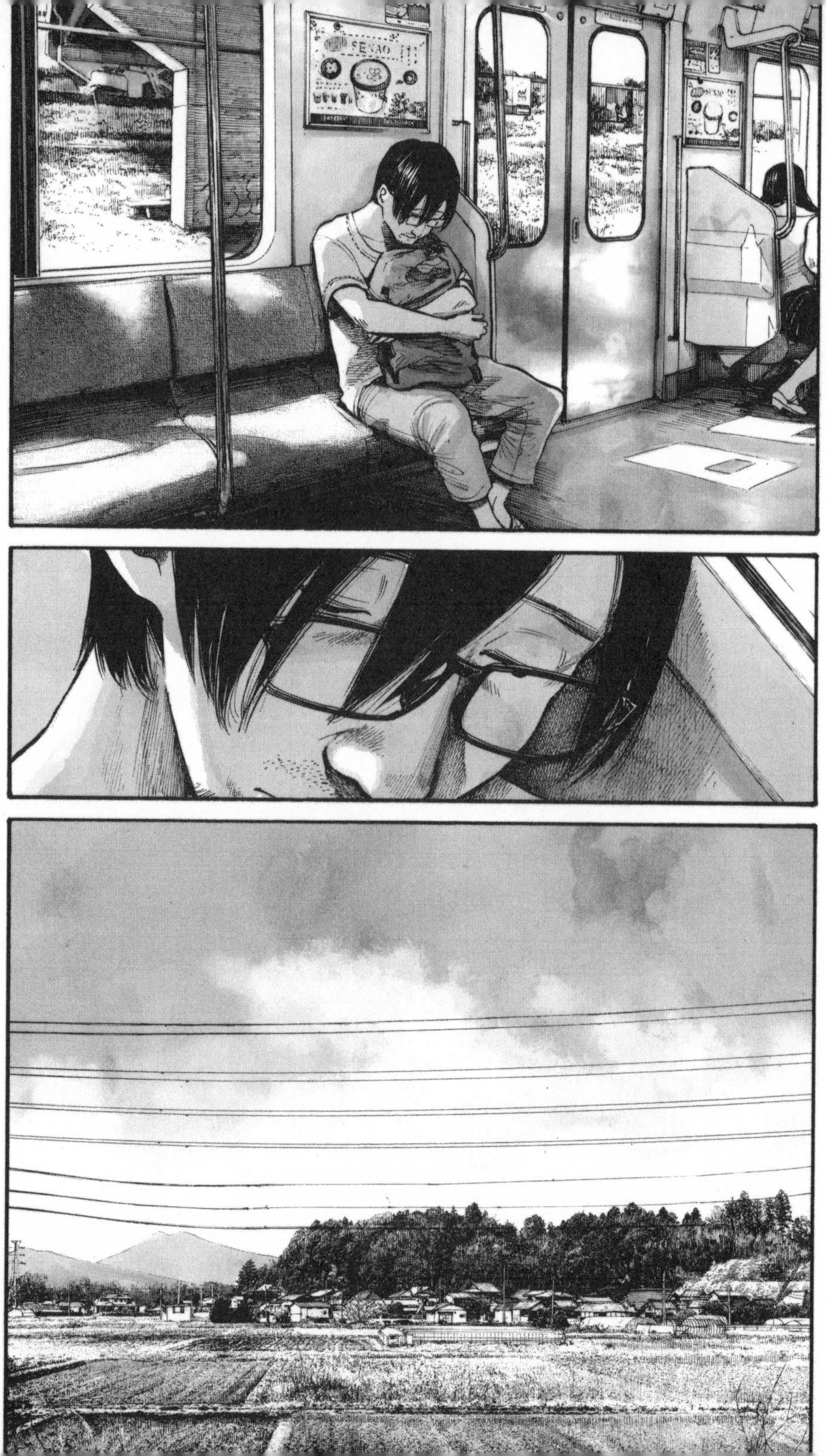
SENAO

At the end of summer, my wife moved out and I got rid of my studio and moved back home.

And now, a few months later, I still haven't unpacked or cleaned up or done any work. But the hardest part is being alone and not being able to see the cat whenever I want.

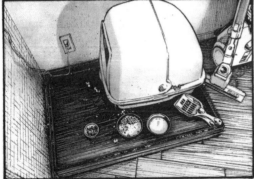

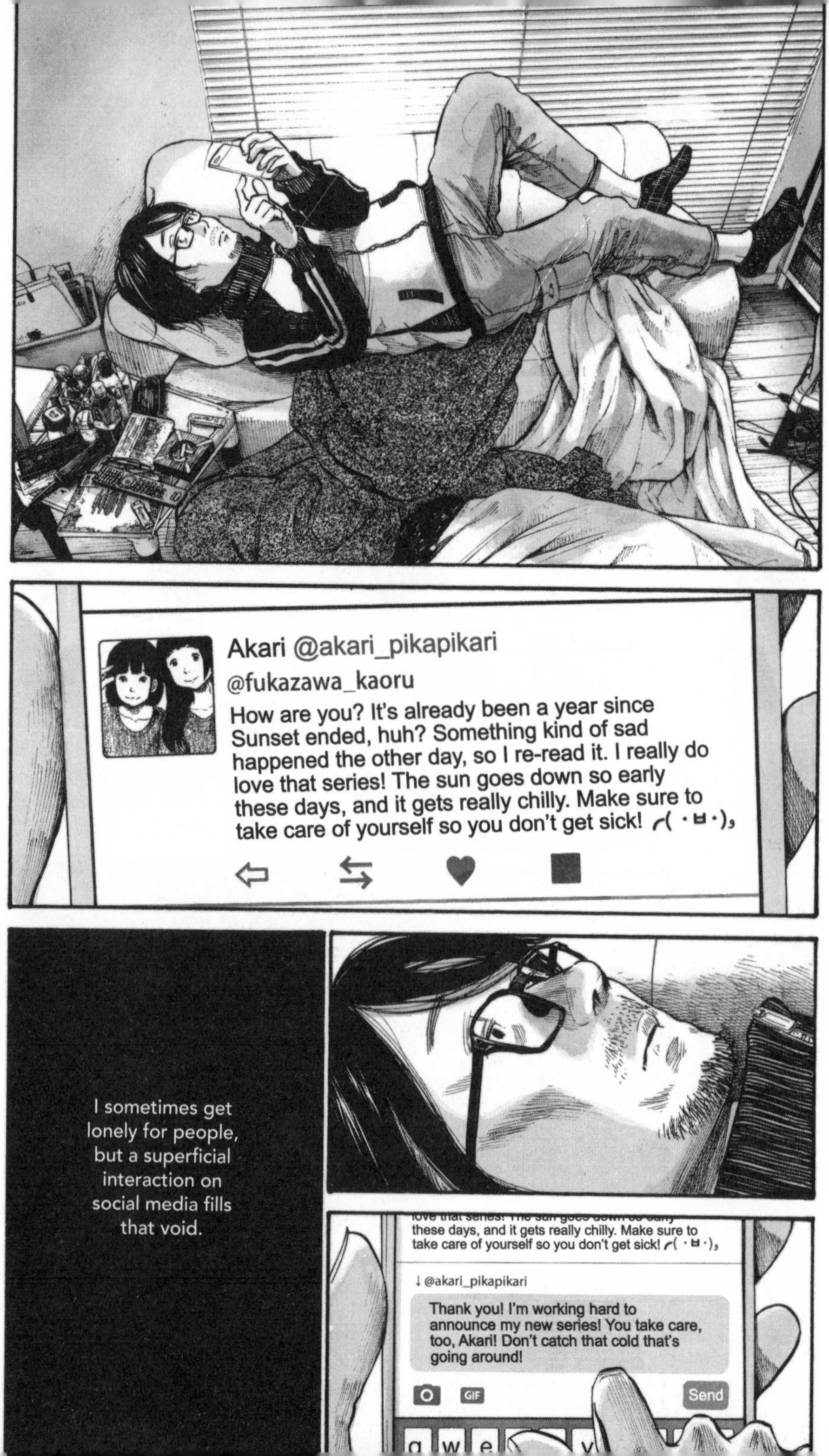
Akari @akari_pikapikari
@fukazawa_kaoru
How are you? It's already been a year since Sunset ended, huh? Something kind of sad happened the other day, so I re-read it. I really do love that series! The sun goes down so early these days, and it gets really chilly. Make sure to take care of yourself so you don't get sick! ╭(･ㅂ･)و
these days, and it gets really chilly. Make sure to take care of yourself so you don't get sick! ╭(･ㅂ･)و
↓@akari_pikapikari
Thank you! I'm working hard to announce my new series! You take care, too, Akari! Don't catch that cold that's going around!
GIF
Send
I sometimes get lonely for people, but a superficial interaction on social media fills that void.

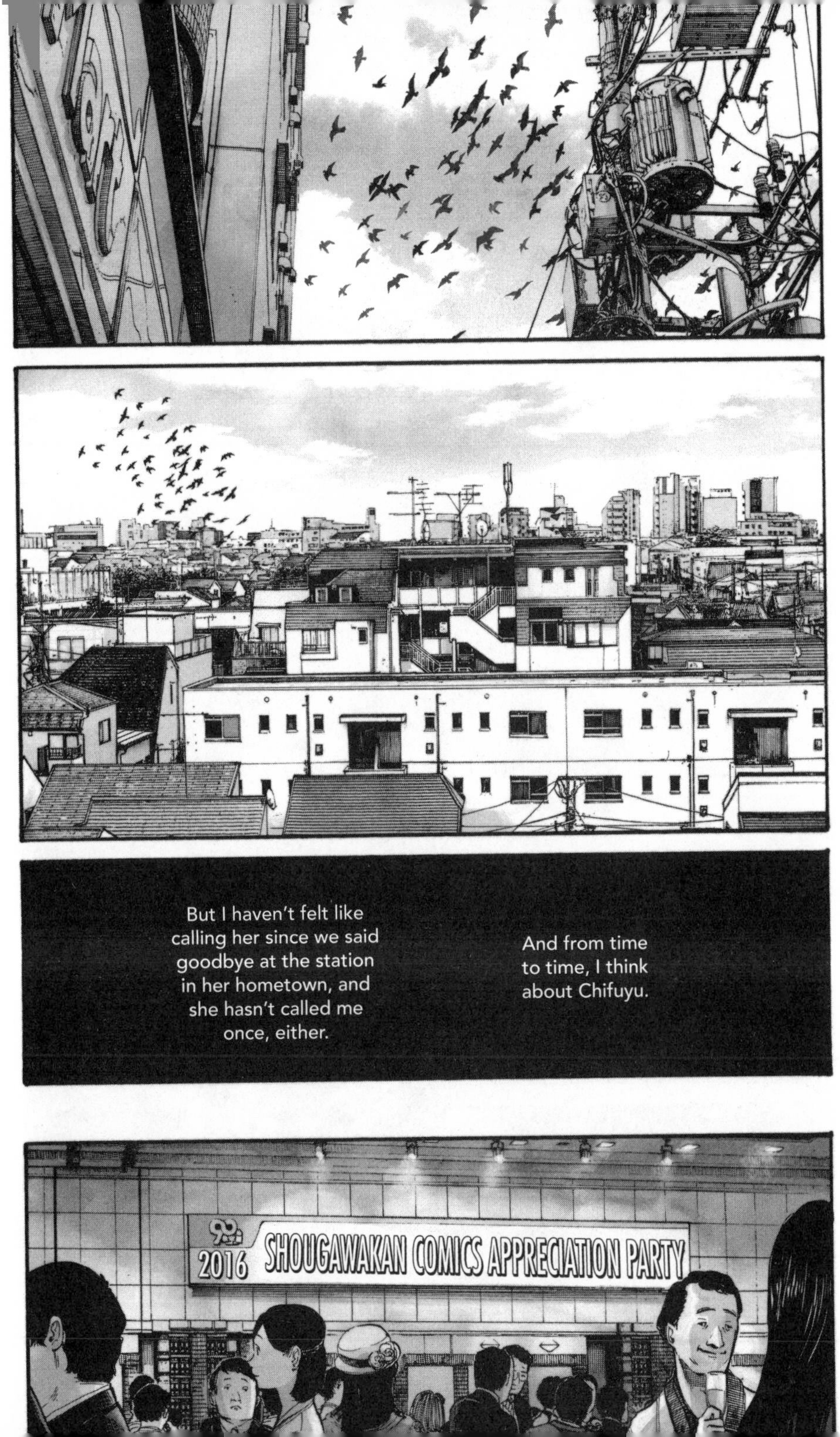
And from time to time, I think about Chifuyu.
But I haven't felt like calling her since we said goodbye at the station in her hometown, and she hasn't called me once, either.
2016
SHOUGAWAKAN COMICS APPRECIATION PARTY

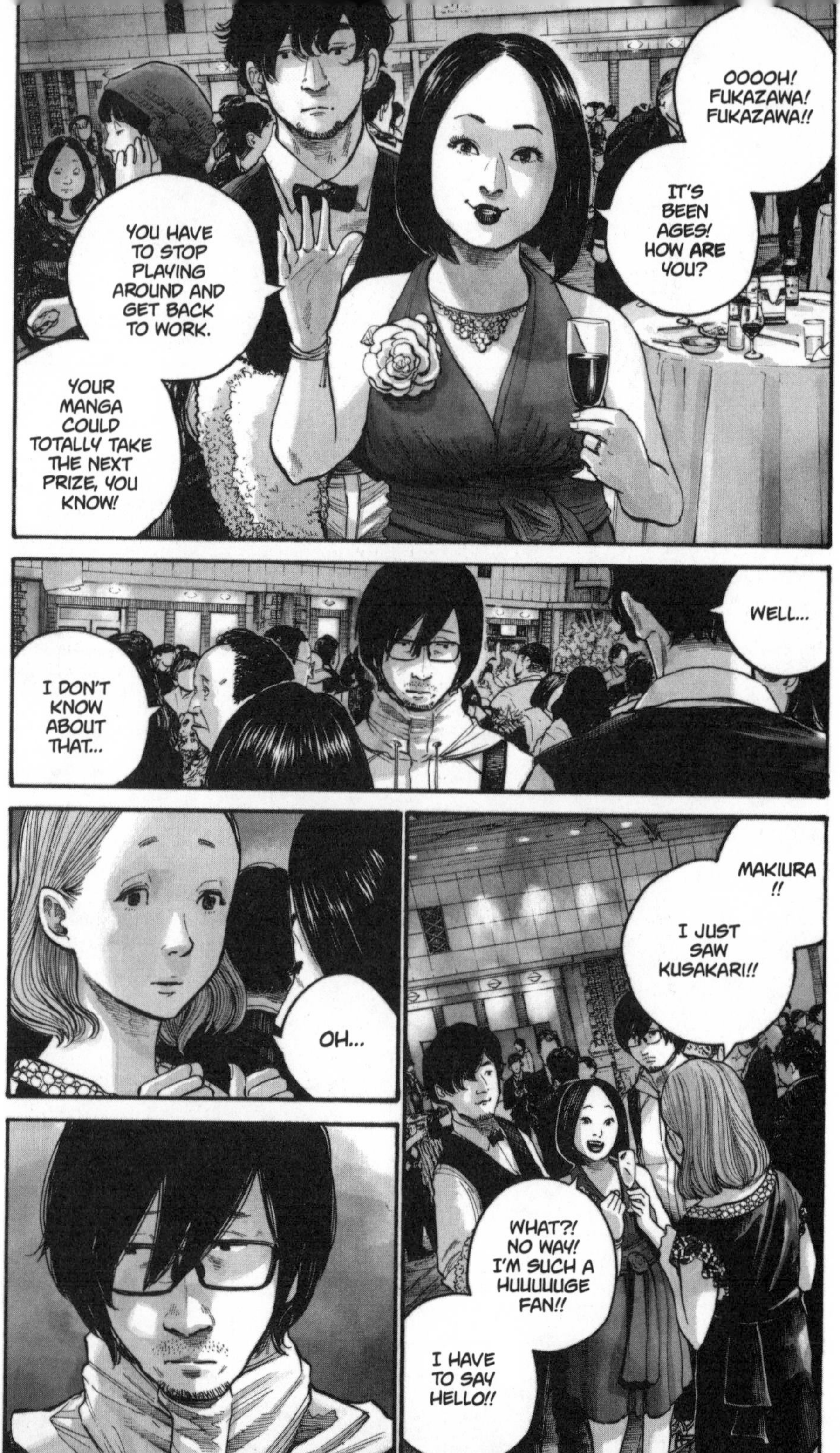
OOOOH! FUKAZAWA! FUKAZAWA!!
IT'S BEEN AGES! HOW ARE YOU?
YOU HAVE TO STOP PLAYING AROUND AND GET BACK TO WORK.
YOUR MANGA COULD TOTALLY TAKE THE NEXT PRIZE, YOU KNOW!
WELL...
I DON'T KNOW ABOUT THAT...
MAKIURA!!
I JUST SAW KUSAKARI!!
WHAT?! NO WAY! I'M SUCH A HUUUUUGE FAN!!
I HAVE TO SAY HELLO!!
OH...

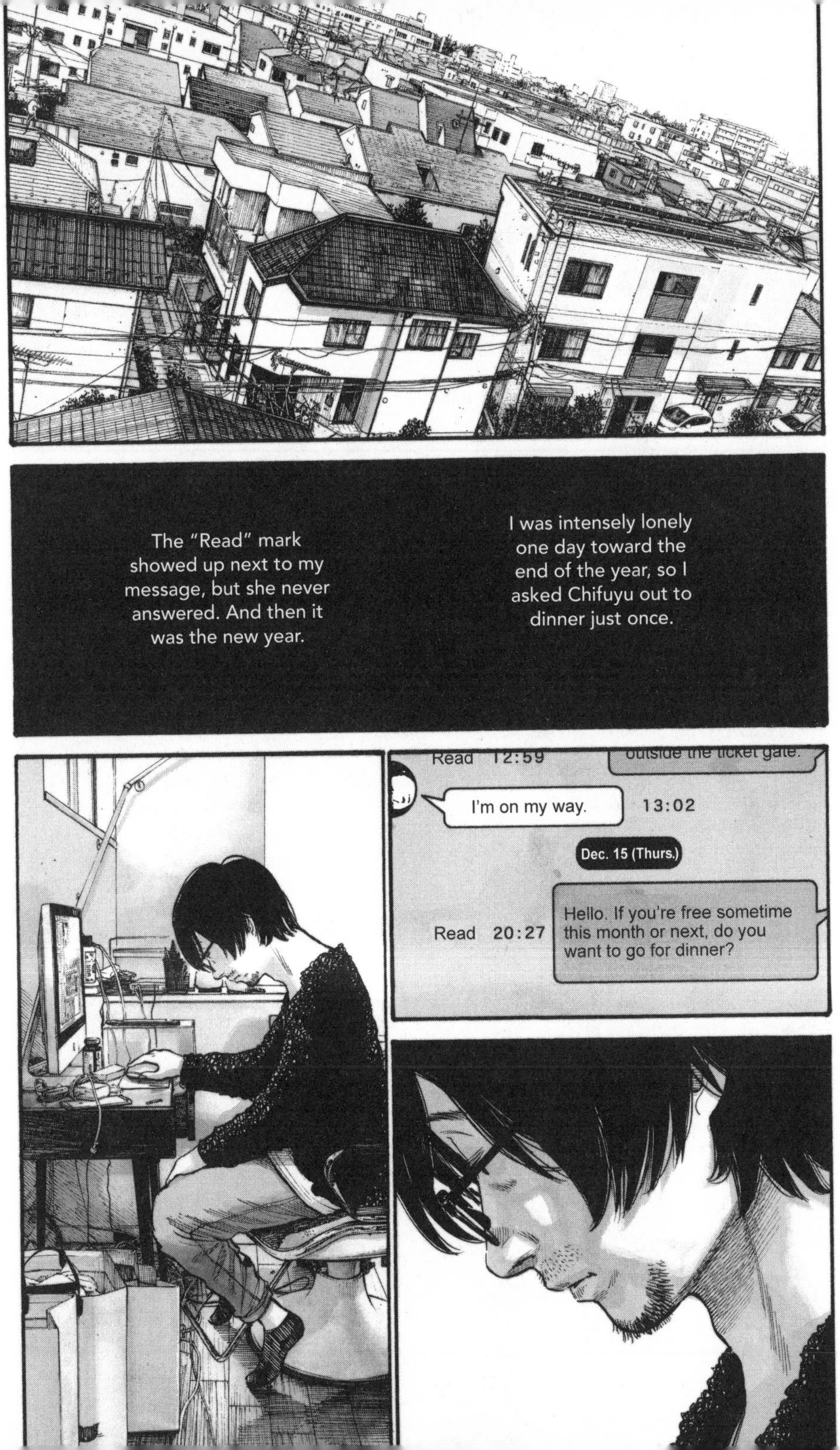

I was intensely lonely one day toward the end of the year, so I asked Chifuyu out to dinner just once.
The "Read" mark showed up next to my message, but she never answered. And then it was the new year.
outside the ticket gate.
Read 12:59
I'm on my way.
13:02
Dec. 15 (Thurs.)
Read 20:27
Hello. If you're free sometime this month or next, do you want to go for dinner?

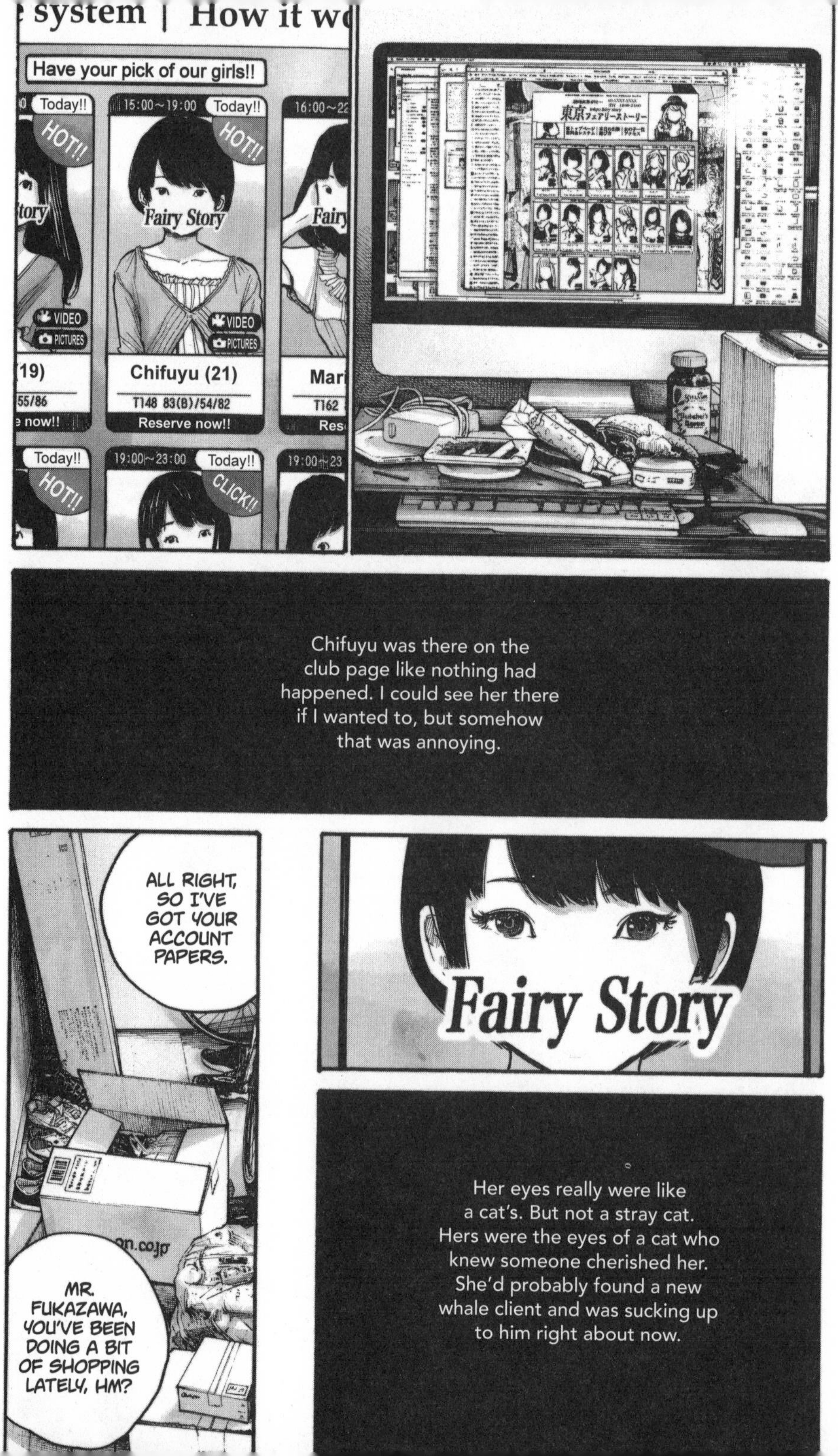
東京
フェアリーストーリー
system | How it w
Have your pick of our girls!!
Today!!
HOT!!
15:00～19:00
Today!!
HOT!!
Fairy Story
VIDEO
PICTURES
Chifuyu (21)
T148 83(B)/54/82
Reserve now!!
16:00～22
(19)
55/86
Mari
T162
19:00～23:00
Today!!
CLICK!!
Today!!
HOT!!
Chifuyu was there on the club page like nothing had happened. I could see her there if I wanted to, but somehow that was annoying.
Fairy Story
Her eyes really were like a cat's. But not a stray cat. Hers were the eyes of a cat who knew someone cherished her. She'd probably found a new whale client and was sucking up to him right about now.
ALL RIGHT, SO I'VE GOT YOUR ACCOUNT PAPERS.
MR. FUKAZAWA, YOU'VE BEEN DOING A BIT OF SHOPPING LATELY, HM?

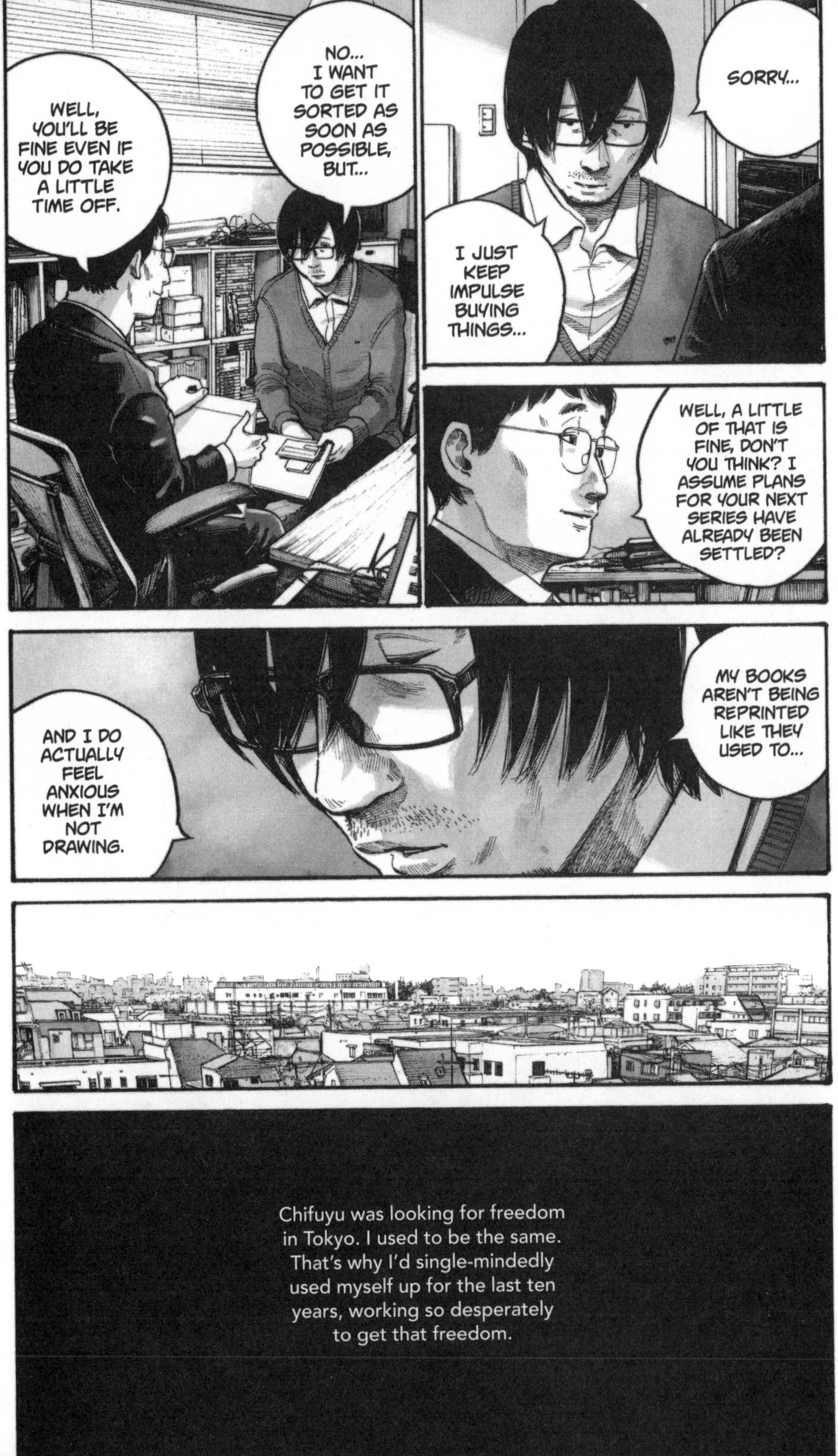
WELL, YOU'LL BE FINE EVEN IF YOU DO TAKE A LITTLE TIME OFF.
NO... I WANT TO GET IT SORTED AS SOON AS POSSIBLE, BUT...
SORRY...
I JUST KEEP IMPULSE BUYING THINGS...
WELL, A LITTLE OF THAT IS FINE, DON'T YOU THINK? I ASSUME PLANS FOR YOUR NEXT SERIES HAVE ALREADY BEEN SETTLED?
AND I DO ACTUALLY FEEL ANXIOUS WHEN I'M NOT DRAWING.
MY BOOKS AREN'T BEING REPRINTED LIKE THEY USED TO...
Chifuyu was looking for freedom in Tokyo. I used to be the same. That's why I'd single-mindedly used myself up for the last ten years, working so desperately to get that freedom.

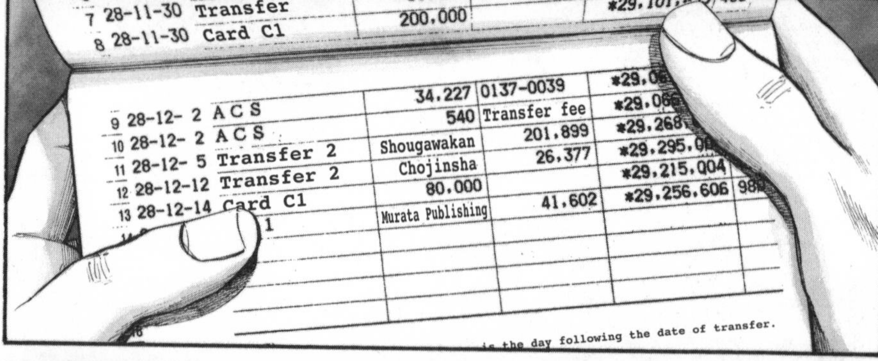
7 28-11-30 Transfer
8 28-11-30 Card C1 200,000
34,227 0137-0039
9 28-12- 2 A C S 540 Transfer fee
10 28-12- 2 A C S Shougawakan 201,899
11 28-12- 5 Transfer 2 Chojinsha 26,377
12 28-12-12 Transfer 2 80,000 *29,215,004
13 28-12-14 Card C1 Murata Publishing 41,602 *29,256,606
the day following the date of transfer.

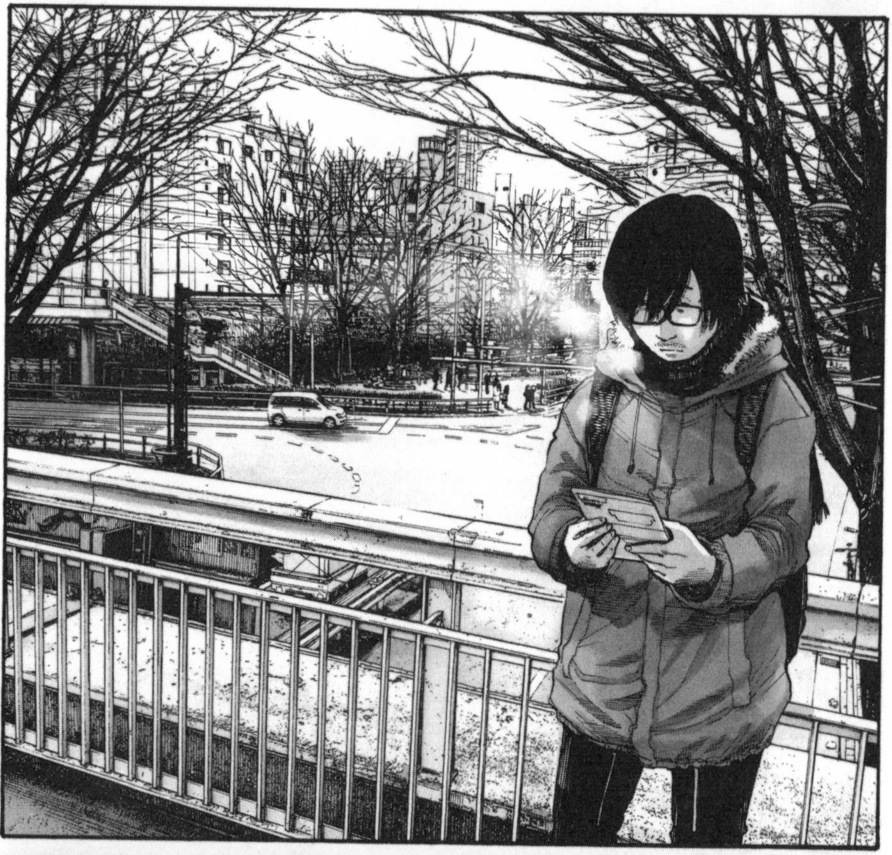

And in exchange for
ten years of servitude,
I'd managed to get just a
couple of years of freedom.

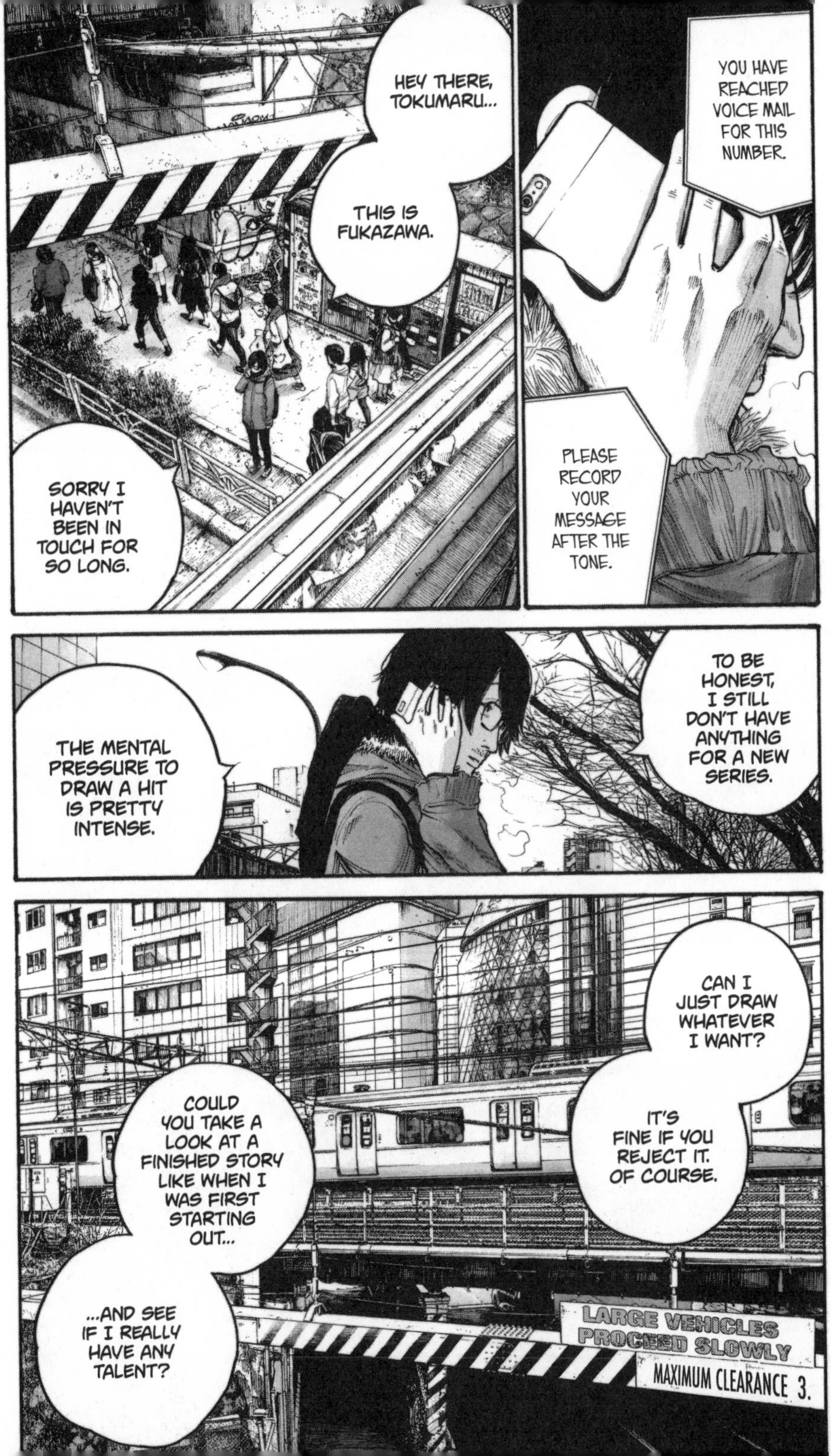
YOU HAVE REACHED VOICE MAIL FOR THIS NUMBER.
PLEASE RECORD YOUR MESSAGE AFTER THE TONE.
HEY THERE, TOKUMARU...
THIS IS FUKAZAWA.
SORRY I HAVEN'T BEEN IN TOUCH FOR SO LONG.
TO BE HONEST, I STILL DON'T HAVE ANYTHING FOR A NEW SERIES.
THE MENTAL PRESSURE TO DRAW A HIT IS PRETTY INTENSE.
CAN I JUST DRAW WHATEVER I WANT?
IT'S FINE IF YOU REJECT IT. OF COURSE.
COULD YOU TAKE A LOOK AT A FINISHED STORY LIKE WHEN I WAS FIRST STARTING OUT...
...AND SEE IF I REALLY HAVE ANY TALENT?
LARGE VEHICLES PROCEED SLOWLY
MAXIMUM CLEARANCE 3.

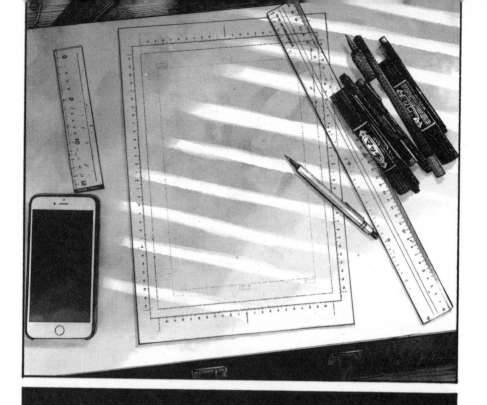

When I sat down with
a blank page for the first
time in a long time, it spread
out endlessly before me.
I had trouble breathing.

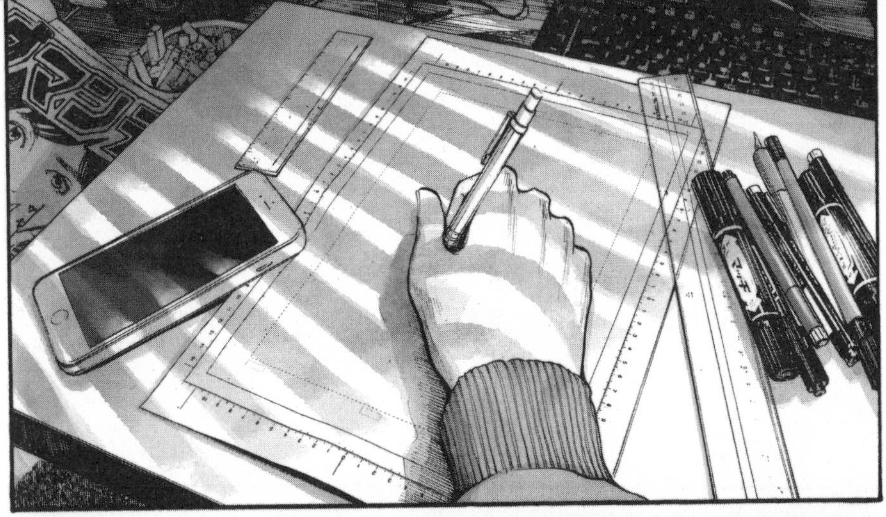

If I were still in my teens,
I might have raced along
innocently on the infinity
of that empty page.

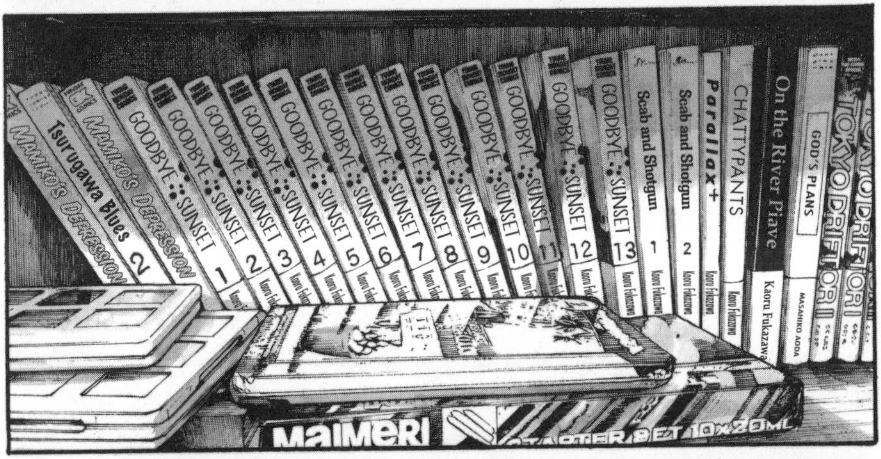
Mamiko's Depression
Tsurugawa Blues 2
Mamiko's Depression
GOODBYE SUNSET 1
GOODBYE SUNSET 2
GOODBYE SUNSET 3
GOODBYE SUNSET 4
GOODBYE SUNSET 5
GOODBYE SUNSET 6
GOODBYE SUNSET 7
GOODBYE SUNSET 8
GOODBYE SUNSET 9
GOODBYE SUNSET 10
GOODBYE SUNSET 11
GOODBYE SUNSET 12
GOODBYE SUNSET 13
Scab and Shotgun 1
Scab and Shotgun 2
Parallax+
CHATTYPANTS
Kaoru Fukazawa
On the River Piave
Kaoru Fukazawa
GOD'S PLANS
MASAHIKO AODA
TOKYO DRIFTOR II
TOKYO DRIFTOR I
MAIMERI
STARTER SET 10x20ML

If I were in my twenties,
I would've been spurred on by
the anxiety and frustration of
not being someone yet.
I could've used all that angst.

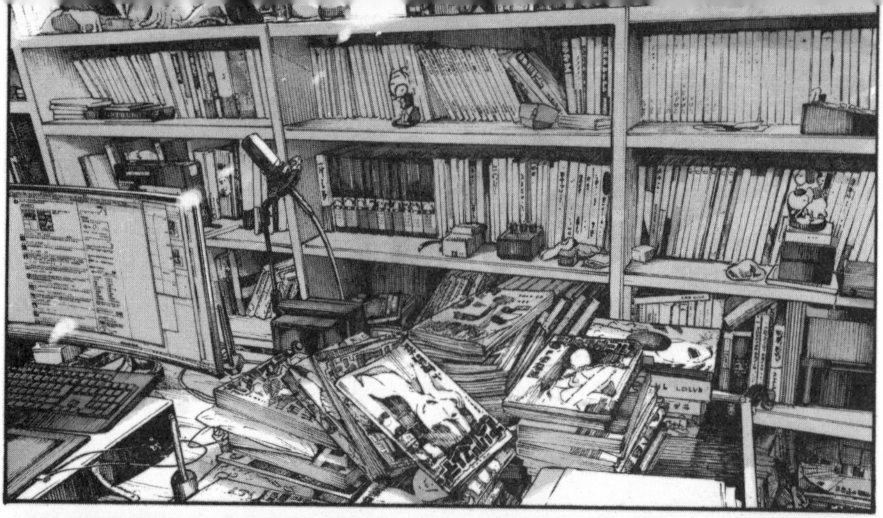

I slipped through most of my thirties knowing what it was like to be accepted by others and feeling the pain of the expectations those people put on me.

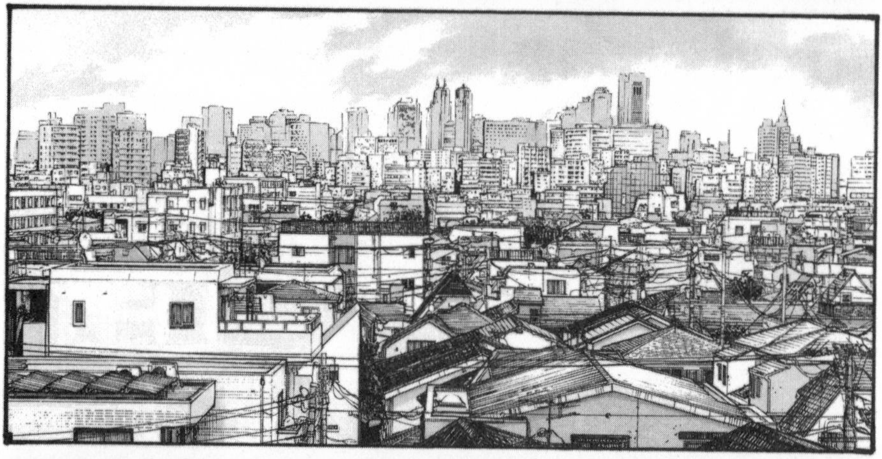

All that's left to me here and now is a worn-out body and some money in the bank.

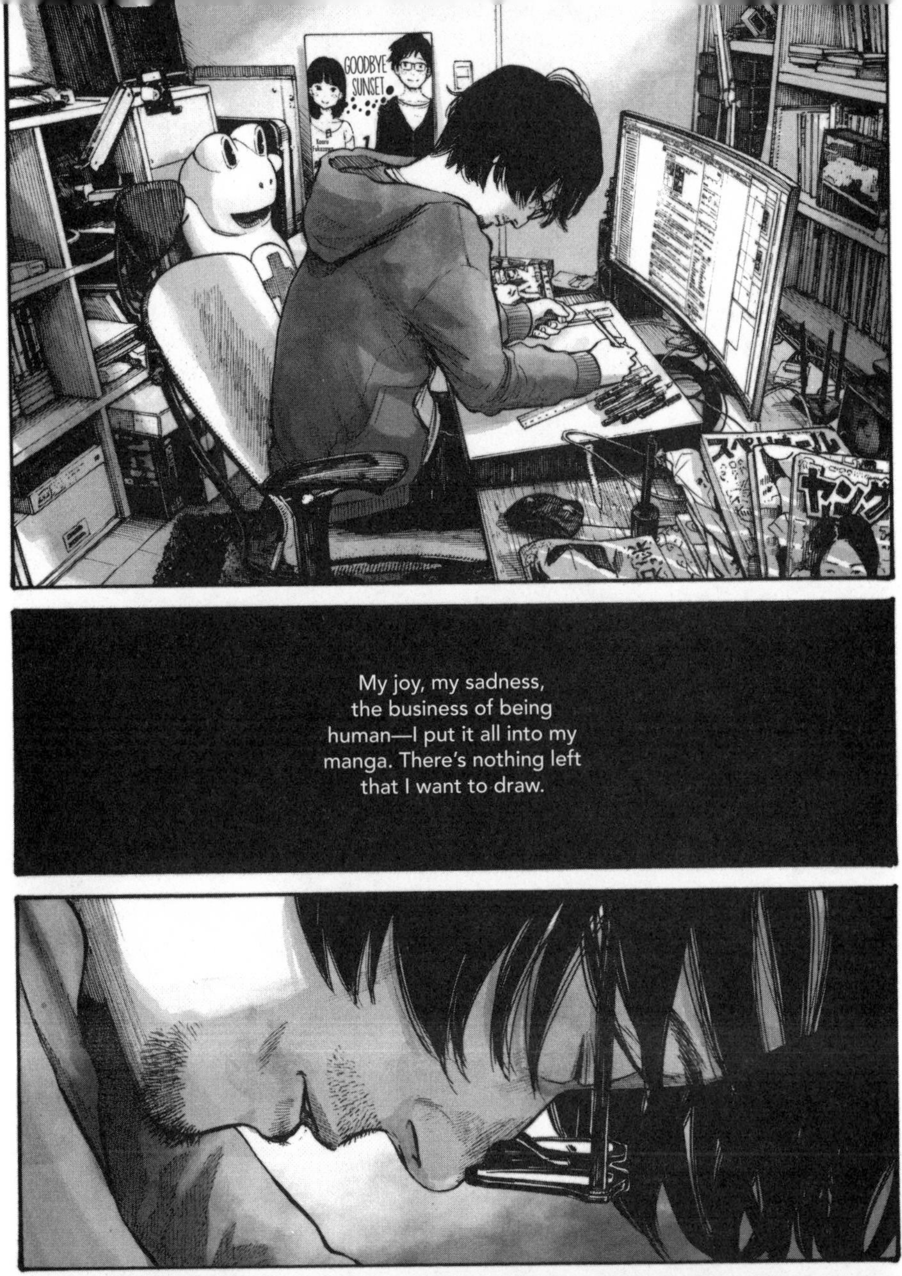
GOODBYE SUNSET
My joy, my sadness, the business of being human—I put it all into my manga. There's nothing left that I want to draw.

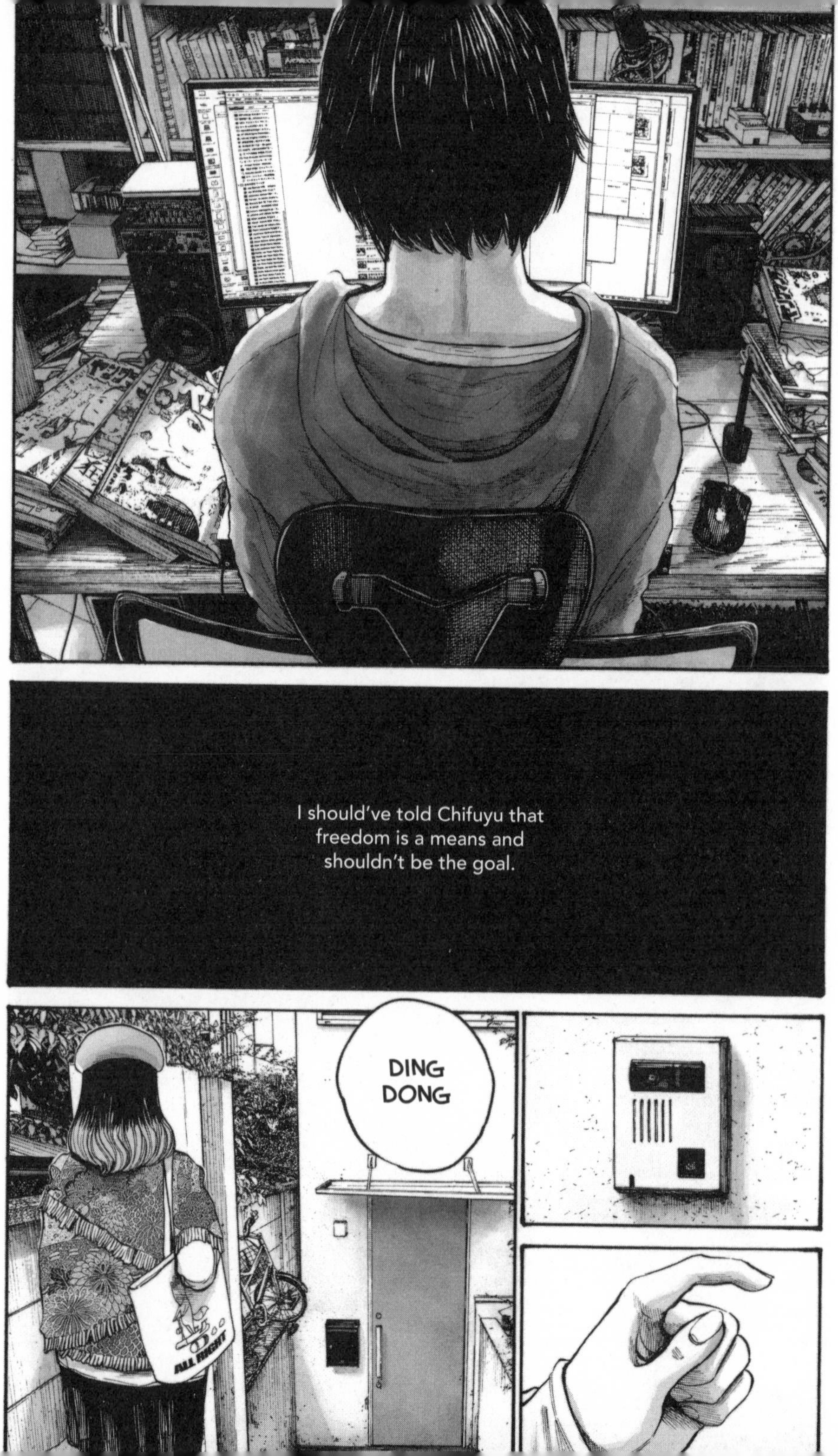
I should've told Chifuyu that freedom is a means and shouldn't be the goal.
DING DONG

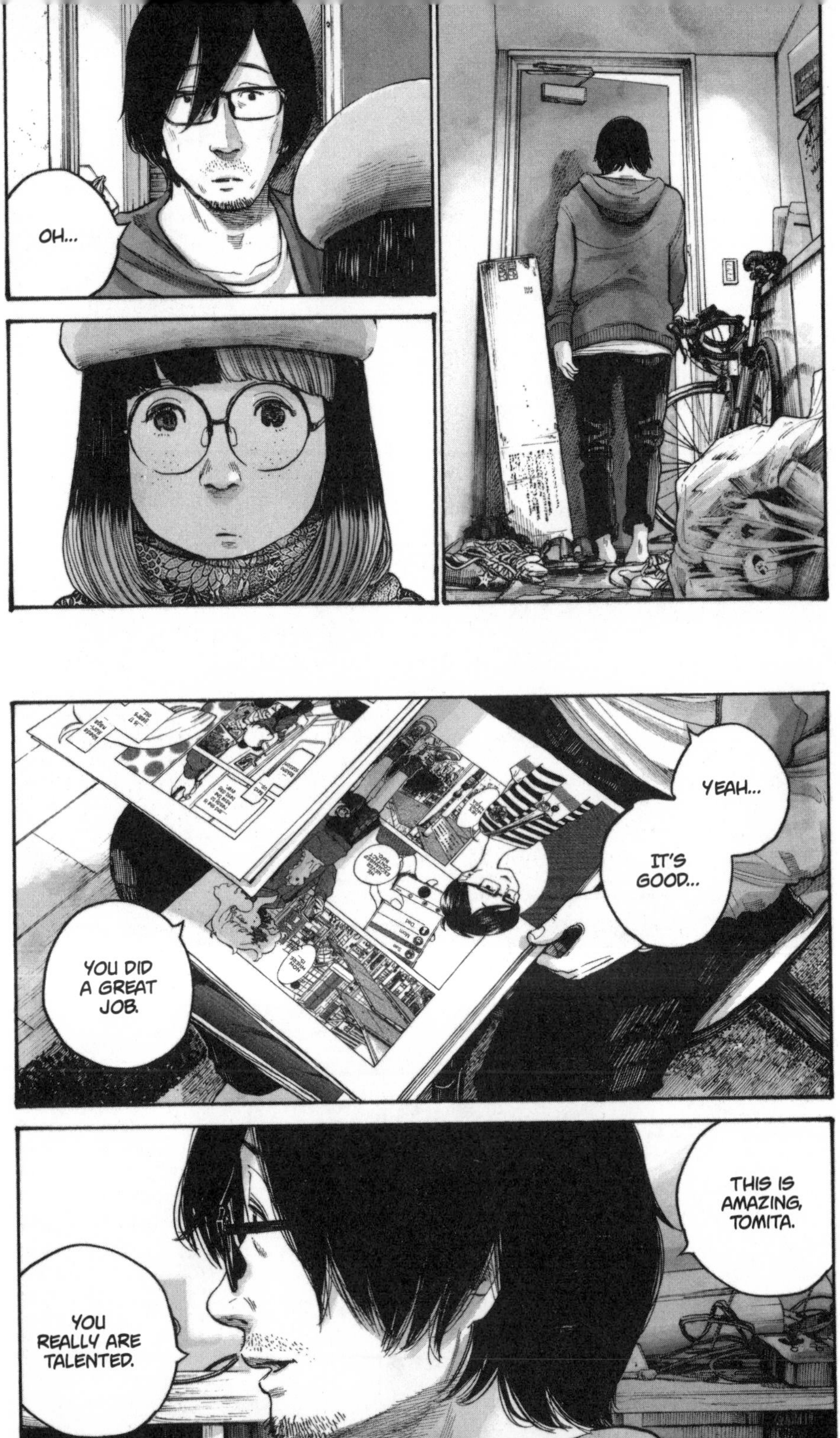
OH...
YEAH...
IT'S GOOD...
YOU DID A GREAT JOB.
THIS IS AMAZING, TOMITA.
YOU REALLY ARE TALENTED.

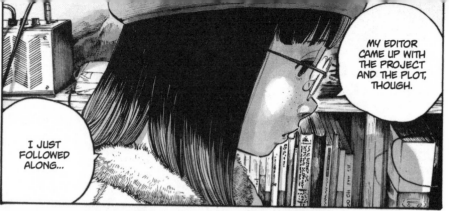

MY EDITOR CAME UP WITH THE PROJECT AND THE PLOT, THOUGH.

I JUST FOLLOWED ALONG...

BUT IT'S YOUR SKILL THAT MADE IT COME TO LIFE AS A MANGA.

HAVE SOME FAITH IN YOURSELF.

THIS WILL DEFINITELY BE A GOOD EXPERIENCE FOR YOU.

OH, SORRY. DID YOU WANT SOMETHING TO DRINK?

FUKAZAWA... UM!

RIGHT ...

I GUESS SO.

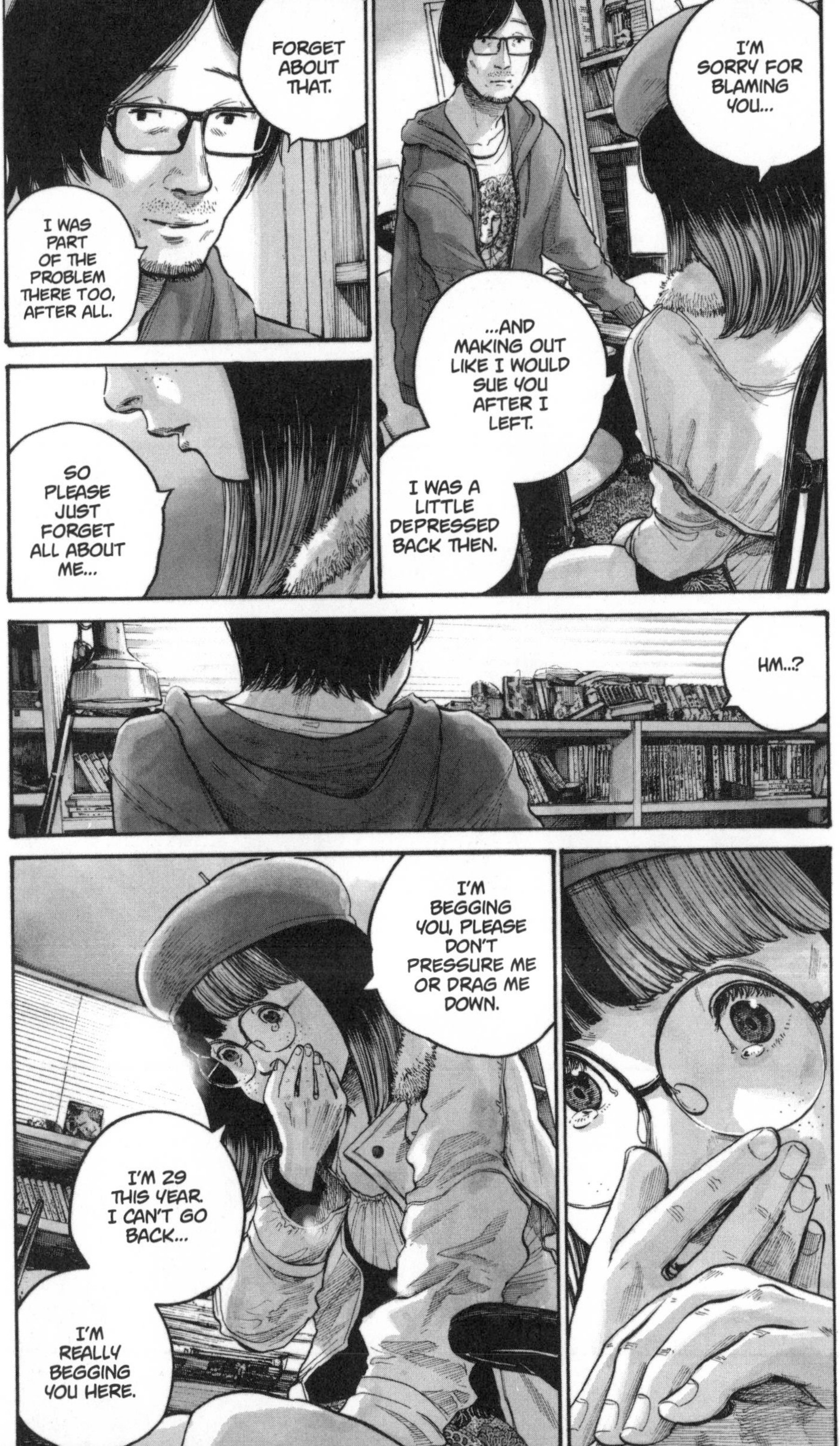
I'M SORRY FOR BLAMING YOU...
...AND MAKING OUT LIKE I WOULD SUE YOU AFTER I LEFT.
I WAS A LITTLE DEPRESSED BACK THEN.
FORGET ABOUT THAT.
I WAS PART OF THE PROBLEM THERE TOO, AFTER ALL.
SO PLEASE JUST FORGET ALL ABOUT ME...
HM...?
I'M BEGGING YOU, PLEASE DON'T PRESSURE ME OR DRAG ME DOWN.
I'M 29 THIS YEAR. I CAN'T GO BACK...
I'M REALLY BEGGING YOU HERE.

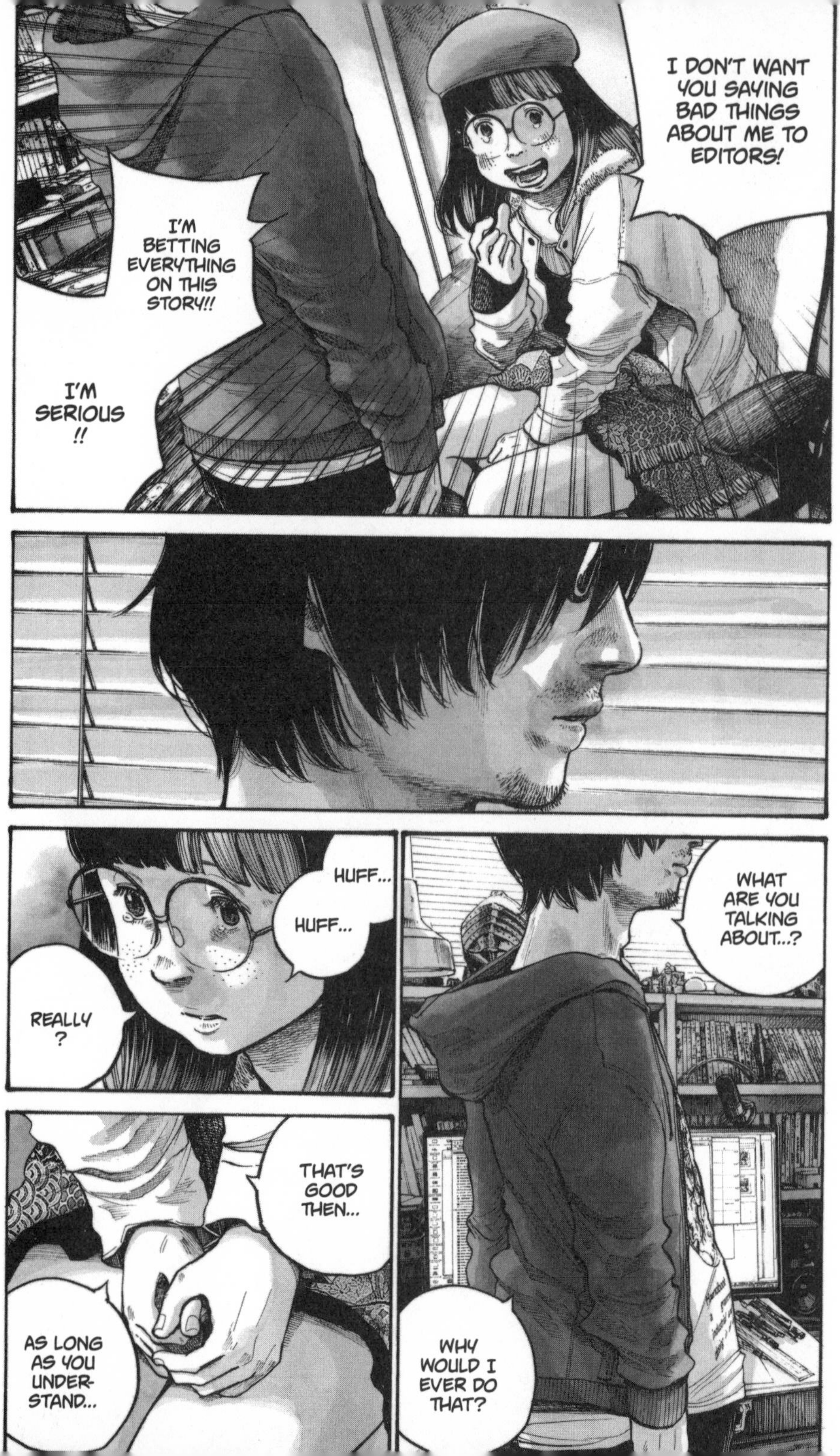
I DON'T WANT YOU SAYING BAD THINGS ABOUT ME TO EDITORS!
I'M BETTING EVERYTHING ON THIS STORY!!
I'M SERIOUS !!
WHAT ARE YOU TALKING ABOUT...?
WHY WOULD I EVER DO THAT?
HUFF...
HUFF...
REALLY ?
THAT'S GOOD THEN...
AS LONG AS YOU UNDER-STAND...

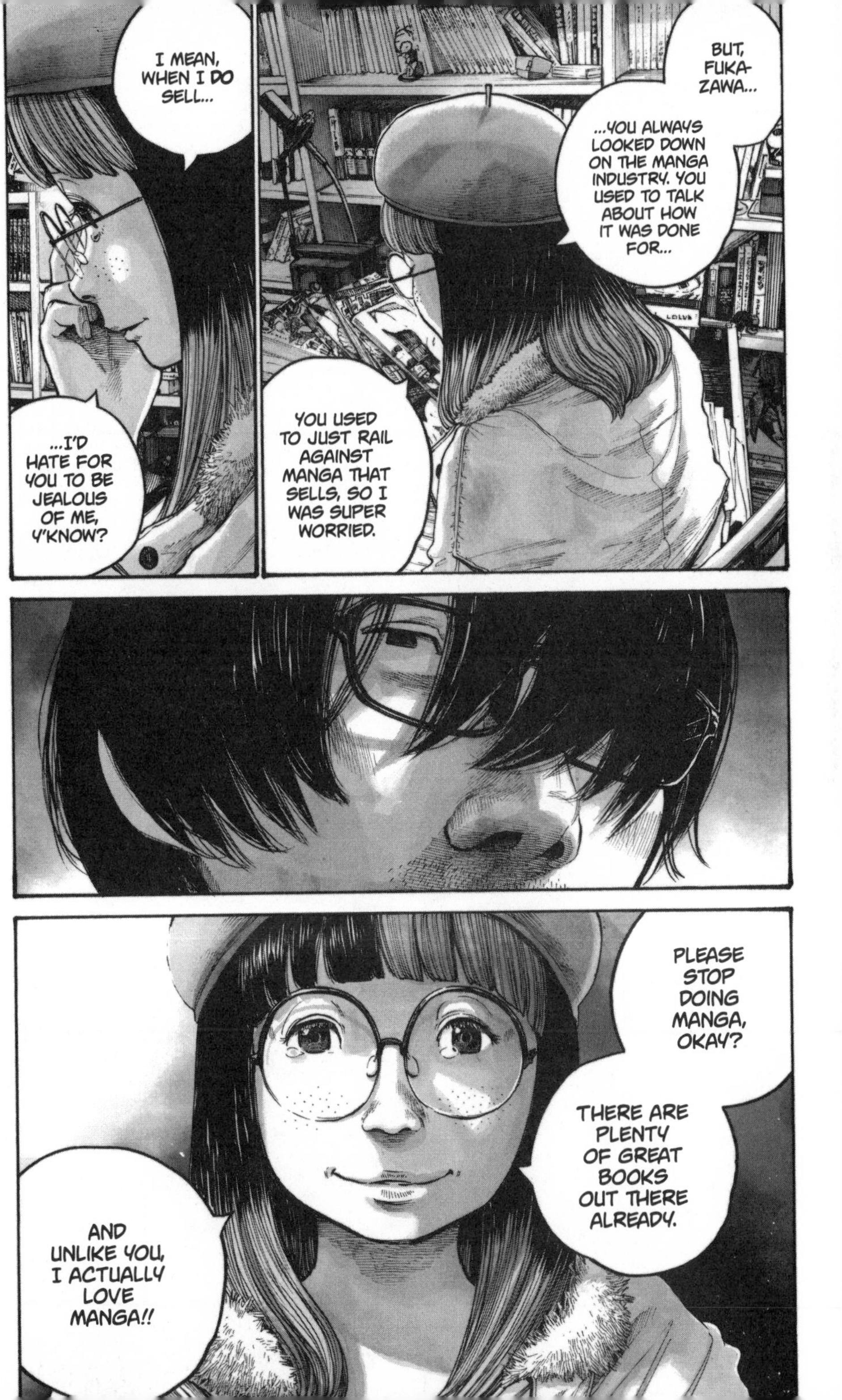
BUT, FUKA-ZAWA...
...YOU ALWAYS LOOKED DOWN ON THE MANGA INDUSTRY. YOU USED TO TALK ABOUT HOW IT WAS DONE FOR...
YOU USED TO JUST RAIL AGAINST MANGA THAT SELLS, SO I WAS SUPER WORRIED.
I MEAN, WHEN I DO SELL...
...I'D HATE FOR YOU TO BE JEALOUS OF ME, Y'KNOW?
PLEASE STOP DOING MANGA, OKAY?
THERE ARE PLENTY OF GREAT BOOKS OUT THERE ALREADY.
AND UNLIKE YOU, I ACTUALLY LOVE MANGA!!

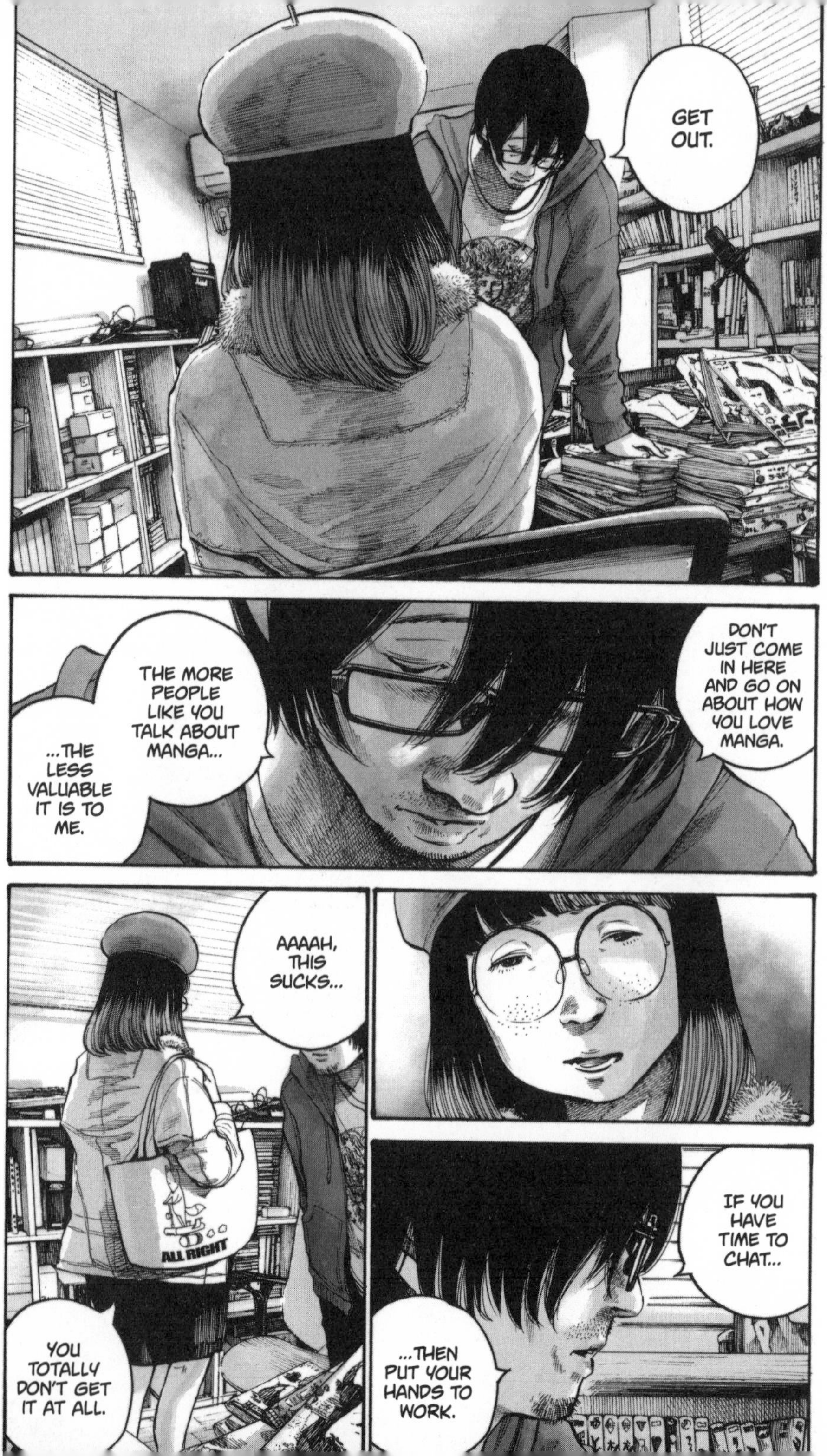
GET OUT.
DON'T JUST COME IN HERE AND GO ON ABOUT HOW YOU LOVE MANGA.
THE MORE PEOPLE LIKE YOU TALK ABOUT MANGA...
...THE LESS VALUABLE IT IS TO ME.
IF YOU HAVE TIME TO CHAT...
...THEN PUT YOUR HANDS TO WORK.
AAAAH, THIS SUCKS...
ALL RIGHT
YOU TOTALLY DON'T GET IT AT ALL.

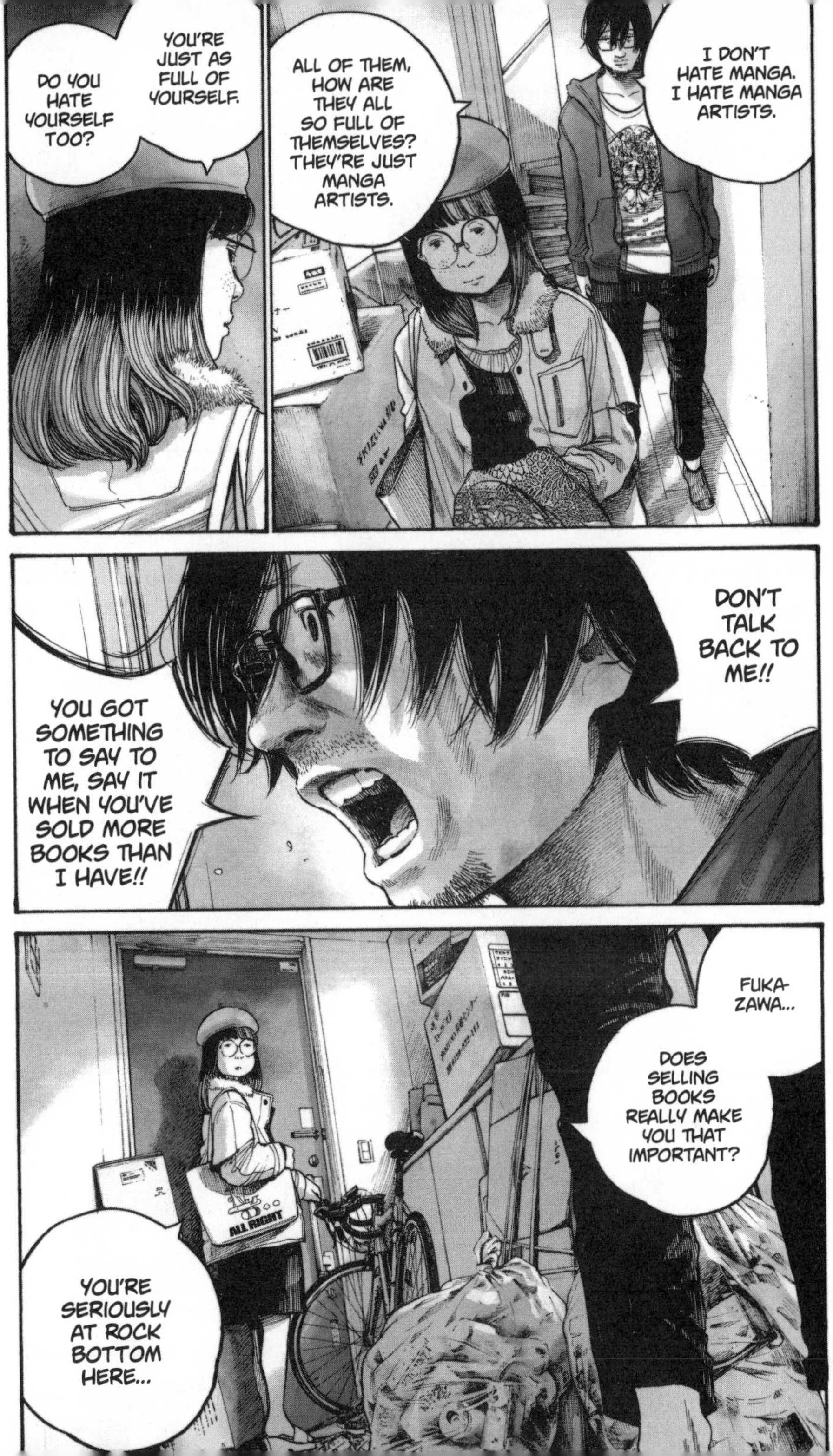
I DON'T HATE MANGA. I HATE MANGA ARTISTS.
ALL OF THEM, HOW ARE THEY ALL SO FULL OF THEMSELVES? THEY'RE JUST MANGA ARTISTS.
YOU'RE JUST AS FULL OF YOURSELF.
DO YOU HATE YOURSELF TOO?
DON'T TALK BACK TO ME!!
YOU GOT SOMETHING TO SAY TO ME, SAY IT WHEN YOU'VE SOLD MORE BOOKS THAN I HAVE!!
FUKA-ZAWA...
DOES SELLING BOOKS REALLY MAKE YOU THAT IMPORTANT?
ALL RIGHT
YOU'RE SERIOUSLY AT ROCK BOTTOM HERE...

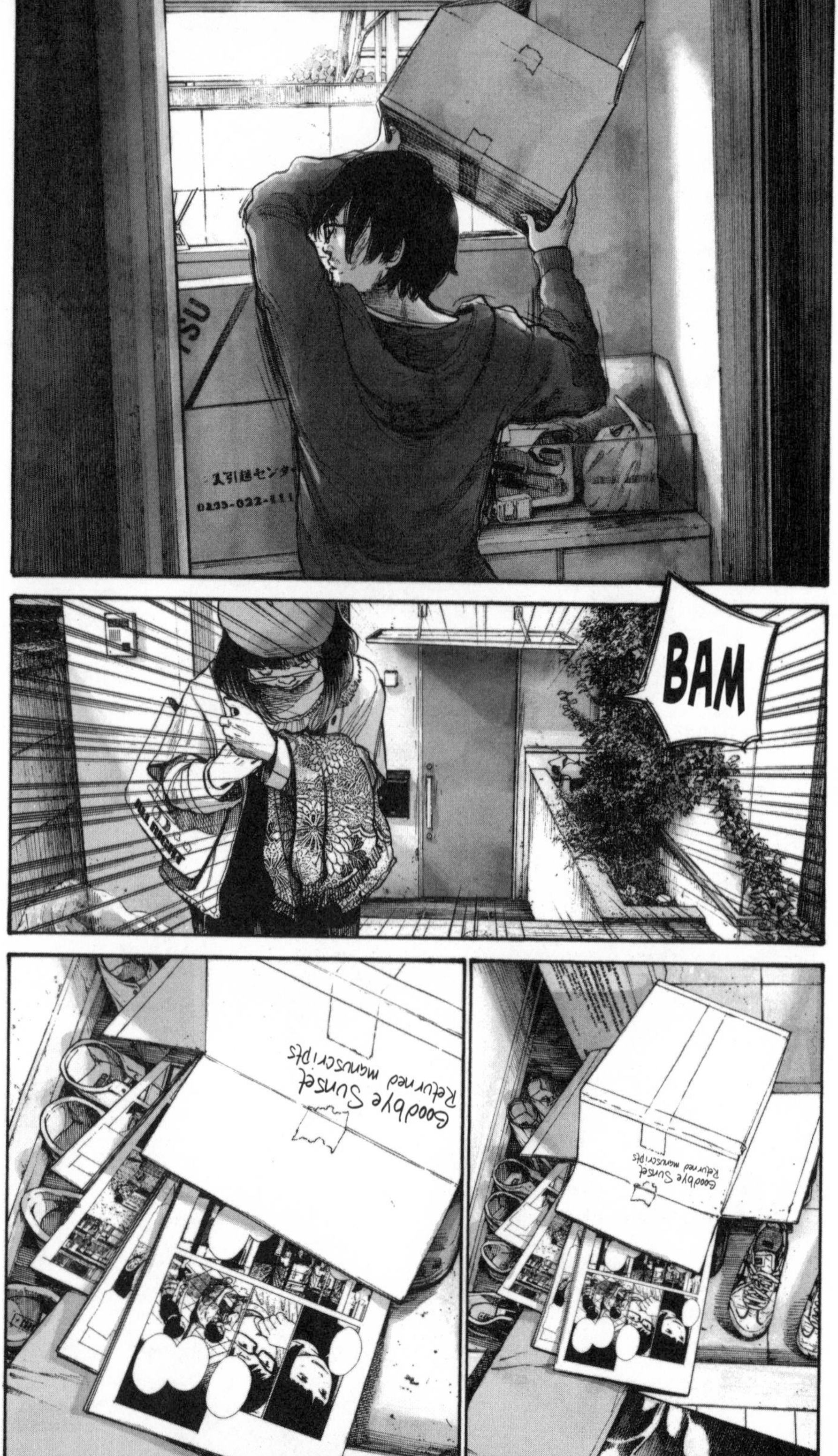
BAM
Goodbye Sunset
Returned manuscripts
Goodbye Sunset
Returned manuscripts

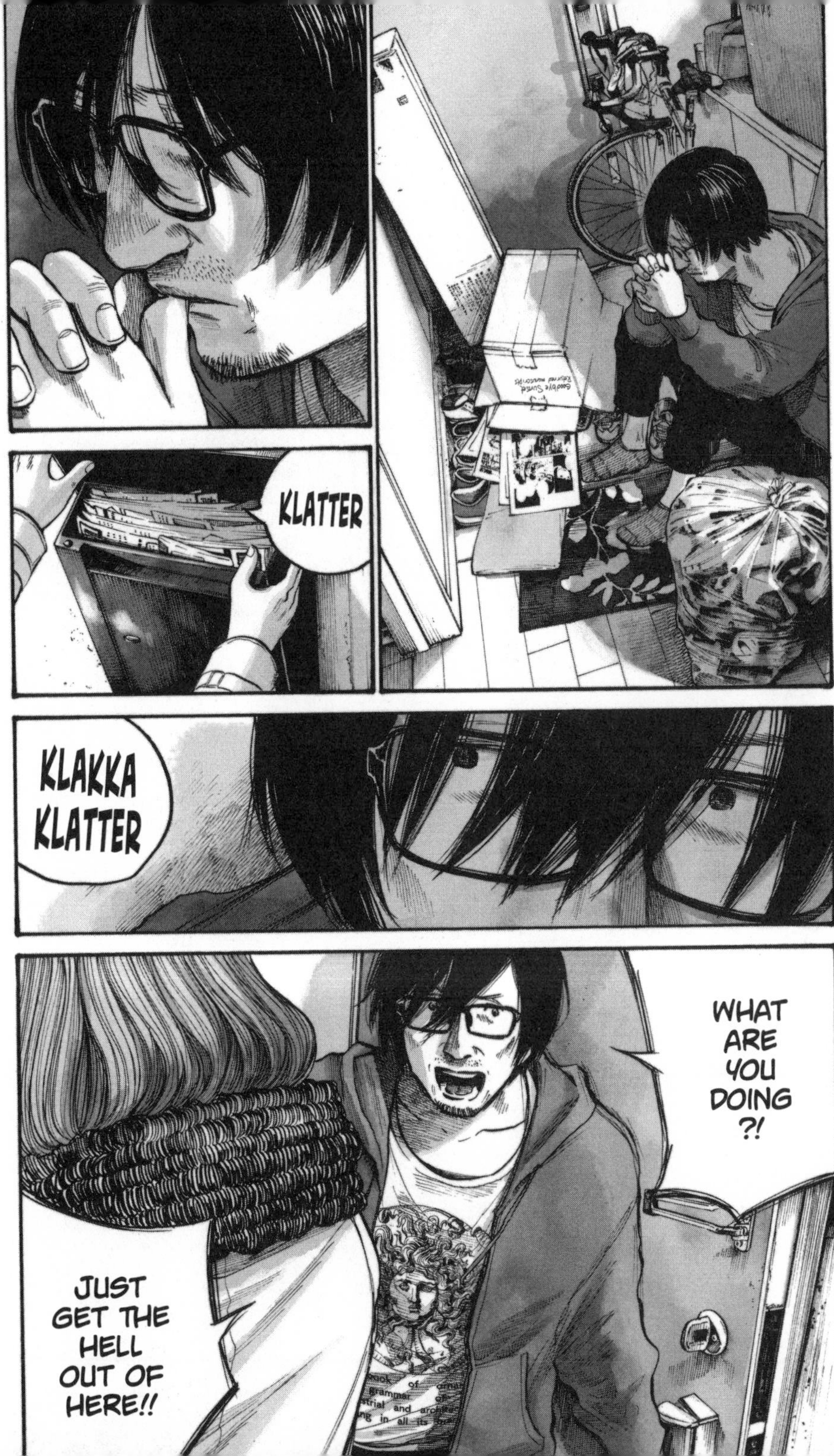
KLATTER
KLAKKA KLATTER
WHAT ARE YOU DOING ?!
JUST GET THE HELL OUT OF HERE!!

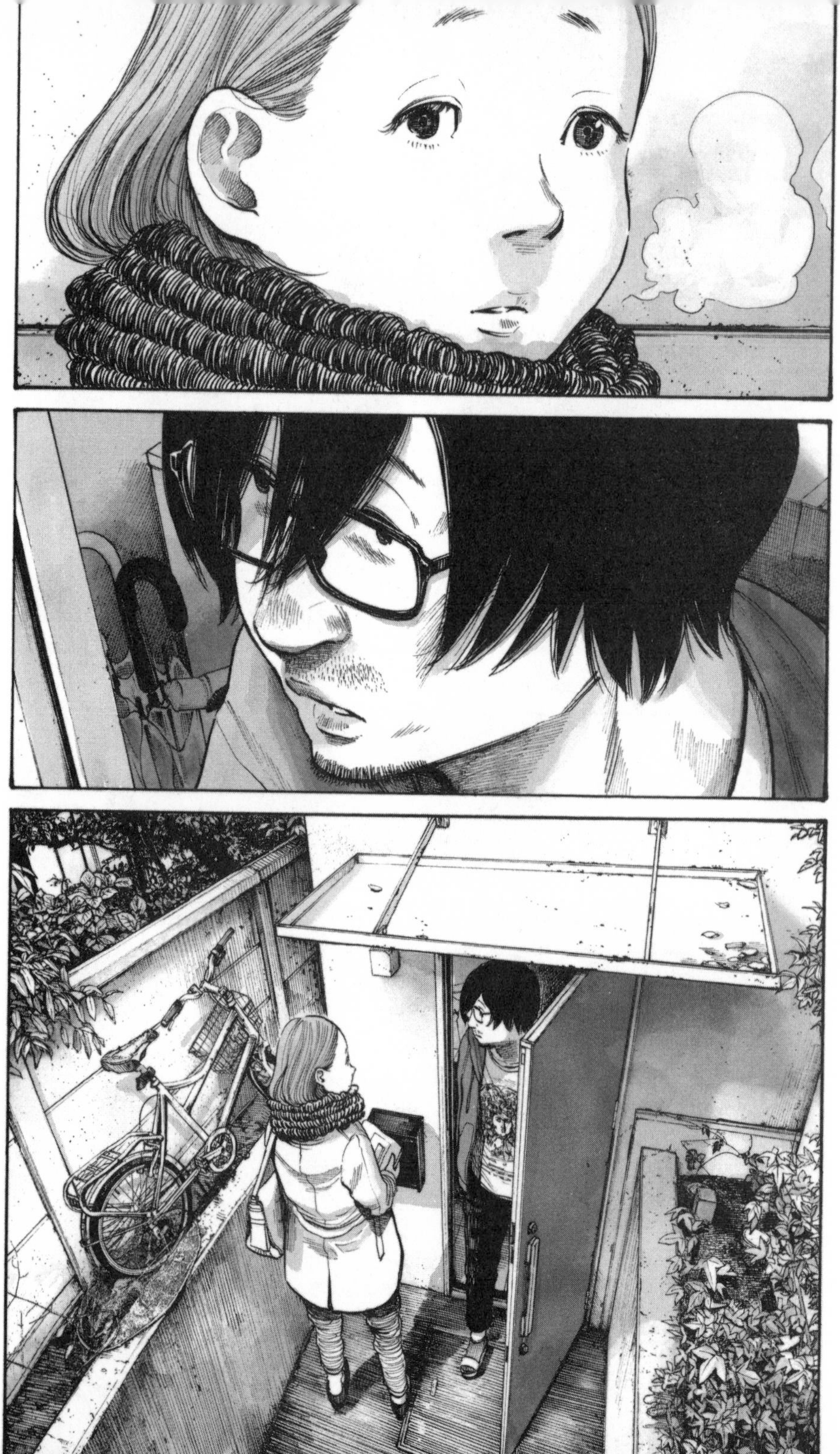

CHAPTER 7

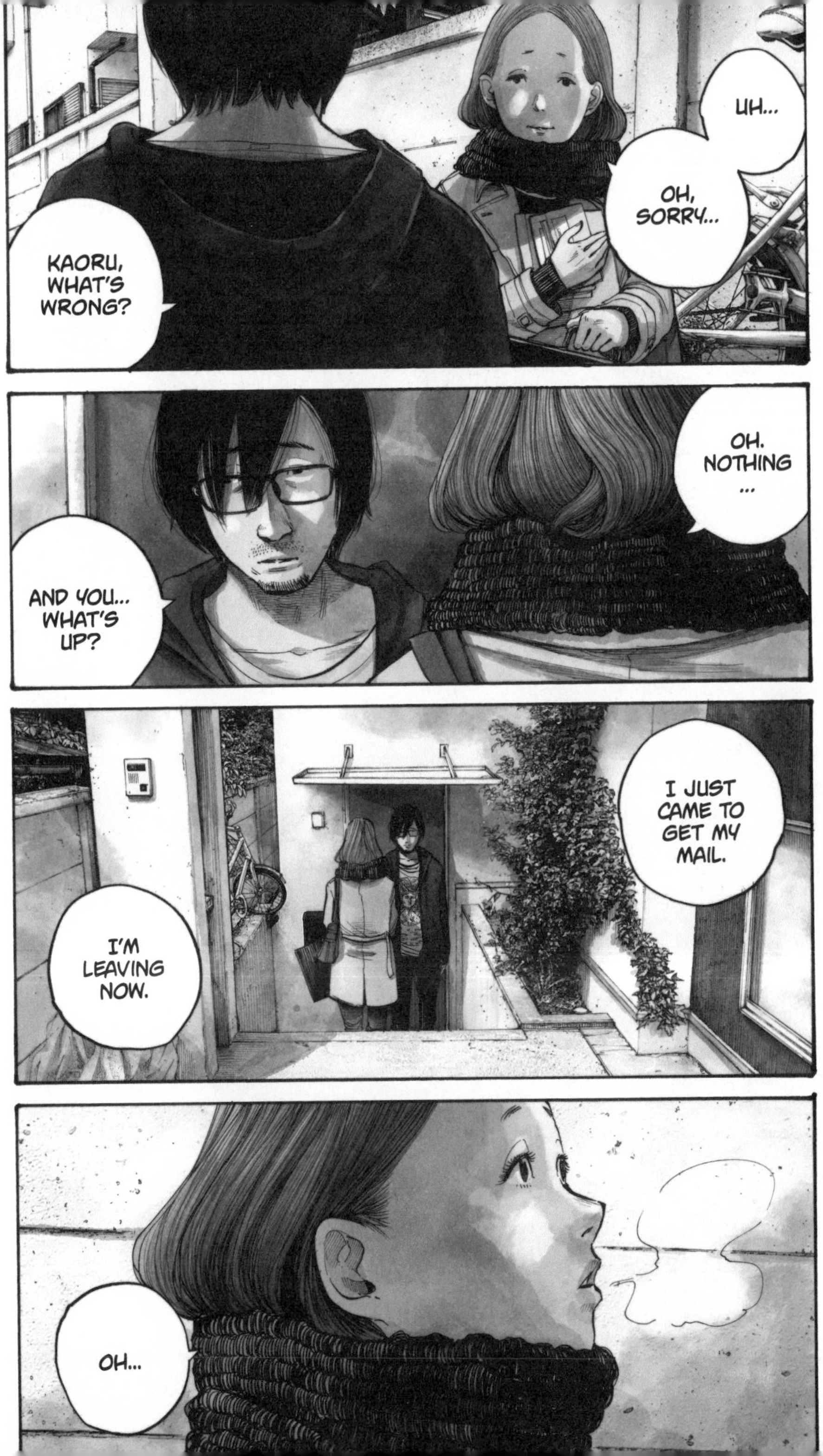
UH...
OH, SORRY...
KAORU, WHAT'S WRONG?
OH. NOTHING ...
AND YOU... WHAT'S UP?
I JUST CAME TO GET MY MAIL.
I'M LEAVING NOW.
OH...

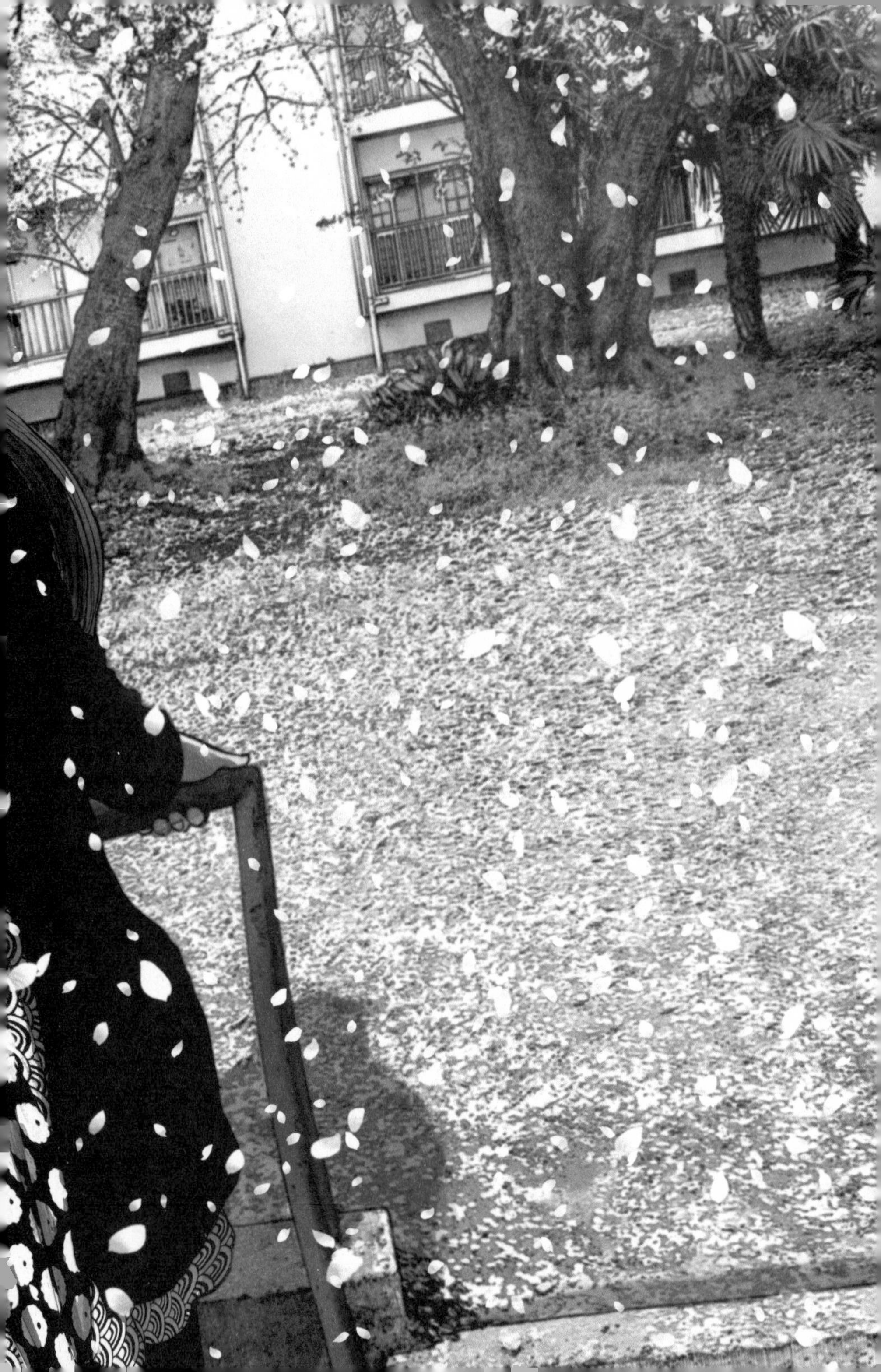

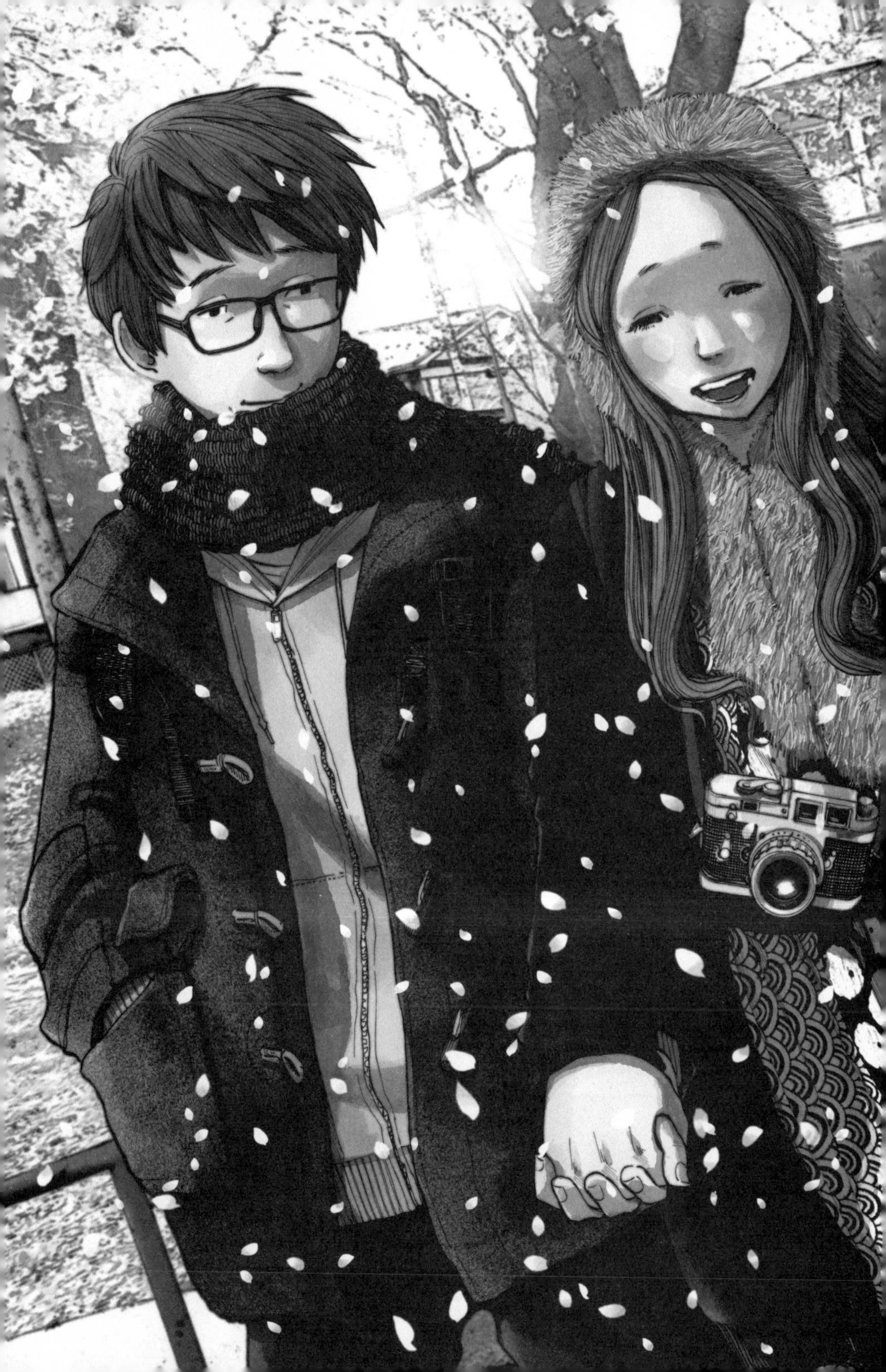

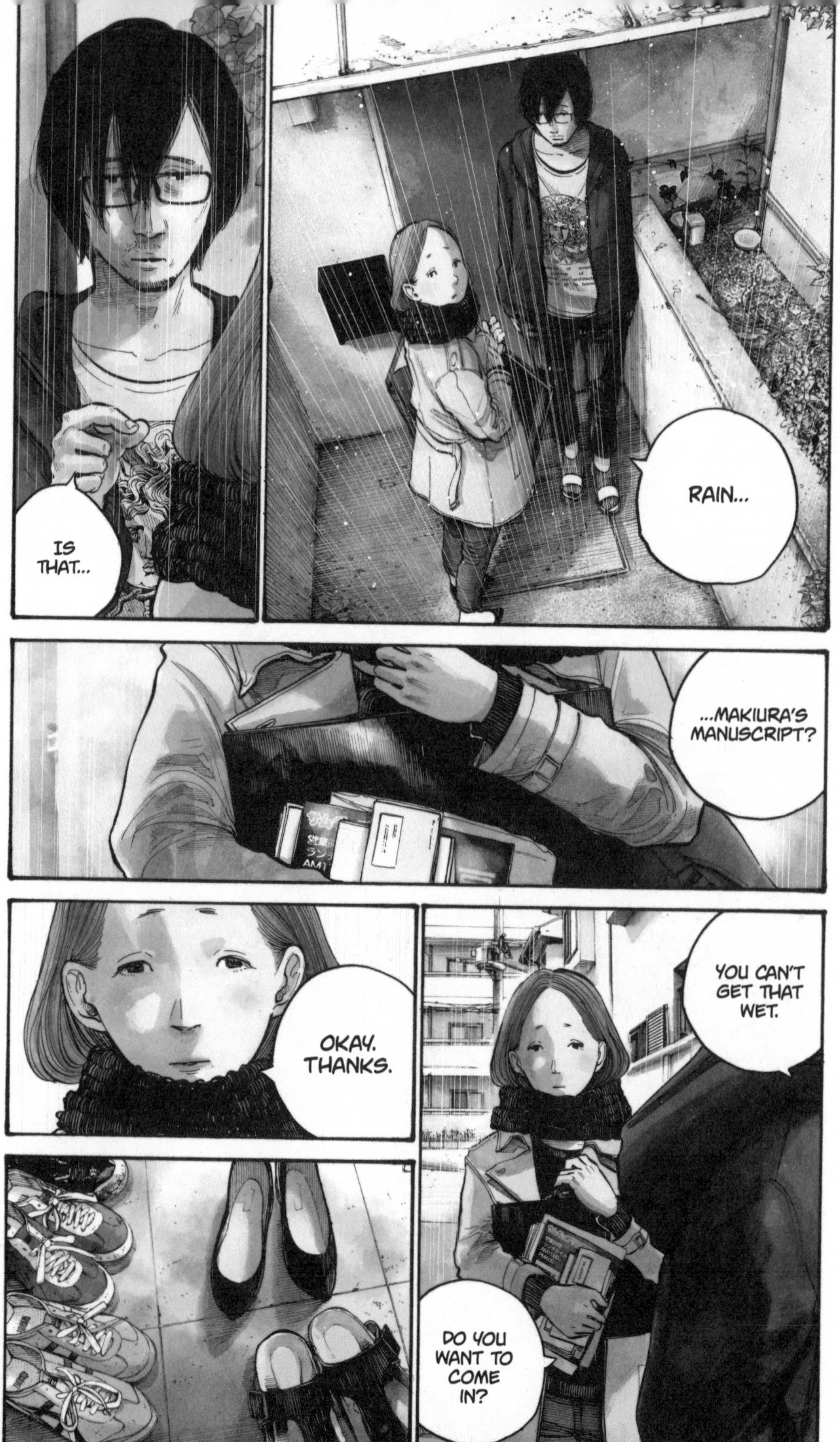

RAIN...
IS THAT...
...MAKIURA'S MANUSCRIPT?
YOU CAN'T GET THAT WET.
DO YOU WANT TO COME IN?
OKAY. THANKS.

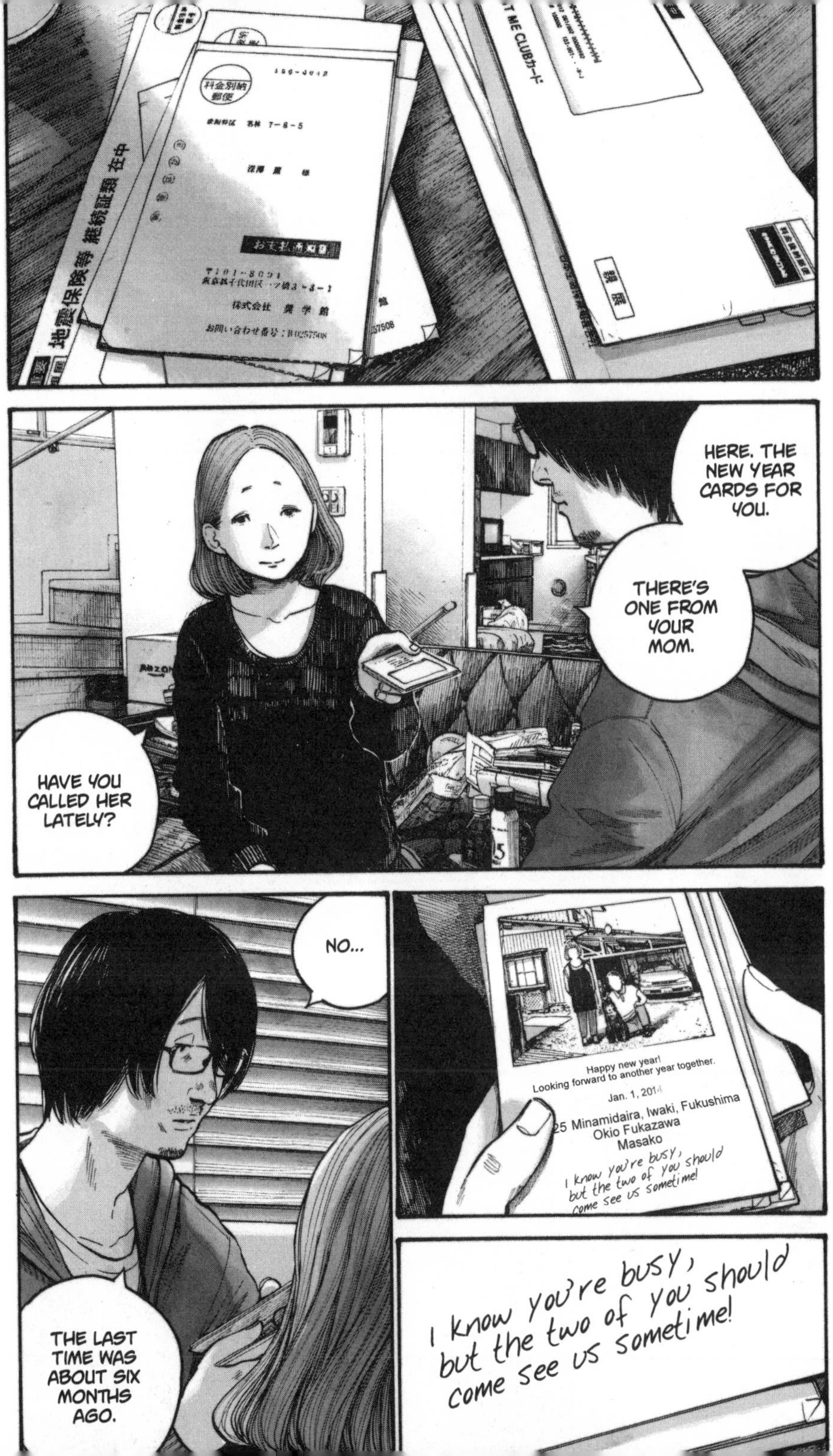
地震保険等 継続証明類 在中
料金別納 郵便
HERE. THE NEW YEAR CARDS FOR YOU.
THERE'S ONE FROM YOUR MOM.
HAVE YOU CALLED HER LATELY?
Happy new year!
Looking forward to another year together.
Jan. 1, 2014
25 Minamidaira, Iwaki, Fukushima
Okio Fukazawa
Masako
I know you're busy, but the two of you should come see us sometime!
I know you're busy, but the two of you should come see us sometime!
NO...
THE LAST TIME WAS ABOUT SIX MONTHS AGO.

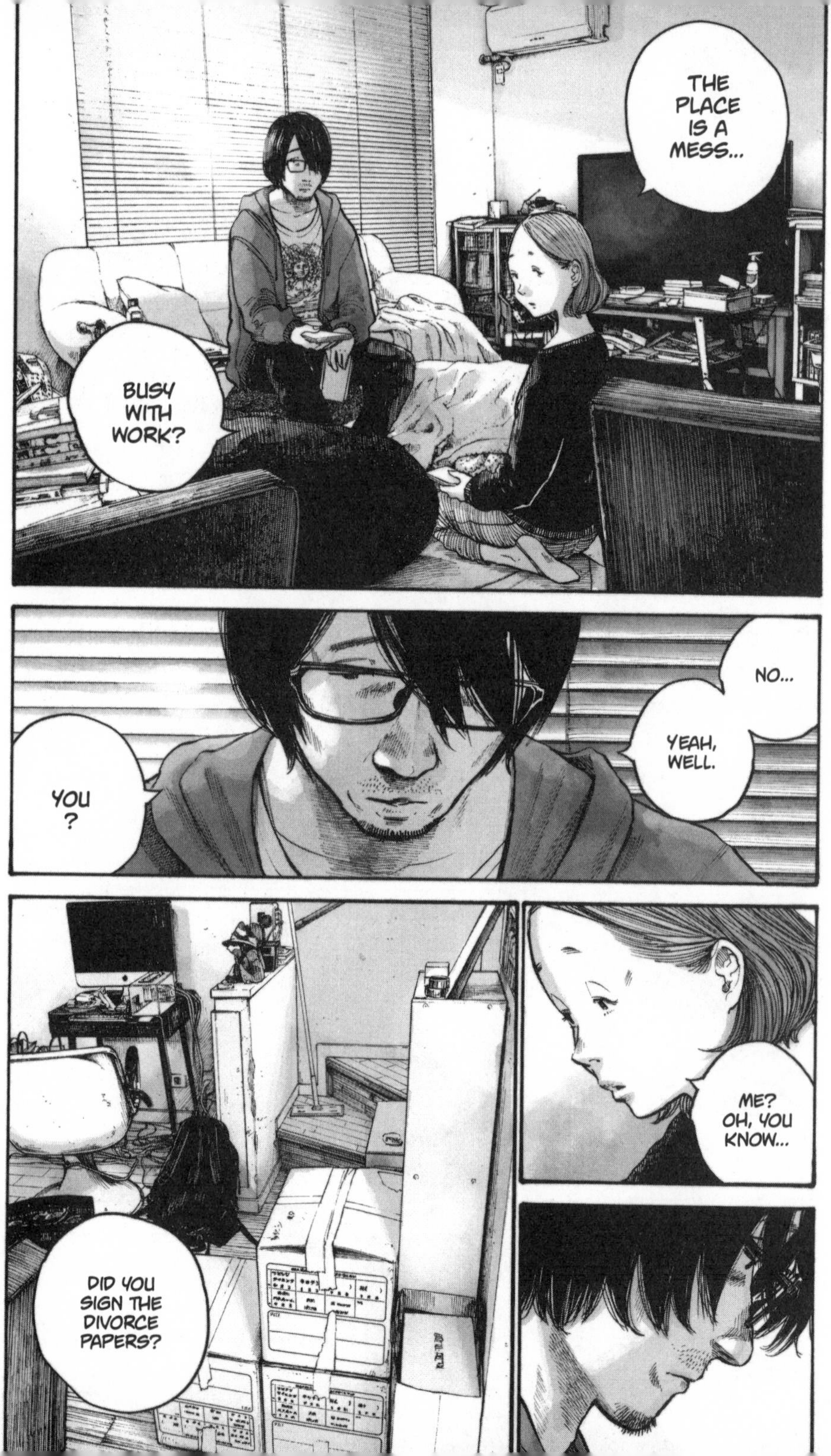
THE PLACE IS A MESS...
BUSY WITH WORK?
NO...
YEAH, WELL.
YOU?
ME? OH, YOU KNOW...
DID YOU SIGN THE DIVORCE PAPERS?

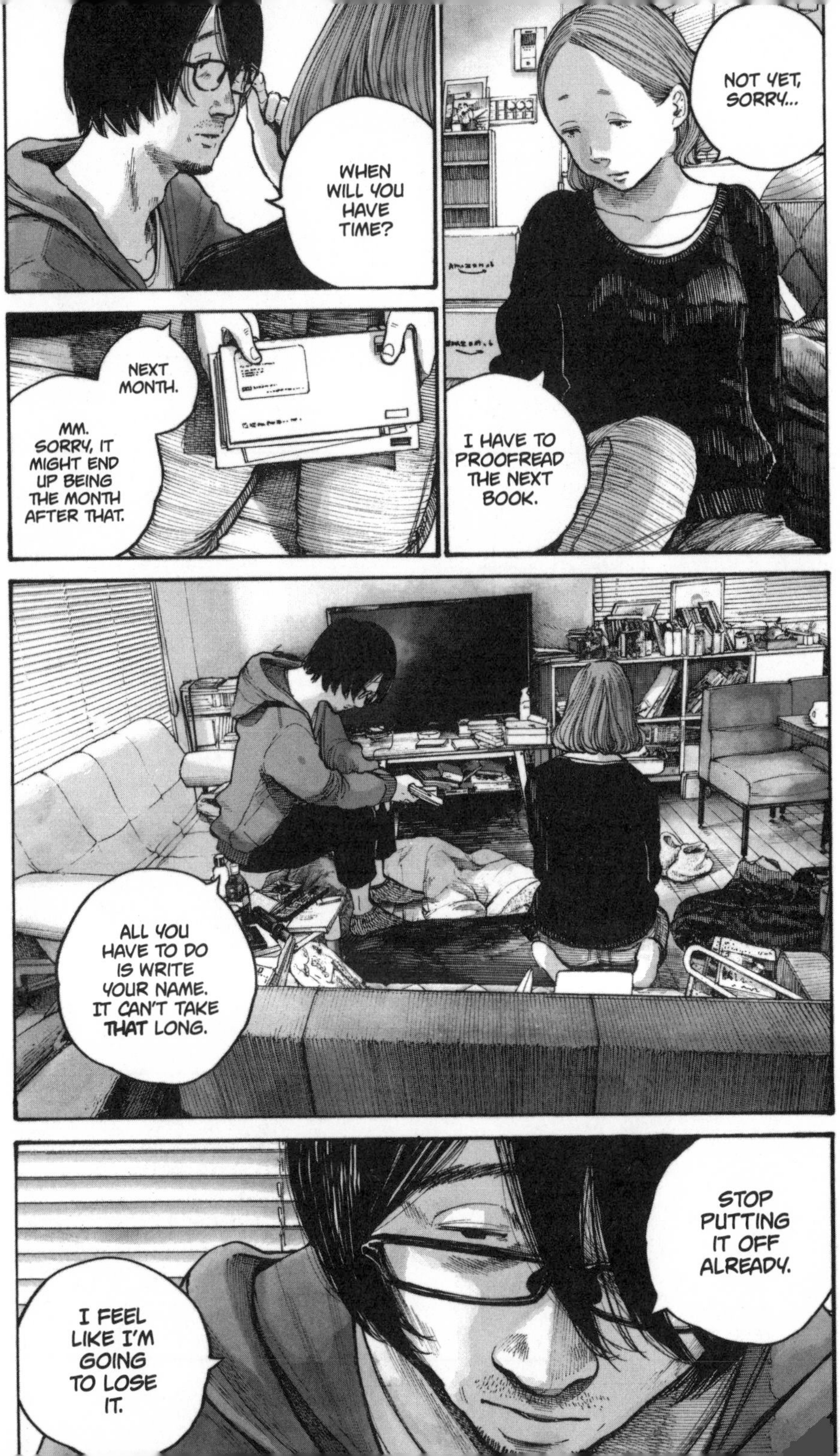
NOT YET, SORRY...
I HAVE TO PROOFREAD THE NEXT BOOK.
WHEN WILL YOU HAVE TIME?
NEXT MONTH.
MM. SORRY, IT MIGHT END UP BEING THE MONTH AFTER THAT.
ALL YOU HAVE TO DO IS WRITE YOUR NAME. IT CAN'T TAKE **THAT** LONG.
STOP PUTTING IT OFF ALREADY.
I FEEL LIKE I'M GOING TO LOSE IT.

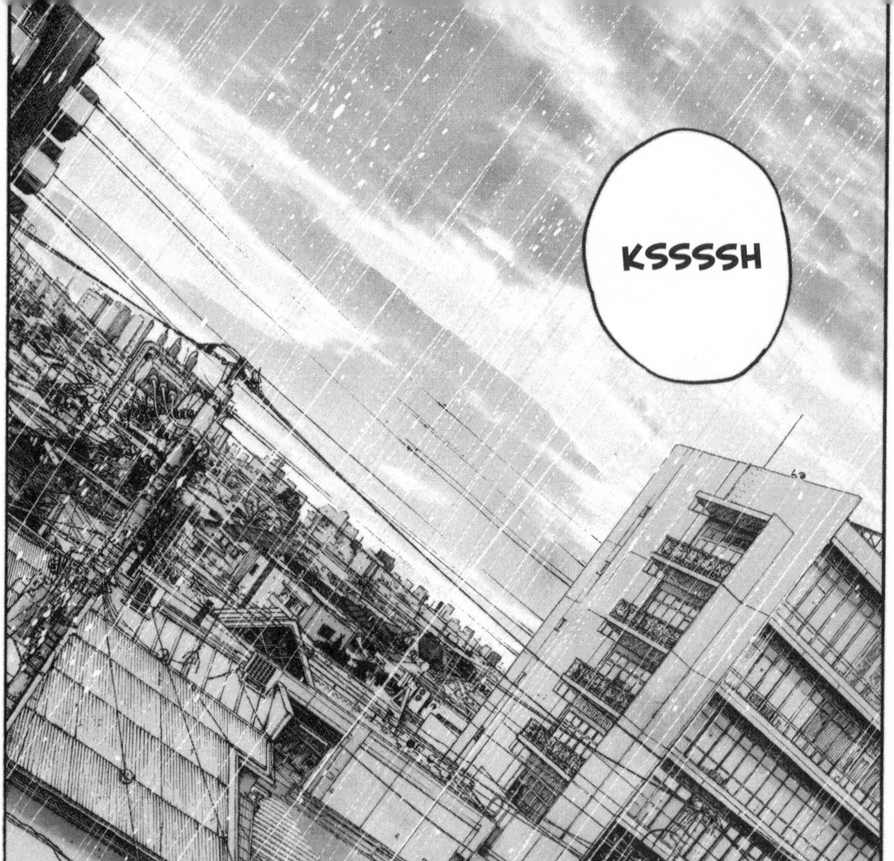
KSSSSH

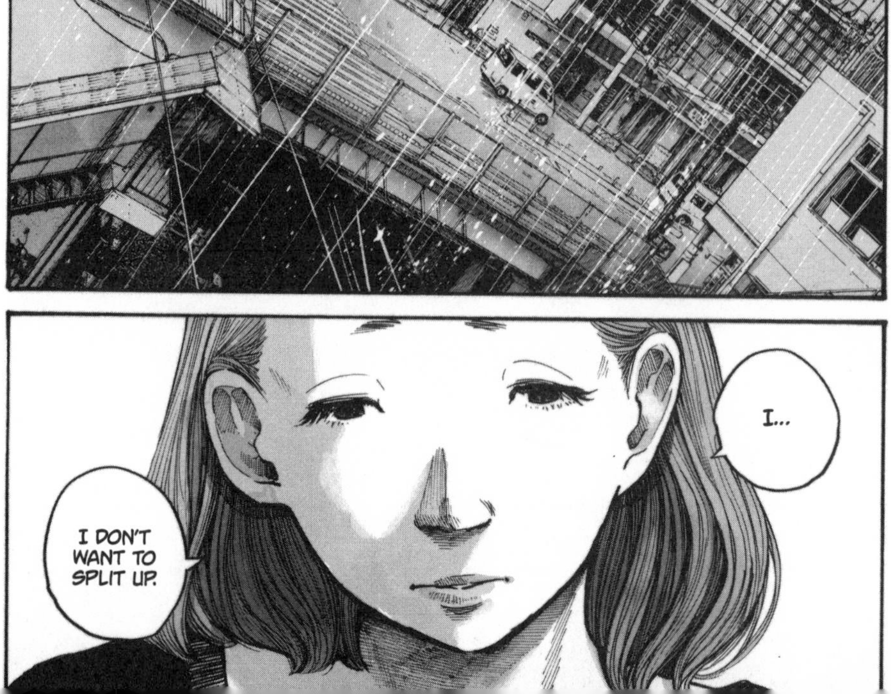
I...
I DON'T WANT TO SPLIT UP.

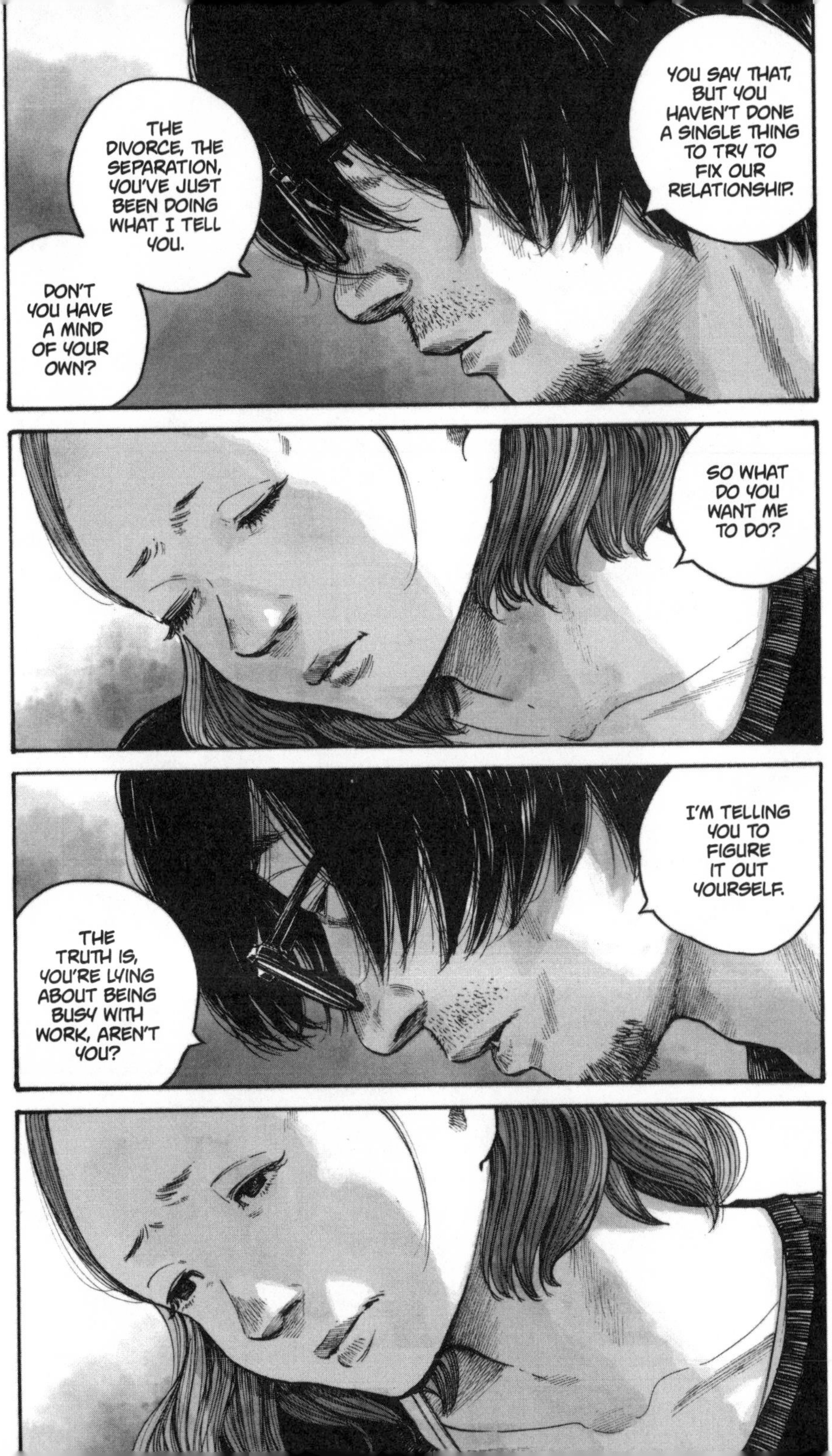
YOU SAY THAT, BUT YOU HAVEN'T DONE A SINGLE THING TO TRY TO FIX OUR RELATIONSHIP.
THE DIVORCE, THE SEPARATION, YOU'VE JUST BEEN DOING WHAT I TELL YOU.
DON'T YOU HAVE A MIND OF YOUR OWN?
SO WHAT DO YOU WANT ME TO DO?
I'M TELLING YOU TO FIGURE IT OUT YOURSELF.
THE TRUTH IS, YOU'RE LYING ABOUT BEING BUSY WITH WORK, AREN'T YOU?

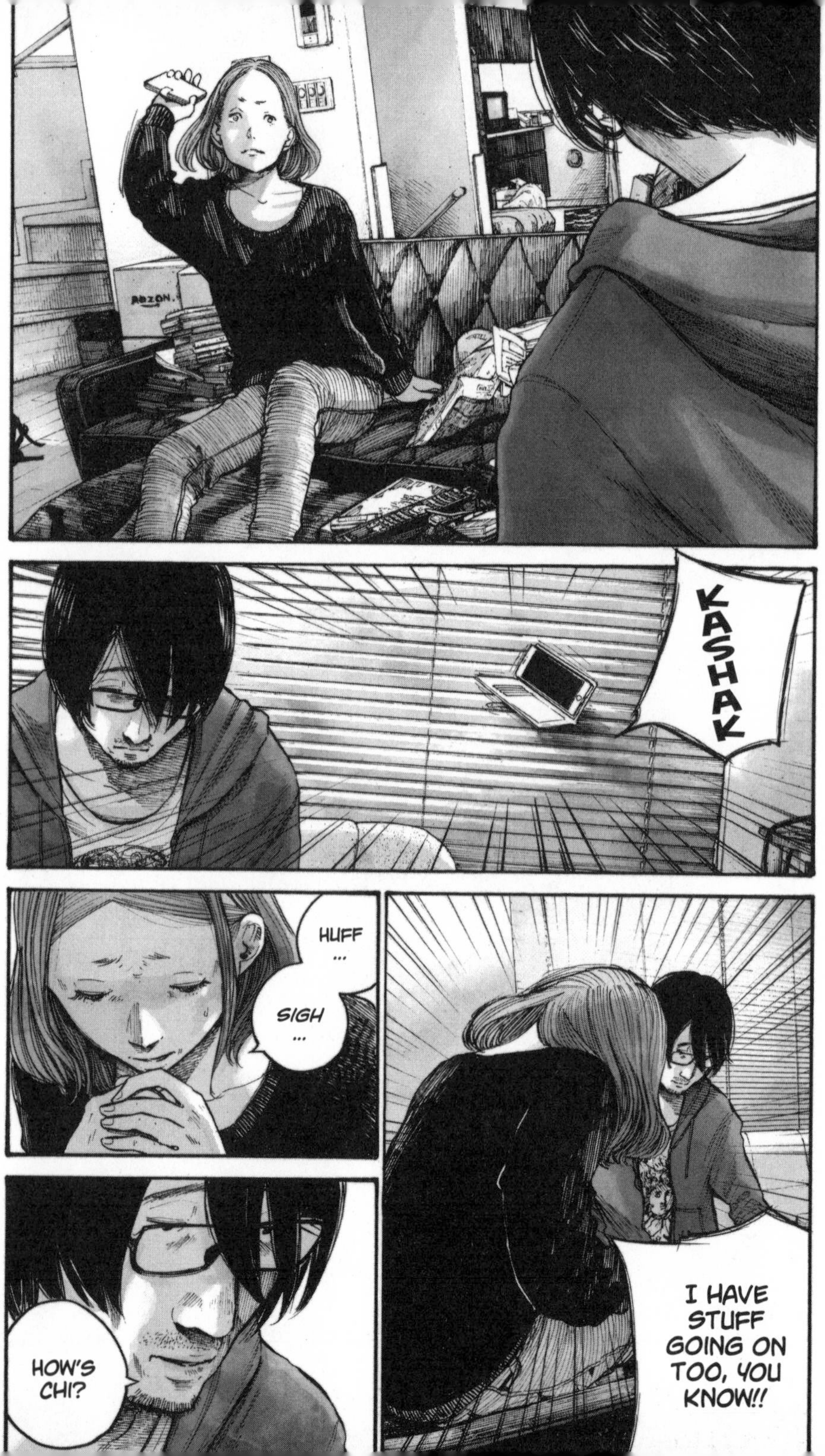
KASHAK
I HAVE STUFF GOING ON TOO, YOU KNOW!!
HUFF...
SIGH...
HOW'S CHI?

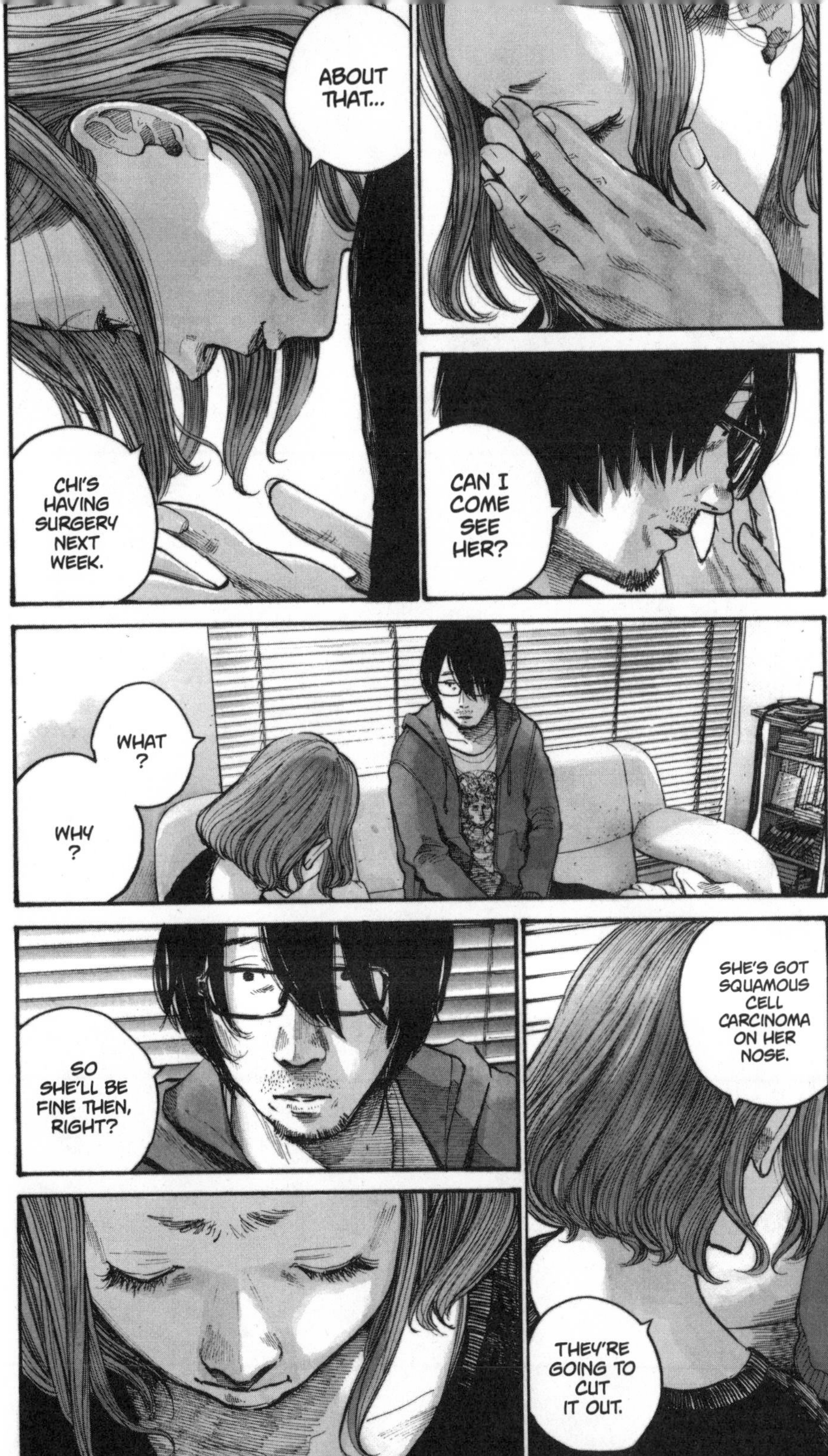
CAN I COME SEE HER?
ABOUT THAT...
CHI'S HAVING SURGERY NEXT WEEK.
WHAT?
WHY?
SHE'S GOT SQUAMOUS CELL CARCINOMA ON HER NOSE.
THEY'RE GOING TO CUT IT OUT.
SO SHE'LL BE FINE THEN, RIGHT?

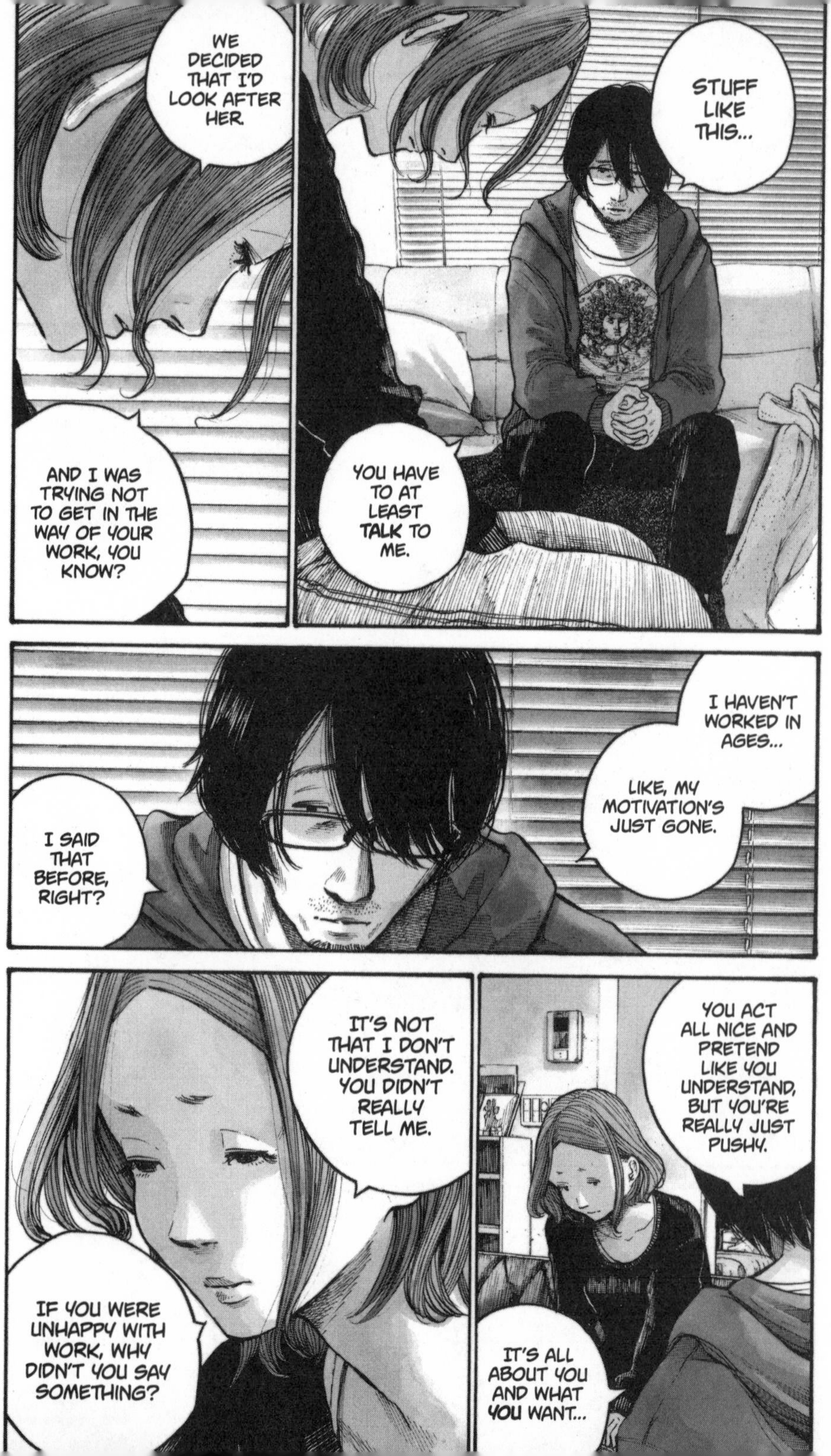
STUFF LIKE THIS...
YOU HAVE TO AT LEAST TALK TO ME.
WE DECIDED THAT I'D LOOK AFTER HER.
AND I WAS TRYING NOT TO GET IN THE WAY OF YOUR WORK, YOU KNOW?
I HAVEN'T WORKED IN AGES...
LIKE, MY MOTIVATION'S JUST GONE.
I SAID THAT BEFORE, RIGHT?
YOU ACT ALL NICE AND PRETEND LIKE YOU UNDERSTAND, BUT YOU'RE REALLY JUST PUSHY.
IT'S ALL ABOUT YOU AND WHAT YOU WANT...
IT'S NOT THAT I DON'T UNDERSTAND. YOU DIDN'T REALLY TELL ME.
IF YOU WERE UNHAPPY WITH WORK, WHY DIDN'T YOU SAY SOMETHING?

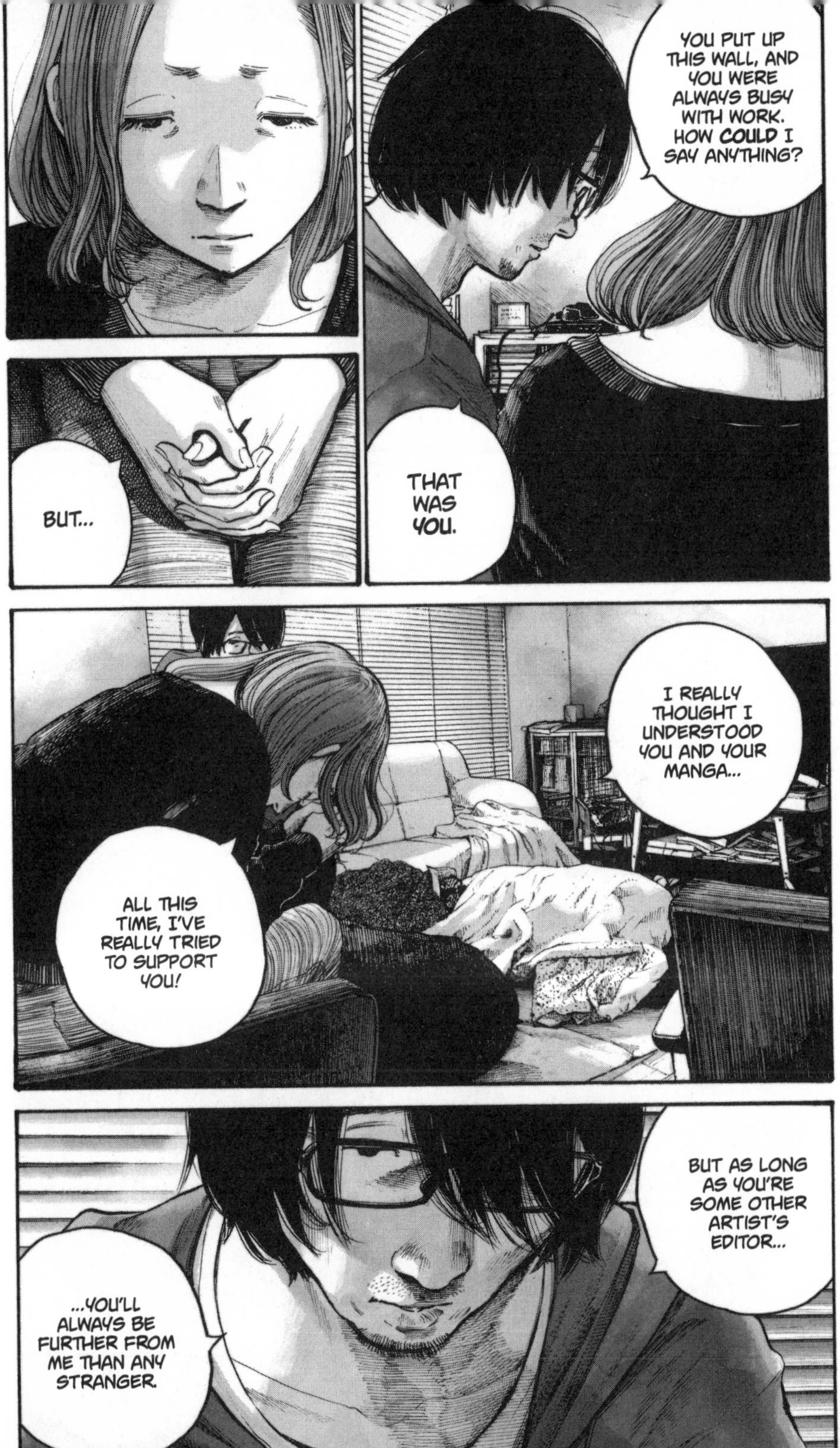
YOU PUT UP THIS WALL, AND YOU WERE ALWAYS BUSY WITH WORK. HOW **COULD** I SAY ANYTHING?
THAT WAS YOU.
BUT...
I REALLY THOUGHT I UNDERSTOOD YOU AND YOUR MANGA...
ALL THIS TIME, I'VE REALLY TRIED TO SUPPORT YOU!
BUT AS LONG AS YOU'RE SOME OTHER ARTIST'S EDITOR...
...YOU'LL ALWAYS BE FURTHER FROM ME THAN ANY STRANGER.

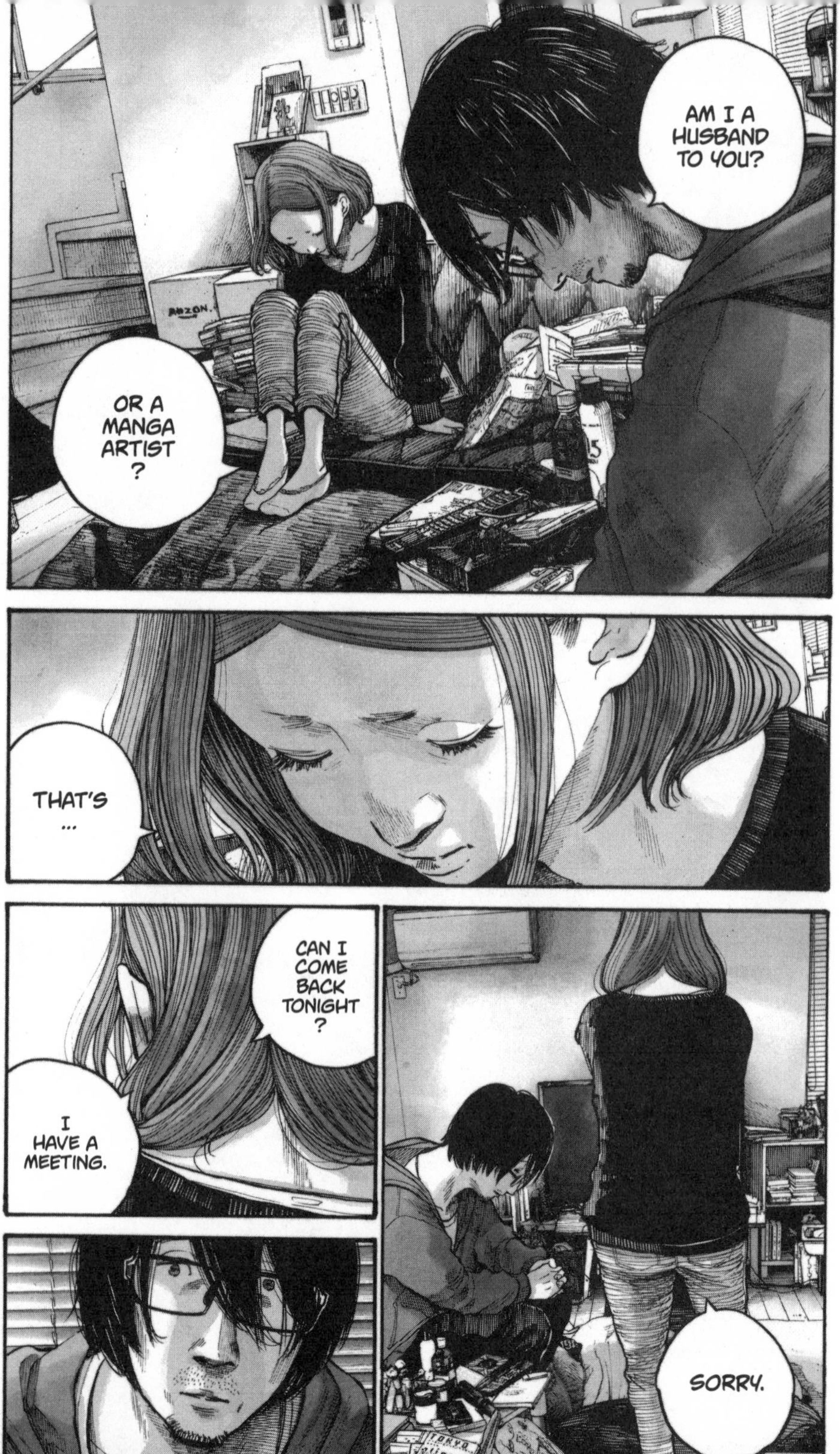
AM I A HUSBAND TO YOU?
OR A MANGA ARTIST ?
THAT'S ...
CAN I COME BACK TONIGHT ?
I HAVE A MEETING.
SORRY.

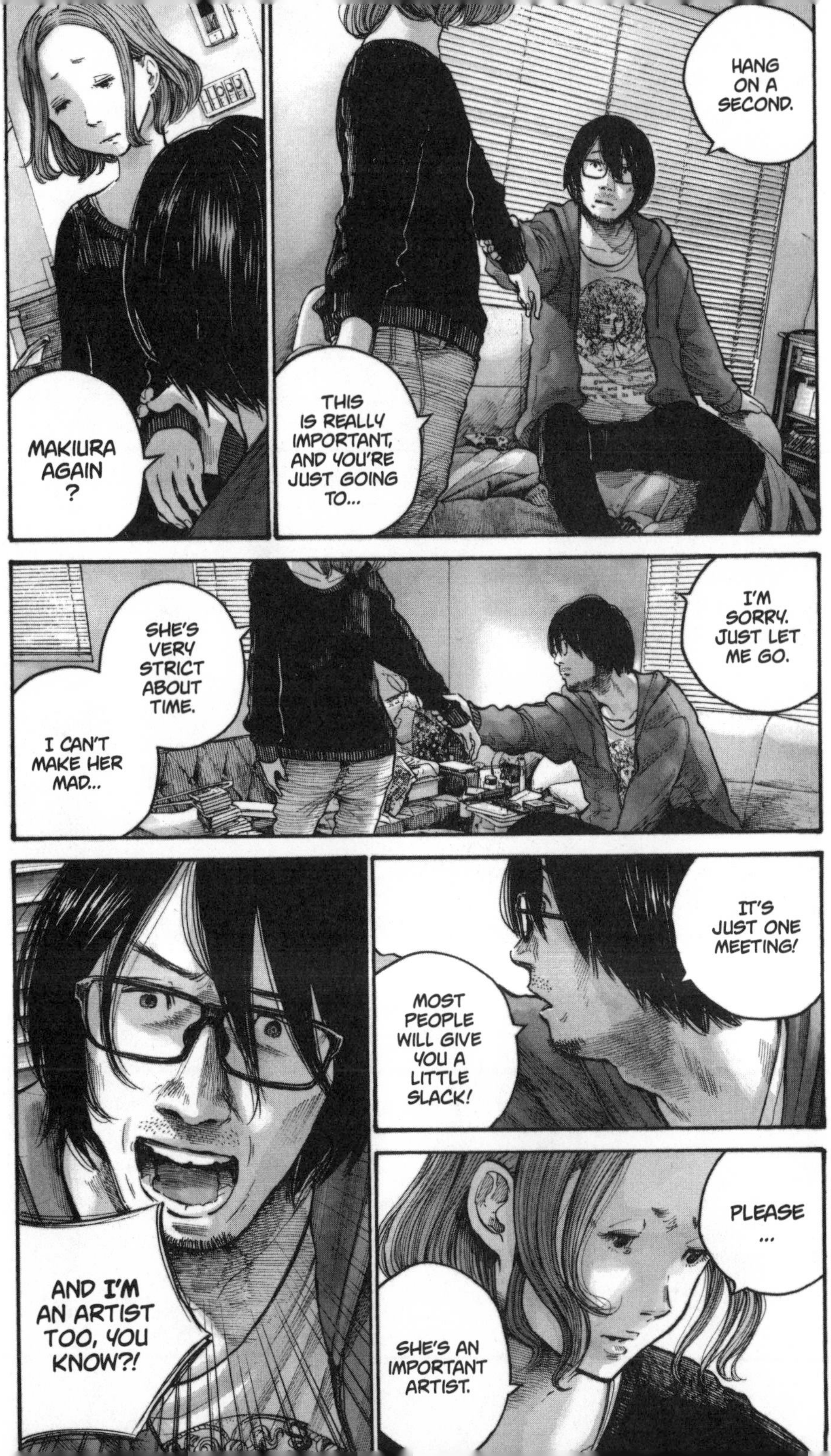
HANG ON A SECOND.
THIS IS REALLY IMPORTANT, AND YOU'RE JUST GOING TO...
MAKIURA AGAIN ?
I'M SORRY. JUST LET ME GO.
SHE'S VERY STRICT ABOUT TIME.
I CAN'T MAKE HER MAD...
IT'S JUST ONE MEETING!
MOST PEOPLE WILL GIVE YOU A LITTLE SLACK!
PLEASE ...
SHE'S AN IMPORTANT ARTIST.
AND I'M AN ARTIST TOO, YOU KNOW?!

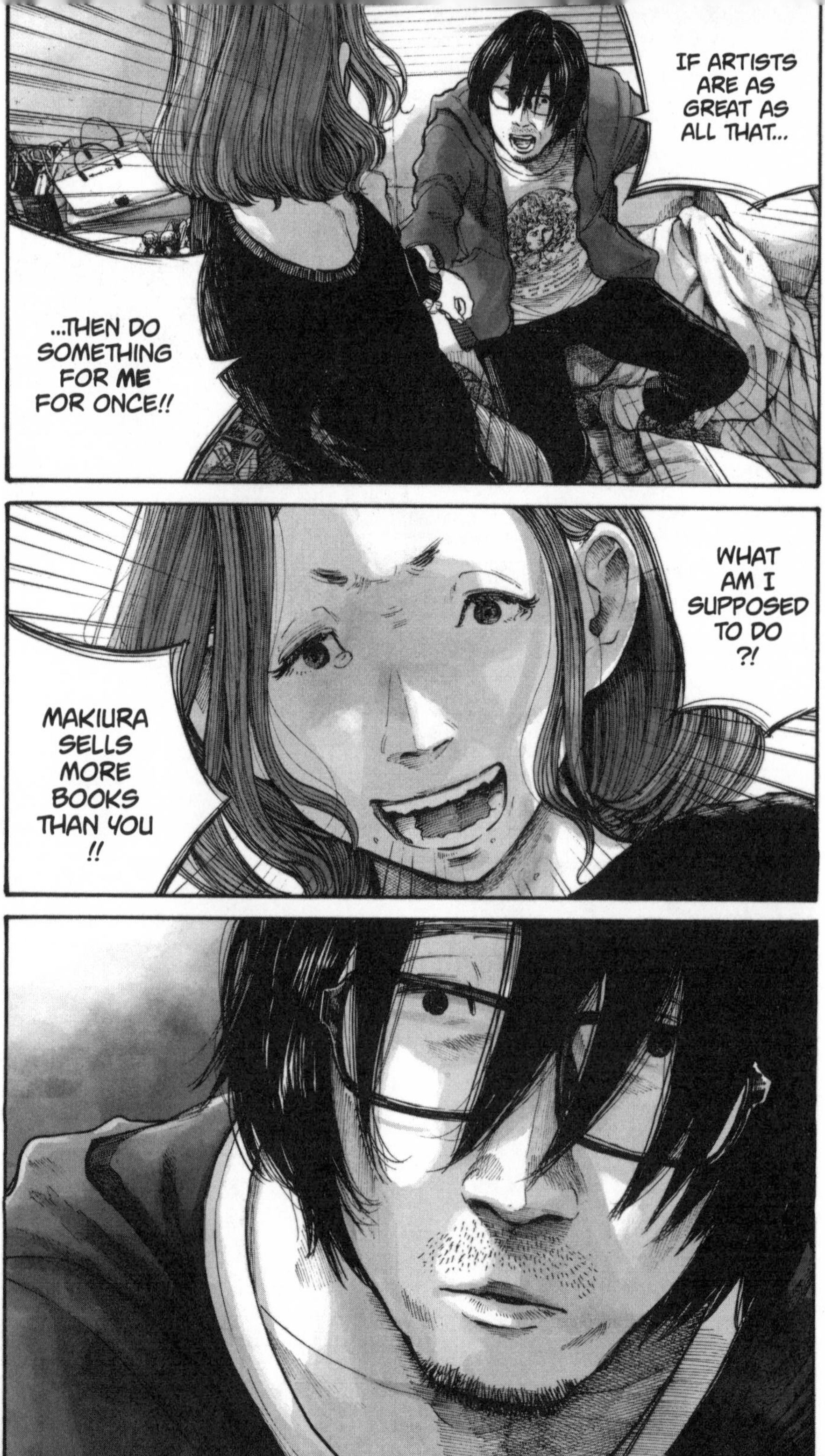
IF ARTISTS ARE AS GREAT AS ALL THAT...
...THEN DO SOMETHING FOR ME FOR ONCE!!
WHAT AM I SUPPOSED TO DO ?!
MAKIURA SELLS MORE BOOKS THAN YOU !!

AH...
HEY...
HEY ?
...KAORU ?
STOP IT. HEY–!!
C'MON ?!
HEY ?!
NO NO NO NO !!

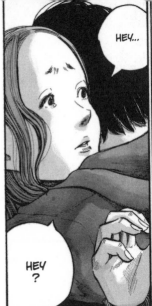

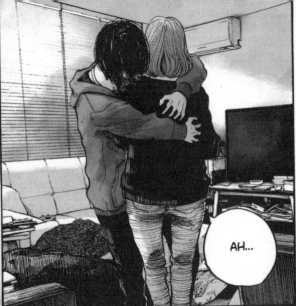

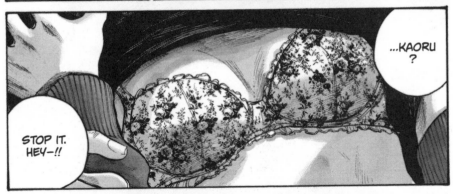

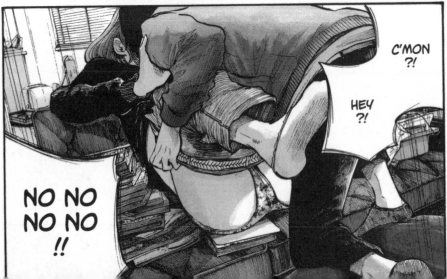

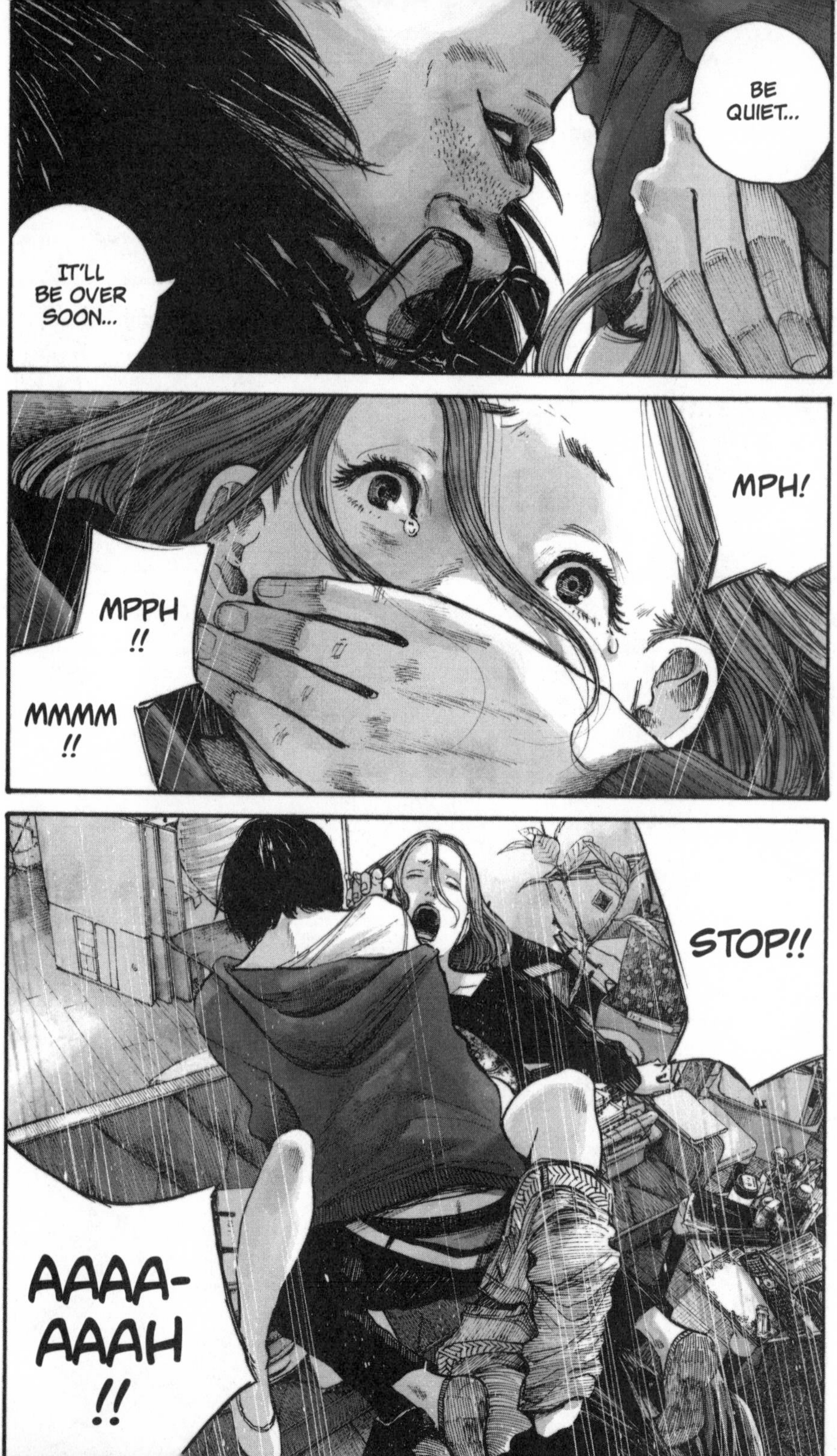
BE QUIET...
IT'LL BE OVER SOON...
MPH!
MPPH!!
MMMM!!
STOP!!
AAAA-AAAH!!

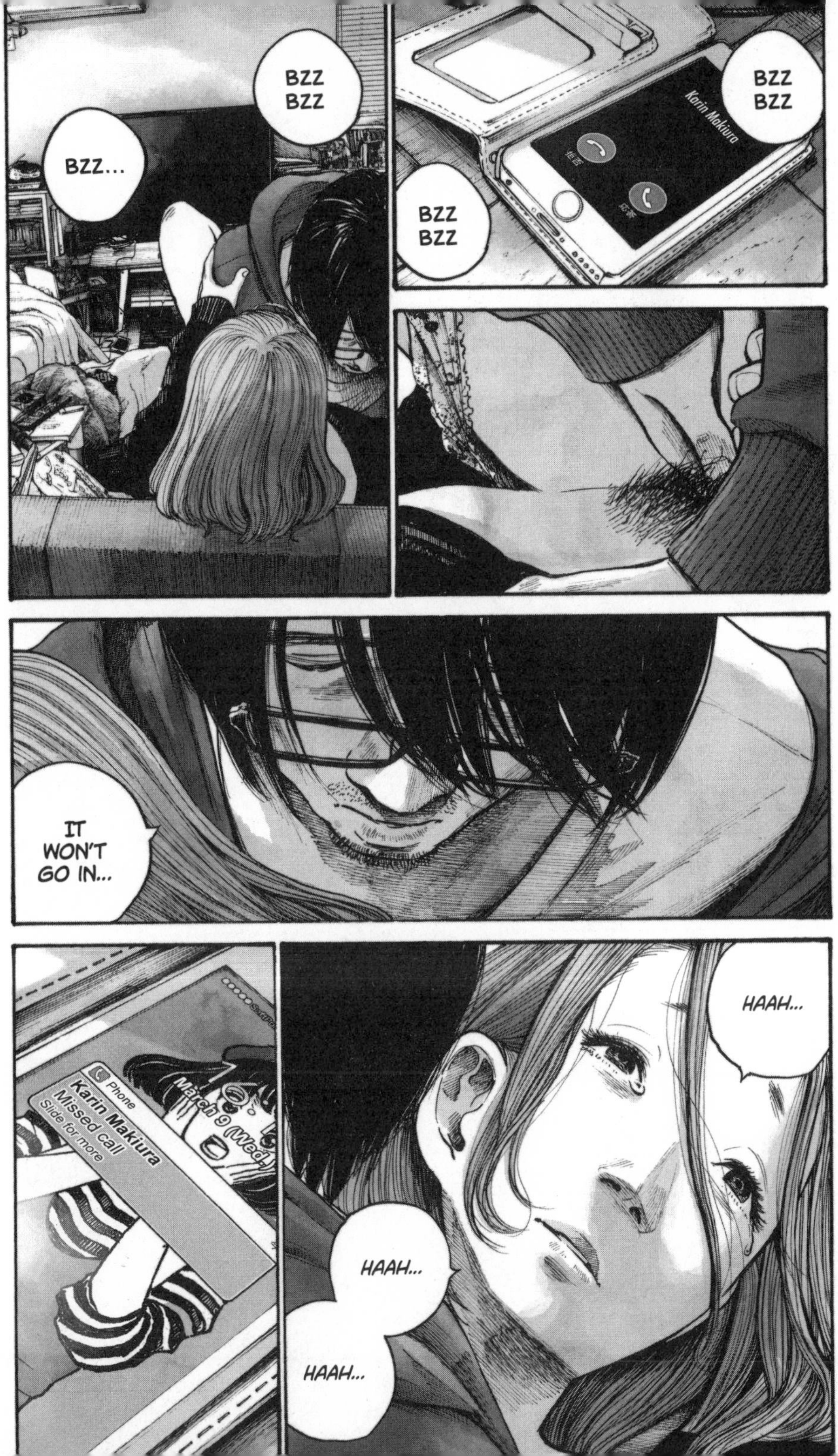
BZZ BZZ
Karin Makiura
拒否
応答
BZZ BZZ
BZZ BZZ
BZZ...
IT WON'T GO IN...
HAAH...
HAAH...
HAAH...
Phone
Karin Makiura
Missed call
Slide for more
March 9 (Wed.

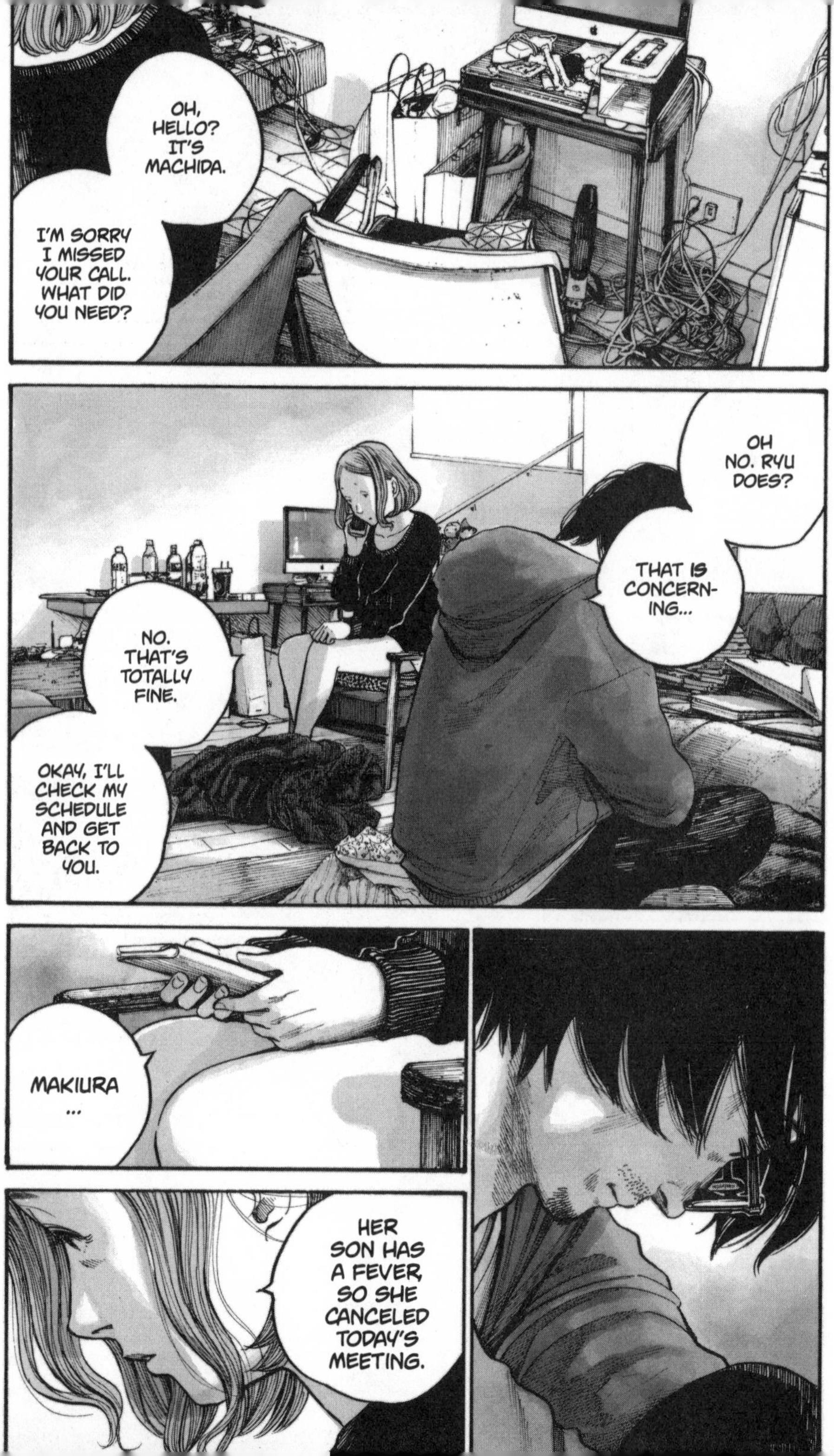
OH, HELLO? IT'S MACHIDA.
I'M SORRY I MISSED YOUR CALL. WHAT DID YOU NEED?
OH NO. RYU DOES?
THAT IS CONCERNING...
NO. THAT'S TOTALLY FINE.
OKAY, I'LL CHECK MY SCHEDULE AND GET BACK TO YOU.
MAKIURA ...
HER SON HAS A FEVER, SO SHE CANCELED TODAY'S MEETING.

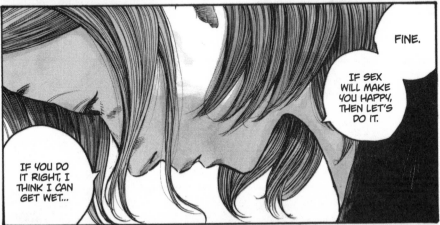

FINE.

IF SEX WILL MAKE YOU HAPPY, THEN LET'S DO IT.

IF YOU DO IT RIGHT, I THINK I CAN GET WET...

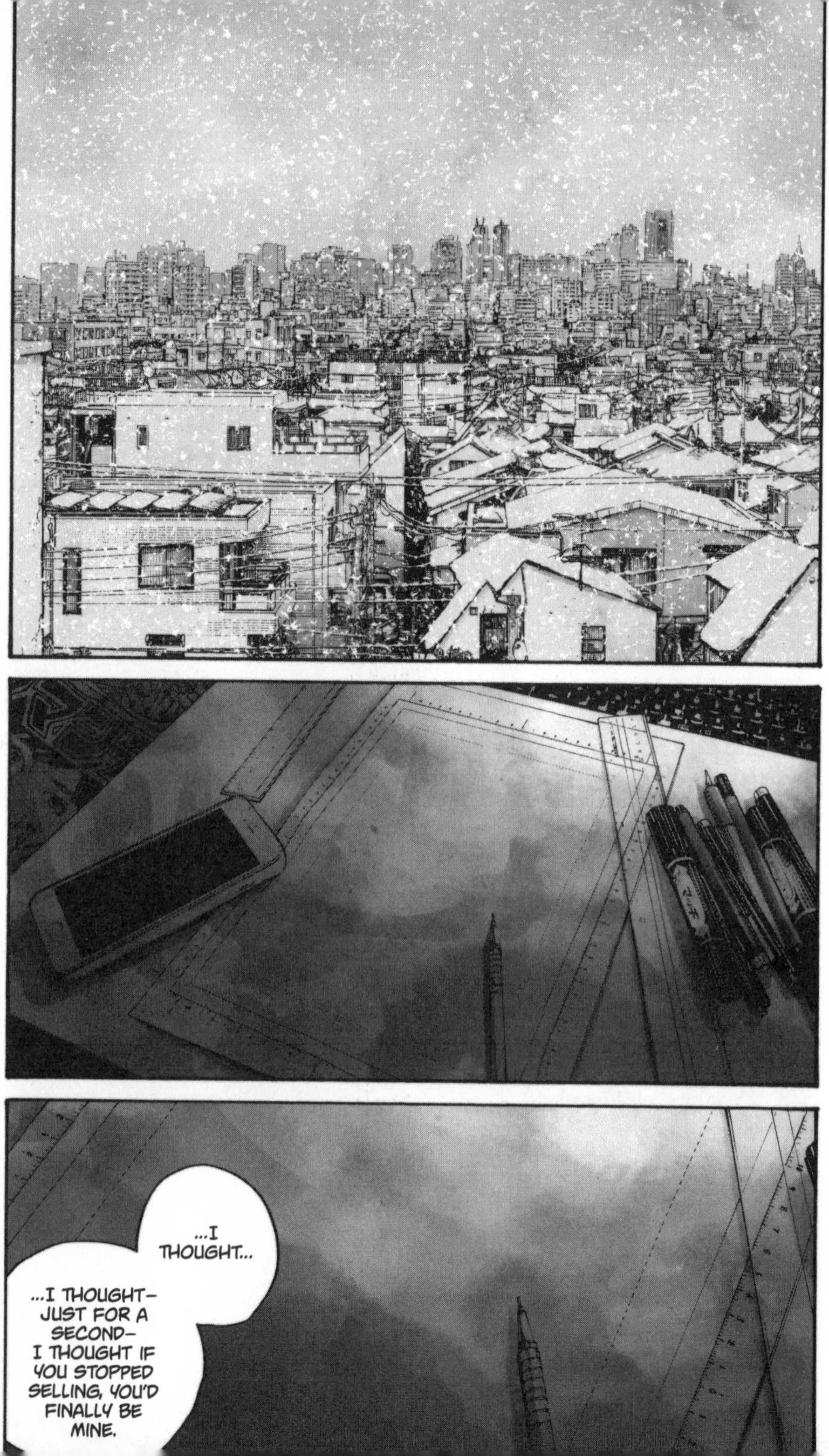
...I THOUGHT...
...I THOUGHT— JUST FOR A SECOND— I THOUGHT IF YOU STOPPED SELLING, YOU'D FINALLY BE MINE.

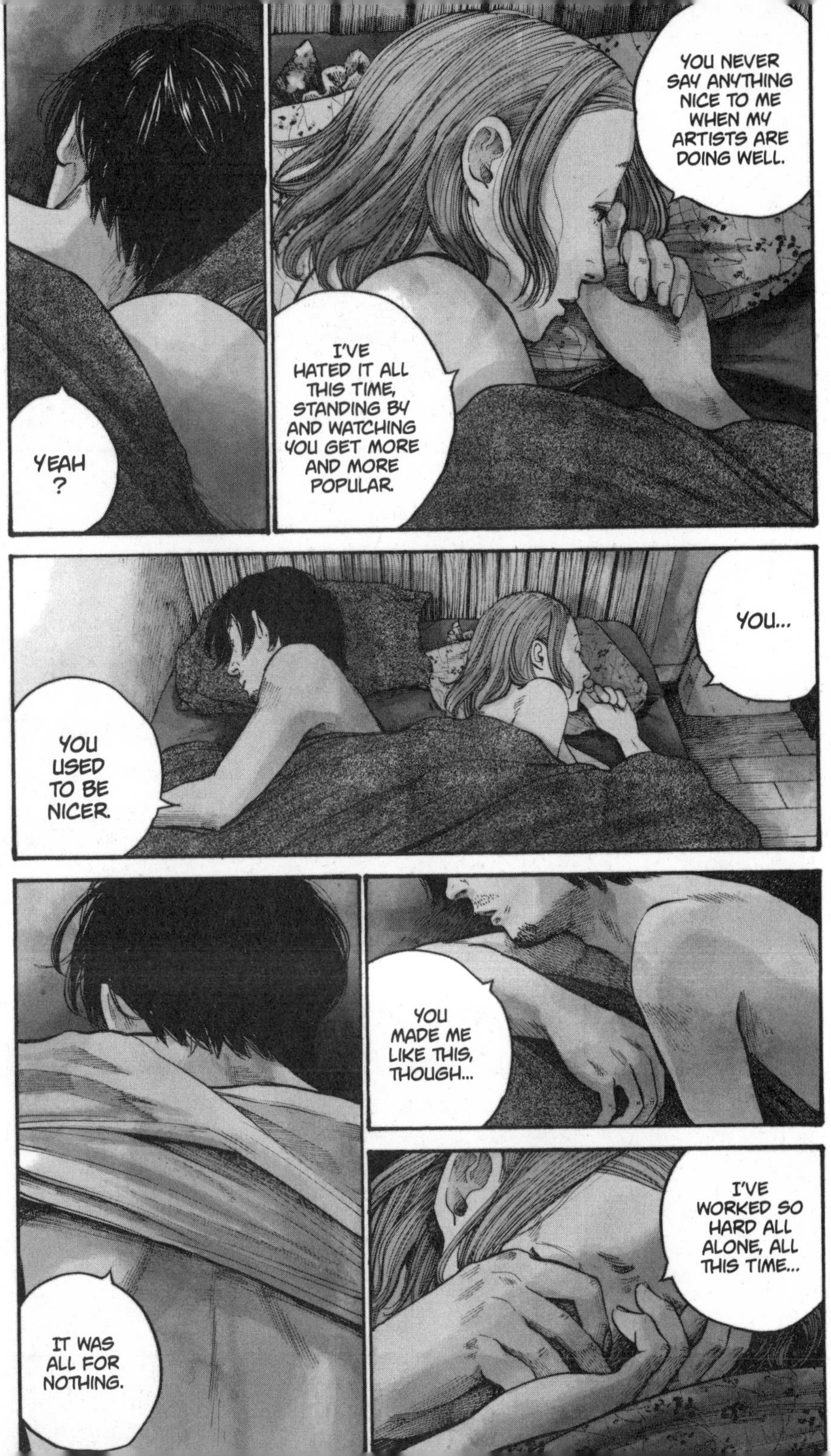
YOU NEVER SAY ANYTHING NICE TO ME WHEN MY ARTISTS ARE DOING WELL.
I'VE HATED IT ALL THIS TIME, STANDING BY AND WATCHING YOU GET MORE AND MORE POPULAR.
YEAH ?
YOU...
YOU USED TO BE NICER.
YOU MADE ME LIKE THIS, THOUGH...
I'VE WORKED SO HARD ALL ALONE, ALL THIS TIME...
IT WAS ALL FOR NOTHING.

KAORU...

YOU'RE AWFUL...

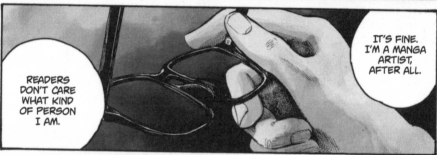

IT'S FINE. I'M A MANGA ARTIST, AFTER ALL.

READERS DON'T CARE WHAT KIND OF PERSON I AM.

SOB

SOB

I FINALLY GET IT...

BASICALLY, I JUST HAVE TO SELL BOOKS.

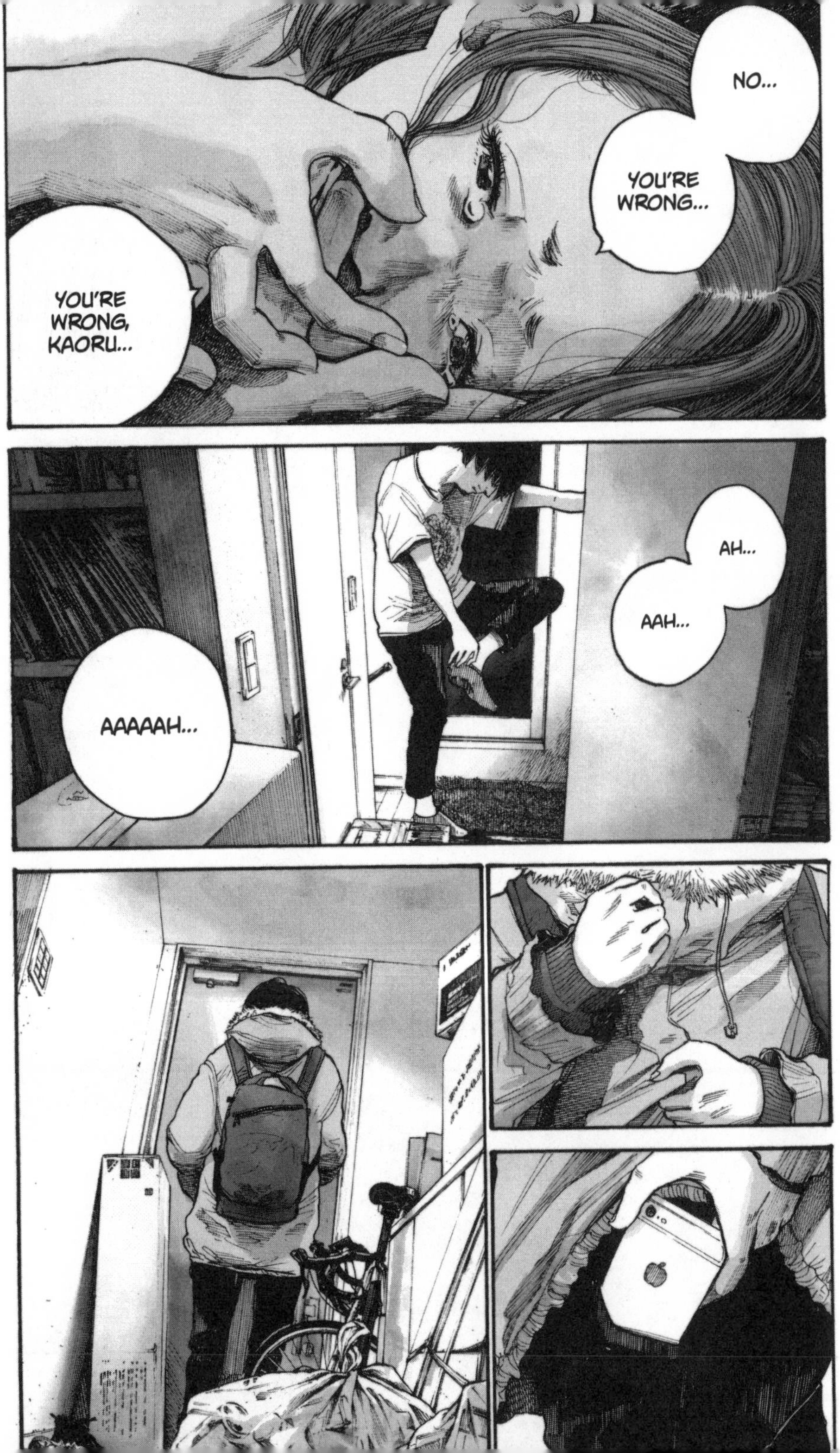
NO...
YOU'RE WRONG...
YOU'RE WRONG, KAORU...
AH...
AAH...
AAAAAH...

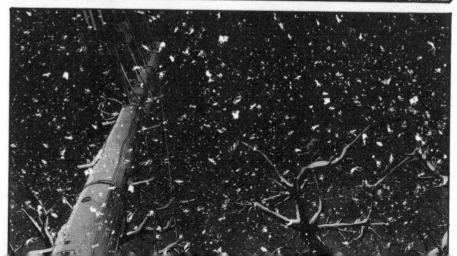

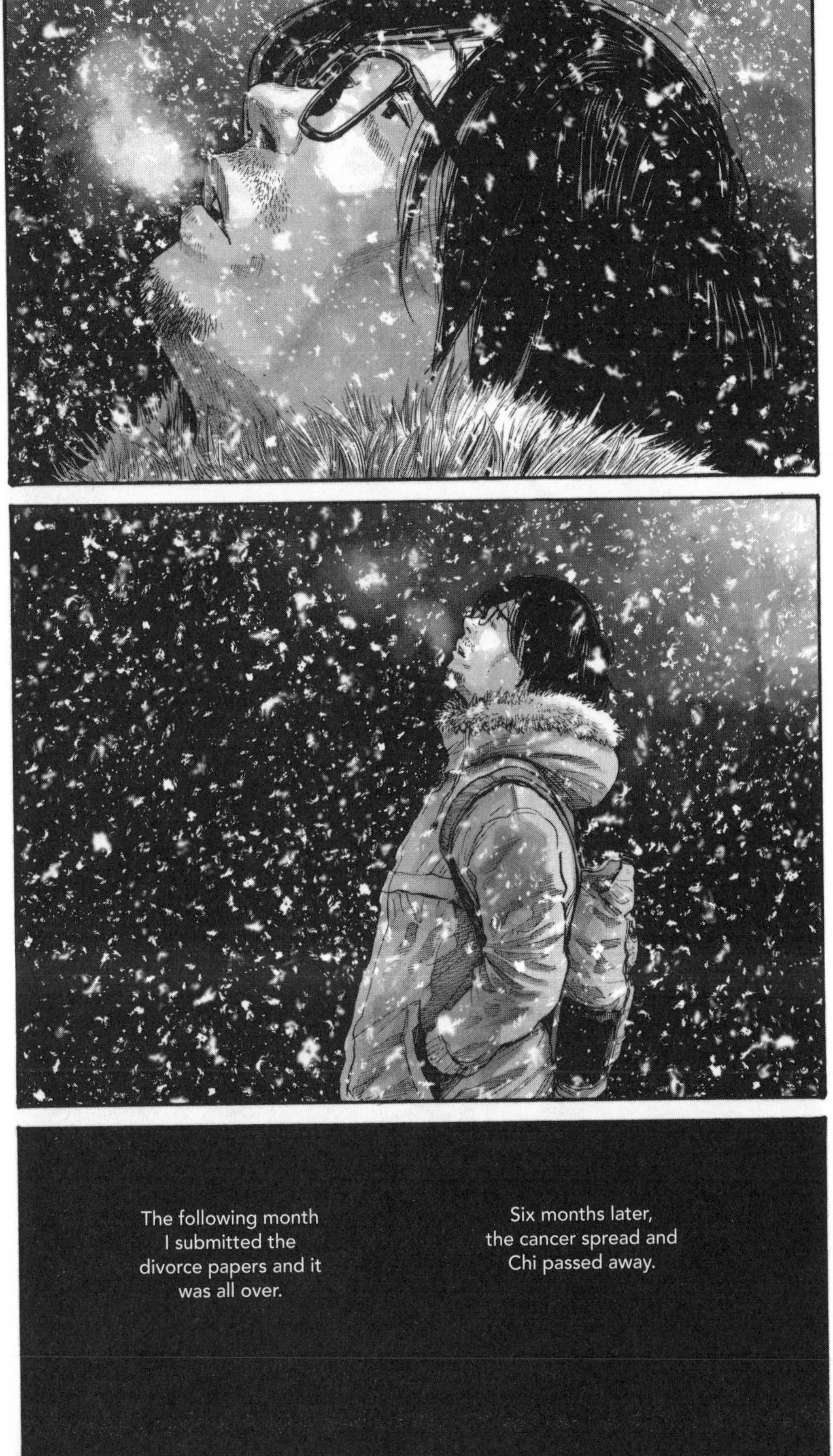
Six months later, the cancer spread and Chi passed away.
The following month I submitted the divorce papers and it was all over.

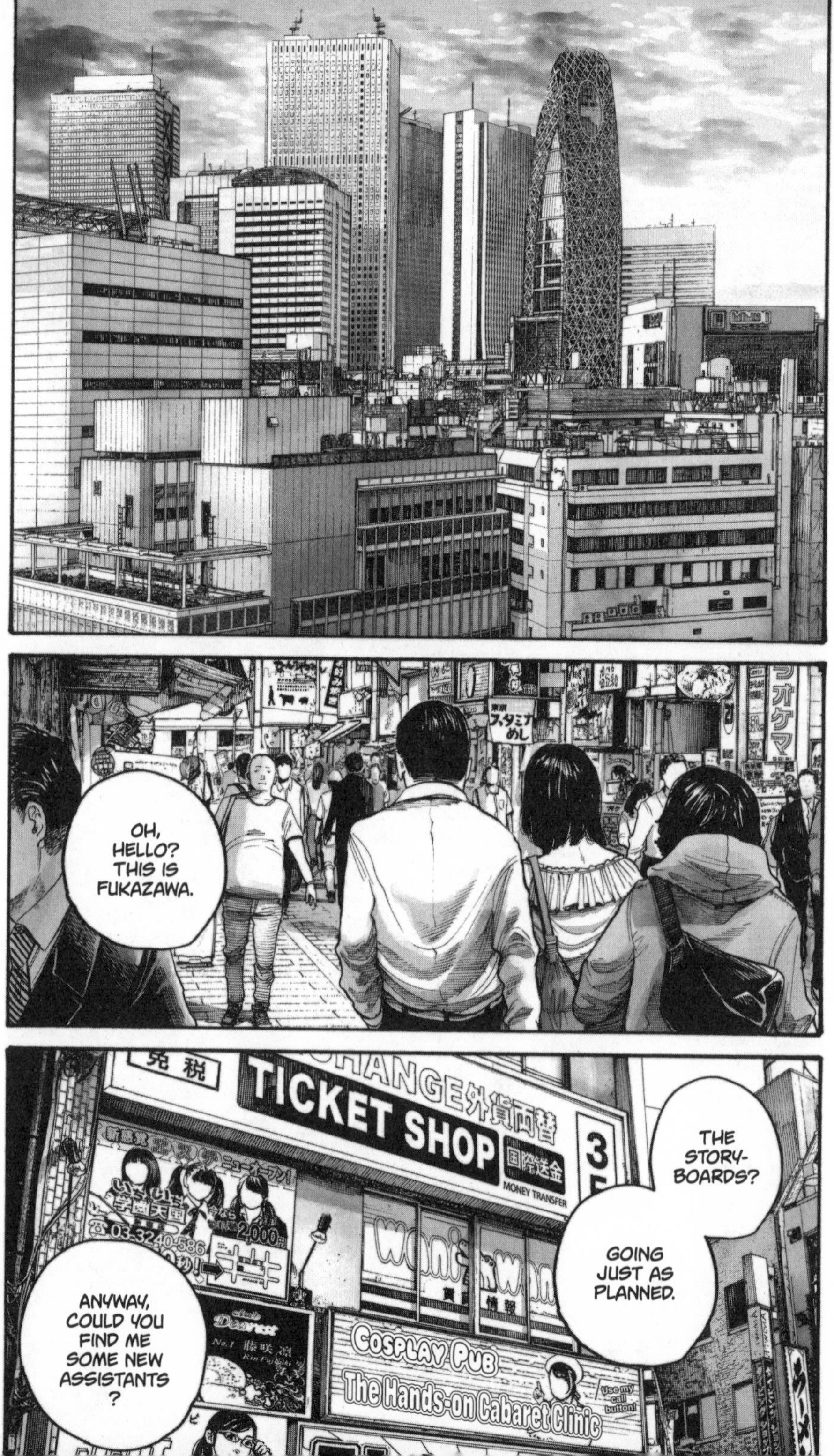
東京
スタミナめし
OH, HELLO? THIS IS FUKAZAWA.
免税
TICKET SHOP
外貨両替
国際送金
MONEY TRANSFER
COSPLAY PUB
The Hands-on Cabaret Clinic
Use my call button!
THE STORY-BOARDS?
GOING JUST AS PLANNED.
ANYWAY, COULD YOU FIND ME SOME NEW ASSISTANTS?

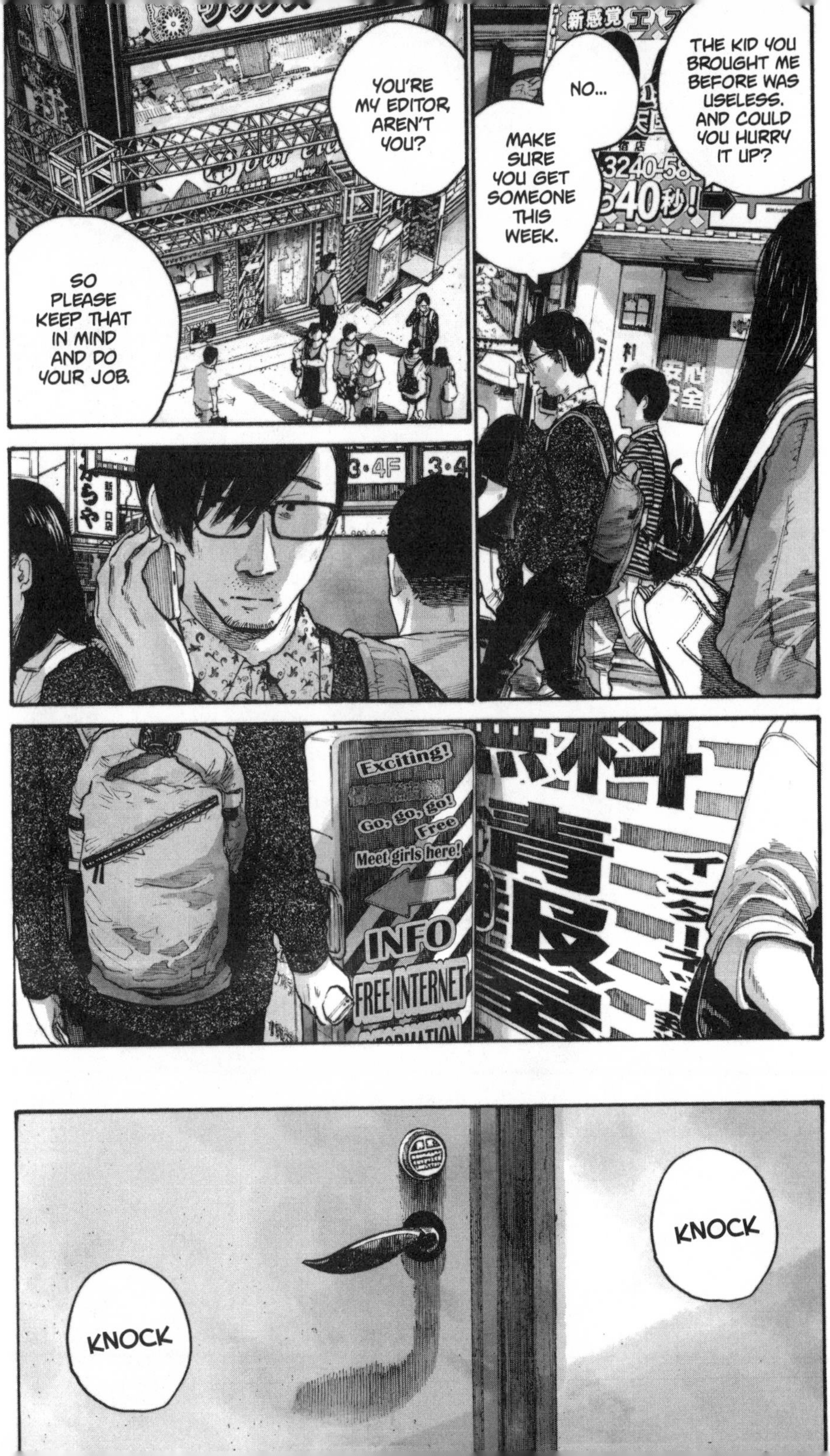
新感覚
THE KID YOU BROUGHT ME BEFORE WAS USELESS. AND COULD YOU HURRY IT UP?
NO...
MAKE SURE YOU GET SOMEONE THIS WEEK.
YOU'RE MY EDITOR, AREN'T YOU?
SO PLEASE KEEP THAT IN MIND AND DO YOUR JOB.
3·4F
Exciting!
Go, go, go!
Free
Meet girls here!
INFO
FREE INTERNET
KNOCK
KNOCK

HELLO...

I'M MARIMEKKO.

I'M SORRY YOU GOT SOMEONE AS UGLY AS ME.

UM. UM. UH...

PLEASE BE GENTLE WITH ME.

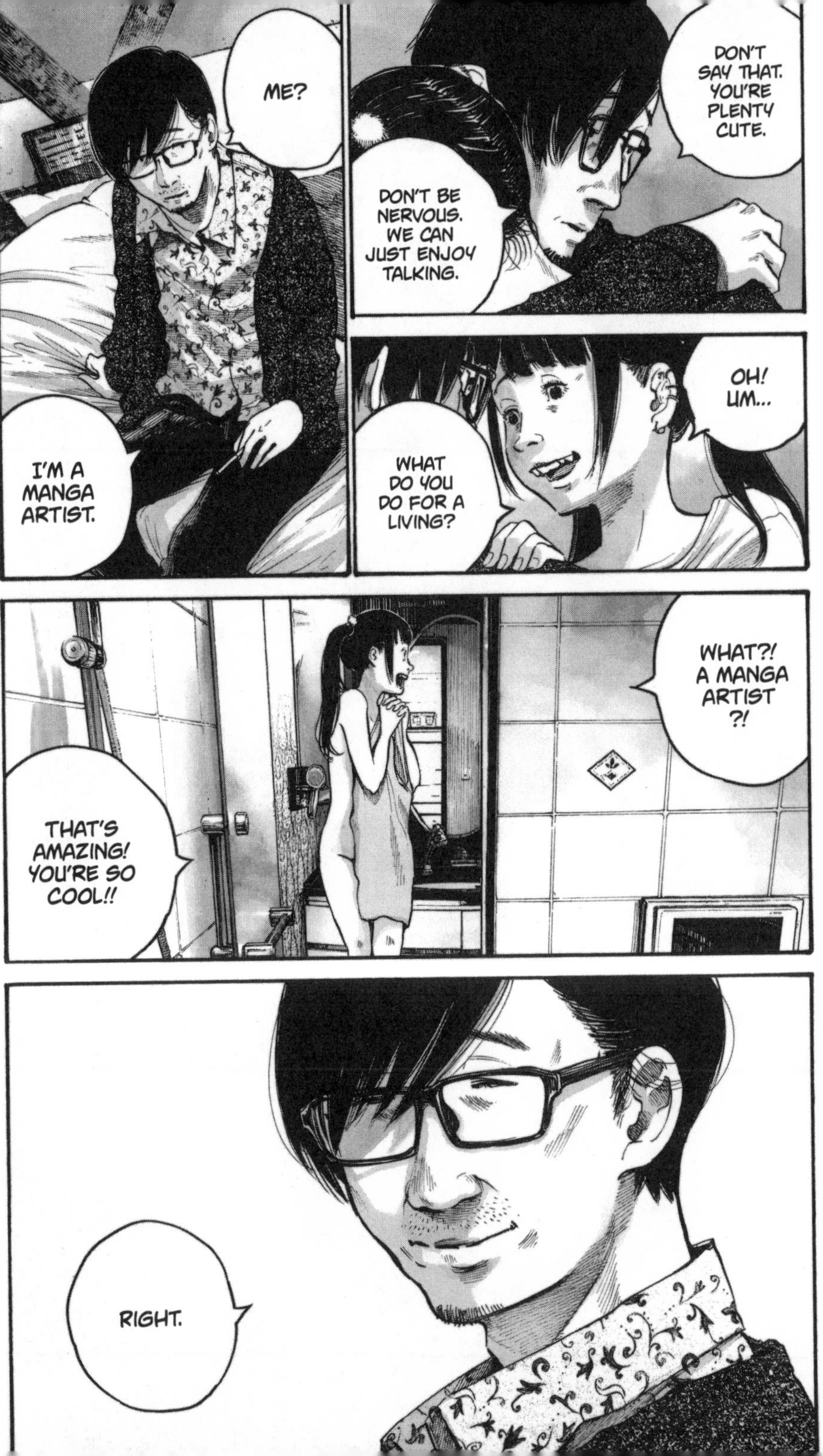
DON'T SAY THAT. YOU'RE PLENTY CUTE.
DON'T BE NERVOUS. WE CAN JUST ENJOY TALKING.
OH! UM...
WHAT DO YOU DO FOR A LIVING?
ME?
I'M A MANGA ARTIST.
WHAT?! A MANGA ARTIST?!
THAT'S AMAZING! YOU'RE SO COOL!!
RIGHT.

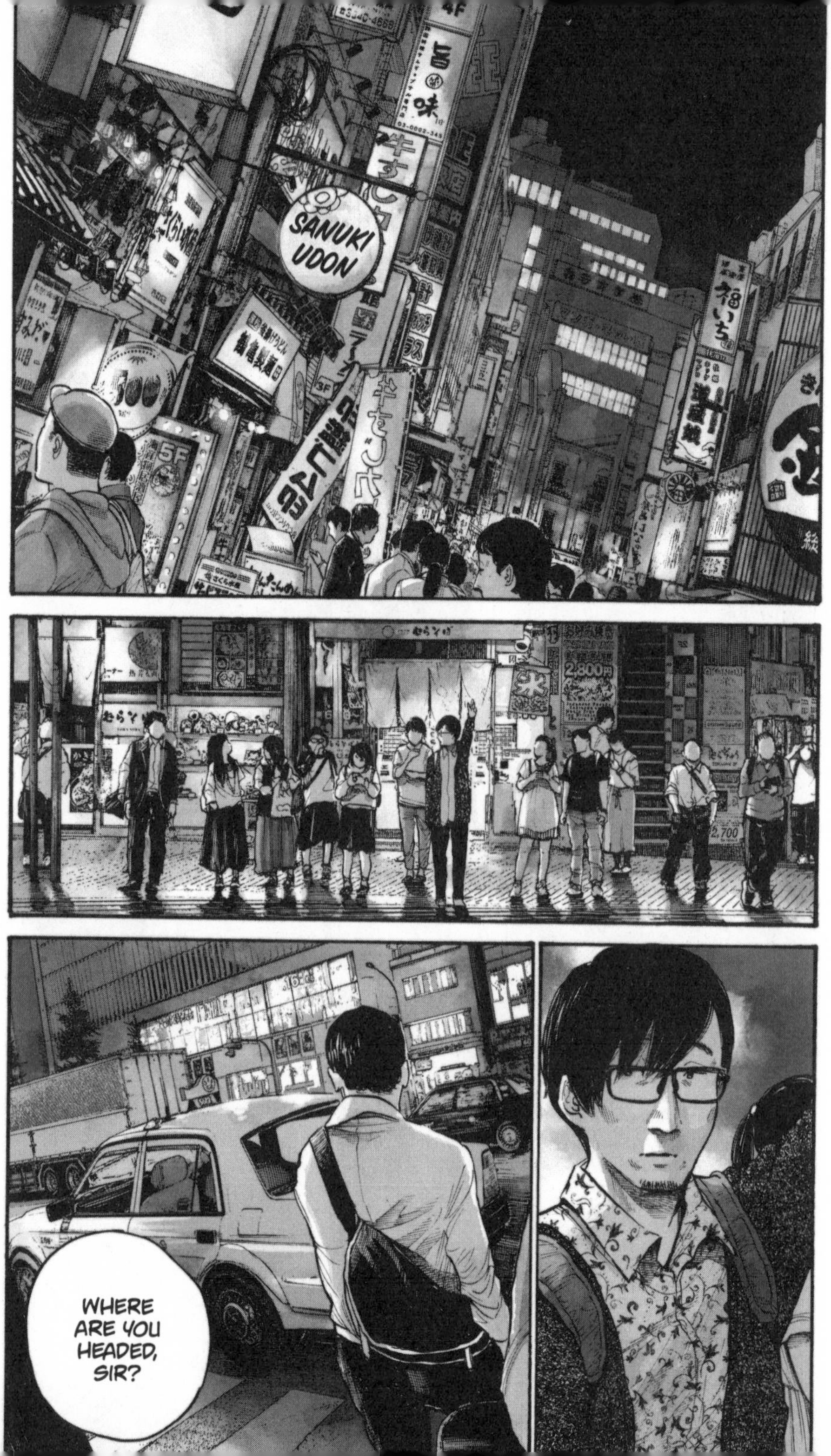
SANUKI UDON
5F
WHERE ARE YOU HEADED, SIR?

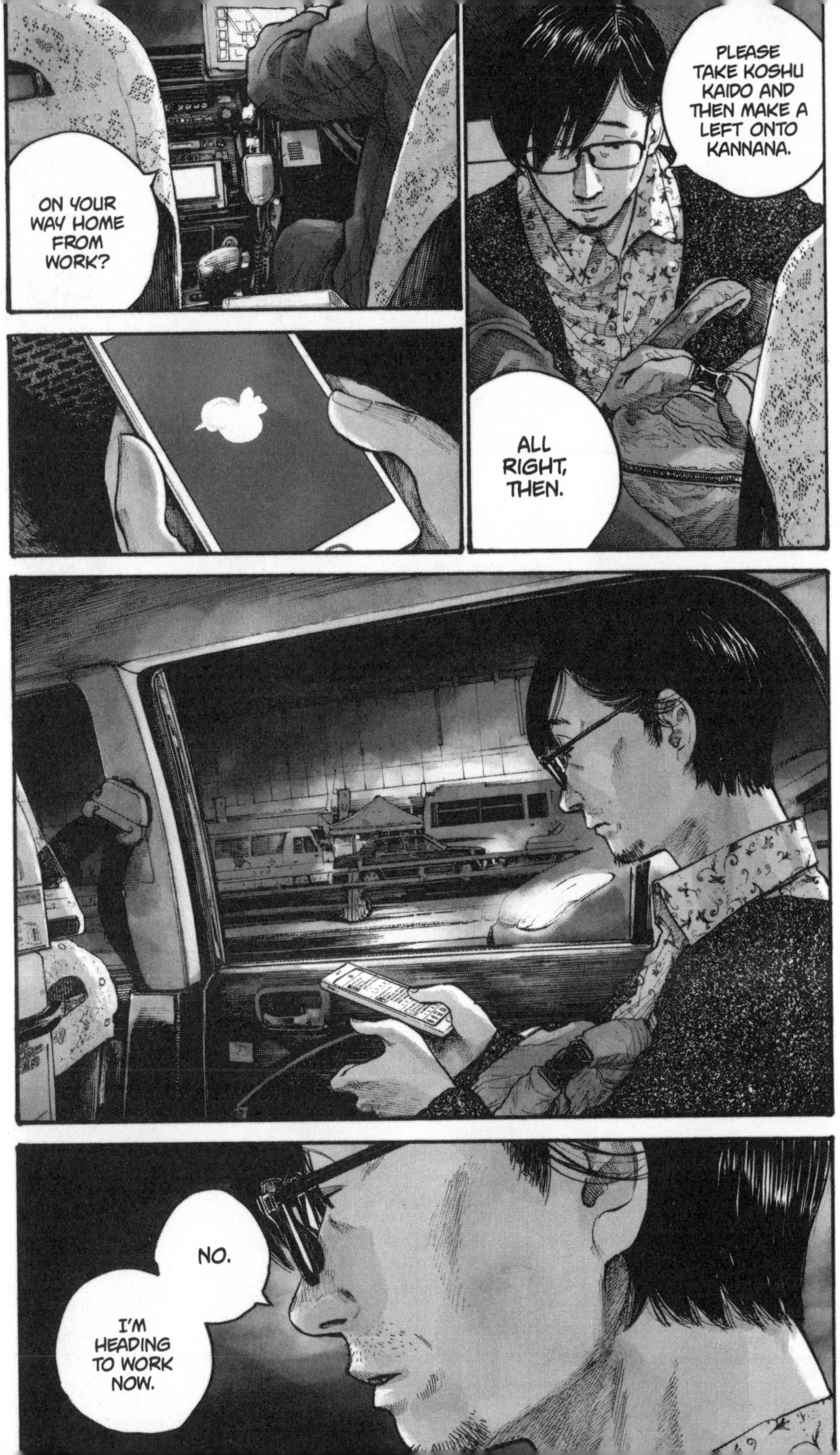
PLEASE TAKE KOSHU KAIDO AND THEN MAKE A LEFT ONTO KANNANA.
ALL RIGHT, THEN.
ON YOUR WAY HOME FROM WORK?
NO.
I'M HEADING TO WORK NOW.

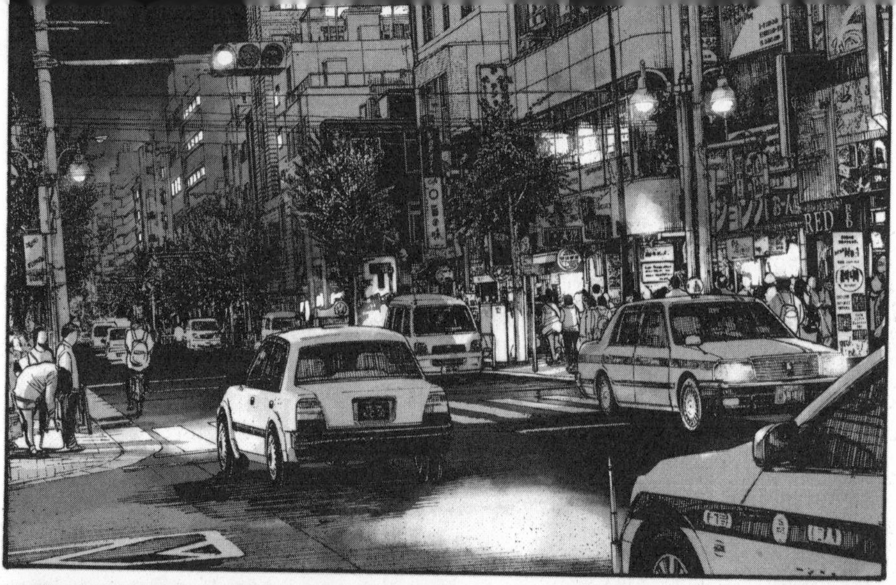
RED
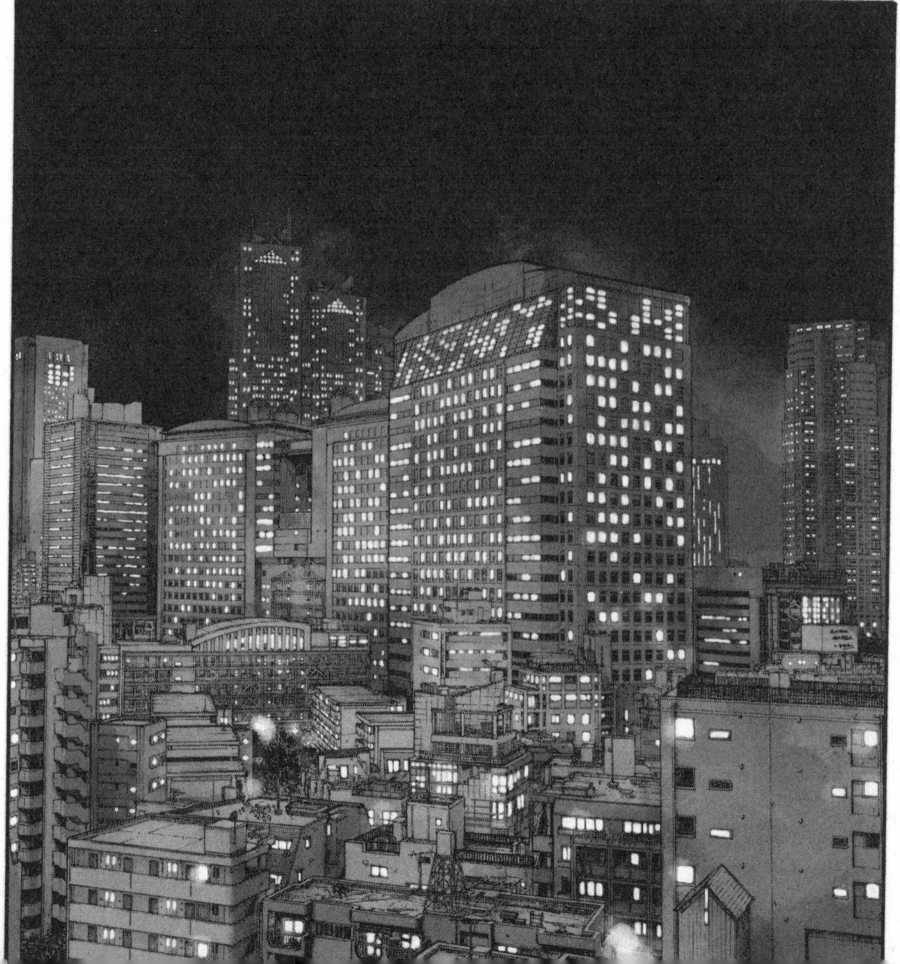

FINAL CHAPTER

Back when I was an up-and-coming manga artist, I was going out with this woman who had been in university with me. She was a year younger than me. Her narrow stray-cat eyes were really a hint at her nature, how her heart was closed off to others.

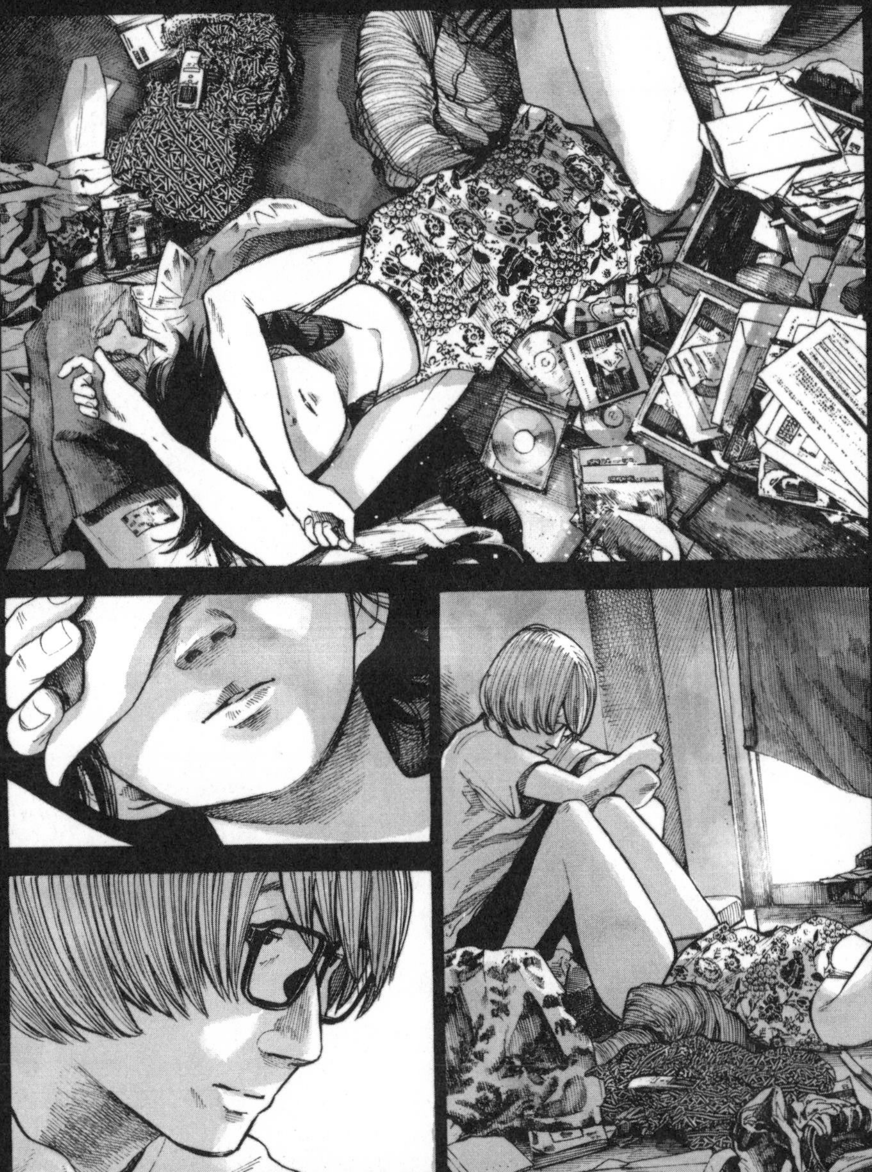

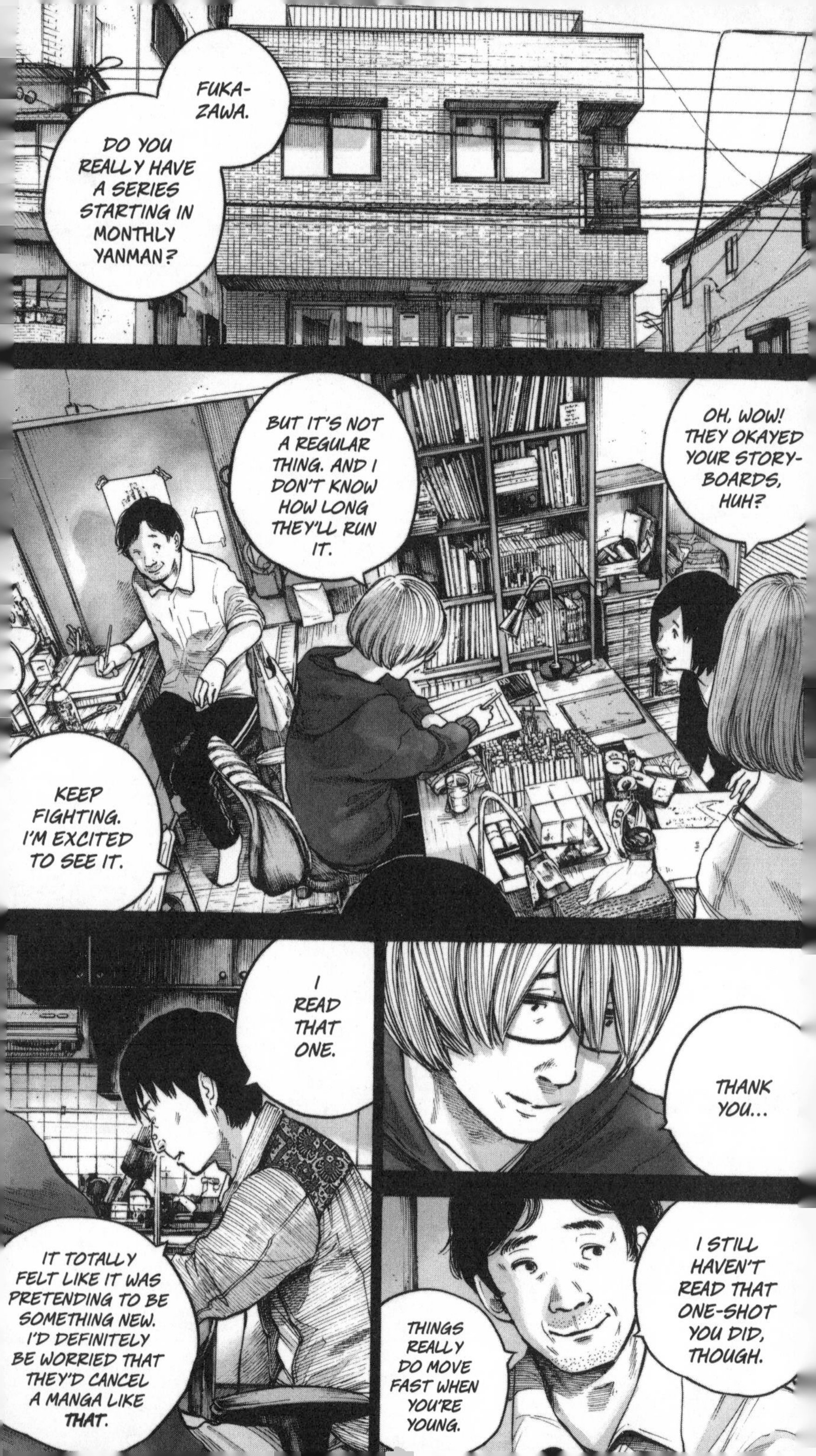
FUKA-ZAWA.
DO YOU REALLY HAVE A SERIES STARTING IN MONTHLY YANMAN?
OH, WOW! THEY OKAYED YOUR STORY-BOARDS, HUH?
BUT IT'S NOT A REGULAR THING. AND I DON'T KNOW HOW LONG THEY'LL RUN IT.
KEEP FIGHTING. I'M EXCITED TO SEE IT.
THANK YOU...
I STILL HAVEN'T READ THAT ONE-SHOT YOU DID, THOUGH.
THINGS REALLY DO MOVE FAST WHEN YOU'RE YOUNG.
I READ THAT ONE.
IT TOTALLY FELT LIKE IT WAS PRETENDING TO BE SOMETHING NEW. I'D DEFINITELY BE WORRIED THAT THEY'D CANCEL A MANGA LIKE THAT.

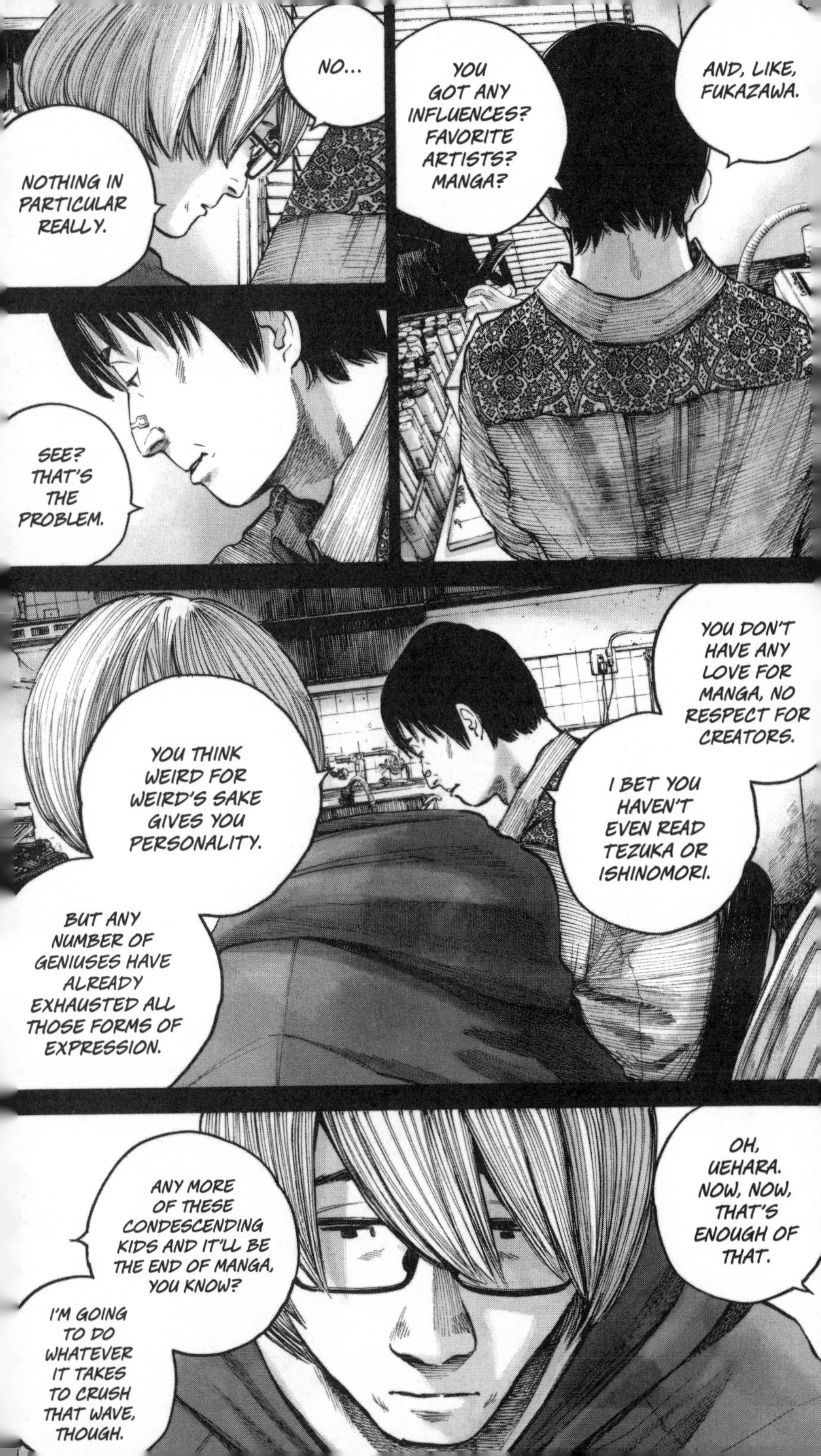
AND, LIKE, FUKAZAWA.
YOU GOT ANY INFLUENCES? FAVORITE ARTISTS? MANGA?
NO...
NOTHING IN PARTICULAR REALLY.
SEE? THAT'S THE PROBLEM.
YOU DON'T HAVE ANY LOVE FOR MANGA, NO RESPECT FOR CREATORS.
I BET YOU HAVEN'T EVEN READ TEZUKA OR ISHINOMORI.
YOU THINK WEIRD FOR WEIRD'S SAKE GIVES YOU PERSONALITY.
BUT ANY NUMBER OF GENIUSES HAVE ALREADY EXHAUSTED ALL THOSE FORMS OF EXPRESSION.
OH, UEHARA. NOW, NOW, THAT'S ENOUGH OF THAT.
ANY MORE OF THESE CONDESCENDING KIDS AND IT'LL BE THE END OF MANGA, YOU KNOW?
I'M GOING TO DO WHATEVER IT TAKES TO CRUSH THAT WAVE, THOUGH.

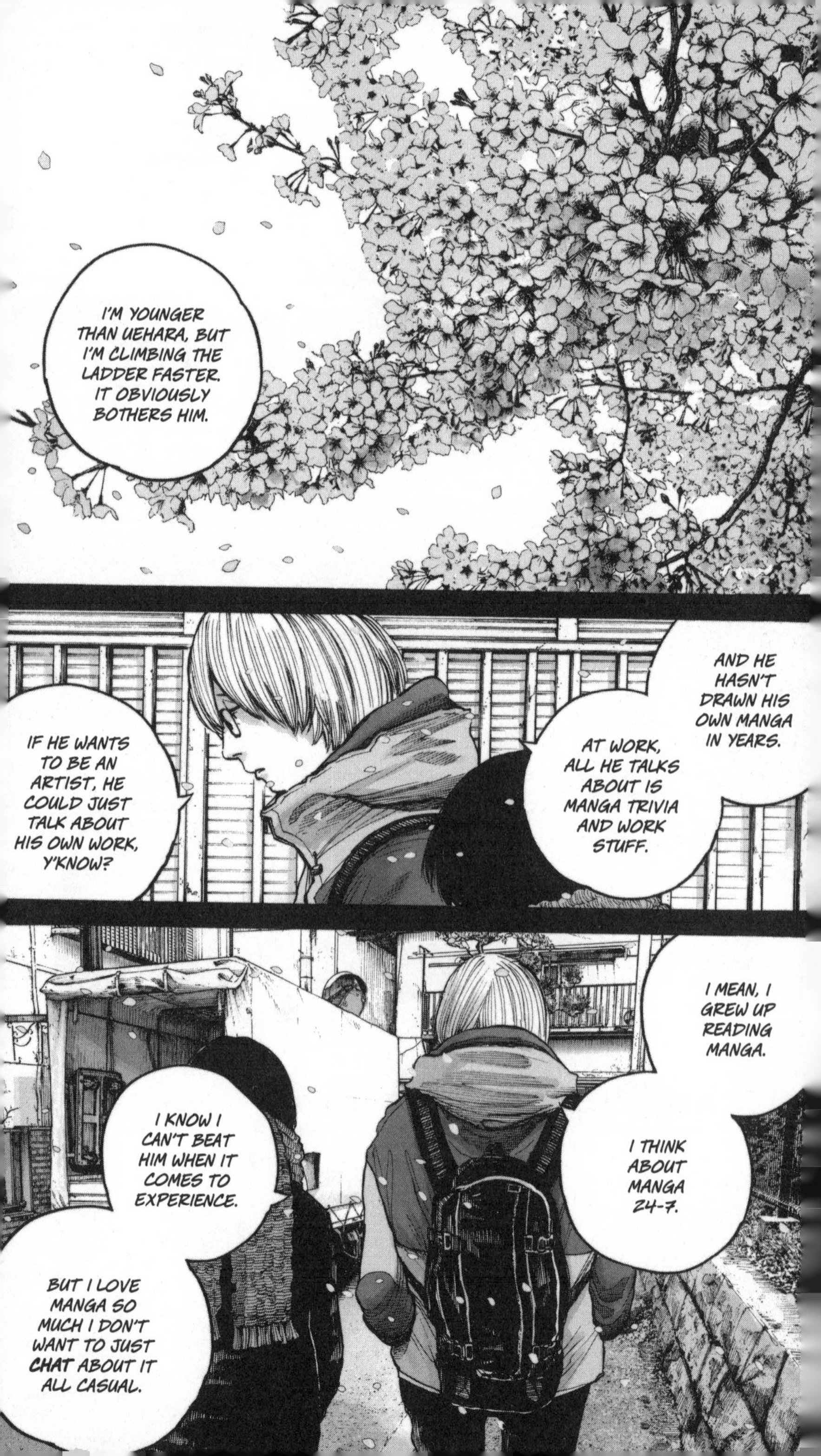
I'M YOUNGER THAN UEHARA, BUT I'M CLIMBING THE LADDER FASTER. IT OBVIOUSLY BOTHERS HIM.
AND HE HASN'T DRAWN HIS OWN MANGA IN YEARS.
AT WORK, ALL HE TALKS ABOUT IS MANGA TRIVIA AND WORK STUFF.
IF HE WANTS TO BE AN ARTIST, HE COULD JUST TALK ABOUT HIS OWN WORK, Y'KNOW?
I MEAN, I GREW UP READING MANGA.
I THINK ABOUT MANGA 24-7.
I KNOW I CAN'T BEAT HIM WHEN IT COMES TO EXPERIENCE.
BUT I LOVE MANGA SO MUCH I DON'T WANT TO JUST CHAT ABOUT IT ALL CASUAL.

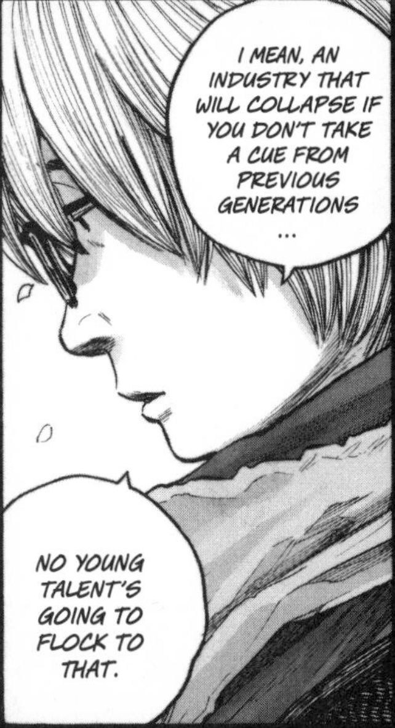
I MEAN, AN INDUSTRY THAT WILL COLLAPSE IF YOU DON'T TAKE A CUE FROM PREVIOUS GENERATIONS ...
NO YOUNG TALENT'S GOING TO FLOCK TO THAT.

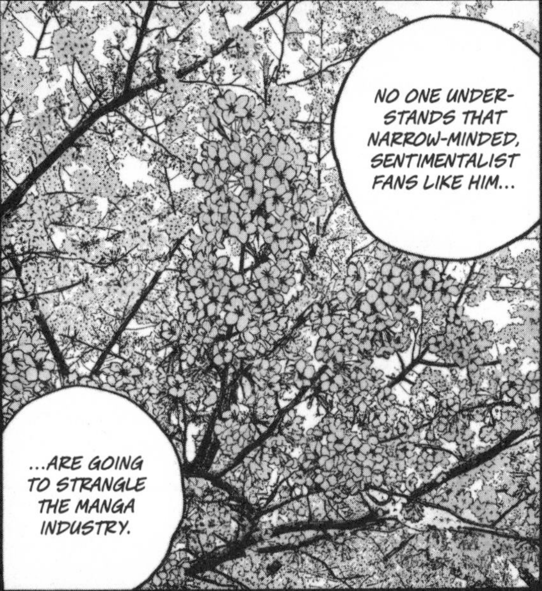
NO ONE UNDER-STANDS THAT NARROW-MINDED, SENTIMENTALIST FANS LIKE HIM...
...ARE GOING TO STRANGLE THE MANGA INDUSTRY.

I'd only just graduated university, and I passed the days in an anxious gloom, a new manga artist with absolutely no prospects.

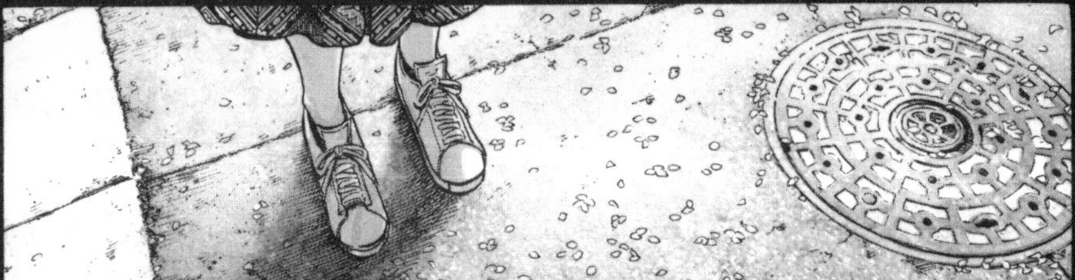

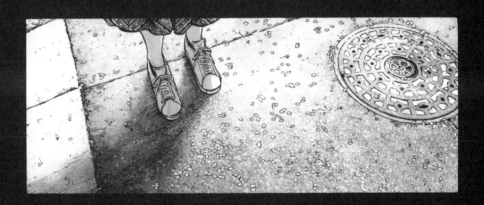

She was the first person to say anything nice about my manga.

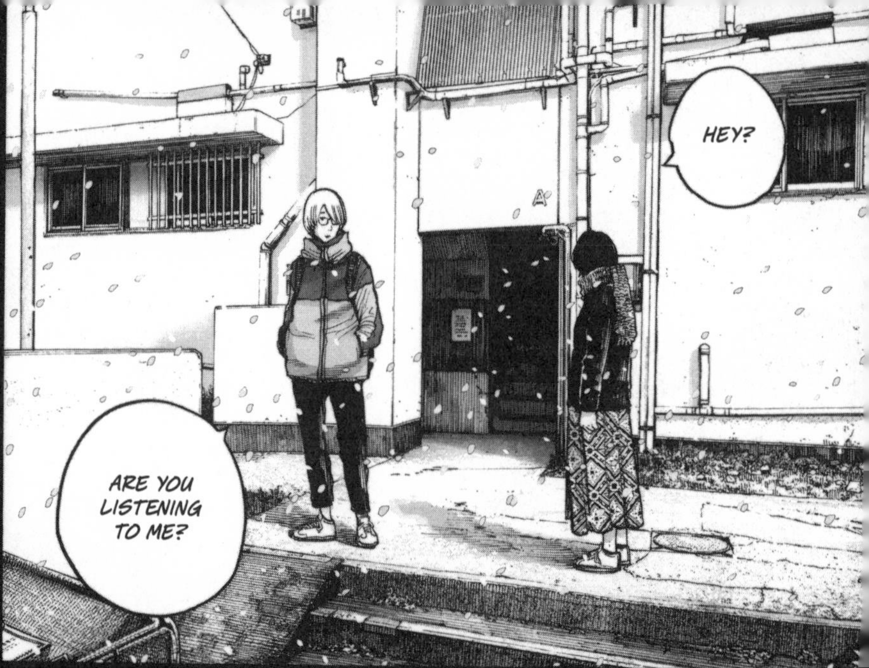
HEY?
ARE YOU LISTENING TO ME?

The mere fact of her acknowledgment was the sole reason I could keep going back then.

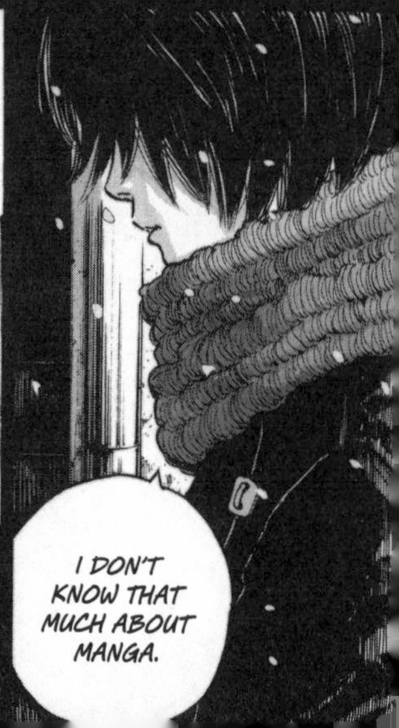
I DON'T KNOW THAT MUCH ABOUT MANGA.

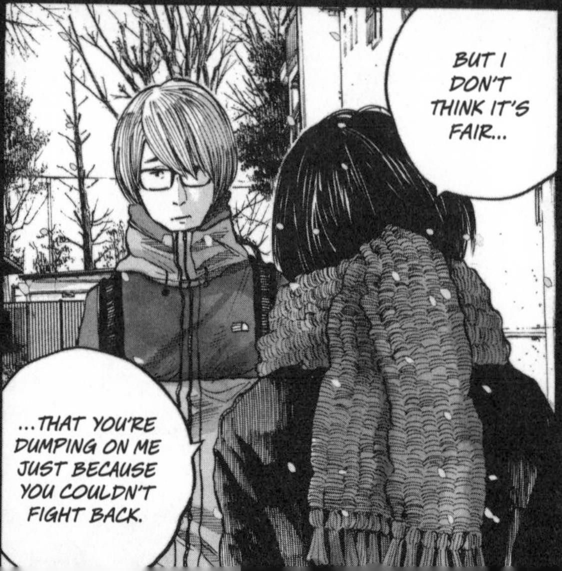
BUT I DON'T THINK IT'S FAIR...
...THAT YOU'RE DUMPING ON ME JUST BECAUSE YOU COULDN'T FIGHT BACK.

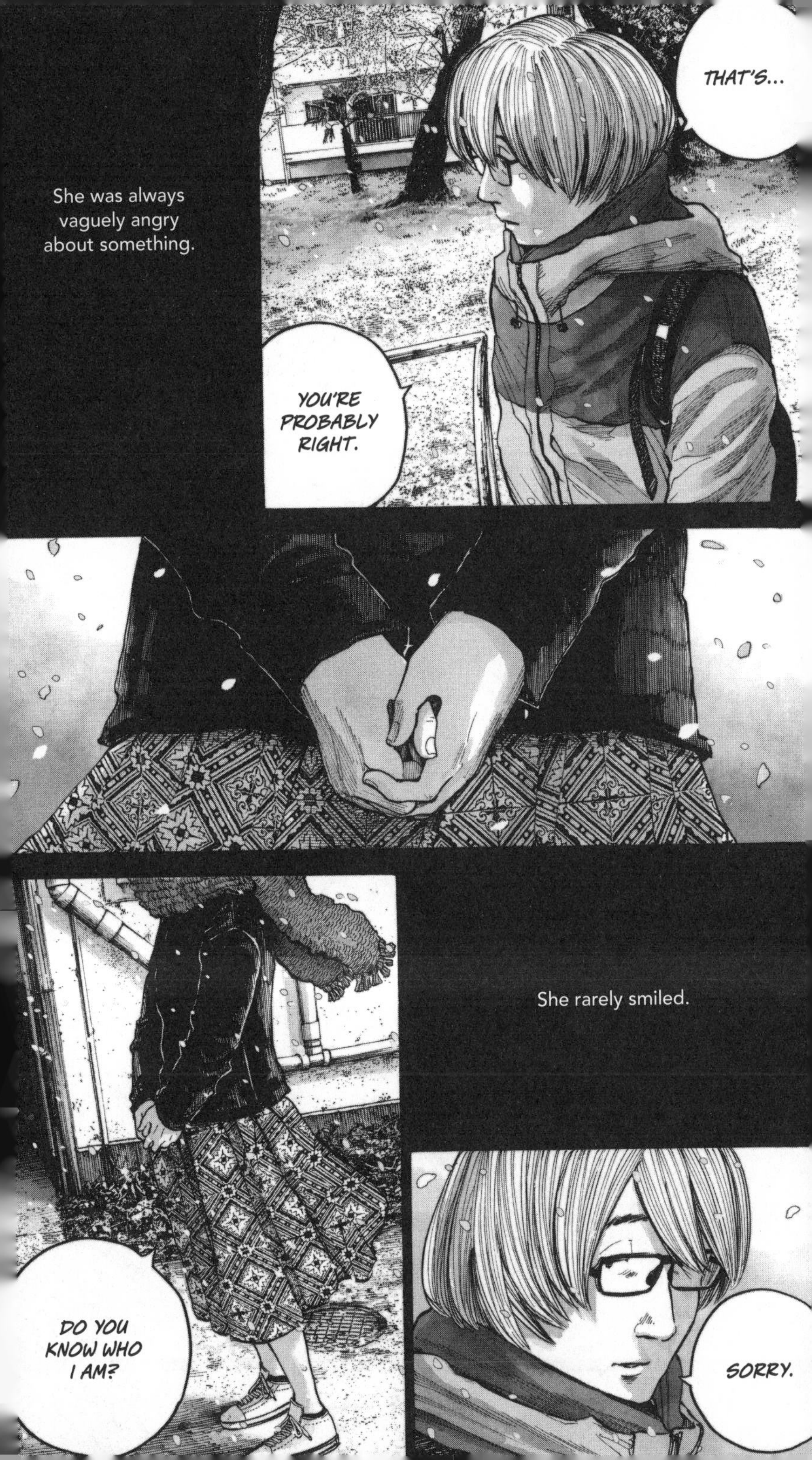
THAT'S...
YOU'RE PROBABLY RIGHT.
She was always vaguely angry about something.
She rarely smiled.
SORRY.
DO YOU KNOW WHO I AM?

Sometimes she'd go on about things that made no sense.

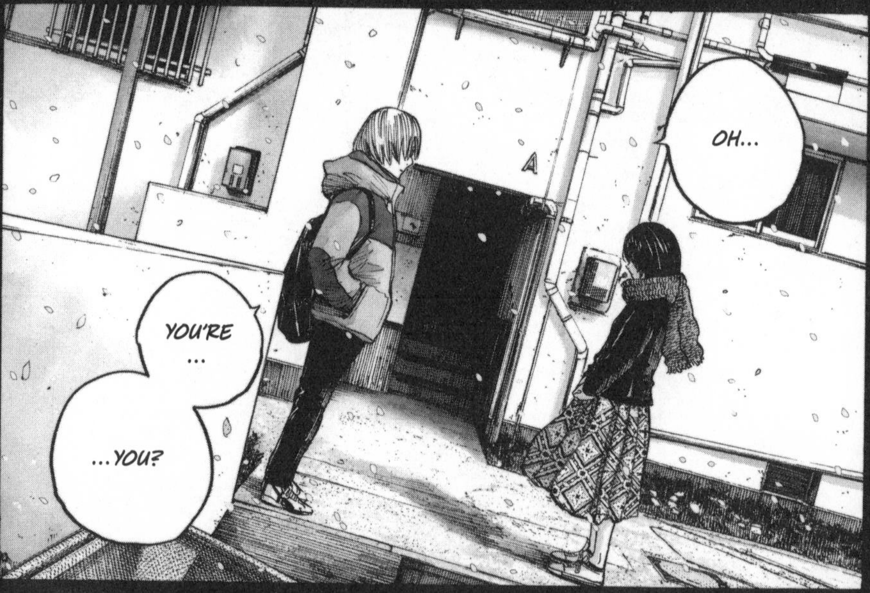
OH...
YOU'RE ...
...YOU?

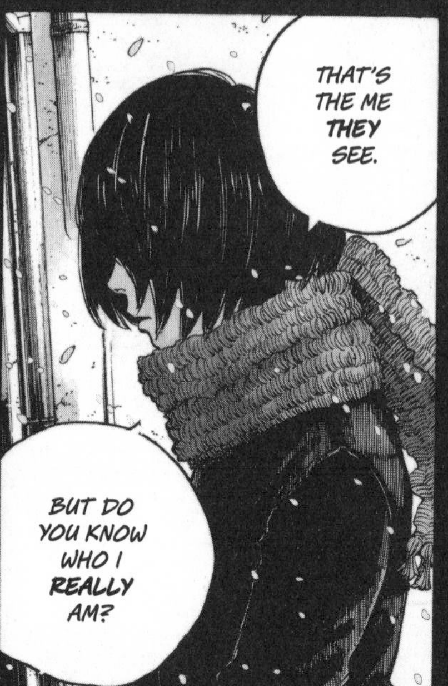
THAT'S THE ME THEY SEE.
BUT DO YOU KNOW WHO I REALLY AM?

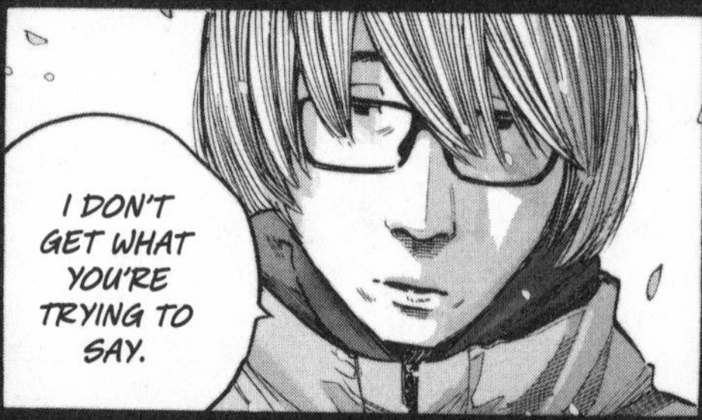
I DON'T GET WHAT YOU'RE TRYING TO SAY.

And I was a little afraid of her.

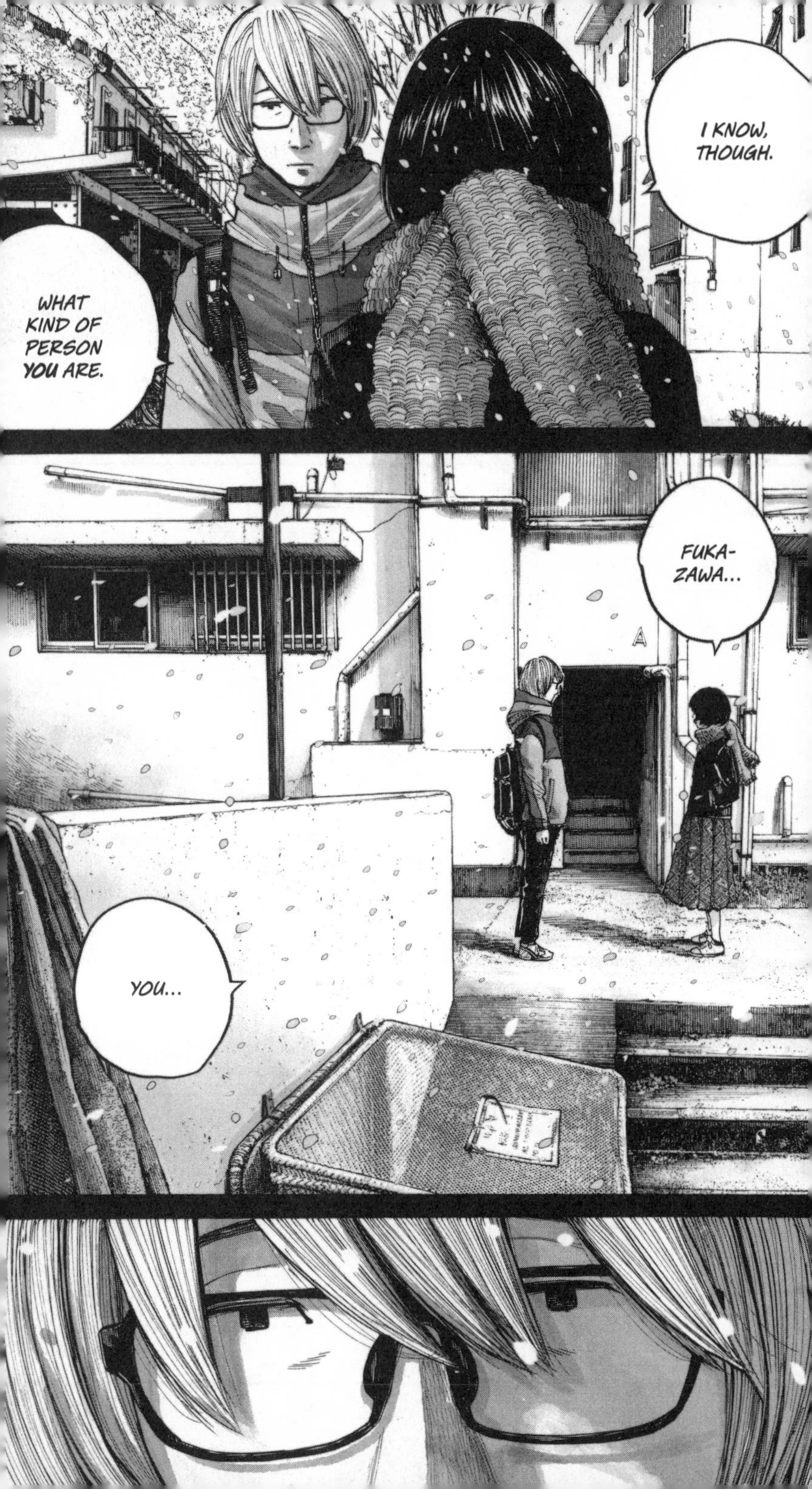
I KNOW, THOUGH.
WHAT KIND OF PERSON YOU ARE.
FUKA-ZAWA...
YOU...

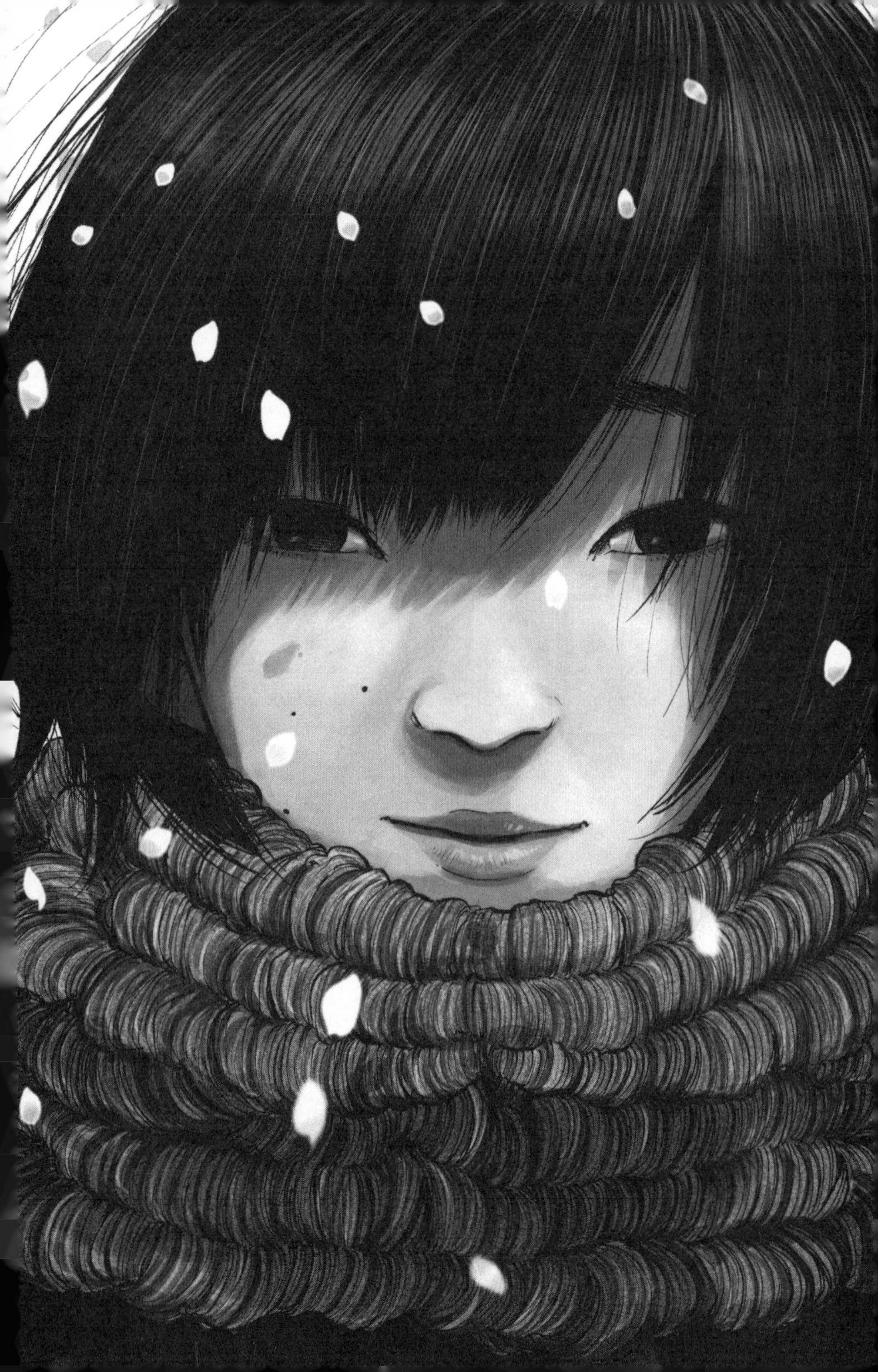

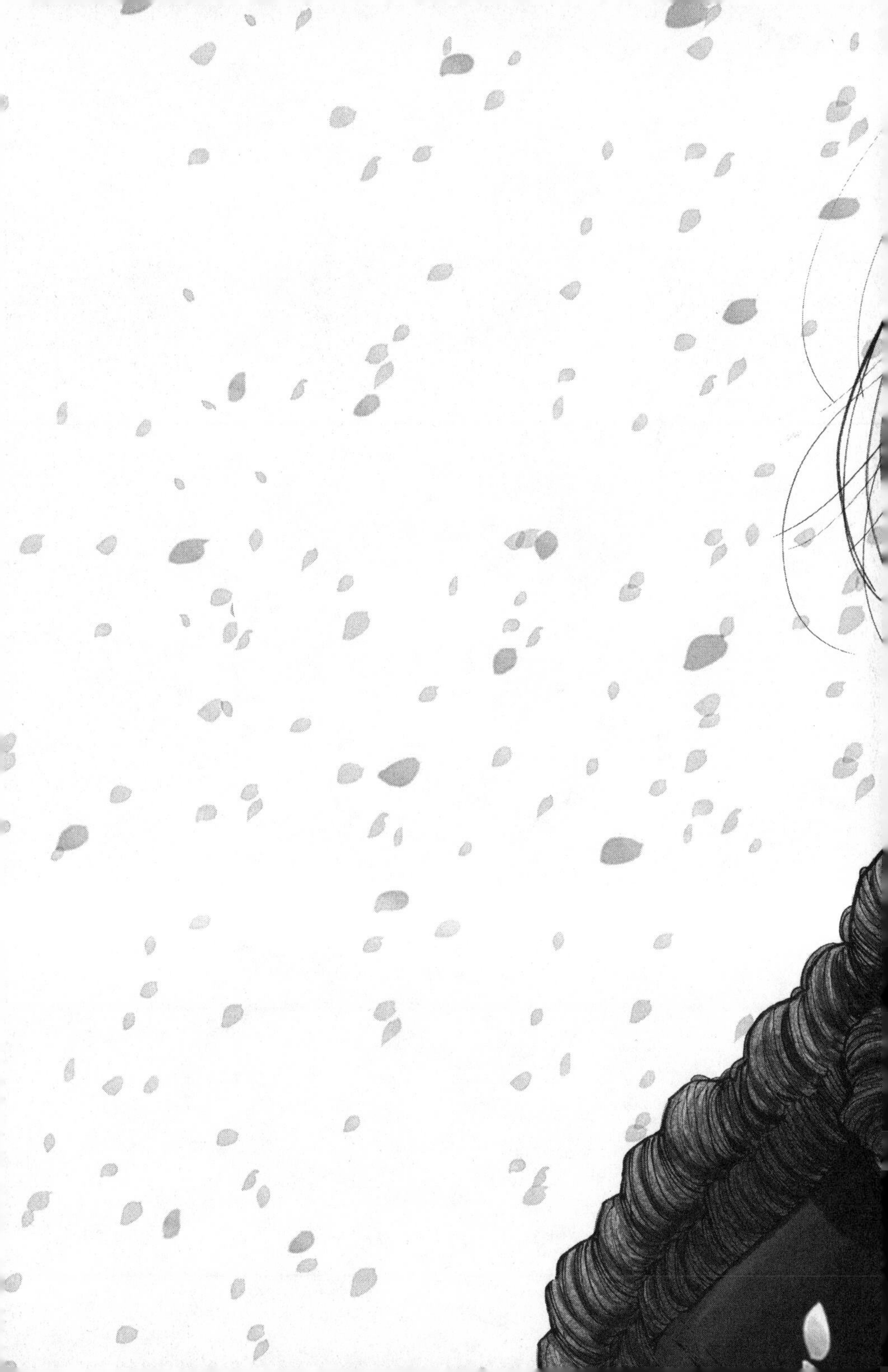

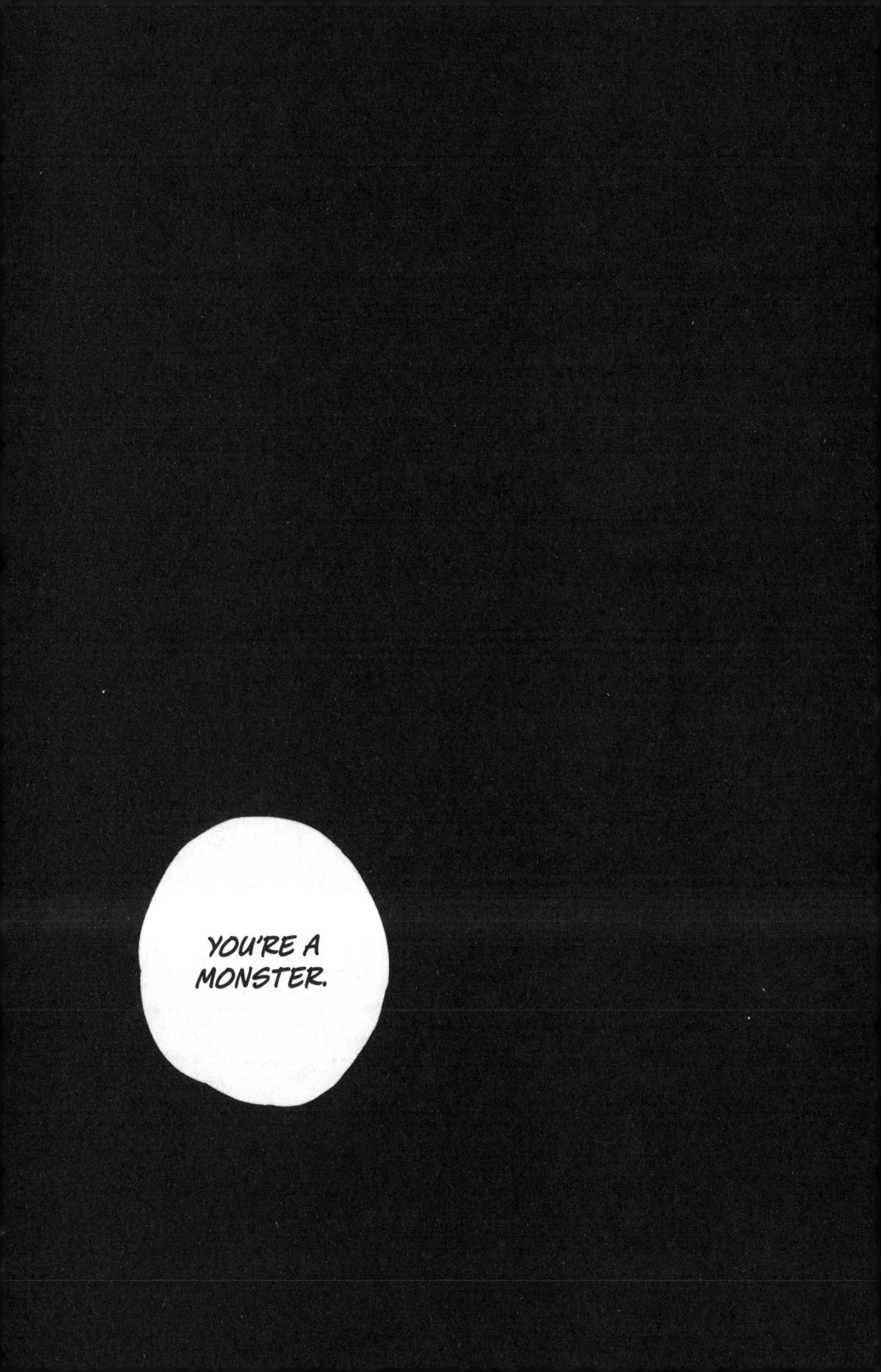
YOU'RE A MONSTER.

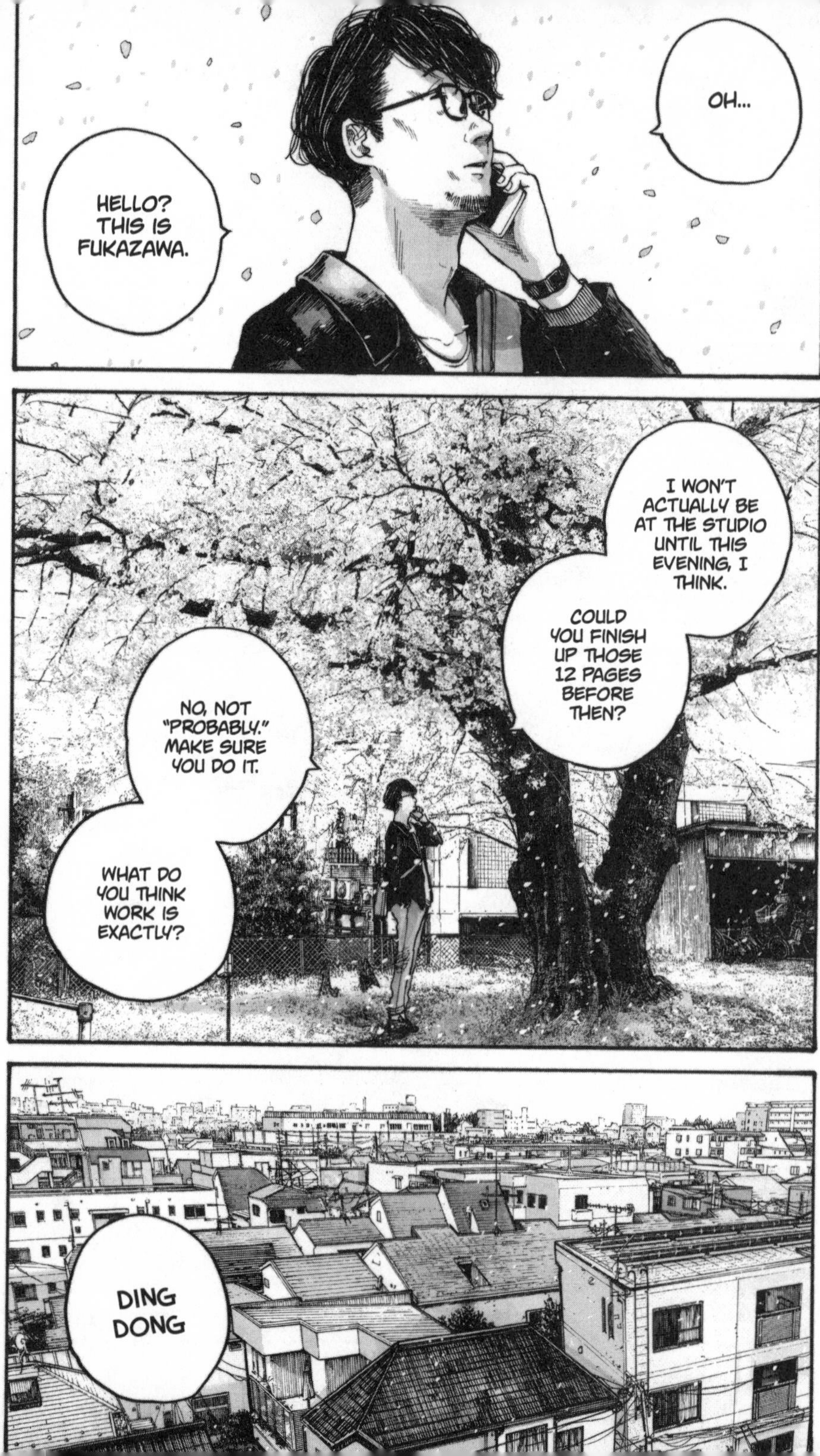
OH...
HELLO? THIS IS FUKAZAWA.
I WON'T ACTUALLY BE AT THE STUDIO UNTIL THIS EVENING, I THINK.
COULD YOU FINISH UP THOSE 12 PAGES BEFORE THEN?
NO, NOT "PROBABLY." MAKE SURE YOU DO IT.
WHAT DO YOU THINK WORK IS EXACTLY?
DING DONG

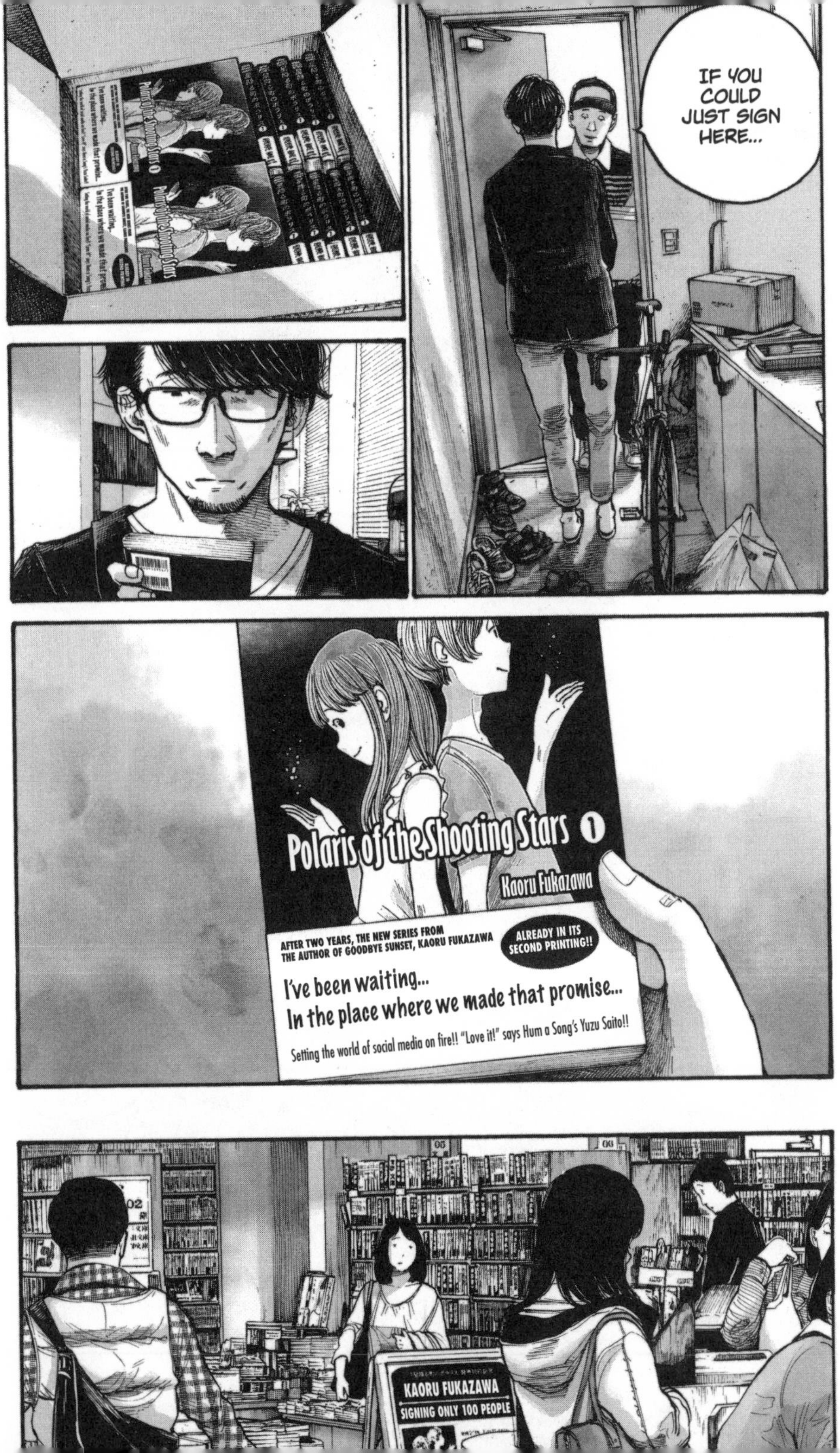
IF YOU COULD JUST SIGN HERE...
Polaris of the Shooting Stars 1
Kaoru Fukazawa
AFTER TWO YEARS, THE NEW SERIES FROM THE AUTHOR OF GOODBYE SUNSET, KAORU FUKAZAWA
ALREADY IN ITS SECOND PRINTING!!
I've been waiting...
In the place where we made that promise...
Setting the world of social media on fire!! "Love it!" says Hum a Song's Yuzu Saito!!
KAORU FUKAZAWA
SIGNING ONLY 100 PEOPLE

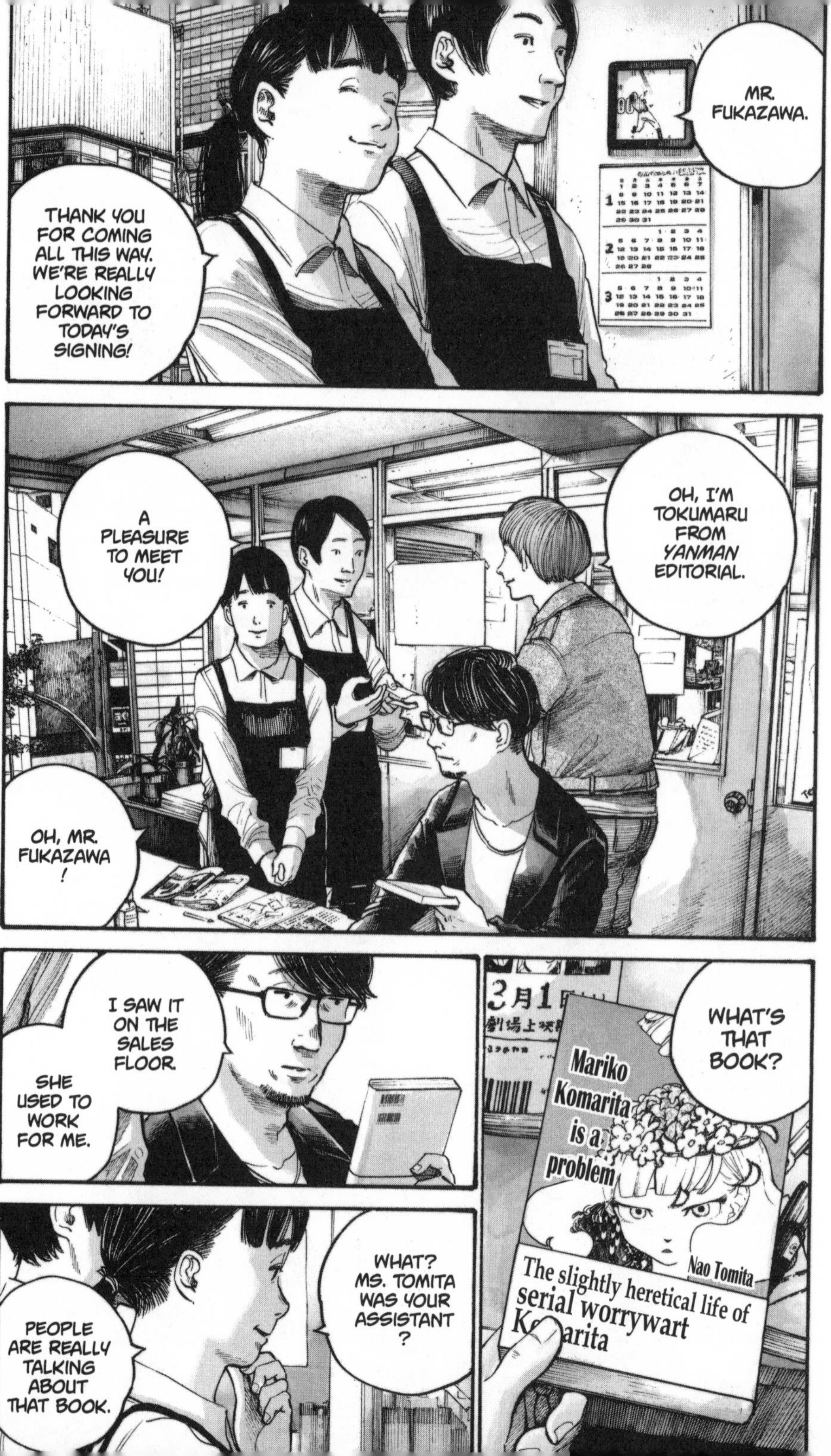
MR. FUKAZAWA.
THANK YOU FOR COMING ALL THIS WAY. WE'RE REALLY LOOKING FORWARD TO TODAY'S SIGNING!
OH, I'M TOKUMARU FROM YANMAN EDITORIAL.
A PLEASURE TO MEET YOU!
OH, MR. FUKAZAWA!
WHAT'S THAT BOOK?
Mariko Komarita is a problem
Nao Tomita
The slightly heretical life of serial worrywart
I SAW IT ON THE SALES FLOOR.
SHE USED TO WORK FOR ME.
WHAT? MS. TOMITA WAS YOUR ASSISTANT?
PEOPLE ARE REALLY TALKING ABOUT THAT BOOK.

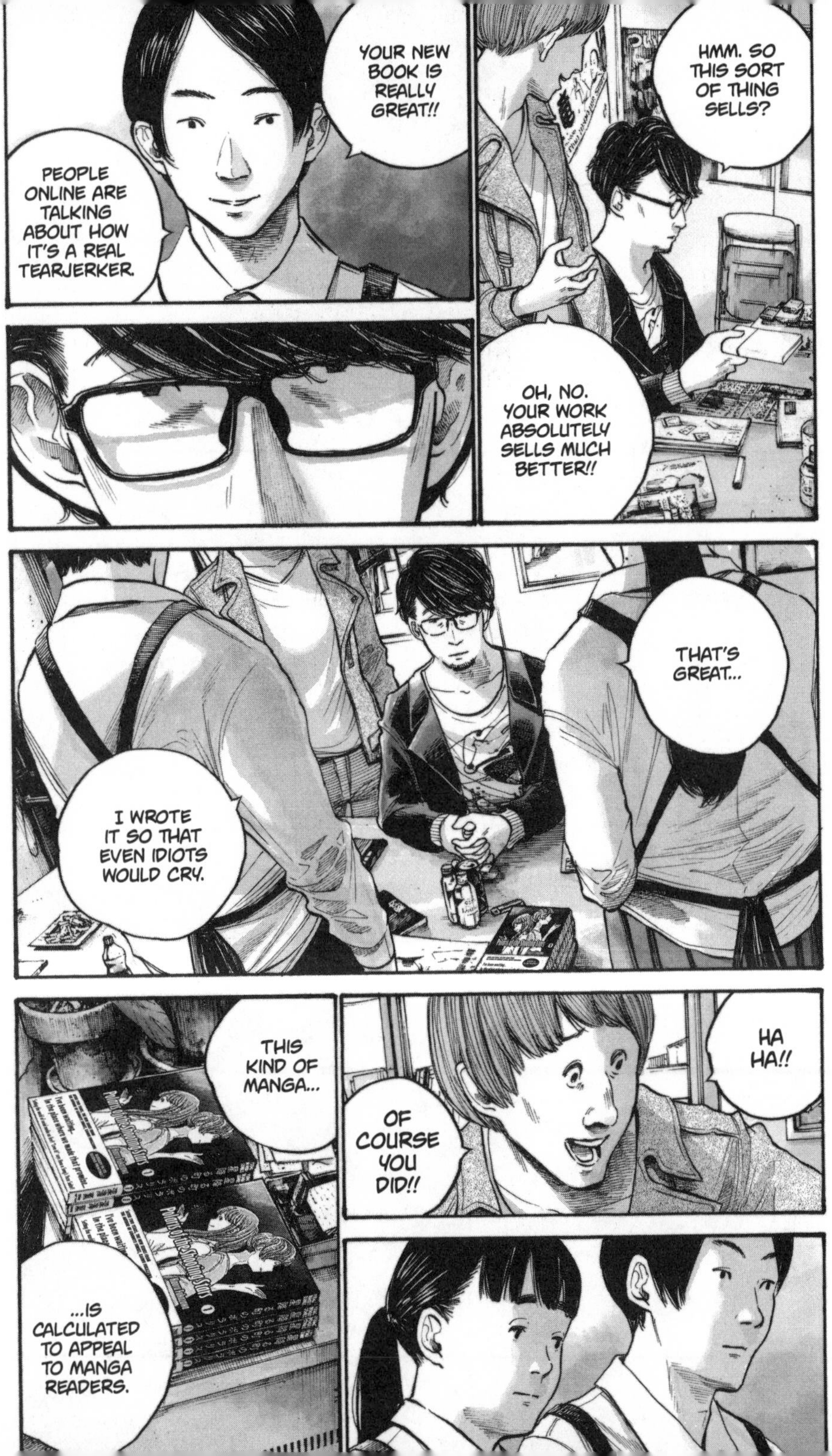
HMM. SO THIS SORT OF THING SELLS?
OH, NO. YOUR WORK ABSOLUTELY SELLS MUCH BETTER!!
YOUR NEW BOOK IS REALLY GREAT!!
PEOPLE ONLINE ARE TALKING ABOUT HOW IT'S A REAL TEARJERKER.
THAT'S GREAT...
I WROTE IT SO THAT EVEN IDIOTS WOULD CRY.
HA HA!!
OF COURSE YOU DID!!
THIS KIND OF MANGA...
...IS CALCULATED TO APPEAL TO MANGA READERS.

WHEN IT COMES TO ENTERTAINMENT, SOOTHING ALWAYS WINS OUT.

THAT'S THE LAW. AS LONG AS IT SELLS.

 Kaoru Fukazawa Polaris V1 on sale now @fukuzawa_kaoru
2017/04/03
Polaris V1 goes on sale today!! I'm so overwhelmed that the day has come when I can bring it to all you readers! Thanks so much to my staff and everyone involved with the book. I'm doing a signing this afternoon in Shinjuku. Please stop by!!

 21   150 ♥ ■ 285

Polaris of the Stars Vol. 1

Kaoru Fukazawa signing

BOOKS KINOKUNIYA

I'M TOTALLY IN LOVE WITH RUI!

PLEASE KEEP GOING WITH THIS SERIES!!

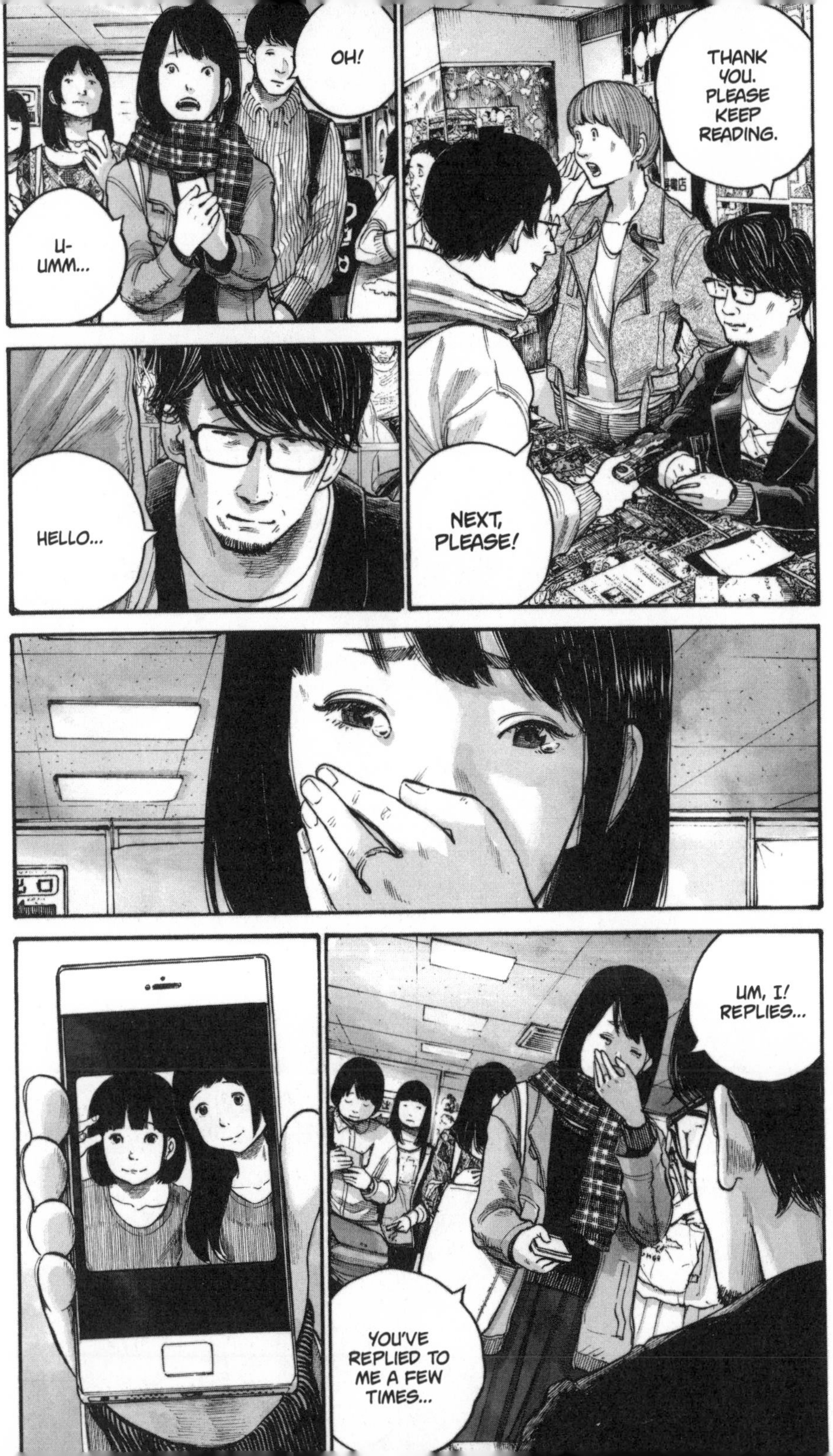
THANK YOU. PLEASE KEEP READING.
NEXT, PLEASE!
OH!
U-UMM...
HELLO...
UM, I! REPLIES...
YOU'VE REPLIED TO ME A FEW TIMES...

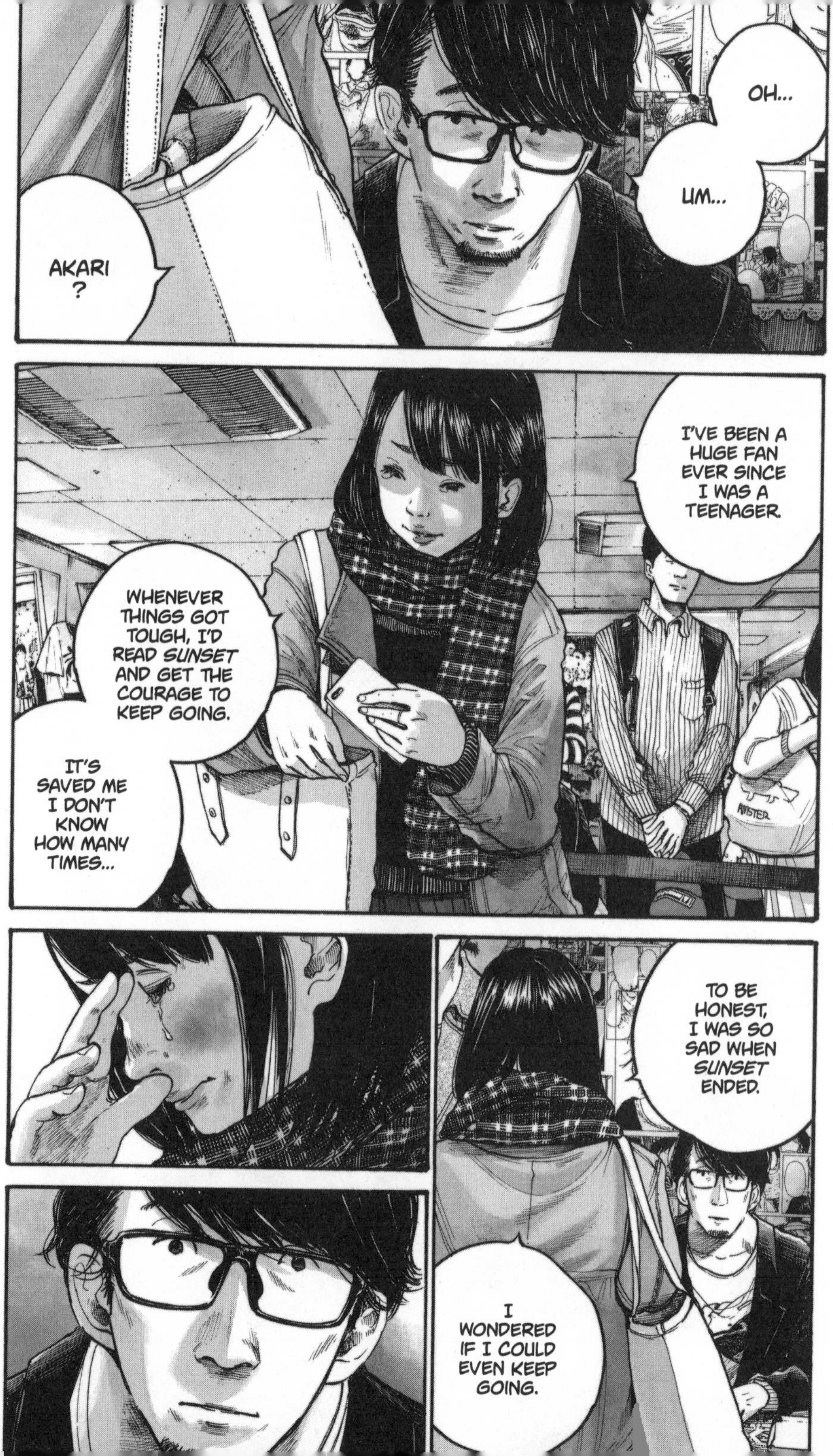
OH...
UM...
AKARI ?
I'VE BEEN A HUGE FAN EVER SINCE I WAS A TEENAGER.
WHENEVER THINGS GOT TOUGH, I'D READ *SUNSET* AND GET THE COURAGE TO KEEP GOING.
IT'S SAVED ME I DON'T KNOW HOW MANY TIMES...
TO BE HONEST, I WAS SO SAD WHEN *SUNSET* ENDED.
I WONDERED IF I COULD EVEN KEEP GOING.

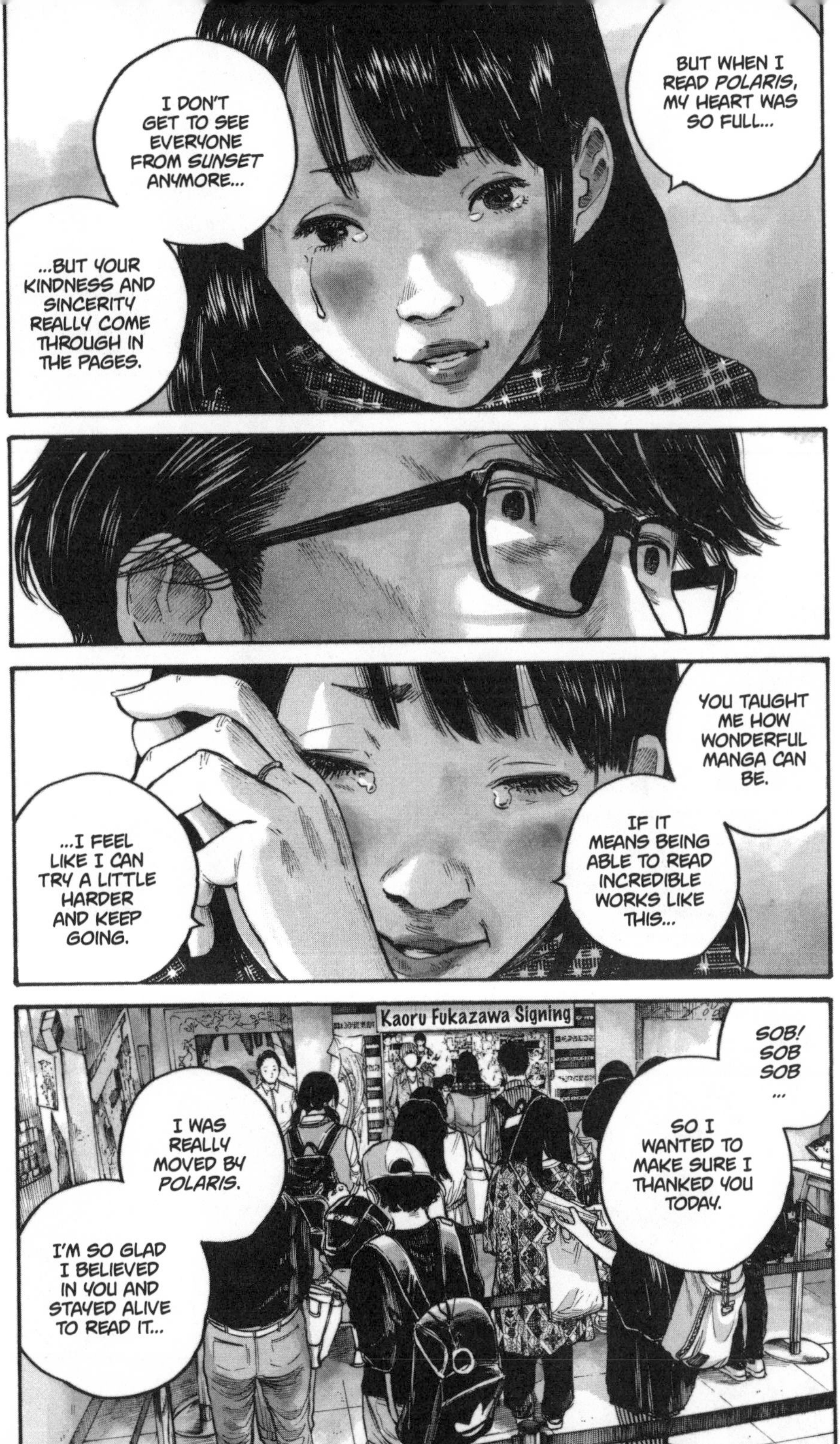
BUT WHEN I READ *POLARIS*, MY HEART WAS SO FULL...
I DON'T GET TO SEE EVERYONE FROM *SUNSET* ANYMORE...
...BUT YOUR KINDNESS AND SINCERITY REALLY COME THROUGH IN THE PAGES.
YOU TAUGHT ME HOW WONDERFUL MANGA CAN BE.
IF IT MEANS BEING ABLE TO READ INCREDIBLE WORKS LIKE THIS...
...I FEEL LIKE I CAN TRY A LITTLE HARDER AND KEEP GOING.
Kaoru Fukazawa Signing
SOB! SOB SOB ...
SO I WANTED TO MAKE SURE I THANKED YOU TODAY.
I WAS REALLY MOVED BY *POLARIS*.
I'M SO GLAD I BELIEVED IN YOU AND STAYED ALIVE TO READ IT...

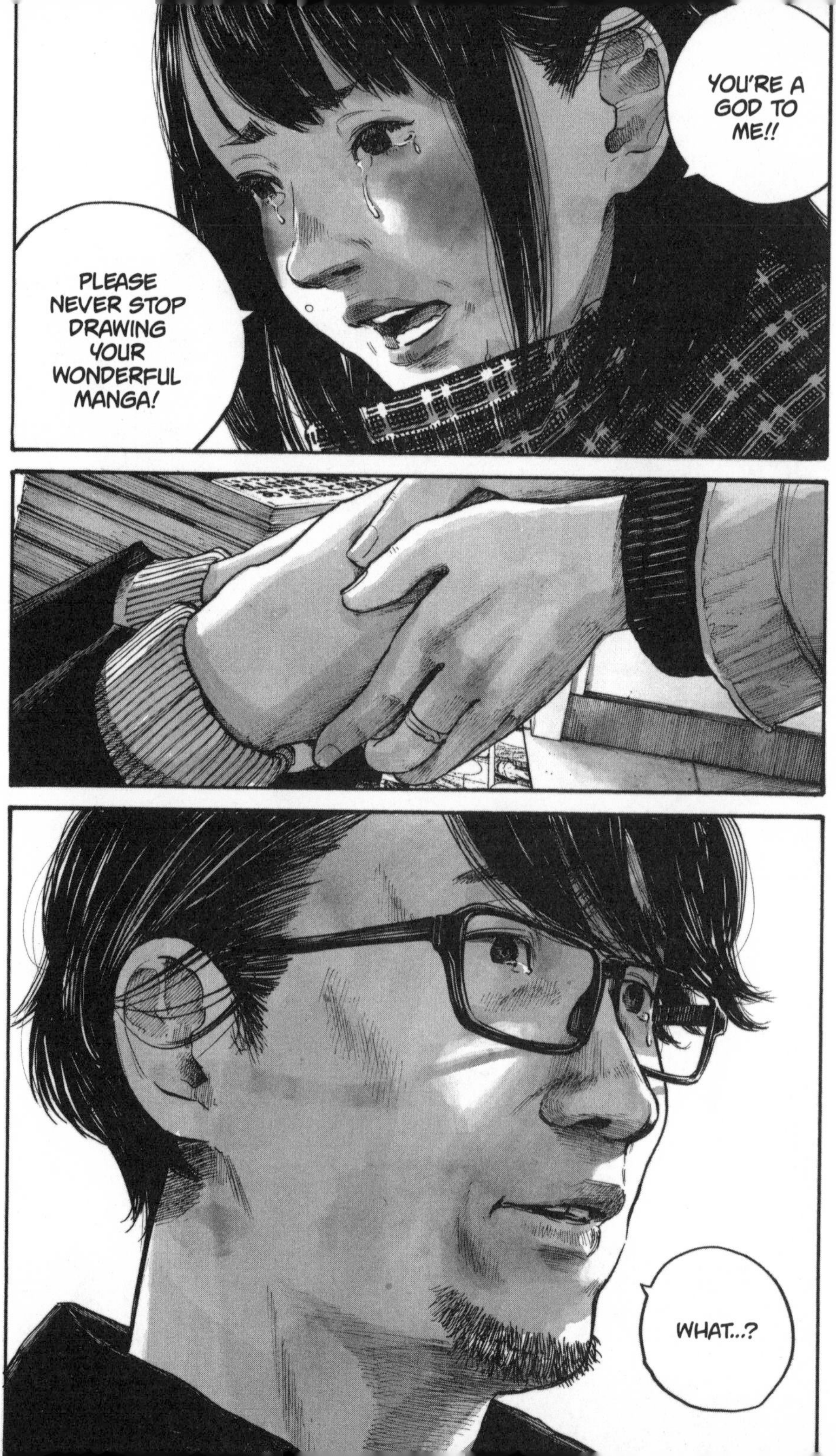
YOU'RE A GOD TO ME!!
PLEASE NEVER STOP DRAWING YOUR WONDERFUL MANGA!
WHAT...?

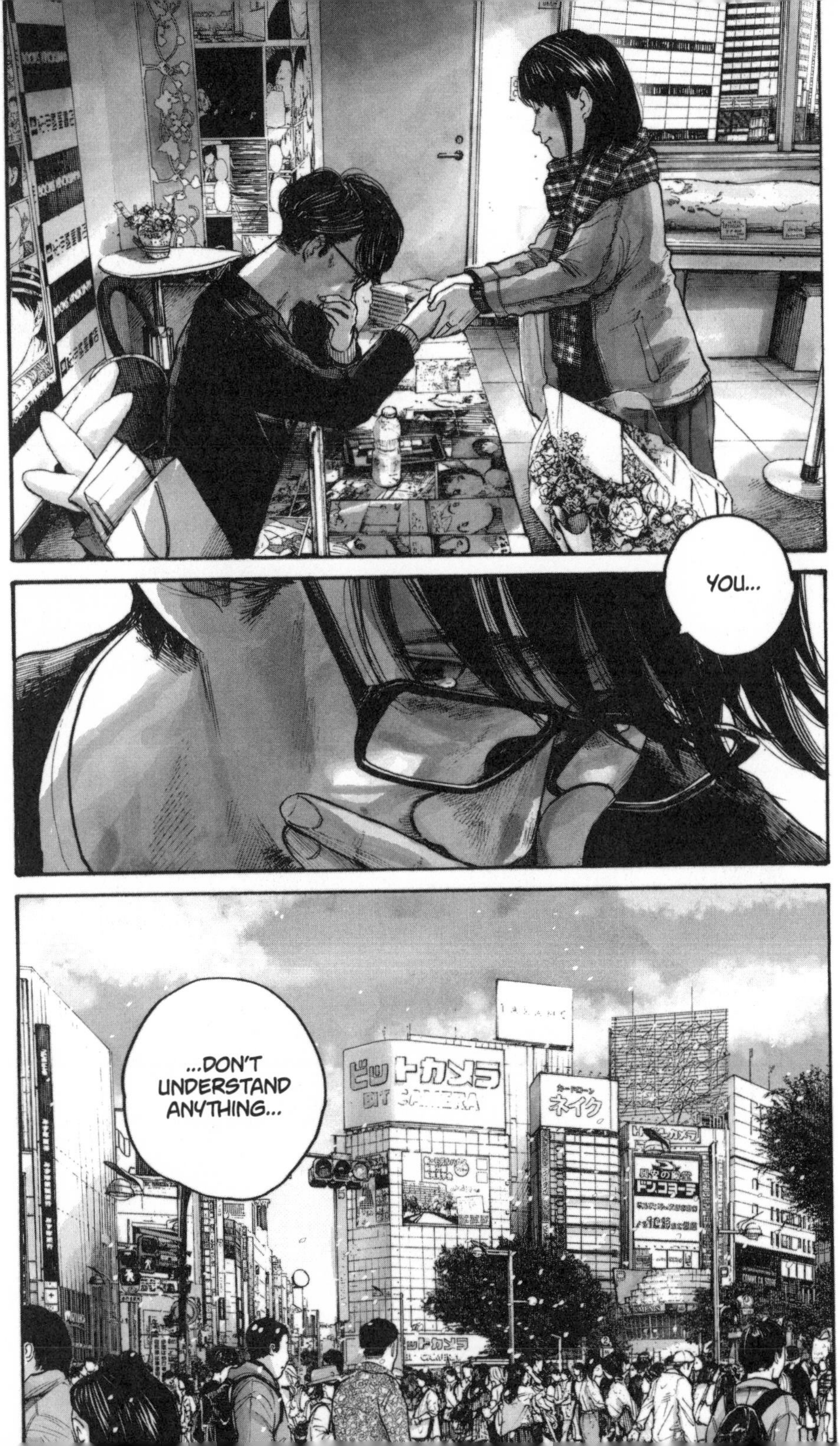
YOU...
...DON'T UNDERSTAND ANYTHING...

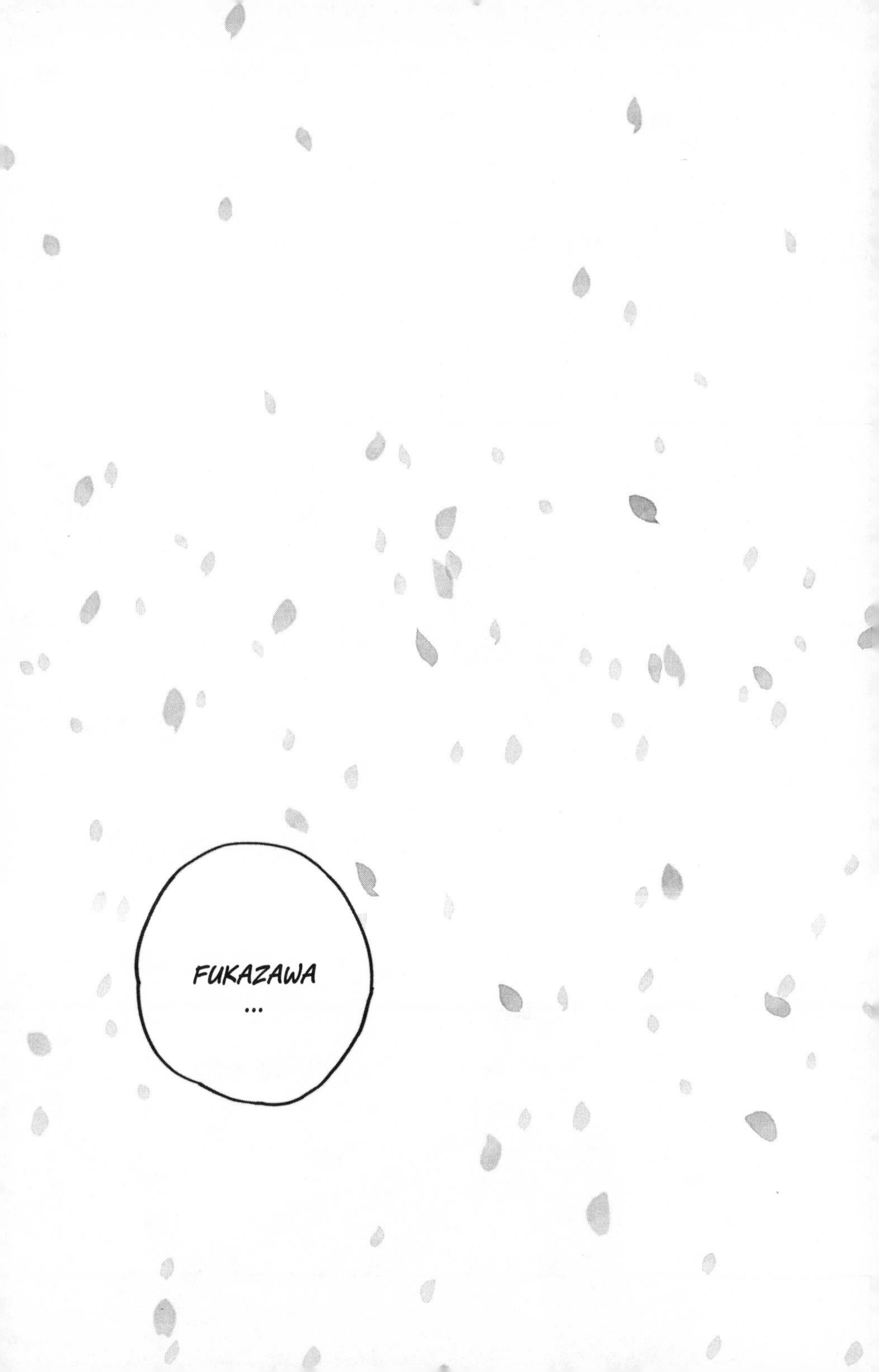
FUKAZAWA ...

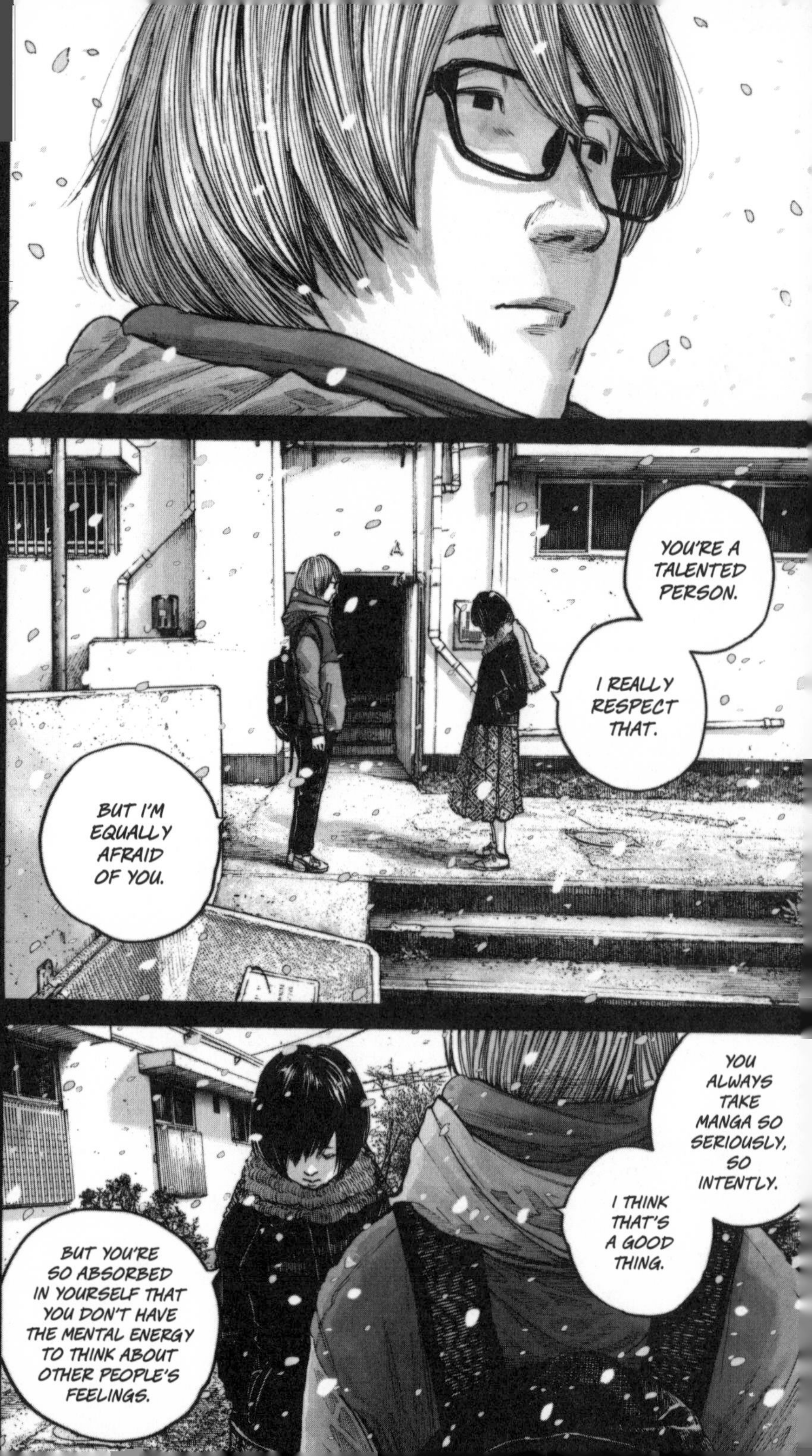
YOU'RE A TALENTED PERSON.
I REALLY RESPECT THAT.
BUT I'M EQUALLY AFRAID OF YOU.
YOU ALWAYS TAKE MANGA SO SERIOUSLY, SO INTENTLY.
I THINK THAT'S A GOOD THING.
BUT YOU'RE SO ABSORBED IN YOURSELF THAT YOU DON'T HAVE THE MENTAL ENERGY TO THINK ABOUT OTHER PEOPLE'S FEELINGS.

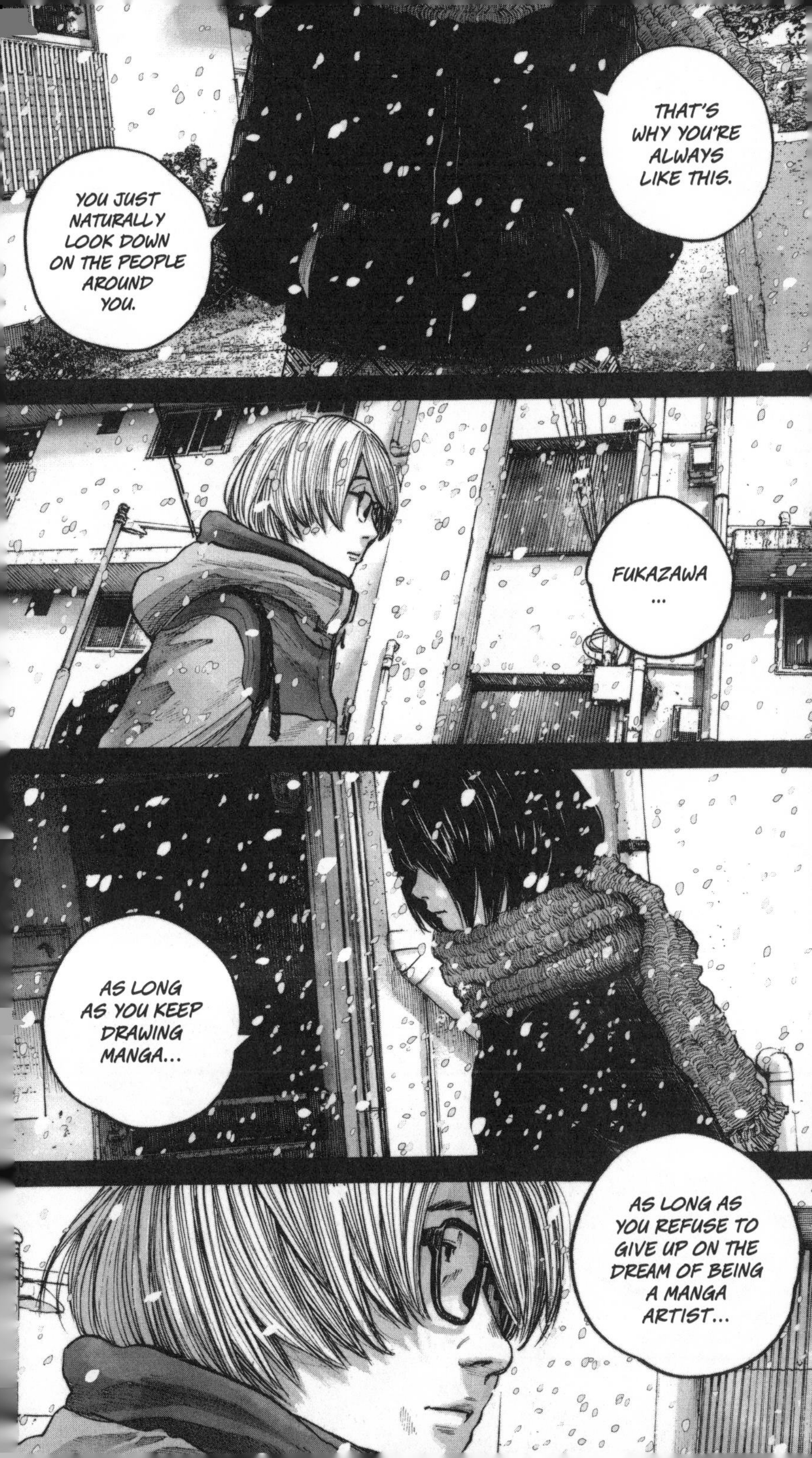
THAT'S WHY YOU'RE ALWAYS LIKE THIS.
YOU JUST NATURALLY LOOK DOWN ON THE PEOPLE AROUND YOU.
FUKAZAWA ...
AS LONG AS YOU KEEP DRAWING MANGA...
AS LONG AS YOU REFUSE TO GIVE UP ON THE DREAM OF BEING A MANGA ARTIST...

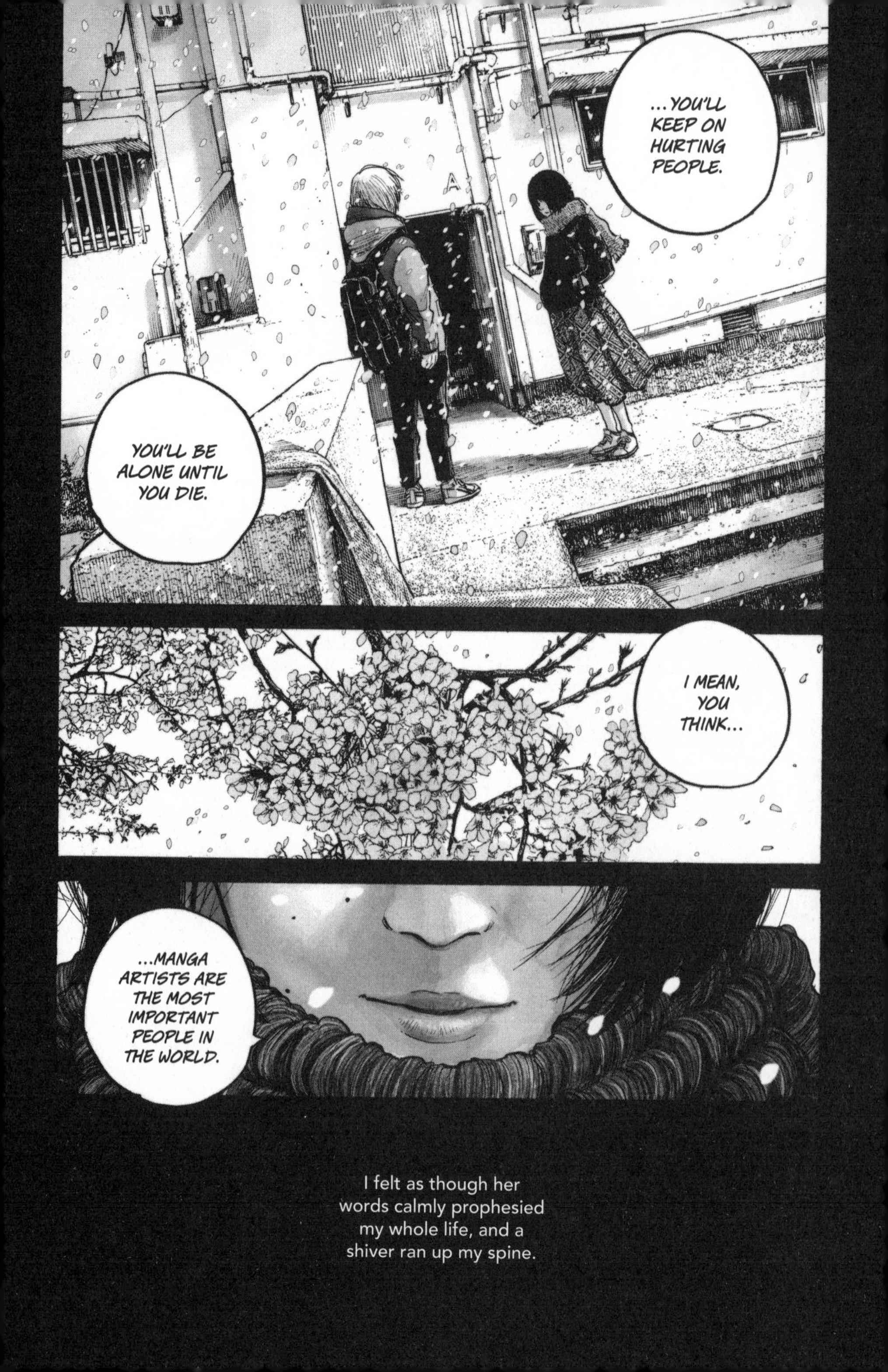
...YOU'LL KEEP ON HURTING PEOPLE.
YOU'LL BE ALONE UNTIL YOU DIE.
I MEAN, YOU THINK...
...MANGA ARTISTS ARE THE MOST IMPORTANT PEOPLE IN THE WORLD.

I felt as though her
words calmly prophesied
my whole life, and a
shiver ran up my spine.

BUT STILL...

I should've made her
take them back, by force if
necessary. I felt something
like a murderous impulse
quietly race through me.

*...YOU'LL
KEEP
PUSHING
AHEAD,
WON'T
YOU?*

How ugly was the version of
me reflected in her eyes?

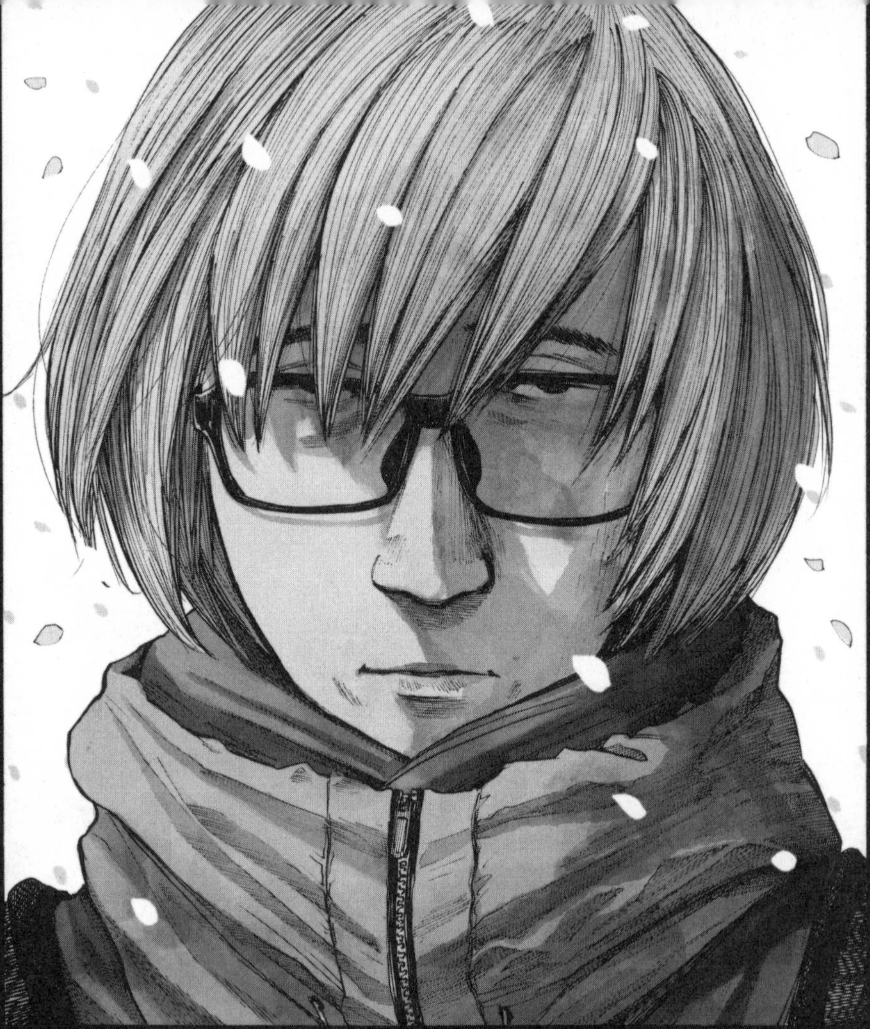

And that's why I
get nervous when
I meet cat-eyed
women, even now.

Fin

PRODUCTION STAFF

Ran Atsumori

Yuka Tatami

Miki Imai

Naoto Tomita